Lecture Notes in Computer Science   8995

Commenced Publication in 1973
Founding and Former Series Editors:
Gerhard Goos, Juris Hartmanis, and Jan van Leeuwen

More information about this series at http://www.springer.com/series/7411

Jelena Mirkovic · Yong Liu (Eds.)

Passive and Active Measurement

16th International Conference, PAM 2015
New York, NY, USA, March 19–20, 2015
Proceedings

 Springer

Editors
Jelena Mirkovic
Information Sciences Institute
University of Southern California
Marina Del Rey, CA
USA

Yong Liu
New York University
New York, NY
USA

ISSN 0302-9743   ISSN 1611-3349   (electronic)
Lecture Notes in Computer Science
ISBN 978-3-319-15508-1   ISBN 978-3-319-15509-8   (eBook)
DOI 10.1007/978-3-319-15509-8

Library of Congress Control Number: 2015931068

Springer Cham Heidelberg New York Dordrecht London

Printed on acid-free paper

Springer International Publishing AG Switzerland is part of Springer Science+Business Media
(www.springer.com)

Preface

We are excited to welcome you to the Passive and Active Measurement Conference (PAM) 2015 in New York, NY, USA. PAM seeks to bring together the network research and operations communities, to consider network measurement and analysis techniques, particularly those in the earlier stages of research.

PAM's focus is on research and practical applications of network measurement, measurement of networked applications, content distribution networks, online social networks, overlay networks, and more. Measurement technology is needed at all layers of the stack: for power profiling of hardware components; at the MAC/network/transport layers; as well as up the stack for application profiling and even to collect user feedback. Measurement technologies are being designed for the digital home, residential access networks, wireless and mobile access, enterprise, ISP, and data center networks.

PAM encourages a broad range of submissions across these recently important topics. We aim to understand the role that measurement techniques can play in networked environments and applications, across different layers, and how they can serve as critical building blocks for broader measurement needs. At the same time, PAM also continues with its original goal, to expand the techniques, tools, and practical uses of network measurement technology.

Submission Statistics

This year, PAM has received 100 submissions. Each submission was reviewed by at least three reviewers, judging its technical content, intellectual merit, and clarity of writing. After the initial review process, the reviewers discussed all submissions until they reached consensus to accept or reject. There were 27 accepted papers.

March 2015

Jelena Mirkovic
Yong Liu

Organization

PAM 2015 was organized and supported by the following committees.

Conference Organizers

Yong Liu (General Chair)	New York University, USA
Jelena Mirkovic (Program Chair)	University of Southern California/Information Sciences Institute, USA
Anyi Wang (Publicity Chair)	New York University, USA

Steering Committee

Nevil Brownlee	University of Auckland, New Zealand
Rocky K.C. Chang	Hong Kong Polytechnic University, Hong Kong
Michalis Faloutsos	University of New Mexico, USA
Aleksandar Kuzmanovic	Northwestern University, USA
Fabio Ricciato	University of Salento, Italy
Matthew Roughan	University of Adelaide, Australia
Nina Taft	Google, USA

Program Committee

Emile Aben	RIPE NCC, The Netherlands
Pere Barlet-Ros	UPC BarcelonaTech/Talaia Networks, Spain
Genevieve Bartlett	University of Southern California/Information Sciences Institute, USA
Robert Beverly	Naval Postgraduate School, USA
Rocky K.C. Chang	Hong Kong Polytechnic University, Hong Kong
Italo Cunha	Universidade Federal de Minas Gerais, Brazil
Alberto Dainotti	CAIDA, University of California, San Diego, USA
Alessandro D'Alconzo	Forschungszentrum Telekommunikation Wien, Austria
Xenofontas Dimitropoulos	FORTH, Greece and ETH Zurich, Switzerland
Kensuke Fukuda	National Institute of Informatics, Japan
Dongsu Han	KAIST, Korea
Gentian Jakllari	University of Toulouse, France
Thomas Karagiannakis	MSR, UK
Ethan Katz-Bassett	University of Southern California, USA
Amir Khakpour	Verizon EdgeCast, USA
Youngseok Lee	Chungnam National University, Korea
Richard Nelson	The University of Waikato, New Zealand
Maria Papadopouli	University of Crete and FORTH, Greece
Gyan Ranjan	Narus, Inc. USA

Dario Rossi   Télécom ParisTech, France
Subhabrata Sen   AT&T Labs Research, USA
Affan Syed   FAST-NU, Pakistan
Xuetao Wei   University of Cincinnati, USA
Udi Weinsberg   Facebook, USA

Contents

Wireless and Embedded

Software Defined Networking

DNS and Routing

~Open Resolvers: Understanding the Origins of Anomalous Open DNS Resolvers

Andrew J. Kaizer[✉] and Minaxi Gupta

Indiana University - Bloomington, Bloomington, USA
akaizer@indiana.edu

Abstract. Recent distributed denial-of-service attacks on the Internet have been exploiting necessarily open protocols, such as DNS. The Spamhaus attack is one of the largest ever examples of such attacks. Although much research has been conducted to discuss how to mitigate these threats, little has been done to understand why open resolvers exist in the first place. In particular, 60 % of the open resolvers have anomalous behavior and causes for their behavior remain a mystery, which hurts mitigation efforts. Our research produces the first detailed investigation of the 17 million anomalous open resolvers and find that these are primarily ADSL modems made by four manufacturers. These devices behave anomalously and respond to DNS queries with the wrong source port due to improper NAT configurations and are unfortunately hard to fix without a concerted effort by ISPs and manufacturers. We also find that anomalous open resolvers are clustered, which has the potential for them to be exploited in more crippling DDoS attacks.

1 Introduction

Over the last several years, attackers have utilized a wide variety of techniques to launch DoS attacks. TCP-based DoS attacks have long been in use, with new exploits being uncovered such as the recent Wordpress XML-RPC pingback attack [1]. However, most of the recent devastating attacks have been leveraging open UDP protocols, such as DNS and NTP, to amplify and launch crippling distributed denial of service (DDoS) attacks. One of the most prominent attacks of this type occurred in Spring 2013 against Spamhaus, where attackers leveraged approximately 31,000 open DNS resolvers – that accept DNS queries on behalf of any client around the world – to generate over 300 Gbps of network traffic against Spamhaus's servers [9]. This highly public attack has spurred considerable focus to the problem of open DNS resolvers, with sources such as the Open Resolver Project running weekly scans to determine the number of open resolvers and advice from Team Cymru on how to close open resolvers [5,7].

While open resolver scans have found approximately 30 million devices functioning as open resolvers in 2013, there is a large percentage – approximately 60 % – whose behavior is anomalous and can hinder mitigation efforts, as simple solutions to identify open resolvers would fail to account for them correctly. Specifically, these anomalous open resolvers (AORs) *appear* to resolve DNS

© Springer International Publishing Switzerland 2015
J. Mirkovic and Y. Liu (Eds.): PAM 2015, LNCS 8995, pp. 3–14, 2015.
DOI: 10.1007/978-3-319-15509-8_1

queries correctly but respond back to clients using the wrong source port[1], which makes it appear that no response was received. In turn, this obscures the involvement of DNS in these attacks. Unfortunately, there is a lack of explanation about AOR behavior. The Open Resolver Project has continually noted their behavior, but no explanation has been provided [7]. Another open resolver scan conducted by an FCC working group – WG5 – on DNSSEC deployment found a large number of responses coming back with erroneous source ports, but provided no explanation for why this behavior was occurring [2]. Note that the AOR behavior is not explained by source port randomization that is in place in many DNS resolvers for DNS queries since the source ports used in AOR responses are sequential.

In order for clients to correctly receive responses from an AOR, they would need to be listening for all incoming responses to the port they sent their DNS query on and not just for a response from UDP port 53. This requires using raw sockets on the client-side and creates hurdles in identifying AORs as one has to consider all incoming responses on a specific port and verify that the response is a valid DNS response with the correct payload. A graphical example of the behavior of an AOR can be seen in Fig. 1.

Given the rich potential for AORs to be exploited in DNS-based DDoS attacks, the key goal of this paper is to explain the underlying causes for their behavior so better informed mitigation efforts can be undertaken. Toward this goal, we conduct an IPv4 wide scan to identify AORs by separating them from open resolvers. Once the AORs are found, we run a suite of tests to fingerprint what specific devices are participating in this behavior and find that they are primarily ADSL modems and routers made by Huawei, TP-Link, ZTE, and D-Link. The fingerprinting process is then used to isolate behavior and infer that AORs are a result of improper NAT configurations. We also experimentally develop a NAT rule that leads to the observed AOR behavior. Unfortunately, consumers cannot easily secure their own ADSL modems from being exploited as AORs since the particular NAT configuration changes are not accessible to them. Thus, concerted efforts from manufacturers and ISPs are required to eliminate consumer devices from becoming AORs.

Beyond the fact that malicious actors can easily find AORs, our experiments reveal that many of the AORs are highly clustered in autonomous systems (ASes). This means that if an attacker can successfully identify several ASes with these devices in them, then scanning the rest of these ASes will result in many additional vulnerable devices that can be exploited to easily find AORs and amplify effortlessly in launching DDoS attacks. In turn, this can cause more fierce and sustained DDoS attacks.

2   Overview of Methodology

The experimental design was split into two phases. In the first phase, we conduct an IPv4 wide scan to determine where AOR devices are located. This involved

---

[1] The response does not come from UDP port 53 as expected for DNS responses.

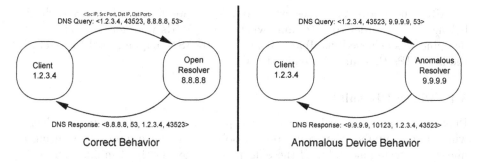

Fig. 1. The left figure: response from DNS resolver is sent from expected src port, 53. The right figure: response from AOR is sent from unexpected src port, 10123.

locating all open resolvers. In the second phase, we fingerprint and conduct tests to identify the causes for AORs' anomalous behavior. For the second phase, we focus on AORs belonging to ASes that met at least one of two criteria. The AS had a large number of AORs or a sizable percentage of the total IP pool in the AS were AORs.

The AS granularity was selected, instead of individual prefixes, to account for the fact that IP addresses inside an ISP – which are part of ASes – are not guaranteed to be contiguous. For example, an ISP may have 200.0.0.0/24 and 1.2.0.0/24, both of which have AORs in them. The two prefixes share no obvious commonality until their AS is accounted for. As a result, these criteria allowed us to focus our exploration where we would have a high success rate to find AORs and not unnecessarily intrude upon ASes that do not have these devices, where our scans might be considered as an attack on that network.

3 Phase I: Identifying AORs

In this phase, we linearly query the entire IPv4 space for open resolvers so that we could uncover AORs. Specifically, we use a local test machine and query each IPv4 address for the *A record* for the host name of a domain we control, www. coffeestaples.com. To identify cases where a response comes back incorrectly, we make each DNS request uniquely identifiable by using the target IP address as a portion of the host name. For example, the host name in the request to 1.2.3.4 would be *1.2.3.4.coffeestaples.com*. The timeout in our requests was set to one second to strike a reasonable trade-off between speed of data collection while accounting for commonly expected DNS response times.

The authoritative DNS server for www.coffeestaples.com, which is responsible for providing responses for the queries, is also hosted locally with logging enabled. This logging, along with the unique tags on the requests, allows us to determine whether the authoritative DNS server received the query directed to the target, even if the response is lost in transit. Based on our methodology, *any unique IP identifier in the hostname that appears in our authoritative log but does not appear with a valid source port in a DNS response to our local test machine was considered an AOR.*

After the above processes were completed, we found what AS each IP belonged to, in order to determine where these AORs were located. This ASN mapping was achieved via Team Cymru's IP-to-ASN mapping tool to generate the list of IPs that an AS broadcasts [4].

3.1 Phase I Results

Phase one scanning revealed a total of approximately 29 million open resolvers, which is the number that other open resolver scans have found when using a linear scan technique [2,7]. Of these devices, approximately 12 million were true open resolvers and 17 million were AORs.

From our initial scan we observed that the AORs were more concentrated by prefix than the correctly behaving open resolvers. For correctly behaving open resolvers, we observed 12 million devices in approximately 1.8 million/24 prefixes. The 17 million AORs were observed in only 1.06 million/24 prefixes – *more AORs for fewer prefixes.*

Next, we clustered AOR IP addresses into their respective ASes. We observed an even higher degree of concentration with this approach: the 18 ASes with the most AORs accounted for 50 % of all AORs; the top 34 represented 67 %; the top 50 represented 75 %. The worst offending AS accounted for 8.02 %, approximately 1.4 million devices. Table 1 shows the top-10 ASNs with the highest concentration of AORs.

Table 1. Top-10 ASNs with the highest number of AORs which account for 35.21 % of all AORs.

Rank	ASN	ASN Name	AS Country	AS Size	% of AORs in AS	% Total AORs Running Total
1	8151	Uninet S.A. de C.V	Mexico	12357888	11.08 %	8.03 %
2	45899	VNPT Corp	Vietnam	3273472	20.66 %	11.99 %
3	22927	Telefonica de Argentina	Argentina	3646720	18.08 %	15.86 %
4	17974	PT Telekomunikasi Indonesia	Indonesia	3689984	15.24 %	19.15 %
5	9121	Turk Telekomunikasyon Anonim Sirketi	Turkey	6934528	8.05 %	22.43 %
6	45758	TripleT Internet ISP Bangkok	Thailand	1069056	44.71 %	25.23 %
7	9737	TOT Public Company Limited	Thailand	1238528	38.52 %	28.03 %
8	13285	TalkTalk Communications Limited	United Kingdom	3506432	13.30 %	30.76 %
9	8452	TE-AS	Egypt	3925504	9.87 %	33.03 %
10	3269	Telecom Italia S.p.a	Italy	18880256	1.97 %	35.21 %

We conclude that *AORs are clustered*, which implies that it is easy for attackers to find large numbers of AORs quickly. The clustering also suggests that ISPs are likely responsible for providing AOR devices to their clients. Since if these were consumer purchased devices, they might exhibit less clustering since consumers might purchase a wider array of devices.

4   Phase II: Identifying AOR Behavior

The second phase of our methodology seeks to fingerprint AORs and also understand why AORs behave anomalously. As stated earlier, we focus on AORs belonging to ASes that met at least one of two criteria: The AS has a large number of AORs or a sizeable percentage of the total IP pool in the AS are AORs. For each AS under consideration, we retrieve the IP addresses it announces using Hurricane Electric (www.bgp.he.net). For each IP address that responds back on an invalid source port, which implies an AOR, we then conduct several fingerprinting tests to determine if a device make/model can be determined. Finally, randomly selected devices are chosen for further testing based on how long the device maintains the anomalous source port and how it handles responses sent to the anomalous source port. This further testing allows us to test if the AOR behavior is attributable to either a NAT or a firewall, which are common features of the devices the ISPs give to their clients.

4.1   Fingerprinting Methodology

Our scanning process utilized scapy – a Python packet creation and manipulation program – on a local test machine where we had super user access [8]. This was a necessity to handle raw sockets. The combination of scapy and Python provided the best framework for other tasks related to fingerprinting, such as strong support for building HTTP and FTP requests.

The scan process worked by scanning specific ASes for AORs. For each IP address scanned, worker processes listened for incoming responses. All incoming responses would be added to a queue for fingerprinting, whose goal was to determine what specific devices were exhibiting this AOR behavior. Using the methodology above, we are able to scan approximately 1 million IP addresses in 60 min to achieve a throughput of around 550 outgoing packets per second. We fingerprinted all IPs in 14 ASes with large concentrations of AORs.

4.2   Protocols for Effective Fingerprinting of AORs

Fingerprinting AORs is a hard problem. The primary point of difficulty is that for a device to respond to a request on a specific service or protocol, it needs to be open to external network traffic on the protocol of interest that is *accidentally volunteering* identifying device details: HTTP, FTP, and telnet are all services that may do this on the devices that we found exhibiting the anomalous behavior. Any devices following good practices and only allowing *intranet* access, should make it difficult – if not impossible – to extract the necessary information to identify it.

During fingerprinting, we found that there are two generic, high-coverage services we could utilize: HTTP and FTP. These two services were the only two that reliably gave us specific model/manufacturer of the device. Other services, such as telnet or ssh, would state the version of the service they were running, but not device details. Other efforts to find additional services to use in finger-printing – e.g. telnet, SSH, CWMP (a WAN management protocol), bit level inspection of the responses – was attempted, but none were found to be overly successful [6]. Even in rare cases where a response was observed from an AOR, we found that the case was not broadly applicable due to low coverage, so we excluded all such cases from the AS-wide scans.

The following list describes the fingerprinting cases we considered:

HTTP. Sending requests for a default landing page '/' via Python's urllib2 functionality had the best coverage in identifying devices [10]. For many devices, the title of the webpage in its HTML source would reveal details about the device such as its model or its manufacturer. For each AS, we also inspected cases where the title did not give enough details and attempted to extract more information from either the content of the page itself or found an additional webpage that volunteered information based on the device itself. Both content and other URLs are applied to specific devices in specific AS, due to the fact that two devices with the same model usually did not share certain special URLs or content due to minor customization differences among ASes/ISPs.

HTTP Authorization Headers. Many devices would not respond with a default landing page, but instead would send authorization headers which often leaked the device model under the *www-authenticate* field of the HTTP header. In these cases we could simply extract that value.

FTP. Device information was sometimes leaked in the FTP *welcome message* – namely, many FTP welcome messages stated exactly what the device you were trying to connect to was. Python's ftplib was used to extract these details [3]. In certain cases, if a title was found during the HTTP phase but was too generic, we would make an FTP request to observe if we could identify a more specific model. The FTP case would not be run if a device could be extracted during the HTTP process.

4.3   Fingerprinting Results

The countries and AS included in our phase II scans of 14 ASes are: Mexico (AS8151), Vietnam (AS45899), Argentina (AS22927), Thailand (AS45758, AS9737), Egypt (AS8452), Belarus (AS6697), Colombia (AS19429, AS3816), Kazakhstan (AS9198), Romania (AS9050), Slovakia (AS6855), Ecuador (AS14420), and Russia (AS28812). Countries that have two AS scanned were selected because the number of vulnerable devices in each AS was similar enough that selecting one over the other made little sense. The overall results of fingerprint scanning resulted in finding 5.218 million AORs and attributing a device type to 2.872 million AORs. The vast majority of the responses we observed were valid DNS responses, with only 7500 responses that had a failure DNS rcode.

The common trait among almost all the devices is their functionality: they are all-in-one ADSL modems which have router, firewall, and NAT functionality built in. If we inspect Table 2, we see that almost all devices listed are ADSL modems, with some consumer grade web cameras and DVRs also in the mix. Furthermore, we see the results are dominated by handful of manufacturers: Huawei, TP-Link, ZTE, and D-Link. The top-10 device responses that our fingerprinting process found were as follows: Huawei HG530, ZXV10 W300, TD-W8901G, TD-8817, Huawei HG520b, TD-8840T, HG530, TD854W, HG521c, and HG520c. These ten accounted for 41.14 % of the approximately 5.2 million AORs observed. An explanation for why these devices are found in large numbers compared to other devices observed as AORs is cost. When ISPs listed multiple devices a consumer could purchase, these modems were often among the least expensive, which means consumers would gravitate towards purchasing these devices.

Table 2. The list of top-10 fingerprinted devices observed in the 14 ASes scanned. This represents 2.1 million devices (41.14 % of all AORs observed).

Device Type	% of Total	Device Type	% of Total
Huawei HG530	19.72 %	TD-8840T	2.08 %
ZXV10 W300	5.05 %	HG530	1.84 %
TD-W8901G	3.09 %	TD854W	1.70 %
TD-8817	2.76 %	HG521c	1.27 %
Huawei HG520b	2.44 %	HG520c	1.19 %

4.4 Determining Root Cause of Anomalous Behavior

We begin by noting that AOR behavior is not explained by source port randomization that many DNS clients use for their DNS queries to a resolver. In the case of AORs, it is the response that comes back on an incorrect source port, which rules this type of behavior out. Moreover, one way source port randomization, as in the case of AORs, is never done since it would cause the receiver to ignore the response, which would always come back on an unexpected port. Another reason this fails to explain AOR behavior is that the source ports used in AOR responses are sequential and not random.

After we identified what manufacturer/make the AORs were and that they were clustered, we needed to determine what could lead to this underlying behavior. The AORs we observed were primarily ADSL routers that were sold by ISPs, which have three key roles: routers, firewall, and NAT. The router is unlikely to be the cause for anomalous behavior, as it simply routes packets. A firewall drops or allows packets based on rule sets, but it can also change the underlying information[2], so a firewall could lead to the AOR behavior observed. The anomalous behavior could also be NAT based, which is responsible for re-routing packets that meet certain conditions as they enter and exit the network. We devised to determine if the NAT or the firewall was the underlying cause of the behavior. The four tests are as follows:

Port Range - The port range test checks if source ports in incoming DNS responses look similar to how NAT assigns ports. It creates a raw socket to listen on a specific port and then makes a request to an AOR. When a response comes back, an ICMP packet is generated by the system and sent to the target[3]. After this ICMP is sent, our system resends the request and sees how the source port changes by watching the response. We note if the source port does not change, changes linearly, changes randomly, or stays within a range. If it changes, that suggests NAT as the culprit, as NATs will release an assigned port that has received an ICMP unreachable message as no longer in use.

Port Accessibility: Part I - This test checks the output of sending a DNS request to the AOR using the same erroneous source port that it sent the response from as the destination port. The goal of this test is determine if the AOR's behavior is simply a response using a wrong port or if there exists a *mapping* between the wrong port and the DNS software that is also listening when our requests are sent to UDP port 53. A response would be a key indicator that NAT was responsible for the AOR behavior, instead of a firewall, as it would mean that an external mapping existed between the anomalous port and the DNS process.

Port Accessibility: Part II - While the previous test keeps the IP address of the sending machine the same as the one that received a DNS response from the AOR, this test sends DNS queries to AORs from other IP addresses as well while keeping all other details the same as in the previous test. The goal of this test is also to find out if a mapping exists between the anomalous port and the DNS process. A positive response would again indicate that a NAT was responsible for AOR behavior.

Port Statefulness - The port statefulness test is designed to explore how long the state of the anomalous port is maintained at the AOR. It does so by observing if an AOR response used the same anomalous port with multiple client requests, and for how long an AOR maintained that state. Since UDP is a stateless protocol, any statefulness would have to be maintained by a feature in the device. In particular, if the behavior lasted for a consistent amount of time and passed the port accessibility tests, then the behavior would have to be NAT based as it would be keeping statefulness on a mapping between ports.

---

[2] Modern firewalls, such as iptables, have the capacity to re-route packets if they meet a certain rule.

[3] This ICMP behavior occurs on Linux machines when dealing with UDP raw sockets because we are not bound to the port, therefore the kernel responds with an ICMP regarding that no one is listening (bound) to that port.

4.5   Anomalous Behavior Results

One of the surprising outcomes of the port range test is that AORs maintain a fixed source port-range for these AORs. *Of the 5.2 million results, 99.67% fell within the range of UDP ports 10000–30000.* Using our test case for determining how these source ports are assigned, we observed a linear behavior; e.g. if we got a DNS response back on source port 21953, the next source port would be 21954[4]. Once a device hits 30000, we would observe the source port roll back to 10000. This range of 10 k–30 k is arbitrary, so it is surprising to see it consistently appear across ASes.

Likewise, with respect to how long these AORs kept the same source port [the statefulness test], we observed a 150 s timeout that was consistent across ASes. After waiting 150 s, we would observe a new source port based on the behavior we described above. These ranges and timeout values do not conform to the standard – laid out in RFC4787 about UDP responses on NAT – and therefore represent some sort of common source to this anomalous behavior [11].

For the accessibility results, we notice that after an anomalous source port has been granted, *any machine* can communicate with the resolver that is behind the target on either UDP53 or the anomalous source port. The target device will always respond back to our client machines on that same anomalous port, regardless of who the request came from (X or Y) and what port was targeted (53 or the anomalous port). Additionally, this AOR behavior will not cause accessibility issues for DNS requests made by intranet clients, because the NAT translation will be corrected to the original source port when it comes back into the network and will not be translated again as it will not leave the network again. Therefore only requests coming from the Internet will suffer from this behavior.

Overall, we conclude that NAT is the reason for AOR behavior. Alternative hypotheses, such as manufacturer of a specific piece of software being responsible, fail to explain the behavior of AORs, since then, we would not expect to see it across many different devices and ASes.

4.6   NAT Rule to Explain AOR Behavior

In order to further ascertain the NAT-based explanation for AORs, we setup a virtual environment and tested a variety of possible iptables rules that alter packets. iptables was selected because the AOR devices that we could find specifications for stated that the code was built on top of a Linux base code that included iptables as one of its default programs.

We found that the behavior would likely be caused by an iptables rule of the following nature: *iptables -t nat -A postrouting -p udp –dport 53 -j SNAT - to :10000–30000.* This type of rule would change outgoing packets that hit the source NAT [-j SNAT] and convert the source port to 10000–30000 UDP [-p UDP]. The 150 s timeout would have required the alteration of IP masquerade

---

[4] The next number may also be a bit bigger than x + 1 because other interactions with the AOR may have incremented the counter forward.

(a NAT style 1-to-many component of iptables) timeout settings, accessible via *ipchains -M -S tcp tcpfin udp*, where the *udp* option would have 150 as its value.

5 Discussion

Here, we describe how AORs can be exploited, why they may be difficult to patch, and further detail some of the tradeoffs involved when fingerprinting AORs.

5.1 Exploitation Potential of AORs

The key concern about the AORs is their potential for DDoS. It is trivial to locate large numbers for use in a DNS amplification attack the moment an attacker finds ASes to exploit. We discussed earlier how the DDoS attack on Spamhaus utilized 31,000 open resolvers to achieve a 300 Gbps attack. For an attack based on AORs, we could choose any of the top 80 ASes from Table 1 to find at *least* 31,000 AORs. If we only consider the top 35 ASes, we could enlist 100 k+ devices to at *least* triple our attack capacity to over 900 Gbps. This scale of attack could make the next DNS amplification attack even more damaging, even if the attacker only cycles through devices in each ASN to try and avoid saturating the local ISP connections.

5.2 Issues in Correcting AORs

While patching AORs is hardly controversial, because of efforts around shutting open resolvers, actually patching them poses practical complications. First, the steps necessary to patch AORs will not be the same as those for patching true open resolvers. This is because many of the ADSL modems that made up the bulk of the AORs we identified make use of DNS relay technology, to carry out DNS queries. Thus, they are not necessarily true resolvers. Since the terminology of a DNS relay is nonstandard, we do not know if the DNS relay is a full resolver that can handle rules to restrict the clients it serves. As a result, there may not be a full resolver to be patched on AORs. Instead, the iptables rules that make up the device's NAT/firewall rules will need to be corrected to not accept arbitrary Internet-based DNS requests.

A further complication comes that AORs are consumer devices that may not allow easy access to iptables or the native DNS resolver. We tested this issue with a TD-8817[5], and could not find a way to directly modify the rules that lead to this behavior. Using the limited NAT/firewall configuration settings only allowed blocking all UDP 53 traffic which only hides the problem and would be cumbersome for consumers to implement. As a result, without manufacturer or ISP cooperation, the number of AORs may decline more slowly than true open resolvers as they will only be patched when a ISPs upgrade their devices

---

[5] We selected the TD-8817 (4th most common AOR) because it was sold in the US and we could gain access to it. The same cannot be said for the other devices.

to versions that do not exhibit AOR behavior or push updates to the AOR to correct the anomalous behavior.

5.3 Fingerprinting Tradeoffs

One of the goals of the phase II scanning process was to make it perform quickly without sacrificing accuracy in the fingerprinting process we detailed in Sect. 4.2. Reasonable speed is important in order to allow the scans to be conducted fast enough to avoid too much IP address turnover from IP leases expiring and to ensure double counting devices assigned a new IP address was kept to a minimum. In order to keep our fingerprinting scan within a desirable coverage and time bounds we took two approaches. Leaving out cases that have no coverage in an AS and leaving out cases that cover only a very small, specialized subset.

With respect to leaving cases with no coverage out. Each AS that we scanned was initially surveyed on multiple/16 prefixes for AORs in that subset of the AS. The results of these smaller scans were then used to develop the special cases that was discussed in Sect. 4.2 regarding HTTP response content. This pre-scanning was also done to select fingerprinting cases we already developed that applied to each AS and leave out cases that had no coverage. This helps us avoid the slow down related to running cases which were never found in an AS. Discarding no coverage cases had minimal risk when tested experimentally: the speedup was considerable and loss of coverage was negligible.

Avoiding adding too many specialized cases to our fingerprinting process also helped the scan run in a reasonable time with minimal coverage tradeoff. For example, we could look for HTTP services on unlikely ports: 81, 8080, 8000, 8001, 8081, etc. All the previous ports were observed in at least one of our more detailed device pre-scans, but when we added these cases to be used in the AS-wide scan process, they yielded very few additional device identifications while adding considerable overhead to the scanning process.

6 Related Work

Although no related work has explored these AORs results directly, several organizations have conducted open DNS resolver scans. Both the FCC working group and the open resolver project have conducted IPv4 wide scans and identified this anomalous behavior [2,7]. The DNS Measurement Factory has been conducting scans for open resolvers based on a more targeted approach, but does not appear to discuss anomalous results [14]. Likewise [15] loosely hypothesized that this AOR behavior may be related to faulty low-grade NAT devices, which is something we have proven in this paper. Our work complements and expands upon this existing work by explaining why the anomalous behavior exists. Our technique of inspecting HTTP authorization headers is also motivated by [15].

Other research has focused on how to attack the results given by DNS resolvers. Dagon, et. al. in 2008 studied the use of open and rogue recursive resolvers to mislead users and resolve them to incorrect sites [12]. Research by [13] addresses the risk of on-path DNS poisoning where non-DNSSEC enabled resolvers can be poisoned by malicious responses that beat the legitimate response back. Although the AOR issue is not directly related to these types of attacks, the presence of AORs can exacerbate the situation.

7   Conclusion

In this paper, we unearthed the devices, manufacturers and root causes for AOR behavior, which can be exploited to produce much stronger DNS amplification attacks. We also found that finding AORs in large numbers is relatively easy since they tend to be clustered in ASes. Unfortunately, there does not appear to be an easy way for consumers to patch AORs, which are mostly ADSL modems, as NAT configurations do not appear to be easily accessible to the user.

It is up to ISPs and manufacturers to act and correct AOR behavior. We hope that by having explored and isolated the issues and risks of AORs, that stakeholders will be compelled to fix this behavior. In doing so, the attack surface of DDoS attacks can be greatly reduced.

References

1. Anatomy of wordpress XML-RPC pingback attacks. https://blogs.akamai.com/2014/03/anatomy-of-wordpress-xml-rpc-pingback-attacks.html
2. Communications security, reliability and interoperability council III — FCC.gov. http://www.fcc.gov/encyclopedia/communications-security-reliability-and-interoperability-council-iii
3. FTP protocol client. https://docs.python.org/2/library/ftplib.html
4. IP to ASN mapping - Team Cymru. https://www.team-cymru.org/Services/ip-to-asn.html
5. Million plus resolver challenge - Team Cymru. https://www.team-cymru.org/Services/Resolvers/instructions.html
6. nmap - Network mapper. http://nmap.org/
7. Open resolver project. http://openresolverproject.org/
8. Scapy - Packet manipulation and construction program. http://www.secdev.org/projects/scapy/
9. Technical details behind a 400 Gbps NTP amplification DDoS attack — CloudFlare blog. http://blog.cloudflare.com/technical-details-behind-a-400gbps-ntp-amplification-ddos-attack
10. urllib2 - Extensible library for opening urls. https://docs.python.org/2/library/urllib2.html
11. Audet, F., Jennings, C.: Ietf RFC 4787 — network address translation (NAT) behavioral requirements for unicast UDP, Jan 2007. http://tools.ietf.org/search/rfc4787
12. Dagon, D., Provos, N., Lee, C., Lee, W.: Corrupted DNS resolution paths: the rise of a malicious resolution authority. In: Proceedings of ISOC Network and Distributed Security Symposium (NDSS) (2008)
13. Duan, H., Weaver, N., Zhao, Z., Hu, M., Liang, J., Jiang, J., Li, K., Paxson, V.: Hold-on: Protecting against on-path DNS poisoning. In: Securing and Trusting Internet Names, IEEE (2012)
14. Measurement factory. Open DNS scanner. http://www.measurement-factory.com/
15. Schomp, K., Callahan, T., Rabinovich, M., Allman, M.: On measuring the client-side DNS infrastructure. In: Internet Measurement Conference, ACM (2013)

Characterizing Optimal DNS Amplification Attacks and Effective Mitigation

Douglas C. MacFarland[1], Craig A. Shue[1]($^{(\boxtimes)}$), and Andrew J. Kalafut[2]

[1] Worcester Polytechnic Institute, Worcester, MA, USA
{dcmacfarland,cshue}@cs.wpi.edu
[2] Grand Valley State University, Allendale, MI, USA
kalafuta@gvsu.edu

Abstract. Attackers have used DNS amplification in over 34 % of high-volume DDoS attacks, with some floods exceeding 300 Gbps. The best current practices do not help victims during an attack; they are preventative measures that third-party organizations must employ in advance. Unfortunately, there are no incentives for these third parties to follow the recommendations. While practitioners have focused on reducing the number of open DNS resolvers, these efforts do not address the threat posed by authoritative DNS servers.

In this work, we measure and characterize the attack potential associated with DNS amplification, along with the adoption of countermeasures. We then propose and measure a mitigation strategy that organizations can employ. With the help of an upstream ISP, our strategy will allow even poorly provisioned organizations to mitigate massive DNS amplification attacks with only minor performance overheads.

1 Introduction

In 2013 and early 2014, attackers used DNS amplification in 34.9 % of high volume DDoS attacks (those creating at least 20 Gbps of attack traffic) and in 18.6 % of all network DDoS attacks [8]. In mid-March 2013, attackers used DNS amplification to launch a high-profile attack against Spamhaus, with attack traffic volume exceeding 300 Gbps [1]. DNS amplification attacks are particularly valuable to attackers for a few reasons: (1) the amplification effect allows attackers to create a disproportionate amount of traffic at the victim, (2) by IP address spoofing and reflection, the attackers can conceal the identities of the attacking systems, preventing them from being blacklisted or cleaned, and (3) the victim cannot blacklist the IP addresses of the reflecting DNS servers without also hindering legitimate DNS resolutions.

In a typical DNS amplification attack, the attacker sends a DNS query packet from an attack system to a DNS server. In the process of creating this query packet, the attacker forges the packet's source IP address field so that it contains the IP address of the targeted victim, rather than the actual sender of the packet. Upon receiving and processing the query packet, the DNS server then dutifully sends a response back to the indicated source address of the query, which in

© Springer International Publishing Switzerland 2015
J. Mirkovic and Y. Liu (Eds.): PAM 2015, LNCS 8995, pp. 15–27, 2015.
DOI: 10.1007/978-3-319-15509-8_2

this case is the address of the victim. When the response packet arrives at the victim, the victim will process the packet, realize it is unsolicited, and discard it. However, at this point, the attack has already succeeded: the DNS response consumed a portion of the victim's bandwidth and computational resources at the victim's DNS resolvers. Even better from the viewpoint of the attacker, since the DNS response packet from the DNS server is larger than the query packet the attacker sent, the attack traffic at the target is increased by a certain amplification factor.

While DNS amplification attacks are well understood, the best defensive strategy is less obvious. In a July 2013 bulletin, the United States Computer Emergency Response Team (US-CERT) made a few recommendations [16]: (1) reduce the number of open DNS resolvers, (2) disable public recursion on authoritative DNS servers, (3) rate limit responses [18], and (4) limit IP address spoofing. Unfortunately, there is little incentive for organizations to employ these recommendations: these actions help other organizations, not the organization performing the remediation. The spoofing prevention measure, in particular, has been encouraged for over a decade, yet over 25 % of Autonomous Systems still allow arbitrary IP spoofing on the Internet [2]. Further, these steps are not actionable for an organization under attack.

While these recommendations may be well intentioned, they likely will not have the desired impact. In particular, efforts to reduce the number of open DNS resolvers will not solve the DNS amplification problem: rather than using an open resolver, attackers can simply query authoritative servers directly and still create effective DDoS conditions.

In this work, we make the following contributions:

1. Measure and Characterize the Attack Potential: We perform DNS queries to the authoritative servers for each of the 129 million DNS domains registered in 9 top-level domains (TLDs) to determine the amplification factor associated with four types of queries. We then focus on the highest amplification factor queries that can be issued and characterize the attack volume that could result. We found that we could create an attack of 1,444 MBytes/s at the target by sending only 44 MBytes/s of attack traffic at the application layer. We found that such attacks could be scaled up, allowing even relatively small botnets to launch damaging attacks, all without the use of open DNS resolvers.

2. Measure the Adoption of Query Rate-Limiting: We randomly sampled 0.5 % of the IP addresses for authoritative DNS servers we previously studied and issued repeated queries to the server to determine whether the domain employed query rate limiting, and if so, what settings were used in the configuration. We found that 2.69 % of the studied domains employed rate limiting. Of those, 7.38 % rate limited at 5 queries per second or less and the remaining 92.62 % used a rate limit between 9 and 14 queries per second.

3. Propose and Evaluate a Novel Mitigation Method: We propose and measure a straightforward mitigation approach that targeted organizations can employ to mitigate attacks. We propose organizations employ remote hosting for their authoritative DNS servers. We then propose organizations request upstream filtering of all DNS traffic, mitigating the DDoS attack. To preserve DNS functionality for the organization, we propose and test a solution to tunnel DNS queries to a remote DNS resolver, such as a remote VM hosted by a cloud provider or ISP. We found that we could automatically activate a remote DNS resolver, activate the tunnel, and forward all local DNS traffic to the remote node in less than 0.67 s, on average. All queries would then have a median additional latency of 16 ms. Accordingly, our approach will allow organizations to weather extremely high-volume DNS amplification attacks with minimal effort.

2 Background and Related Work

Traditional reflection attacks, such as the Smurf attack [15], simply forge the source IP address of a packet to be the address of the intended victim. The attacker sends the packet to an innocent third-party system called a *reflector*. The reflector then issues a legitimate reply that arrives at the victim. When a large number of attack packets are sent to reflectors, or when a reflector is a broadcast network address for many hosts, the combined volume at the victim can be crippling.

In a 2001 article, Paxson [11] described how reflectors can be used as part of a distributed reflector denial of service (DRDoS) attack. He argued for five possible defenses against the attacks: (1) filter reflected attack traffic at the victim, (2) prevent source address spoofing, (3) detect and block spoofed packets at the reflector, (4) allow traceback to the origin even through the reflector, and (5) detect the attack traffic from the compromised systems. With the exception of the first defense, in which the victim employs filtering, each of these defenses requires a third-party organization to detect and block attack traffic. The specific third-party organization affected depends on the details of the attack (e.g., the origin of the attack and the particular reflectors in use), but each of them must implement the solution. Solutions which require 100 % adoption by third-parties are unlikely to succeed, especially when these third-parties have no incentives for adoption. For example, the second option, source address filtering, is comparatively straightforward for organizations to employ, yet over 25 % of Autonomous Systems still allow arbitrary IP spoofing on the Internet [2].

Attackers often try to increase the amount of traffic generated by a reflection attack. These attacks, called *amplification attacks*, typically leverage protocol-specific attributes to increase the attack volume. Recent attacks using NTP amplification [12,17] were able to create floods of 400 Gbps against a victim. In the NTP attack, the attacker found a list of susceptible NTP servers and, spoofing the IP address of the victim, issued a query requesting a list of the last 600 clients that accessed the server. These NTP responses were much larger than the query, creating a massive amplification attack against the victim. Earlier this year, Rossow [13] examined 14 different network protocols to look for reflection attacks that yield significant amplification. While Rossow's analysis did include

DNS, it was not the focus of the work and the analysis was not as comprehensive as our own; we compare and contrast our results in the appropriate sections of our paper. Kührer *et al.* discuss the prevalence of DNS amplifiers, compared to other UDP-based protocols, and discusses fingerprinting techniques [10]; however, they do not expand on the amplification results. The solutions they propose focus on efficient identification, the notification of vulnerable amplifiers for various protocols, and on curtailing ASes that allow spoofing. Their approach is orthogonal to our own solution.

US-CERT recommends that organizations focus on eliminating open DNS resolvers [16], which echoes RFC 5358 [5]. However, this advice ignores the hundreds of thousands of authoritative DNS servers that are, by design, required to answer DNS queries to anyone who asks. These servers are well provisioned and capable of handling large volumes of traffic [7]. Attackers could use these servers to launch crippling attacks, even without using open resolvers. Accordingly, we focus on the risks associated with authoritative servers in this work.

Other reflector and amplification attacks can be damaging. However, we focus on DNS amplification because the protocol is widely used and the amplification attack can be indistinguishable from legitimate usage. Further, measures such as filtering, which may be used to mitigate other amplification attacks, would have unacceptable consequences for DNS (such as leaving a victim without the ability to resolve host names).

3   DNS Amplification Potential

We begin by determining the inherent DNS amplification risks associated with today's DNS authoritative servers. We examined over 129 million domains and over 1.1 million unique DNS authoritative servers to determine the amplification factor associated with common DNS queries.

3.1   Data Collection

As a starting point for our measurements, we used a DNS zone snapshot from July 2, 2013 for a collection of nine generic top-level domains (gTLDs). We obtained the DNS zone files for the biz, com, info, mobi, name, net, org, travel, and us zones from their respective maintainers. These zone files list the domain names and associated name servers for each of the domains registered under these TLDs. We collected records for 129, 300, 870 unique domains, each of which had one or more name servers listed, by host name, as authoritative for the domain. In total, 2, 771, 768 unique host names were listed as name servers, which upon resolving to IP addresses yielded 1, 101, 446 unique name server IP addresses. We collected these records in a distributed fashion and used delays between queries to minimize the impact on other users and the queried servers. We had an opt-out approach for queried providers; however, we did not receive any out-out requests.

Using these zone files, we constructed a set of pairs of the form (domain_name, NS_IP_address). This resulted in $363,263,970$ unique pairs. For each pair, we issued a set of DNS queries to the associated name server for the domain name without indicating any subdomains or hosts (e.g. a query for example.com).

Based on the results reported in our prior work [9], we knew that A records, which provide the IPv4 address for an indicated host name, would be quite common. Queries for A records are commonly issued by hosts on the Internet and are not be likely to be noticed by network operators. Recent DNS amplification attacks have used the ANY record type in their queries, which asks a name server to return any records associated with a host name. Since we used the base domain name, an ANY query would be likely to return the SOA, NS, and MX records associated with the domain, along with an A record for the host name. These four records were the most common in DNS zones in our prior work [9]. While the ANY query may yield the most records, such queries are not as commonly used by normal Internet hosts and their role in attacks may make them more noticeable when queried. Accordingly, we collect data for both the ANY query and the more common A query.

Traditional DNS packets are limited to a maximum length of 512 bytes at the application layer. However, the extension mechanisms for DNS (EDNS) [6] allow larger DNS packets if supported by both the resolver and authoritative server. To communicate support, the resolver sends a pseudo-resource record, OPT, that indicates the supported packet size. The OPT record can indicate DNSSEC support [4], indicating the server should send any associated DNSSEC records.

Attackers have a tactical consideration with using EDNS. Including an OPT record requires the attacker to include an additional 11 byte record in the query. If the server does not support EDNS, or the response would fit within the standard 512 byte limit, the response size remains the same. Accordingly, EDNS use would decrease the amplification factor associated with the query. However, if the EDNS support results in a larger response, it may dwarf the size of the OPT record and increase the amplification factor. Accordingly, we measure amplification, both with and without EDNS enabled (indicating a maximum application layer packet size of 4096 bytes as recommended by RFC 6891).

We also issued queries for AAAA records associated with IPv6. However, they were not widely used and did not provide a meaningful amplification over the other queries types. Accordingly, we omit any further discuss of these records.

In summary, we issued the following DNS queries for each domain: (1) A record without EDNS or DNSSEC support, (2) A record with EDNS and DNSSEC support, (3) ANY record without EDNS or DNSSEC support, and (4) ANY record with EDNS and DNSSEC support.

We issued the queries from July 29, 2013 to Aug. 1, 2013. To perform the massive number of queries quickly, we used a dedicated querying process and a separate packet capture process to collect and store each of the DNS responses sent to our server. Some packets may have been dropped, but for expediency, we accepted these losses and did not attempt a retransmission. Accordingly, each of the results we report will be conservative estimates of possible amplification.

3.2   Analysis of Servers and DNS Responses

We now examine the DNS responses. We exclude analysis of malformed packets, since we are unable to properly parse them, which amounts to 0.07 % of the data set. In Table 1, we show the overall success rates of our queries and statistics on the degree of amplification resulting from each. We calculated all packet sizes at the application layer (i.e., the DNS headers and payload). This excludes extraneous factors, such as the IPv4/IPv6 or UDP/TCP headers, and focuses on DNS. In Fig. 1, we show the amplification factor distribution for each of the data sets. For each query type, the attacker receives at least a 129 % increase in traffic volume at the application layer using DNS reflection. However, only 0.35 % of A record queries and 1.54 % of ANY queries had a packet size greater than the 512 byte limit when EDNS was enabled. Accordingly, the query overhead of using EDNS reduced the average amplification factor for both the A and the ANY groups. Simply put, an attacker does not benefit from using EDNS in the average case since few responses must be shortened to fit within 512 bytes.

Table 1. DNS Responses to Queries. Results are presented in the aggregate along with statistics on the top 1 million largest responses of each group.

Query Type		Response Rate	Top Million Queries Total (MB)		Amplification Ratio	
Record	Uses EDNS		Sent	Received	All Queries	Top 1 million
A	no	90 %	34	485	2.74	14.42
A	yes	89 %	44	725	2.29	**16.37**
ANY	no	84 %	35	534	6.22	15.32
ANY	yes	85 %	44	1,444	5.03	**32.77**

While this degree of amplification may be worthwhile for an attacker, a more potent strategy may be to focus on the queries and responses that yield the greatest amplification factor. To highlight the benefits of doing so, we provide statistics on the top 1 million packets, by response size, of each data set in Table 1. These packets make up roughly 0.3 % of each data set. Additionally, while EDNS did not help an attacker sending queries to random domains, it does benefit the attacker who focuses on those providing the most amplification. In both groups, EDNS yielded a notable increase in amplification among the million largest amplifying responses. This selective querying can help an attacker increase the amplification ratio to over 14.42 in the worst case and up to 32.77 in the best case.

The attacker receives the best amplification while using ANY queries, but we note that this record type may raise suspicions. An attacker that wishes to use A record queries to avoid detection can still achieve an amplification factor of 16.37. As an anecdotal result, in issuing the roughly 1.5 billion DNS queries associated with this study, our organization was contacted only once by a queried

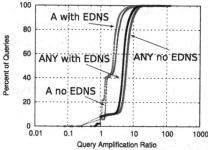

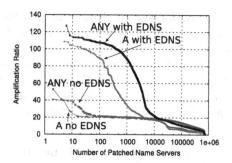

Fig. 1. Cumulative distribution function of the amplification ratio compared to the percent of queries for each data set.

Fig. 2. Amplification ratios ordered from the most amplifying server to the least. Some data points are aggregated for readability.

organization. That report was from an automated system indicating that the `ANY` query it received from our querying host may be the result of an attacker launching a reflection attack against us. Organizations may begin filtering `ANY` queries to reduce the amplification factor, but the amplification potential of `A` queries is unlikely to change.

To provide context for these results, we consider the theoretical maximum amplification, at the application layer, for DNS with EDNS using the recommended maximum response size of 4096 bytes. The DNS header itself is 12 bytes, with an additional $n + 5$ bytes for a query record, with a domain name of length n, and another additional 11 bytes for the OPT record to enable EDNS. The average maximum amplification with EDNS can then be expressed as $\frac{4096}{N+28}$ where N is the average domain name length in the queries. In our dataset, the average domain name length was 17 characters, which yields a maximum average amplification of roughly 91.02. Our overall amplifications are much lower than this, indicating most queried systems are not providing maximum-sized responses. However, looking at our top 10 % of amplifying name servers, we see an amplification of 78.13 indicating longer domain names on average with nearly maximum length responses. These highly amplifying servers are closer to the ratios reported in Rossow's DNS_{NS} set [13]. However, our dataset-wide averages are much lower than those in Rossow's data set. These are likely due to our different methodologies: Rossow used the Common Crawl project while we used the zone files themselves. Our data sets are larger and we did not pre-filter based on the deployment of DNSSEC, reducing potential sources of bias.

While attackers want to maximize the amplification factors associated with attacks, they must also ensure they use a large, distributed base of reflectors. If the attackers focus on a small number of highly amplifying reflectors, the reflector bandwidth may become a bottleneck. Even worse, the defenders may be able to filter a small number of reflector IP addresses with little collateral damage. To highlight this point, we note that although we received responses from 669,090 reflecting name servers, a much smaller pool of servers are responsible for the

1 million highest amplifying queries. For the top 1 million A record queries, the number of servers ranges from 24,782 in the "without EDNS" group to 24,841 servers in the "with EDNS" group. For the top 1 million ANY queries, the number of servers ranges from 22,508 in the "without EDNS" group to 28,101 in the "with EDNS" group. In other words, less than 3.8 % of authoritative name servers are associated with the highest degrees of amplification. In Fig. 2, we demonstrate the amplification ratios associated with each name server.

3.3 Impact of Record Type on Response Size

In Table 2, we show the contributions each resource record makes to the typical DNS packet from the Top 1 million EDNS groups. Attackers may consider which record types have the largest payload for the response and compose queries to elicit these responses. Not all record types are present in each packet. For example, the SOA record typically signals that no valid records are being returned. Thus, it is unsurprising it typically represents a large percentage of the responses where it appears. Likewise records associated with DNSSEC tend to be large, constituting a majority of the packet size in the instances where those records occur.

Interestingly, the use of DNSSEC to ensure the authenticity of DNS records has the unintended consequence of improving DNS amplification attacks. As one countermeasure, DNS servers may choose to apply rate-limiting separately to DNSSEC records. If a server continually asks for a response, the servers may discontinue providing DNSSEC records in duplicate responses before cutting the server off entirely. This would effectively decrease the amplification factor of an attack. However, it would limit clients' ability to get authenticated records in cases of high DNS packet loss. Operators may wish to consider these tradeoffs.

Table 2. Average number of bytes by resource record type for Top 1 million EDNS groups, as well as the occurrence percentages. We omit negligible results for readability.

Record Type	Packet Bytes (Percent)		Packet Occurrence %	
	A	ANY	A	ANY
A	171 (22.13 %)	115 (7.63 %)	87.2 %	97.7 %
AAAA	158 (19.60 %)	181 (15.76 %)	60.7 %	48.8 %
NS	220 (28.54 %)	126 (8.39 %)	85.9 %	99.5 %
SOA	70 (11.10 %)	63 (3.37 %)	12.5 %	67.1 %
TXT	-	141 (9.17 %)	-	19.1 %
All DNSSEC	623 (71.3 %)	1,688 (84.1 %)	40.2 %	60.0 %
RRSIG	590 (67.5 %)	1,308 (65.2 %)	40.2 %	60.0 %
DNSKEY	-	444 (20.8 %)	-	47.4 %
NSEC3	89 (14.4 %)	-	11.8 %	-

4   Measuring the Adoption of DNS Rate Limiting

A recent standard specified the rate-limiting of DNS responses at the DNS server to limit the use of DNS amplification in practice [18]. US CERT recommended organizations employ such rate-limiting, where possible, with a limit of five identical responses to the same origin per second [16]. However, CERT acknowledged that some popular DNS servers, notably Microsoft's DNS server, lack response rate limiting functionality, making rate-limiting impractical for many organizations. At the time of writing, this repeated response rate-limiting is the only standardized scheme available at DNS servers. We thus focus our measurement study on this approach.

CERT also acknowledged that rate-limiting may cause legitimate DNS queries to go unanswered if there is significant packet loss or other patterns. In our own prior work [14], where we monitored the DNS queries being issued to the authoritative servers at the Oak Ridge National Laboratory, we found that over 26,000 DNS resolvers re-issued a repeated query before the expiration of the five-minute TTL associated with the record. We found about 35 % of the repeated queries were issued within the first 10 s of the original resolution request, likely due to DNS packet loss. Further, we saw that some large Internet service providers load balanced their clients' DNS requests across caching DNS resolvers on contiguous IP addresses. Because the DNS rate limiting standard recommends rate-limiting at the /24 network prefix, it is possible that the combination of packet loss and load balancing will cause legitimate servers to exceed the rate-limit. This will deny clients access to the organization's services. Organizations have an incentive to avoid rate limiting or to set a high rate-limit value to avoid losing business or negatively affecting their customers.

To determine the impact of rate limiting, we used a random 0.5 % sample of name servers from our previous study and issued a set of repeated queries to each to find out what limit, if any, the server used for repeated requests. We issued these queries on May 3, 2014. We used an iterative process, ranging from 3 repeated queries to 15 repeated queries, with all queries in a set being issued within a single millisecond. Between iterations, we delay roughly 6 min to ensure any rate-limits are reset.

Using this methodology, we declare a particular name server as employing response rate limiting if there is a consecutive sequence from some number, x, to our limit of 15 in which each set of queries is missing at least one response. However, if a set of y queries, where $y > x$, successfully receives all of its responses, it is unlikely that the server uses a rate limit of x, since rate limiting is deterministic by nature. We note that this is a conservative approach, which may cause us to overestimate rate limiting adoption, since some responses could be lost due to chance. However, our methodology will not detect limits set at more than 15 queries a second.

In doing this probing, we found only 149 (2.69 %) of the studied name servers employed rate limiting. Of those, 7.38 % rate limited at 5 queries/second or less. The remaining 92.62 % used a rate limit between 9 and 14 queries/second.

These results show that rate-limiting is rarely used in practice and thus is unlikely to be a significant factor in a DNS amplification attack.

5   Countermeasure: Tunnel to Remote Resolver

Under normal flooding-based DDoS attacks, the victim can employ filtering at the victim's organization. However, victim organizations often also enlist filtering support from the organization's upstream Internet provider. These providers often have greater capacity and can employ filters before the traffic would reach the organization's last-mile link, which is often a bottleneck link. These providers can also employ such filtering at each ingress router to achieve more scalable, distributed filtering for providers with many peering points.

While a similar approach could also be used to filter all DNS response packets destined to the victim organization, this would also prevent legitimate DNS traffic both to and from that organization. Inbound traffic to the organization's authoritative DNS servers can be outsourced to one of the many entities, such as CloudFlare [3], which offer robust, off-site DNS hosting services using anycasting techniques. Since these approaches only focus on protecting externally accessible resources, they do not protect resolvers performing outbound local DNS resolutions.

We propose to address this problem in a simple way: create an off-premises DNS resolver for the organization and create a tunnel, using virtual private network protocols such as IPSec or SSL, between the off-premise resolver and the organization's on-site DNS resolver. We can then configure the on-site resolver to forward all DNS requests through the tunnel to the off-site DNS resolver while configuring the off-site resolver to operate recursively on behalf of the organization. Organizations could then simply request their upstream Internet providers to filter all DNS response traffic to the organization. This will filter the attack traffic, but will not affect the tunneled traffic between the resolvers, allowing organizations to maintain full DNS resolver functionality.

Many cloud providers would allow an organization to cheaply store and run a virtual machine that acts as an off-site DNS resolver. Since the resolver requires minimal computational resources, such hosting would be widely available for less than a dollar per day of use. As long as the organization's upstream provider can filter the attack, organizations could shrug off DNS amplification attacks of arbitrary size with minimal expense. With widespread adoption, the value of amplification attacks would decrease for attackers and their use may decline.

To demonstrate the feasibility of the approach, we used PlanetLab to host a DNS resolver off-site. The remote node was located in Rhode Island, USA, while our local resolver was hosted at our organization in Massachusetts, USA. We used BIND 9.5 as the DNS software on both our local resolver and on the remote PlanetLab resolver. We used OpenSSL to create an encrypted tunnel between the resolvers. We pre-install the DNS and OpenSSL software on each machine.

We then measured the amount of time required to transition from the resolver performing queries locally to performing the queries through the remote resolver.

We found that our solution's average start time was 1.36 s across 10,000 trials with a 0.55 s standard deviation. This overall time is the sum of the time required to start the remote BIND instance, establish the SSL tunnel, alter the configuration file on the local BIND resolver, and to reload the local resolver to apply these changes. We also determine the client's perspective of perceived downtime during the switch to the solution, after it has been set up, using a host that issued a query every 100 ms. Across 10,000 runs, it took an average of an additional 0.66 s (standard deviation of 0.81 s) from initiating the change until the first response was received by the client.

While using a remote resolver, the latency associated with each query increased to accommodate the propagation delays between the local and remote resolvers, as shown in Table 3. This had an impact on the latency for lookups. We first measured the delay between issuing a DNS query and receiving its response at the remote machine (which we label the baseline). We then measured the delay between issuing a DNS query and receiving the response at the local resolver, which forwards the query over the encrypted tunnel and to the remote machine for a recursive resolution (which we label the solution). The mean additional latency was 16 ms. Naturally, the geographical location and connectivity of the remote resolver will impact the overall latency. However, we can see that the overhead of the solution itself is minimal.

Table 3. Latency comparison of DNS resolutions on directly from the remote resolver to those forwarded by a targeted network to the remote resolver.

Approach	Query Response Time (ms)			Standard Deviation	Number of Queries
	Minimum	Median	Mean		
Baseline	7	69	128	166	1,547
Forwarded	22	85	94	62	1,344

We note that the adversary could learn about the victim's use of a remote resolver by having a client inside the victim's network, which can cause queries to traverse the remote resolver, and by operating an authoritative server that would be queried by the remote resolver. However, the victim can easily adapt to this by creating N remote resolvers, requiring the attacker to divide their resources. The victim organization may also monitor the attack, discover the colluding entities, and secure the internal client.

While this solution does require the cooperation of a third-party, that third-party is the victim organization's ISP, which has a financial interest in assisting its customer. Furthermore, the involvement of the ISP is minimal, constituting the addition of a simple filter rule.

6   Conclusion

In this work, we analyze the attack potential associated with DNS amplification attacks that focus on using authoritative servers as amplifiers. We find that attackers can launch damaging attacks of 1,444 MBytes/s of traffic at the target by sending only 44 MBytes/s of attack traffic from the source, and that botnets could scale up such attacks easily. We find that less than 3.8 % of authoritative servers are responsible for the highest amplification factors. Further, we note that DNSSEC played a significant role in amplification: by securing the DNS infrastructure, defenders are increasing the amplification potential of DNS reflector attacks. Further, we note that DNS response rate limiting has minimal adoption, with less than 3 % of name servers using the approach.

While much discussion has focused on open resolvers, they functionally serve as distributed mirrors of the top amplifying authoritative servers. These resolvers could also let attackers bypass rate-limiting at servers; however, with less than 3 % of servers using rate-limiting, open resolvers only seem valuable to have a larger base to distribute attacks.

While attackers have powerful tools at their disposal, we provide a simple mechanism that allows a victim organization to mitigate an on-going attack while incurring only modest latency increases in the organization's own DNS queries. Further, we note that organizations may be able to decrease their role in DNS amplification attacks by rate-limiting DNSSEC responses when repeatedly queried by a single source.

References

1. Bright, P.: Spamhaus DDoS grows to Internet-threatening size, March 2013. http://arstechnica.com/security/2013/03/spamhaus-ddos-grows-to-internet-threat ening-size/
2. Center for Measurement and Analysis of Network Data, Naval Postgraduate School: Spoofer project: State of IP spoofing, February 2014. http://spoofer.cmand.org/summary.php
3. CloudFlare: Cloudflare advanced ddos protection. https://www.cloudflare.com/ddos
4. Conrad, D.: Indicating resolver support of DNSSEC. IETF RFC 3225, December 2001
5. Damas, J., Neves, F.: Preventing use of recursive nameservers in reflector attacks. IETF RFC 5358, October 2008
6. Damas, J., Vixie, P.: Extension mechanisms for DNS (EDNS(0)). IETF RFC 6891, April 2013
7. Elz, R., Bush, R., Bradner, S., Patton, M.: Selection and operation of secondary dns servers. IETF RFC 2182, July 1997
8. Incapsula Inc: 2013–2014 ddos threat landscape report, April 2014. http://www.imperva.com/docs/RPT_2013-2014_ddos_threat_landscape.pdf
9. Kalafut, A.J., Shue, C.A., Gupta, M.: Touring DNS open houses for trends and configurations. IEEE/ACM Trans. Netw. PP(99), 1 (2011)
10. Kührer, M., Hupperich, T., Rossow, C., Holz, T.: Exit from hell? reducing the impact of amplification ddos attacks. In: USENIX Security Symposium (2014)
11. Paxson, V.: An analysis of using reflectors for distributed denial-of-service attacks. ACM SIGCOMM Comput. Commun. Rev. **31**(3), 38–47 (2001)

12. Prince, M.: Technical details behind a 400gbps NTP amplification DDoS attack, February 2014. http://blog.cloudflare.com/technical-details-behind-a-400gbps-ntp-amplification-ddos-attack

13. Rossow, C.: Amplification hell: Revisiting network protocols for DDoS abuse. In: Network and Distributed System Security (NDSS) Symposium (2014)

14. Shue, C., Kalafut, A.: Resolvers revealed: Characterizing DNS resolvers and their clients. ACM Trans. Internet Technol. (TOIT) 12(4), July 2013

15. US-CERT: Smurf ip denial-of-service attacks. Advisory (CA-1998-01), January 1998. http://www.cert.org/historical/advisories/CA-1998-01.cfm

16. US-CERT: Dns amplification attacks. Alert (TA13-088A), July 2013. https://www.us-cert.gov/ncas/alerts/TA13-088A

17. US-CERT: NTP amplification attacks using CVE-2013-5211. Alert (TA14-013A), January 2014

18. Vixie, P., Schryver, V.: Dns response rate limiting (DNS RRL), April 2012. http://ss.vix.su/~vixie/isc-tn-2012-1.txt

Measuring BGP Route Origin Registration and Validation

Daniele Iamartino[1,2]([⊠]), Cristel Pelsser[1], and Randy Bush[1]

[1] Internet Initiative Japan, Tokyo, Japan
[2] Politecnico di Milano, Milano, Italy
daniele.iamartino@mail.polimi.it

Abstract. BGP, the de-facto inter-domain routing protocol, was designed without considering security. Recently, network operators have experienced hijacks of their network prefixes, often due to BGP mis-configuration by other operators, sometimes maliciously. In order to address this, prefix origin validation, based on a RPKI infrastructure, was proposed and developed. Today, many organizations are registering their data in the RPKI to protect their prefixes from accidental mis-origination. However, some organizations submit incorrect information to the RPKI repositories or announce prefixes that do not exactly match what they registered. Also, the RPKI repositories of Internet registries are not operationally reliable. The aim of this work is to reveal these problems via measurement. We show how important they are, try to understand the main causes of errors, and explore possible solutions. In this longitudinal study, we see the impact of a policy which discards route announcements with invalid origins would have on the routing table, and to a lesser extent on the traffic at the edge of a large research network.

1 Introduction

Mis-originations, an Autonomous System (AS) announcing an IP prefix to which it has no rights, regularly appear in the Internet. Sometimes they arise from BGP misconfigurations. They may also result from malice. A notorious prefix mis-origination was the "YouTube incident" [9] where Pakistan Telecom advertised one of YouTube's IPv4 prefixes. The original intent was to censor traffic from Pakistan destined to YouTube. However, when PT "leaked" the prefix to the world, the event had a much larger impact than desired; traffic destined YouTube was blackholed at global scale. A more recent example is the "Indosat event" [17,19]. In April 2014, Indosat originated 417,038 prefixes normally announced by other ASs. This is believed likely due to a mis-configuration, a maintenance event gone bad [17]. In August 2014, a bitcoin miner [16] was attacked with the goal of diverting the traffic from the miners to relay the result of their computation and divert the monetary benefit of their work. The attack on bitcoin miners was malicious. This last example shows the limitations of route origin validation. Attackers will find another way to perform the attack if route origin validation is widely deployed.

© Springer International Publishing Switzerland 2015
J. Mirkovic and Y. Liu (Eds.): PAM 2015, LNCS 8995, pp. 28–40, 2015.
DOI: 10.1007/978-3-319-15509-8_3

In the current taxonomy, there are three pieces to improving BGP security, the RPKI, RPKI-based origin validation, and in the future path validation. In this paper, we focus on RPKI and RPKI-origin validation.

The RPKI is an X.509 based hierarchy congruent with the Internet IP address allocation administration, the IANA on top, then Regional Internet Registries (RIRs), and ISPs, ...It is the substrate on which origin and path validation are based. It is currently deployed by all five RIRs, AfriNIC, APNIC, ARIN, LACNIC, and RIPE.

RPKI-based origin validation uses RPKI data to allow routers to verify that the AS originating an IP prefix is in fact authorized to do so. This is not crypto checked, as a BGP update message does not carry signatures, so can be violated. But it should prevent the vast majority of accidental'hijackings' on the Internet today, e.g. the Pakistani accidental announcement of YouTube's address space. RPKI-based origin validation is in shipping code from Cisco and Juniper, and others soon.

A Route Origination Authorization (ROA) is an RPKI object which verifiably asserts that a specified AS is authorized to originate BGP announcements for a given set of prefixes [15]. A ROA is composed of an AS number, a list of IP prefixes, and for each prefix, a maximum length. The maximum length is a macro to authorize the AS to advertise more specific prefixes than the original prefix, up to the length as specified.

It is important to understand the status of deployment of route origin validation. For this purpose, we have been collecting data from the RPKI infrastructure since April 2012. Here we analyse these data to show the scale of deployment of ROA registrations. We find that registration is significantly deployed in Europe and Latin America, but is extremely poorly deployed in north America, Asia/ pacific, and Africa. We illustrate some of the events that occurred while publishing entities, the RIRs, learned to operate the RPKI system. There were serious problems regarding reliability of the RIR's RPKI infrastructure. Overall, it varied from bad to acceptable.

The incentive for operators to register ROAs is high, as it protects their resources. In order for this to be effective other operators need to deploy route origin validation in their ASs. That is, their routers need to check the validity of each route's origin. The drive to do this is multifold. It protects one's customer traffic from following a bogus/malicious route and it protects one's infrastructure from accepting many more routes than usual from a given peer (this can lead to a session reset or the restart of the router). It will also become common good practice, on the same level as prefix filtering, in that the effect of misconfigurations are contained close to the source of the event instead of affecting the entire Internet infrastructure. The second part of our study focuses on the validation of routes based on the registered ROAs. We take the views from public BGP monitors [8], and study the evolution of route origin validity over a 2.5 year time period with the objective to show that mis-origination occurred and could have been detected. In addition, we are interested in mis-matches between information registered in the RPKI and advertised routes. We try to understand these as they may highlight misunderstanding of the technology by network operators or poor tools or controls at the publishers. Does the validity of a route depend on the location where the advertisement is received? We try to answer that question next by looking at the validity status of routes at multiple locations.

Among the invalid prefixes, 81 % are covered by a valid prefix or a prefix not registered in the RPKI. A network operator strictly enforcing route-origin validation would not drop many prefixes. 54 % of the invalid prefixes result from a mis-match between the prefix length and the MaxLength in the ROAs. The other major issue results from ISPs not helping their multi-homed customers to register their sub-allocations.

Last, performing route origin validation means BGP routes selected by routers may change and thus can affect traffic forwarding. We try to understand the traffic impact by looking at the statistics of an operational router within an American research network. The router counts traffic forwarded by routes with valid, notfound, and invalid origin. This tells us the amount of traffic that would be dropped by the router should different BGP policies be adopted. It shows that if an operator was to configure its routers to strictly drop routes with invalid origin, the effect on the traffic would be negligible.

The paper is organized as follows. We describe our methodology and data sets in Sect. 2. In Sect. 3 we look first at the extent of RPKI ROAs publication across the different administrative regions. Second, we study the different causes of mis-match between route advertisements and RPKI registrations. Third, we present traffic statistics for each class of routes (valid origin, invalid, and unknown). We present some related work in Sect. 4, and conclude in Sect. 5.

2   Methodology

2.1   Validation Process

As we are analyzing historical data, to determine the validity of a BGP route advertisement at some point in time, the first step is to get all the published ROAs for a given time and build a radix tree. The radix tree will then be used to validate the route entries of subsequent BGP RIB dumps.

Each ROA file is composed of an AS number, multiple IP prefixes, and a maximum length for each prefix. For all X.509 validated ROA files, we extract tuples (ASN, Prefix, MaxLen, Expiration time). We insert these tuples as nodes of a radix tree where the key is the IP Prefix of the tuple. That is, each node of the radix tree is identified by the IP prefix that it is covering. Note that more than one ROA record might exist for a particular prefix. Consequently, each node may contain more than one ROA record.

After building the radix tree, we take the BGP RIB dump following the download of the ROAs from the RPKI infrastructure, and before the next download of ROAs. We validate the content in each RIB dump separately. Each dump gives us a view of the validity at a different point in time. For each announcement found in a RIB dump, we search for the longest prefix match in the radix tree. If no such node is found, we mark the announcement as "ROA not found".

Then, for each ROA present in the node, we check if the max length of the node covers the announced prefix and if the AS number specified in the ROA record is equal to the origin AS number of the announcement. If these conditions are met, the ROA validates the route announced for the prefix. If no validating ROA is found in the given node, we traverse upward to shorter prefixes until we either find a validating ROA or there is no parent node. If we moved upward in the tree and never found a matching ROA, the route is marked as invalid, else its origin AS is deemed valid.

In a RIB dump, there may be multiple announcements for a single prefix, as a monitor may learn the same prefix from different BGP peers. We validate each announcement separately.

2.2 Datasets

This study relies on a number of datasets: (1) the download of ROAs from the RPKI infrastructure every hour from March 2012 to August 2014, (2) BGP RIB dumps from RouteViews [8] for the same period. RouteViews RIB dumps are available every two hours, and (3) the marked statistics taken from a live router in a research network. We perform most validation on the LINX RIB dumps. To determine the sensitivity of route origin validity at different locations we also consider the ISC, Sao Paulo, Sidney, and WIDE RouteViews monitors.

Regarding the first dataset, as the IANA has not been allowed to provide an RPKI root, we chose trust anchors following the recommendation of the IETF SIDR working group [15], using the rcynic tool [7] to download ROAs from the RIPE, LACNIC, AfriNIC, APNIC and CA0 trust anchors, with two exceptions; for legal reasons, we only have ARIN data starting from August 2014 and we add the CA0 data. ARIN has a policy of providing access to the data only to those who have signed a document. CA0 is the trust anchor for some legacy and experimental address space that ARIN will not register.

As ROAs can not cover AS-SETs, we excluded from our study the minuscule portion of BGP announcements which have an AS-SET for the origin AS.

When we validate the origins of advertisements in a RIB dump, we take the ROAs gathered during the rcynic run prior but closest in time to the time-stamp of the RIB dump.

3 Results

3.1 RPKI Deployment

First we look at the extent of RPKI registration deployment. Table 1 shows the number of IPv4 host addresses (/32 s) covered by ROAs by each RIR publication point. The 3rd column shows the total number of IPv4 addresses delegated by each RIR. We observe that while ARIN has allocated most of the address space, it lags far behind the other Northern RIRs in registrations, giving many North Americans a distorted view of RPKI deployment. The same is true for APNIC.

Table 1. Deployment status of the registration of IPv4 addresses on September 8, 2014 (data from [1]) compared to the allocation of IPs by these RIRs on the same day [2–6].

Publication point	Number of IPv4 addresses covered by a ROA	Number of IPv4 allocated	Percentage coverage
RIPE NCC	125,133,312	797,906,680	15.68 %
ARIN	30,187,520	1,733,372,928	1.74 %
LACNIC	19,089,408	189,833,472	10.05 %
AfriNIC	2,814,464	119,534,080	2.35 %
APNIC	744,960	872,194,816	0.08 %
Total	177,969,664	3,712,841,976	4.79 %

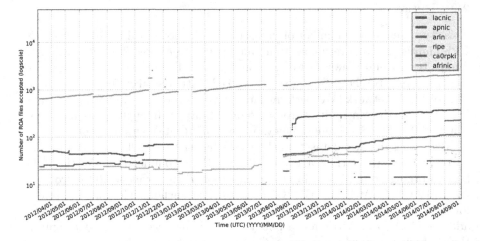

Fig. 1. Accepted (valid) ROA files below the six trust anchors. The discontinuous increases in number of ROAs observed for RIPE NCC occur during key rollovers. LACNIC and APNIC face a loss of valid ROAs for roughly seven months, likely due to an expiration of their X.509 certificate. There is a hole in our data, for all trust anchors between July and August 2013.

RIPE NCC is currently the leader in terms of both absolute and relative amount of allocated address space covered by ROAs, and LACNIC is quite active.

In Fig. 1 we can see, for each RIR, the number of ROAs authenticated by rcynic between March 2012 and September 2014. There is a one-month hole between July and August 2013 due to a problem in our data collection. We only started collecting ARIN's data in August 2014, due to ARIN's legal barriers placed on RPKI use. We see LACNIC data being interrupted from the end of December 2012 to mid August 2013; we believe the reason for this is X.509 expiration of their trust anchor. That this went undetected is operationally quite disturbing. Also the APNIC repository had a similar event for seven months between January and August 2013. Between November 2012 and February 2013 we can see the effects of key roll-over on the RIPE data. We started to collect CA0 data on August 2013. We observe regular drops in the number of ROAs for CA0 because this data is hosted on a machine that is regularly disconnected from the Internet for extended periods of time giving time for objects to expire without being renewed on time.

3.2   Validity Status of Prefix Announcements Over Time

For this analysis we use a BGP RIB dump taken every 30 days on the LINX monitor of Route-Views. In a RIB dump we usually find several announcements for the same prefix received from different BGP peers. For origin-validation purposes, each announcement is identified by: its time-stamp, the prefix announced, and the origin AS (the right-most AS on the AS_PATH). Note that in the case of a RIB dump file, the time-stamp is always equal to the global time-stamp of the RIB dump. We validate each announcement as described in Sect. 2.1. In a given RIB dump, we might have several announcements with different origin AS for the same prefix. Consequently, we classify every prefix in one of the following groups:

- **Valid only:** All announcements observed for this prefix are valid.
- **Invalid only:** All announcements observed this prefix are invalid.

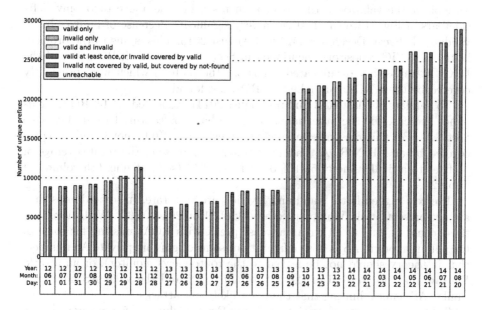

Fig. 2. Validity status of routes seen by route-views LINX monitor between June 2012 and September 2014. The first (green, pink and yellow) bar shows the status of prefixes independently from the existence of covering prefixes. The second bar (blue, red and grey) illustrates the reachability of a prefix considering that an invalid prefix might be covered by another valid or "ROA not found" prefix (Color figure online).

Table 2. A few data points to compare valid and invalid prefixes to the reachability of these prefixes should the LINX monitor drop invalid prefixes. Most invalid prefixes are still reachable because of the existence of a covering prefix that is either marked as "valid" or "ROA not found".

Date	Total prefixes seen	Valid prefixes	Invalid prefixes	Valid and invalid prefixes	Percentage of RPKI-covered prefixes	Reachable prefixes	Unreachable prefixes	Percentage of invalid covered
2012/06/01	432,516	7,253	1,621	0	2.05 %	8,648	226	86.05 %
2012/11/28	454,601	9,258	2,123	13	2.50 %	11,149	245	88.45 %
2012/12/28	458,955	5,097	1,368	16	1.41 %	6,276	205	85.01 %
2013/09/24	504,733	17,567	3,400	8	4.15 %	20,537	438	87.11 %
2014/05/22	525,241	23,531	2,693	31	4.99 %	25,731	525	80.50 %
2014/07/21	534,519	24,511	2,916	18	5.13 %	26,904	541	81.44 %
2014/08/20	538,926	25,973	3,168	17	5.41 %	28,565	593	81.28 %

- **Valid and invalid:** We found both valid and invalid announcements for the prefix. That is, some announcements have a different origin ASs.
- **ROA not found:** There is no ROA covering this prefix.

As seen in Sect. 3.1, only 4.79 % of IP addresses are covered by ROAs. This means that a lot of prefix advertisements will fall in the "ROA not found" category. For readability, we do not show this case in the following figures. When we look at the validity of the advertisements using the above taxonomy (left-side bars of Fig. 2) we can first see a very significant decrease of prefixes being validated between December 2012 and August 2013. This is due to the problem in the LACNIC repository mentioned in Sect. 3.1. Almost all ROA files of the LACNIC repository disappeared. Thus, all the prefixes which were previously covered by these ROAs are labelled "ROA not found".

To validate the last RIB dump (August 2014), we added ARIN ROAs. This is not the case for the other months, as we had not captured those data (see Sect. 3.1). For this reason, some prefixes which were "ROA not found" become covered by an ARIN ROA, leading to a slight increase of the total coverage of prefixes to a final value of 5.41 % on August 2014 (see last line, 6th column of Table 2).

Prefixes tagged both "valid and invalid" are very rare. In some dumps they are not present at all. We observed a peak of 31 on 2014/05/22. We believe that these could be due to either an anycast prefix with ROAs missing for some of the potential origin AS, a misconfiguration (some origins are private AS numbers that in theory should not be leaked to the route-views monitor), or an attack. We saw that, for several of these, the failing AS and the valid AS have very similar AS names, hinting that these are likely not attacks.

Table 2 shows some of the data points of Fig. 2. Column 3–5 correspond to the elements of the first bar for some times on the x-axis in the figure. We can further deduce the amount of 'ROA not found' prefixes by looking at column 6. In June 2012, 97.95 % of the prefixes were not covered by any ROAs. This decreases to 94.59 % in August 2014.

Table 3. Reachable and unreachable prefixes from different route-views monitors on 20 August 2014

Monitor name	All prefixes seen	RPKI-covered reachable prefixes seen	RPKI-covered un- reachable prefixes seen	Percentage of unreachable	Percentage of RPKI-covered prefixes
ISC	540,197	27,587	591	2.14 %	5.21 %
LINX	538,926	28,565	593	2.07 %	5.41 %
Sao Paulo	547,554	28,521	580	2.03 %	5.31 %
Sydney	538,378	28,741	596	2.07 %	5.44 %
WIDE	528,883	27,457	588	2.14 %	5.30 %

3.3 Taking Coverage into Account

It is often assumed that operators who validate advertisements will drop invalids. In order to better understand the effect of that policy on reachability, we cannot simply look at prefixes separately. We need to consider the coverage of invalids by other prefixes. Let's assume that a BGP border router receives the same routes as our LINX monitor. It drops all "invalid only" prefixes. In addition, in the deployment phase, we expect operators to also accept announcements for prefixes with no ROA. If a prefix is "valid" or "valid and invalid", we consider it as reachable, because it means that at least one valid announcement for that prefix was present. When a prefix is marked "invalid only", there are some cases when it could be reached:

- The invalid prefix is **up-covered by another valid** prefix (Example: announcement of 10.1.2.0/24 is invalid, but 10.1.0.0/16 is also announced and valid, so the monitor can reach 10.1.2.0/24 anyway exploiting the covering valid announcement)
- The invalid prefix is **completely down-covered by other valid** prefixes (Example: announcement of 10.1.0.0/16 is invalid, but 10.1.0.0/17 and 10.1.128.0/17 are also announced and valid)
- The invalid prefix is **up-covered by a "ROA not found"** prefix (Example: announcement of 10.1.2.0/24 is invalid, but 10.1.0.0/16 is also announced and there is no covering ROA for the latter)

So we can finally say that a given prefix is **reachable** if it is "ROA not found", "valid only", "valid and invalid" or "invalid only" covered as in one of the three cases above. Instead, when a prefix is "invalid only" and there is no coverage by another valid or "ROA not found", we mark it as **unreachable**. The right-side bars of Fig. 2 show the reachability of prefixes considering coverage. Table 2 list of few of the key values in columns 7–9. We note that around 80 % of invalid prefixes are in fact reachable. They are "rescued" by another valid or a "ROA not found" covering prefix.

3.4   The Effect of Monitors

Up to now we considered the data from the LINX monitor because it has a lot of peering links. This monitor is interesting because it receives a lot of heterogeneous announcements. Here we aim to see if our observations are highly dependent on that monitor. For that purpose, we consider 4 additional route-views collection points: **ISC** (Palo Alto CA, USA), **SAOPAULO** (Sao Paulo, Brazil), **SYDNEY** (Sydney, Australia), **WIDE** (Tokyo, Japan). The main difference between monitors is that they do not receive routes for the same amount of prefixes (see Table 3). However, the percentage of RPKI-covered prefixes seen is very similar. We think that in order to detect specific events, it might be better to combine the data from all monitors, but for the purpose of our measurements it's enough to consider one of the biggest. The percentage of unreachable prefixes due to an invalid origin is almost the same at any of the 5 locations considered.

3.5   The Causes Behind Invalids

What are the reasons behind failed route origin validations? For every "invalid only" or "valid and invalid" prefix, we look at the reason why the ROA record(s) present in the longest-prefix matching node of the radix tree does not match the advertisement under validation. We analyze all invalid prefixes, discarding their potential coverage by other prefixes, contrary to Sect. 3.3. We divide the failed validations into three categories:

- **Invalid maximum prefix length:** For example, the monitor receives an announcement for 10.1.2.0/24 but the ROA record covers only 10.1.0.0/16-16.
- **Invalid origin AS number:** The monitor receives an announcement by AS666 for 10.1.2.0/24 but the ROA record authorize 10.1.2.0/24 only from AS42.

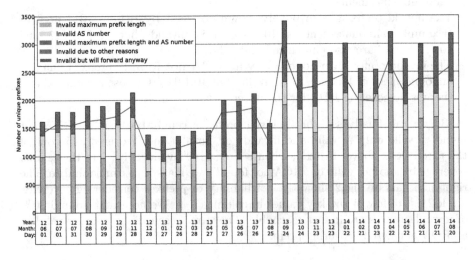

Fig. 3. Breakdown of invalid prefixes, by failing cause, as seen by LINX monitor

Table 4. Percentage of invalid prefixes, divided by failing reason: MaxLength/ASN/ both. Data from LINX monitor of route-views project.

Date	Prefixes invalid due to MaxLength	Prefixes invalid due to wrong ASN	Prefixes invalid due to MaxLength and ASN
2012/06/01	989 (61.01 %)	387 (23.87 %)	245 (15.11 %)
2012/11/28	1053 (49.30 %)	644 (30.15 %)	439 (20.55 %)
2014/06/21	1661 (55.61 %)	462 (15.47 %)	864 (28.93 %)
2014/07/21	1690 (57.60 %)	411 (14.01 %)	833 (28.39 %)
2014/08/20	1736 (54.51 %)	584 (18.34 %)	865 (27.16 %)

– **Both maximum length and AS number:** At least two ROAs are found in the longest-prefix matching node for the prefix, one or more of them failing on AS number, the other(s) failing on MaxLength; or there is a single ROA failing for both reasons. This may cover a lot of different causes and we don't have enough information to classify them.

In Fig. 3 we can see that mismatched maximum length is the most widespread cause for invalids (see Table 4 for some numbers relative to the figure). There are less invalids due to non-matching origin ASs.

We can further subdivide the class of "invalid origin AS number" and "both maximum length and AS number" errors by looking for the valid AS within the AS path. This indicates that the up-stream provider registered the covering prefix but did not do their job and create a ROA for their customer's sub-allocation. For example, the service provider (ISP) registers (prefix 10.0.0.0/16, AS42) and allocates 10.0.1.0/24 to its multi-homed customer AS666. The monitor receives the AS path 100 200 42 666. The announcement of the customer is invalid because only AS42 is authorized by the ROA. However AS42 is present in the AS path. We took invalid prefixes of the last RIB dump of August 2014, and for each of them we check whether at least one of the announcements of that prefix contains a correct AS in the AS path. Results are that 57.36 % of "invalid origin AS number" invalid prefixes and 83.23 % of "both maximum length and AS number" invalid prefixes contains the correct AS on the AS path.

Summing the percentages, when we see an announcement coming from the wrong origin AS, in %72 of the cases we can find the correct AS in one of the AS paths of that prefix. As the customer (AS666 in the example) is multi-homed, there are likely one or more other AS Paths also starting from AS666 but not having the allocating up-stream in the path. However, the 54.51 % percentage of MaxLength problems alone is still the overwhelming invalid cause, and could be easily fixed by submission of correct ROA records by organizations.

This study highlights the need for operators to monitor the status of their prefixes with regard to what is registered in the RPKI. In addition, customers should make sure that their provider registers the prefixes they have been allocated or should perform the registration themselves. Most invalids today are

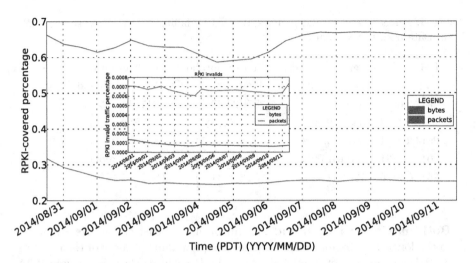

Fig. 4. Percentage of bytes or packets coming or going to an IP address of an RPKI-covered prefix

probably a result from operators learning a new technology and have not yet developed good procedures. By monitoring the validity of their prefixes they should be able to learn from their mistakes and fix them. RIRs and researchers could also publish these problems and notify those who should fix them.

3.6 Effect on Traffic in a Real Network

BGP announcement data can give us an idea about the deployment of origin-validation on the global Internet. However, most of the common traffic on the Internet is usually directed to just few destinations. For this reason, we gathered data about how many "RPKI-protected" packets/bytes are passing across a real router within a large research network. We say that a packet/byte is 'RPKI-protected', if the packet/byte was received from an IP address part of an RPKI-covered prefix or sent to such an IP destination. We observe in Fig. 4 that very little traffic is RPKI-covered, likely because this is an American research network whose prefixes ARIN will not certify. The embedded figure shows the percentages of bytes/packets with invalid source or destination that cross the router. Traffic from/to invalid origins is negligible in this case. This finding is consistent with [10,13].

4 Related Work

The closest works to ours are [13] and [10]. They provide snapshots of route validation in specific deployments. Here we go further as we study route validation over an extended period of time. In addition, we provide statistics regarding the RPKI infrastructure, and the registration of resources and events caused by the operation of the infrastructure.

In [18], Wählisch et al. aim to distinguish misconfiguration from intentional hijacks. For this purpose they rely on route origin validation. On the other hand, PHAS [14] offers a real-time hijacking detection service. PHAS monitors the set of origin ASs observed in public data. It notifies operators that register to the system of changes in observed origin ASs. In the RPKI, publication points can remove resources from the distributed database with the adverse effect that advertisements from some prefixes may not be validated anymore. The work of Heilam *et al.* [12] aims to prevent publication points from removing resources from the system without the consent of the owner(s) of the resources. The objective of [11] is to measure the effect of attacks on the traffic. The authors observe that even with secure routing mechanisms, it is possible to attract a large amount of traffic by advertising routes along valid paths but infringing the BGP policies for targeted prefixes.

5   Conclusion

In this paper, we studied the extend of RPKI deployment. We observed that Europe and Latin America are leading today, with many ROAs registered. Regarding the RIRs RPKI infrastructure, there were serious problems. The entire dataset became unavailable for extended periods of time for a couple of RIRs. We then quantified the state of origin-validation deployment. It is about 5 %, and increasing. Among the invalid BGP announcements, the number of invalid prefixes due to the MaxLength error alone are the majority, and they could be easily fixed by just correct ROA submissions. We also discovered that many invalid prefixes are due to coverage by a ROA of a service provider. This shows that organizations that are still not planning to deploy RPKI should care about what their service provider is doing.

While we found several invalid BGP announcements of prefixes, most of them are "rescued" by another valid or "ROA not found" covering prefix. This means that, today, filtering invalid prefixes could leave few unreachable prefixes, but not as many as one would think. When looking at the actual effect on the traffic crossing a router, we find that dropping invalids leads to negligible amount of traffic being dropped, and hence is safe to do.

Acknowledgments. We thank the operator of the large American research network for setting up the collection of the traffic statistics. Rob Austein was a great help toward understanding the mechanics of the RPKI infrastructure and the different events we observed.

References

1. IPv4 Address Space in ROAs (/24s). http://certification-stats.ripe.net/?type= roa-v4
2. IPv4 Prefixes Delegated by AfriNIC. ftp://ftp.afrinic.net/stats/afrinic/delegated-afrinic-extended-latest

3. IPv4 Prefixes Delegated by APNIC. ftp://ftp.apnic.net/pub/apnic/stats/apnic/del egated-apnic-extended-latest
4. IPv4 Prefixes Delegated by ARIN. ftp://ftp.arin.net/pub/stats/arin/delegated-arin-extended-latest
5. IPv4 Prefixes Delegated by LACNIC. ftp://ftp.lacnic.net/pub/stats/lacnic/dele gated-lacnic-extended-latest
6. IPv4 Prefixes Delegated by RIPE NCC. ftp://ftp.ripe.net/ripe/stats/delegated-ripencc-extended-latest
7. rcynic RPKI validator. http://rpki.net/wiki/doc/RPKI/RP/rcynic
8. University of oregon route views project. http://www.routeviews.org
9. YouTube Hijacking: A RIPE NCC RIS case study, March 2008. http://www.ripe.net/internet-coordination/news/industry-developments/youtube-hijacking-a-ripe-ncc-ris-case-study
10. Fincham, M.: RPKI, NZNOG 2014, February 2014. http://hotplate.co.nz/archive/nznog/2014/rpki/
11. Goldberg, S., Shapira, M., Hummon, P., Rexford, J.: How secure are secure inter-domain routing protocols? Comput. Netw. **70**, 260–287 (2014)
12. Heilman, E., Cooper, D., Reyzin, L., Goldberg, S.: From the consent of the routed: improving the transparency of the RPKI. In: Sigcomm 2014 (2014)
13. Kloots, J.: RPKI Routing Policy Decision-Making, A SURFNET Perspective, February 2014. https://blog.surfnet.nl/?p=3159
14. Lad, M., Massey, D., Pei, D., Wu, Y., Zhang, B., Zhang, L.: PHAS: a prefix hijack alert system. In: Proceedings of USENIX Security Symposium (2006)
15. Lepinski, M., Kent, S.: An Infrastructure to Support Secure Internet Routing, RFC 6480, February 2012
16. Litke, P., Stewart, J.: BGP Hijacking for Cryptocurrency Profit, August 2014. http://www.secureworks.com/cyber-threat-intelligence/threats/bgp-hijacking-for-cryptocurrency-profit/
17. Toonk, A.: Hijack Event Today by Indosat, April 2014. http://www.bgpmon.net/hijack-event-today-by-indosat/
18. Wählisch, M., Maennel, O., Schmidt, T.C.: Towards detecting BGP route hijacking using the RPKI. In: Sigcomm 2012 (Poster) (2012)
19. Zmijewski, E.: Indonesia Hijacks the World, April 2014. http://www.renesys.com/2014/04/indonesia-hijacks-world/

On the Diversity of Interdomain Routing in Africa

Rodérick Fanou[1,2]([✉]), Pierre Francois[2], and Emile Aben[3]

[1] IMDEA Networks Institute, Madrid, Spain
[2] Universidad Carlos III de Madrid (UC3M), Madrid, Spain
{roderick.fanou,pierre.francois}@imdea.org
[3] RIPE NCC, Amsterdam, The Netherlands
emile.aben@ripe.net

Abstract. With IP networking booming in Africa, promotion of BGP peering in the region emerge, and changes in the transit behavior of ISPs serving Africa are expected. However, little is known about the IP transit topology currently forming the African Internet. Enhancing the RIPE Atlas infrastructure, we evaluate the topology interconnecting ISPs based on the continent. We reveal a variety of ISP transit habits, depending on a range of factors such as the official language or the business profile of the ISP. We highlight the emergence of IXPs in Africa, evaluating its impact on end-to-end connectivity. Our results however emphasize the remaining dominance of ISPs based outside Africa, for the provision of intra-continental paths. We study the impact of this aspect on AS path length and end-to-end delay. Such results illustrate that performing measurements from a broad, diversified, range of vantage points is necessary to assess interdomain routing on the continent.

Keywords: RIPE Atlas · IP transit · African Internet · IXP

1 Introduction

Despite major investments in submarine and terrestrial cable deployments in Africa, Internet access is still perceived as of low quality, with high latency and low bandwidth [1,2]. According a study of the African Union [3], Africa spends between US $400 millions and $600 millions per year in transit fees for intra-African traffic. Initiatives such as the African Internet eXchange System have thus been launched to promote the creation of IXPs and regional carriers, and improve the fragmented status of the IP infrastructure [4]. It provides an enabling environment for cross-border interconnection to thrive and become more competitive to reduce transit costs paid by Africa for intra-African traffic exchange. Meanwhile, caches and peering points have been deployed by CDNs (Google, Akamai, Cloudfare, etc.) in the region proving the capacities to offload traffic from the expensive transit links. However, little is known about the current state of the Internet topology in Africa, due to its low representation in

© Springer International Publishing Switzerland 2015
J. Mirkovic and Y. Liu (Eds.): PAM 2015, LNCS 8995, pp. 41–54, 2015.
DOI: 10.1007/978-3-319-15509-8_4

existing measurement projects. Obtaining relevant topological data, especially for access-to-access interconnection is thus essential to understand its current state and observe its foreseen evolution. Recent work focusing on Africa, such as [2,5,6], relied on a very limited set of vantage points, and had different focuses, as explained later.

In this paper, we set as key milestone to obtain an interdomain map that is not biased towards the South African perspective. To this end, we met ISPs in Benin, Burkina Faso, Congo, Ghana, Ivory Coast, Mauritania, Morocco, Niger, Nigeria, Senegal, and Togo, to deploy RIPE Atlas probes within their networks. We complemented our set of probes with those deployed by RIPE Atlas Ambassadors. To obtain insights on the evolution of the peering ecosystem, our measurement campaign covers 6 months, monitoring end-to-end paths among v4 and v6 probes scattered on the continent [7]. We discover a large variety of ISP transit habits, notably correlated with the location, the official language, and the monetary union of the country in which operate the ISP. Our results illustrate that, with the exception of ISPs based in South Africa, the provision of intra-continental paths is dominated by ISPs based outside Africa, while South Africa is being adopted as a hub for East-West African communications. We study the impact of such aspects on the end-to-end delay between ISPs, notably among networks based in the same country. Finally, we illustrate the benefits of new IXPs with respect to end-to-end delay.

The remainder of this paper is structured as follows. Section 2 discusses related work. Section 3 presents our methodology, while Sect. 4 exposes our results. Section 5 concludes the paper and describes our plans for further research.

2   Related Work

An extensive amount of research has been carried out on the discovery of the Internet topology, both at the router level and the AS level [8–10]. Archipelago has the goal of reducing the efforts needed to develop and deploy sophisticated large-scale measurements [11]. Of its 94 monitors, only 5 are deployed in Africa. For this study, a larger deployed base of vantage points was needed. Similarly, although the PingER project [12] involves 46 African countries, only Burkina Faso and South Africa host a monitoring site, preventing us from doing large scale end-to-end measurements.

Gilmore *et al.* mapped, in [5], both the router level and AS level graphs of intra-African traffic. Traceroutes from South Africa towards all the IPs allocated by AFRINIC were performed for a week. To improve their results, they extracted from the RIBs of routers in the South African Tertiary Education Network, the links among ASes registered in AFRINIC and those towards their direct neighbouring ASes. As a consequence, they obtained one way paths from which they infered a tree, of which South Africa is the root. They acknowledged that the link density might look different if the traceroute probes were sent out from other countries in Africa.

Recently, Gupta *et al.* investigated Internet connectivity between Kenya, Tunisia, and South Africa [6], by performing traceroutes from access networks to sites hosting popular content. They noticed that 66.8 % of paths from their vantage points towards Google cache servers located in Africa leave the continent. They generalized, from their results, the nature of intra-domain interconnectivity on the continent. Nevertheless, broadband access networks in those countries are more developed in comparison with most African countries, so that, as acknowledged by the authors, the obtained dataset may not reflect the nature of the paths in other countries.

In contrast, our study presents discoveries of the Internet infrastructure based on measurements performed from access to access networks, as we aim at studying how Africans communicate with one another. We perform these measurements among a large variety of networks, and for a long enough period of time to study the dynamics of the African Internet topology. The paths in our dataset are typically not seen in RouteViews, RIS and PCH datasets, as these do not host monitors in the studied regions. We also show that ISP transit and peering habits vary throughout the continent. By exhibiting newly established IXPs located in Africa, as well as the use of other ones, we show that ISPs do peer now in Africa, illustrating the first benefits of the initiatives promoting peering. An exploration of how these measurements in Africa compare to measurements in other regions is left to future work.

3 Methodology

3.1 Data Collection

Multiple challenges influenced our choice for the measurement infrastructure. First, whereas network operators are reticent to the intrusion of foreign devices, for legitimate security and privacy reasons, we had to find a relevant number of hosting locations for the measurement devices. Such devices have to be robust, as power outages and surges frequently occur in the studied countries. Finally, we preferred an open measurement infrastructure, as we wanted to provide means for network operators and researchers to further study African networking. We chose the RIPE Atlas measurement platform, which consists of over 7400 deployed worldwide [7]. These devices are free, secure, and require no maintenance.

In June 2013, Africa only hosted a few active RIPE Atlas devices, with almost no deployment in the West. To improve the situation, we deployed 21 RIPE Atlas probes in 15 ISPs networks covering 11 countries, focusing on that region. These devices are hosted by either ISPs, universities, or home networks. None of them are behind a wireless access link, to reduce the impact of last mile latency on our results. Collaborating institutions such as AFRINIC and ISOC also deployed a considerable amount of probes in the Southern and Eastern regions, which we used in this study.

We used paris-traceroute for all our measurements to discover as many paths as possible, and not suffer from inconsistent results caused by load balancing, as happens with classic traceroute [13]. Probes performed traceroutes with 16 different paris_id defaults. We used the UDP-traceroute to reduce the potential bias caused by differentiated traffic handling of ICMP packets [14]. We conducted 3 measurement campaigns. During the first one, we performed traceroutes among all probes located in Africa, with a period of 3 h, from November 30, 2013 to April 06, 2014. It results in total in 675,421 traceroute outputs. Second, we issued v4 and v6 traceroutes, at the same frequency, focusing on countries hosting IPv6 enabled probes, from June 01, 2014 to August 01, 2014, in order to compare v4 and v6 routing. It results in total in 408,383 v4 and 21,744 v6 traceroute outputs. Finally, to highlight the launch of the Serekunda IXP in GM[1], we performed hourly, during the second week of August 2014, 3,161 traceroutes among all RIPE Atlas probes in GM, publicly available in a Technical Report [15].

An essential step is to undertake an in-depth sanity-check on the raw data to only consider the valid traceroute outputs during our analysis. Before this filtering process, our raw data involved 214 probes hosted in 90 ASes operating in 32 African countries. The geographical and networking spread of the used probes are available in [15]. As for the granularity of our results, the percentage of ASes allocated by AFRINIC [16] covered per country is 21.7 % on average [15]. With this dataset, we first map IPs into Country Codes (CCs) in order to infer the set of countries traversed by the packets during each traceroute. Second, we map IPs into ASes to infer the ASes sequences.

3.2 Data Analysis

3.2.1 IP to Country Code Mapping and Validation

Geolocation is said to be of poor quality, especially for IPs located in Africa [17]. To geographically locate the 8,328 v4 and 465 v6 public IPs found in the traceroute data as accurately as possible, we thus analyzed 6 public databases (DBs), that we cross-correlated with delay measurements, as explained in this section. We used OpenIPMap (*OIM*) [18], Reverse DNS lookups (*RDNS*), Max-Mind GeoIP2City (*MM*) [19], Team Cymru (*TC*) [20], the AFRINIC DB (*AF*) [16], and Whois (*Whois*).

When all databases providing an entry for an IP returns the same CC, we retain it for that IP. When DBs are inconsistent for an entry, we use a latency-based method to tie-break among them. We ping each IP from up to 10 random RIPE Atlas probes hosted in each country returned by the DBs[2]. We compute the minimum delay recorded per possible country, and assume that the IP is located in the country for which the minimum delay is the lowest. We compare in Table 1 the entries of the selected DBs. The coverage column (Cov.) is the percentage of addresses of our dataset for which the DB provided a valid country field. Trust is the percentage of IPs for which the DB entry is equal to the country that we finally selected for that IP.

5,430 v4 IPs (resp. 292 v6 IPs) out of the 8,328 v4 (resp. 465 v6) have an identical CC mapping among all DBs for which an entry was available.

---

[1] In this paper, we refer to countries using ISO 2-letter country codes, that we list in [15].

[2] The raw data for these delay measurements can be found in [15].

Table 1. Comparison of Geolocation databases

DB	IPv4 entries		IPv6 entries		DB	IPv4 entries		IPv6 entries	
	Cov.	Trust	Cov.	Trust		Cov.	Trust	Cov.	Trust
OIM	26 %	93.8 %	30.1 %	92.8 %	*TC*	86.7 %	71 %	99.1 %	79.4 %
RDNS	56.7 %	88.8 %	46.7 %	78.5 %	*AF*	36.2 %	93 %	56.7 %	83.7 %
MM	83.9 %	74 %	99.1 %	71.4 %	*Whois*	85.6 %	68 %	43.2 %	67.7 %

Our delay-based tie-breaking approach was used to geolocate the rest of the IPs that responded to pings (81.2 % of IPv4, 92.2 % of IPv6). That is for 2,406 v4 IPs (resp. 164 v6 IPs), the ping technique allows us to deduce the country. At the end of this process, 94.1 % v4 IPs (98.1 % v6 IPs) of our dataset are associated with a location. With the obtained geolocation data, we can compute the country path corresponding to the IP path of each traceroute output [17].

3.2.2 IP to as Lookup and Raw Data Sanity Check

We map, using *TC*, public IP addresses of our traceroute data into ASes, with the following filtering procedure: We first keep traceroutes for which the obtained AS Sequence contains source and destination ASes corresponding to the ASes which are known to host the probes. If it is not the case, we check if the first AS on the path is a known direct upstream of the source and the last AS on the path is a known direct upstream of the destination, as observed in the previous set of traceroutes. If these checks succeed, we keep the traceroute as well. Note that we only use this second set of inferred AS sequences for AS Path analysis, and excluded them from our RTT analysis.

To assess the accuracy of the inferred AS Paths, we keep track of intermediate traceroute hops for which the IP has no entry in *TC*, or for which we did not receive a reply [10]. We respectively refer to them as *unresolved* and *unknown* ASes.

We then compress AS Paths into AS Sequences. *Unresolved* or *unknown* hops found between two resolved hops of the same given AS, are considered as belonging to that AS. Consecutive equal AS numbers are compressed into a single AS hop. We only infer an edge between two ASes if there are no *unresolved* or *unknown* hops in the IP path, and if both ASes are consecutive in the AS sequence.

In our first campaign, we identified 4,648 traceroutes with inferred AS path loops. The top 3 ASes in those paths with loops were AS3356 (Level3, US), AS37282 (MainOne, NG) and AS37054 (Data Telecom Service, MG) at respectively 32 %, 15 % and 11 %. Similar results were found in our second campaign. These paths are a small fraction of the total dataset, so we decided to filter them out. Including these paths in our results is part of our ongoing work.

By the end of this raw data cleaning method, we retained, for the first campaign, 87.81 % of v4 traceroutes. For the second one, we retained 97.27 % of v4 traceroutes and 90.11 % of v6 traceroutes. For the last campaign, we retained

86.93 % of v4 traceroutes outputs. The corresponding total numbers are listed in Sect. 3.1. The dataset resulting from this filtering process comprises paris-traceroutes outputs from 181 probes located in 30 African countries, hosted in 90 ASes.

Finally, we estimate the RTT between the source and the destination AS as the difference between the RTT from the source probe to the ingress point of the destination AS, and the RTT from the source probe to the egress point of the source AS.

4   Results

In this section, we first discuss the biases of our dataset, and compare it with the view of the African topology that can be made from public BGP data. We then investigate the dynamics of the observed paths. Next, we discuss the length of the AS Paths, highlighting different trends among the studied regions. We then illustrate the impact of the intercontinental aspect of paths on the RTTs among African ISPs. We finally detect new peering links and IXPs in Africa to shed light on the progress made by some operators towards localizing interdomain routing. We provide a detailed analysis of the coverage of the IP ranges per country, path dynamics, the AS-Centrality of our dataset in [15].

4.1   Dataset Limitations and Public BGP Data

We acknowledge that not all the probes were deployed at the beginning of our initial measurement campaign. The constant evolution of the RIPE Atlas infrastructure on the continent leads us to daily add new probes to the set of probes that we use. As of today, our dataset involves 7.2 % of the ASes allocated by AFRINIC. Shortcomings of IP to AS mapping also have to be considered. For instance, 40.6 % (resp. 35.9 %) of the unique v4 (resp. v6) AS paths either contain one *unknown* or an *unresolved* AS.

We extracted from Routeviews, RIPE RIS, and PCH, all the paths containing one of the 90 ASes hosting a probe (2,258,692 v4 and 840,180 v6 paths), using all available data for 2013 and 2014 [21–23]. We compare these paths with our set of (2,529 v4 and 91 v6) paths containing no *unknown* or *unresolved* ASes. As most of the routes collectors are hosted outside the continent, our dataset is more precise when it comes to end-to-end African paths. Among the 960 v4 (resp. 63 v6) AS adjacencies that we inferred from the discovered paths, 733 v4 (resp. 35 v6) are not visible in these public datasets. Note that most of the AS adjacencies found in both datasets are among ASes based outside the continent. Quite intuitively, entire African AS paths - 2,519 v4 (resp. 79 v6) - are not visible in RouteViews, RIS, and PCH either. The only AS paths found in both datasets actually belong to the set of paths measured from AS3741 (Internet Solutions, ZA); this ISP hosts a RouteViews collector.

4.2   Path Dynamics

Considering the data of our first two campaigns, we identify all unique AS paths for each pair of monitored ASes, and compute their frequency of observation. In the rest of this paper, we refer to the path among two ASes which has the highest frequency of observation, as the preferred path for that AS pair. About 72.6 % (resp. 82 %) of the v4 (resp. v6) preferred paths have been used with a frequency higher than 90 %. Only 4 % of the v4 AS pairs have used their preferred paths at a frequency lower than 50 %, whereas no v6 preferred path has a frequency of usage lower than 50 %.

Some outliers were found in this analysis. Among them, Isocel Telecom (BJ) was showing 42 different AS Paths towards Onatel/FasoNet-AS (BF), and 22 paths were observed in the opposite direction. Link, node failures, and flapping could be listed as the possible reasons of such changes. However, we validated these results by visiting Isocel Telecom, and discovered that this ISP is constantly performing interdomain traffic engineering in order to offer the best possible QoS to its customers. As Onatel is doing the same, a large number of paths were explored between these two ASes.

4.3   As Path Length Distribution

Based on our first two measurement campaigns, we study the distribution of the length of AS Sequences among pairs of ASes. We notably take a perspective focused on West Africa and South Africa, to highlight differentiated trends. We also carry out a specific analysis for pairs of ASes located within the same country. Note that we remove *unknown* and *unresolved* ASes from paths used for plotting graphs of Fig. 1, except for those corresponding to paths length distribution within countries. Thus, the AS paths in those cases could be even longer than what is presented.

On Fig. 1(d), we show the AS path length distribution for all the paths of the dataset. Since ASes in West Africa are based in geographically collocated countries, one could guess that paths would be shorter. However, based on the specific view provided in Fig. 1(a), we discover unusually long AS paths in West African communications. Figure 1(b) and (f) highlight that short paths tend to be found in Southern Africa, and precisely in ZA. Paths among ASes operating in the same country (Fig. 1(c) and (f)), are much shorter in South Africa than in West Africa. IPv6 AS paths, all observed in *SAf*, tend to be short, reflecting similar peering and localized transit habits as for v4 in the region. These observations confirm that focusing solely on measurements from ZA does not provide a representative sample of Internet paths characteristics for the rest of Africa.

4.4   Trends in African Interdomain Routing

We now study the role of transit played by each ISP found in our data. To this end, we use the concept of AS-centrality of an AS, defined as the percentage of paths containing that AS [17], but for which that AS is neither the source

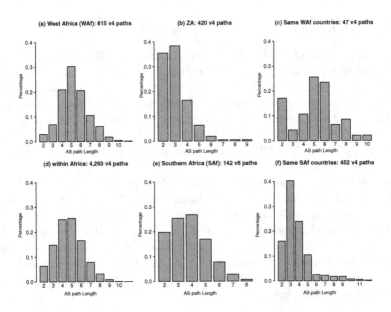

Fig. 1. Path length distributions for all paths and for some African regions

nor the destination. Note that AS-centrality is not equivalent to the betweenness centrality of ASes on the AS graph. We only account for presence within AS paths among pairs of ASes, radically diverging from betweenness centrality in the AS graph. We then define the concept of "joint AS-centrality", which captures the centrality of tuples of ASes present together on AS paths.

We classify the 164 ASes of our dataset into 5 categories, depending on their region of operation: *WAf* (for ASes based in West Africa), *SAf* (Southern Africa), *EAf* (East Africa), *RAf* (ASes operating in Africa but not in any of the previous regions), and *Int* - Intercontinental - (all ASes based outside the continent). Note that we find 61 *Int* Ases.

The 4 most central ASes in our view of the v4 African interdomain topology are all intercontinental ones: Level3 (US) with 23.4 % of the 4,293 AS paths, TATA (US) with 22 %, Cogent (US), 13.6 %, and Orange (FR), 12 %. 65.2 % of the AS pairs were served using at least one of these 4 ASes. The most central African AS, Internet Solutions (ZA) has an AS-centrality of 11.6 %. In contrast, Orange is the dominating ISP when it comes to paths among ASes in the *WAf* category, with an AS-centrality of 37.8 %, while TATA and Level3 respectively own 32 % and 26.1 % of the market share. We notice that a relevant percentage of paths (18.9 %) connecting *WAf* ASes transit via MTN (ZA). The most central local AS is MainOne (NG), found on 17.2 % of the paths.

The reliance on *Int* transit providers is considerably lower within the Southern African region; the top 2 ASes remain Level3 with 20.5 % and TATA (15.3 %), but Internet Solutions (ZA), SAIX-NET, a private IXP owned by Telkom SA (ZA), and MWEB (ZA) follow with respectively 15 %, 12.9 %, and 11.2 %.

SAf ASes appear to benefit from diversity in their transit offerings, and resort a lot to peering, as no ISP was found to completely dominate transit in the region. Note that the reliance of *SAf* ASes on ISPs based on other African regions is insignificant.

Some ASes which are not relevant for v4 routing, show a high AS-centrality when it comes to v6. The top 3 ASes in v6 are Hurricane Electric (US) with 23.9 %, TENET (ZA) with 22.5 %, and Liquid Telecom (GB) with 21.1 %. They are followed by IXPs AS5459 (LINX-AS, GB) and AS1200 (AMSIX, NL) traversed respectively by 19.7 % and 14.7 % of the paths while Level3 and TATA are present on only 9.8 % and 9.1 %.

One can observe a diversity of transit trends based on technico-economical factors. In Fig. 2, we present the centrality of Orange, TATA, and Level3, discussing whether these ASes jointly serve a path, or are lying on the path on their own. The three left-most triplet of barplots are based on all the paths of the dataset, while the last triplet focuses on the *WAf* category.

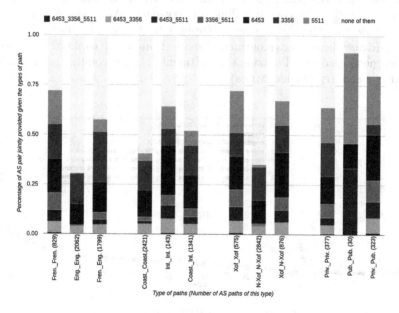

Fig. 2. Joint AS-centrality of AS3356 (Level3, US), AS6453 (TATA, US), and AS5511 (Orange, FR), for paths among various categories of ASes (Color figure online)

French speaking countries mostly rely on Orange, which serves 17 % of the West African AS pairs, without TATA nor Level3. Another 14.5 % of AS pairs are also served by Orange, but jointly with TATA or Level3. Orange completely disappears from our internetworking map when it comes to communications among English speaking countries. Such diverse transit habits are also observed when classifying ASes according to the monetary region to which they belong. Within the XAF-XOF (CFA Franc) monetary union, Orange has a centrality of

36.7 %, but is barely present in the market of communications among ISPs that are not belonging to this union.

From the same figure, we learn that Orange and TATA are lying together on 33 % of the paths among the public owned *WAf* ASes[3], and Orange is lying alone on another 45.8 % of these paths. In [15], we discuss the transit behaviour of these ISPs as a function of their ownership by Orange. No public operator seems to get transit from Level3. However, in the same region, a relevant proportion of pairs of ASes involving a private owned AS are served via Level3. Finally, the second triplet of barplot shows that African inland AS pairs rely much more on TATA (54.17 %) than on Level3 (29.16 %), dominating Orange. Such differences can be explained by the scarcity of Internet transit offerings in inland countries, mostly relying on Satellite transport companies which peer with Level3 and TATA.

4.5   Impact of Transit Localization on End-to-end Delay

We identify, per AS path, the IP path over which the minimum RTT was observed, as well as its corresponding country path. We group AS paths into two categories; continental AS paths (from 1 to 1,073) are those which stay within Africa, whereas intercontinental ones (from 1,074 to 4,082) are via at least one node geolocated outside the continent (i.e. the country path contains at least one country outside Africa).

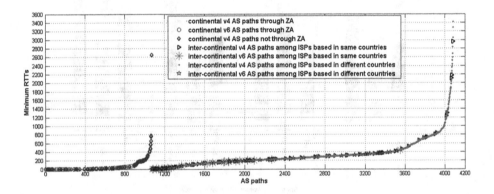

Fig. 3. Minimum RTT distribution

Figure 3 shows the distribution of the minimum RTTs among our probes. Continental paths with very low RTTs mostly correspond to paths among pairs of ASes based in the same country, or those passing through collocated regional ISPs. As highlighted by the yellow crosses, many of such paths are through South Africa, acting as a regional hub. Note that all the continental v6 paths traverse ZA.

---

[3] We categorized the *WAf* ASes as public or private, based on gathered private information.

Slightly longer RTTs (50–150 ms) are seen among AS pairs from geographically distant countries. For instance, a path from a KE ISP to a ZA ISP, only served by African transit ISPs, shows a minimum RTT of 80 ms. A striking result comes from the presence of very long RTTs in paths that are categorized as continental ones. These v4 paths are typically those between Eastern African ISPs and Western African ISPs, which are served by ZA transit ISPs. However, a v4 path, between GA and NG, categorized as continental, appears with an RTT of 2.6 s. Actually, this path is probably mis-categorized, as its IP level traceroutes contains many non answering hops. The following long RTTs are recorded on paths from TZ to ZA via AS37100 (SEACOM, MU), from Internet Solutions (ZA) to Simbanet (TZ) via KE, or from SAIX-NET to TENET in ZA. They are having the same issue of mis-categorization, as per our manual checks, but we have no data allowing us to certify that they leave the continent.

Let us now analyze the paths categorized as intercontinental. Intercontinental paths with a low RTT (i.e. ≺100 ms) also reveal the weakness of geolocation. These AS paths contain *Int* ASes, as per TC, and have also been consistently geo-located in either GB, NL, FR or US by the geo-location databases. These are cases where all geo-location databases are returning the same Country Code, located outside Africa, although delay-based measurements clearly indicate that the device is located on the continent. Our ongoing work includes the correction of such databases, in order to account for the new measurements performed towards these mislocalized IPs.

Most of the measured RTTs in this category however reflect intercontinental transit of continental traffic, with a RTT around 200 ms. 95,4 % of the paths with a RTT between 100 ms and 400 ms are through Europe. Paths with RTTs scattered around 750 ms are mostly from and towards ISPs that are served by Satellite providers, routing traffic through another continent. For example, a path in this group is from Connecteo in BF to AFNET in CI, passing through SkyVision, Level3 (in New York), Level3/Global-Crossing (in London), and MTN (ZA). The paths measured with an RTT above 1000 ms are mostly those served via 2 satellite links. For instance, one is from Connecteo in BF to Sonitel in NE, going through the US and Europe, but arriving in NE via another satellite, provided by IntelSat. Finally, we highlight the RTTs between ISPs operating in same African countries, exchanging packets over intercontinental AS paths. These are notably observed in BJ, CM, MA, MZ, and MU.

4.6   Emergence of New IXPs

Let us now focus our analysis on paths revealing the use of IXPs to exchange traffic. We collected IXP information from [23–25]. We also learned, through word-of-mouth, that new IXPs were being deployed in BJ, SC, and GM. We crossed such information with our traceroute results, and detected IPs used to address interfaces to these IXP in our traceroute data.

We notice some frequently used IXPs, notably JINX, CINX, DINX, and NAP Africa in ZA. Actually, 58,6 % of the continental paths which traverse ZA, go through one of these IXPs. We found the new IXPs in SC, BJ and GM. In SC,

4 members of the new IXP were hosting one of our probes, at the beginning of the 2nd campaign. We could observe a delay around 1 ms among each pair of this clique, formed by CWS, Intelvision, Telecom Seychelles, and Kokonet Ltd. In the data collected during our third measurement campaign, we find probe hosts connected to SIXP, in GM: QCell, Netpage, and GAMTEL. RTTs are around 1.5 ms among QCell and NetPage, while RTTs involving GAMTEL fluctuate between 1 ms and 460 ms. Measurements performed between the GAMTEL probe and the IXP platform itself actually revealed unstability of the link from GAMTEL to SIXP, as detailed in [15].

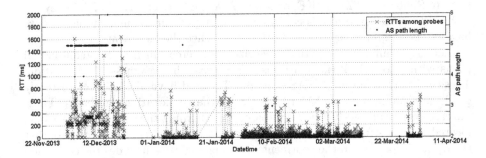

Fig. 4. RTTs from Benin Telecom to Isocel Telecom during Benin-IX (BJ) establishment

Let us now analyze the measurements performed among members of Benin-IX, being Benin Telecom, Isocel Telecom, and OTI Telecom. From December 2013 to the end of our first measurement campaign, in April 2014, RTTs measured among those ASes considerably drop from 314 ms on average between November 30th and December 20th 2013, to 42 ms on average from January 2nd to April 6th 2014. Figure 4 illustrates the benefit brought by this IXP, depicting the RTT among two members of that IXP, as well as the length of the measured AS Sequence. The figure also shows that our probes lost internet connectivity during the establishment of the IXP, as very few traceroutes succeeded during that period.

5   Conclusions and Future Work

In this paper, we assessed the global African interdomain routing topology. To this end, we deployed new RIPE Atlas probes, and carried out active measurements from 214 RIPE Atlas probes located in 90 ASes, covering 32 African countries[4].

---

[4] As of December 10, 2014, the RIPE Atlas platform has evolved to 318 probes hosted in 147 ASes and spread across 44 countries all over Africa [7].

We notice striking differences in transit habits of ISPs, notably depending on the official language of the country, the monetary region, or the business profile of the ISP. These illustrate how critical it is to have a large, diversified set of vantage points before drawing conclusions on the state of interdomain routing on the continent. Our results show a lack of interconnection among African ISPs (South Africa being an exception), confirming the interest of initiatives to promote peering on the continent. We highlight the remaining reliance on intercontinental ISPs for the establishment of continental connectivity. We correlate such trombonning paths with long RTTs among our probes. Nevertheless, new IXPs are emerging in Africa, notably in the West. We illustrate their benefits by showing the improvement in terms of RTT observed among their members.

In the future, we plan to measure the connectivity between African ISPs and the rest of the world. We also plan to provide a model to study the opportunities for cost reduction brought by IXP initiatives on the continent.

Acknowledgement. We are grateful to whoever deploys or hosts a RIPE Atlas probe. We also thank Michuki Mwangi, Nishal Goburdhan, Vesna Manojlovic, Andra Lutu, Camilo Cardona, Ignacio De Castro, and Pablo Camarillo for their insightful comments.

References

1. Les Cottrell, R.: How Bad Is Africa's Internet? January 2013. http://spectrum. ieee.org/telecom/internet/how-bad-is-africas-internet
2. Chetty, M., Sundaresan, S., Muckaden, S., Feamster, N., Calandro, E.: Measuring broadband performance in South Africa. In: Proceedings of the 4th Annual Symposium on Computing for Development, ACM DEV-4 '13. ACM, New York (2013)
3. African Union: Study On Harmonisation of Telecommunication, Information and Communication Technologies Policies and Regulation in Africa, March 2008. http://www.itu.int/ITU-D/projects/ITU_EC_ACP/hipssa/docs/2_ Draft_Report_Study_on_Telecom_ICT_Policy_31_March_08.pdf
4. African Union: African Internet eXchange System. http://pages.au.int/axis
5. Gilmore, J., Huysamen, N., Cronje, P., de Klerk, M., Krzesinski, A.: Mapping the African internet. In: Proceedings Southern African Telecommunication Networks and Applications Conference (SATNAC), Mauritius, September 2007
6. Gupta, A., Calder, M., Feamster, N., Chetty, M., Calandro, E., Katz-Bassett, E.: Peering at the internet's frontier: A first look at ISP interconnectivity in Africa. In: Faloutsos, M., Kuzmanovic, A. (eds.) PAM 2014. LNCS, vol. 8362, pp. 204–213. Springer, Heidelberg (2014)
7. RIPE NCC: Global RIPE Atlas Network Coverage (2014). https://atlas.ripe.net/ results/maps/network-coverage/
8. Mao, Z.M., Rexford, J., Wang, J., Katz, R.: Towards an accurate AS-level traceroute tool. In: Proceedings of ACM SIGCOMM, pp. 365–378 (2003)
9. Subramanian, L., Agarwal, S., Rexford, J., Katz, R.H.: Characterizing the internet hierarchy from multiple vantage points. In: Proceedings of IEEE INFOCOM, p. 12 (2002)
10. Haddadi, H., Rio, M., Moore, A.: Network topologies: inference, modeling, and generation. IEEE Commun. Surv. Tutor. **10**(2), 48–69 (2008). IEEE

11. Hyun, Y.: Archipelago Infrastructure. http://www.caida.org/projects/ark
12. PingER: PingER Project (2013). http://www-iepm.slac.stanford.edu/pinger/
13. Augustin, B., Cuvellier, X., Orgogozo, B., Viger, F., Friedman, T., Latapy, M., Magnien, C., Teixera, R.: Avoiding traceroute anomalies with Paris traceroute. In: IMC '06 Proceedings of the 6th ACM SIGCOMM Conference on Internet Measurement, pp. 153–158, October 2006
14. Cristel, P., Luca, C., Stefano, V., Bush, R.: From Paris to Tokyo: On the suitability of ping to measure latency. In: IMC '13 Proceedings of the 13th IMC, pp. 427–432 (2013)
15. Fanou, R., Francois, P., Aben, E.: African measurement campaigns: Technical Report, September 2014. https://fourier.networks.imdea.org/external/techrep_amc/
16. AFRINIC: AFRINIC database (2014). ftp://ftp.afrinic.net/
17. Karlin, J., Forrest, S., Rexford, J.: Nation-state routing: Censorship, wiretapping, and BGP. CoRR, vol. abs/0903.3218 (2009). http://arxiv.org/abs/0903.3218
18. RIPE NCC: OpenIPMap database (2014). https://labs.ripe.net/Members/emileaben/infrastructure-geolocation-plan-of-action
19. MaxMind: GeoIP (2014). http://www.maxmind.com/en/geolocation_landing
20. Team Cymru: Team Cymru Services. https://www.team-cymru.com/
21. RouteViews Project (2005). http://routeviews.org
22. RIPE, RIS: Raw data
23. Packet Clearing House (PCH): PCH IXP directory (2014). http://prefix.pch.net/images/applications/ixpdir/ip_asn_mapping.txt
24. CAIDA: AS Relationships. http://www.caida.org/data/as-relationships
25. PeeringDB. http://www.peeringdb.com/private/exchange_list.php

Mobile and Cellular

AppPrint: Automatic Fingerprinting of Mobile Applications in Network Traffic

Stanislav Miskovic[1]([⊠]), Gene Moo Lee[3], Yong Liao[2], and Mario Baldi[2]

[1] Symantec Corporation, Sunnyvale, CA 94086, USA
Stanislav_Miskovic@symantec.com, stanislav.miskovic@gmail.com
[2] Narus, Inc., Sunnyvale, CA 94086, USA
[3] University of Texas at Austin, Austin, TX 78712, USA

Abstract. Increased adoption of mobile devices introduces a new spin to Internet: mobile apps are becoming a key source of user traffic. Surprisingly, service providers and enterprises are largely unprepared for this change as they increasingly lose understanding of their traffic and fail to persistently identify individual apps. App traffic simply appears no different than any other HTTP data exchange. This raises a number of concerns for security and network management. In this paper, we propose *AppPrint*, a system that learns fingerprints of mobile apps via comprehensive traffic observations. We show that these fingerprints identify apps even in small traffic samples where app identity cannot be explicitly revealed in any individual traffic flows. This unique AppPrint feature is crucial because explicit app identifiers are extremely scarce, leading to a very limited characterization coverage of the existing approaches. In fact, our experiments on a nation-wide dataset from a major cellular provider show that AppPrint significantly outperforms any existing app identification. Moreover, the proposed system is robust to the lack of key app-identification sources, i.e., the traffic related to ads and analytic services commonly leveraged by the state-of-the-art identification methods.

1 Introduction

Mobile apps are expected to dominatex Internet in the post-PC era [9]. Running on ubiquitously adopted smartphones and tablets, mobile apps support users in numerous daily activities. This attracts both individuals and enterprise users, opening a number of new opportunities. However, managing this relatively young ecosystem is still in its infancy. Even basic identification of hundreds of thousands of apps existing in Internet traffic is a challenge. This has dramatic implications on security and network management because it entails that enterprises and network operators cannot impose any meaningful policies on mobile users. Similarly, being unable to distinguish the traffic of individual apps makes isolation of malicious or infected apps difficult, if at all possible.

The key challenge we address is that mobile apps cannot be presently distinguished at many levels. First, the apps predominantly communicate with their

Done under the Narus Fellow Research Program with equal author contributions.

© Springer International Publishing Switzerland 2015
J. Mirkovic and Y. Liu (Eds.): PAM 2015, LNCS 8995, pp. 57–69, 2015.
DOI: 10.1007/978-3-319-15509-8_5

host services via HTTP [14], which makes protocol- or port-based identification [10] ineffective. Even deep packet inspection largely fails because app traffic may not contain any *explicit app identifiers*, such as app names. In fact, we measured that these identifiers exist only in 1 % of mobile traffic, while the rest is completely unknown to any characterization. Also, a widespread use of cloud and CDN (content delivery network) services invalidates any identification based on service-host IP addresses or domain names.

In this paper, we present *AppPrint*, a system capable of identifying the apps at a granularity of arbitrarily small traffic samples. This means that app identification becomes much more frequent and its traffic coverage increases. In contrast to the state-of-the-art approaches that solely rely on temporally sparse occurrences of explicit app identifiers [2, 3, 6, 8, 11, 14], AppPrint can identify the most likely apps even when such identifiers are not present. For example, an operator of the AppPrint system could slot traffic in intervals as small as 10 s and identify the most likely apps for each slot and for all users in it with a high confidence. This is achievable due to two key AppPrint novelties: (i) learning elaborate app fingerprints from a priori limited app-identification data, and (ii) creating app fingerprints from features that may span multiple different traffic flows.

Specifically, we create app fingerprints as collections of *tokens*, e.g., any generic key-value pairs in URLs or any substrings of HTTP header fields, such as User-Agents or Cookies. Our intuition is that such tokens would be representative of their apps either individually or in groups; either by parameter names (keys) or parameter values. For example, an app can be designed in a specific development framework which makes the names of app parameters unique (i.e., app-identifying). Similarly, if several apps are developed on the same framework, their parameter values as well as the occurrences of specific parameters across flows could be sufficiently unique to identify each app. Leveraging this intuition enables AppPrint to characterize the traffic even when no explicit app identifiers are present. We achieve this by measuring the highest token-set similarity between an observed set of flows and readily learned app fingerprints.

One of the key contributions of AppPrint is its continual learning and refinement of app fingerprints. While the system does require some seeding with explicit app identifiers, it can expand this knowledge towards discovering many new fingerprints in the previously uncharacterised flows. Specifically, AppPrint can be bootstrapped by a single app identifier present in some particular flows (*e.g.*, embedded advertisement flows), and expand that knowledge to fingerprinting many other types of flows (such as social networking flows, audio streaming flows, etc.). We achieve this by effectively measuring collocation persistence between the seeding tokens (e.g., explicit app identifiers) and other tokens in the neighboring flows.

Another key feature of AppPrint is independence of its fingerprint learning and app identification processes. This is crucial for achieving a broad characterization coverage. Specifically, while the learning requires some seeding, the identification process has no such constraints. It can apply any fingerprints learned at any time (even offline) towards revealing the most likely apps "hidden" in the traffic. We developed an algorithm that facilitates this separation and named it MAP-SCORE.

We evaluate AppPrint on a week-long nationwide traffic trace from a major cellular provider in the United States. In this real environment, AppPrint offers an order of magnitude improvement over the state-of-the-art solutions in terms of app identification coverage.

The rest of the paper is organized as follows. Section 2 overviews the related work. Section 3 introduces AppPrint, while Sect. 4 evaluates the proposed methods on the lab traffic that contains app-identification ground truth, as well as on the real ISP traffic. Section 5 summarizes this work.

2 Related Work

A number of papers have identified that network administrators increasingly lose visibility in their traffic due to mobile apps being indistinguishable from generic HTTP communications [4,5,13]. Hence, identifying apps via common approaches of protocol identification or port numbers is no longer effective. This situation calls for a new paradigm.

The most straightforward way to identify apps is to look for app names in HTTP User-Agent fields [14]. However, this has serious limitations on the widely accepted Android platform where app developers do not follow any conventions in creating their user agents [3], i.e., the user agents may not contain app names. Another approach is to look for app identifiers in auxiliary services embedded in the apps, such as ads or analytics (A&A) [2,3,11]. The embedding of such services is common, especially in free apps [7,11,13]. However, the flow coverage of such identification is very low, because A&A flows are present in only a small fraction of traffic - especially for paid apps.

Dai et al. [3] improved app identification capabilities by developing a system that automatically runs Android apps and devises app fingerprints from the generated traffic. This approach can be effective, but it would be difficult to scale it to the size of current app markets with hundreds of thousands of apps. It would be even more difficult to obtain fingerprints that are representative of true human app usage, given that intelligent tools for interaction with diverse app UIs are still lacking. Thus, the obtained fingerprints may not be comprehensive or representative. For example, it would be very difficult for this system to produce representative signatures for apps that require user registration or logins, e.g., the popular Android Facebook app.

Choi et al. [2] proposed installing a monitoring agent in mobile devices. The agent helps in building ground truth knowledge for app identification. With the data collected in a campus network, the authors generated classifiers based on HTTP user-agent fields, HTTP hostname fields, and IP subnets. However, installing such agents on user devices may be challenging due to privacy concerns. Besides, deploying the agent at a large scale has many other practical challenges.

AppPrint shares only the *initial* sources of app-identification knowledge (e.g., User-Agent fields or A&A services) with the existing approaches. These sources are only seeds that help AppPrint to learn and apply its fingerprints towards characterization of a much wider span of traffic flows.

3 Methodology

In this section, we introduce AppPrint by first providing some basic intuition behind its design. We then describe its two core algorithms: (i) *MAP*, a method for discovery and learning of new app fingerprints, and (ii) *SCORE*, a method for identification of apps in the observed traffic (based on MAP's app fingerprints).

3.1 AppPrint Overview

We are motivated by the fact that existing app identification approaches [2,3,6,8,11,14] characterize only a small fraction of mobile traffic. AppPrint tries to increase the characterization coverage by learning a priori inconclusive features that may exist in the traffic and prove to have app identifying properties.

We focus on two types of features: (i) *tokens* that can be specific strings, or parameter names, or parameter values in HTTP headers, and (ii) *traffic flow groups* that can jointly point to an app identity. While it is a priori unknown whether useful instances of these features exist in the traffic, there is a number of reasons for them to be present. For example, app developers commonly collect statistics about their apps. Thus, there must be a way to for the apps to report back to their developers via some specific formatting of data. As an illustration, many apps use Apsalar library [1] that employs "i=" URL parameter to report executable filenames of active apps. This is an app-identifying token. Similarly, apps may require exchange of very specific parameter names to ensure proper execution. For example, Angry Birds app uses a unique "u_audio=" URL parameter to configure sound volume.

Flow grouping is another key source of AppPrint's intelligence. The grouping is invaluable when individual traffic flows do not reveal any app-specific tokens. We learned that mobile apps do exchange such generic traffic, *e.g.*, in order to transfer generic web objects such as pictures and audio. In such cases, AppPrint tries to propagate app identification from the identifiable flows to the ones that cannot be characterized. Moreover, even when none of the grouped flows contains explicit app identifiers, the tokens dispersed over several flows may jointly reveal app identity.

3.2 Initial App Identification Knowledge

Initial seeding knowledge for AppPrint can be obtained by many means. While such bootstrapping is neither the focus nor the contribution of this paper, we describe some aspects of it for completeness.

The values of explicit app identifiers are publicly available in app markets and can be easily collected for the system's bootstrap. We focus on two most popular mobile app markets: Google Play (Android) and Apple's iTunes App Store (iOS). To this end, we developed crawlers that gather the identifiers for all apps existing in these markets. For Android apps, we collect app names (such as TuneIn Radio) and app package denominators (such as tunein.player); for iOS apps, we crawled app names and unique 9-digit app IDs (such as 319295332).

```
GET /Config.ashx?partnerId=xwhZkVKi&provider= ggl&latlon=
     &version=6.1&render=json HTTP/1.1
User-Agent: TuneIn Radio/6.1(Android 15;sdk;Java)
Host: opml.radiotime.com
```

Fig. 1. App identifier "TuneIn Radio" included in the HTTP User-Agent field.

We verified that such tokens do appear in some URL parameters, User-Agent fields, substrings of HTTP referer fields, etc. Also, the tokens are employed by various services embedded in mobile apps, such as advertisements and analytics (A&A). An example of an app name included in the User-Agent field is illustrated in Fig. 1.

3.3 MAP: Auto Fingerprint Generation

The MAP algorithm collects statistics about tokens, thus effectively serving as a knowledge repository of AppPrint. It continually self-learns and refines app fingerprints discovered in the traffic by means of flow grouping. An app fingerprint is a set of one or more tokens that strongly identify an app. MAP keeps a tally of all individual tokens observed in the traffic, as well as the apps to which each token may be attributed. Subsequently, if a token proves to be predominantly associated to an app, it becomes a fingerprint component of that app. Based on this principle, we next develop the MAP algorithm.

Flow grouping: *Flow grouping* is our technique to address the issue of inconclusive data, i.e., the majority of traffic that does not contain any explicit or readily known app identifiers. The idea is to first group the flows that are temporally close to each other. We perform the grouping around the instances of flows which contain known or readily learned strong app identifiers. Then, we let the flow whose app identity can be determined *suggest* or *propagate* that identity to all other tokens in its flow group - even the tokens in the neighboring (unidentifiable) flows. Consequently, in different instances of flow grouping, a token may be *suggestively* associated to different apps. To identify the most likely app, we consider all tokens and their association in the observed flows and let the SCORE algorithm decide.

The key challenge of flow grouping is that individual instances of flow groups may not be sufficient to learn true token-to-app associations. Scenarios like app multitasking and device tethering may cause flows of many apps to appear close in time, thus inducing noise in the grouping process. To eliminate such noise, one could train AppPrint in a controlled environment and ensure grouping of flows that belong to individual apps. We adopt a different strategy that is easier to scale, especially in larger networks such as cellular provider networks, university campuses or enterprise environments. We thus focus on observations of numerous flow groups generated by large user populations during AppPrint's activity. Then, given that users use different apps and run them at different times, the noise should disperse and become easily identifiable: The tokens that

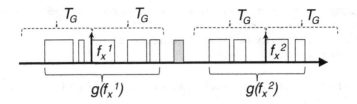

Fig. 2. MAP flow grouping.

persistently collocate with specific apps become fingerprint tokens, while other tokens that associate equally likely with many apps get disregarded. We will verify this approach experimentally in Sect. 4.

An illustration of flow grouping is given in Fig. 2: Flow group $g(f_x^i)$ is formed around an identifiable anchor flow f_x^i, which contains an explicit or strong app identifier. Here, parameter i designates i-th flow grouping for a given mobile user. The grouping is based on two criteria: (i) the flows must originate from the same source (source IP address), and (ii) the flows that cannot be characterized must be less than T_G seconds away from the anchoring flow f_x^i. T_G is a configurable parameter addressed in Sect. 4. This ensures strong time and source locality of app identification. In the illustrated example, flow f_x^i would suggest its app identity to all tokens in the group, *i.e.*, its own tokens and the tokens of other flows in $g(f_x^i)$.

MAP repository: The MAP repository is a knowledge base that reveals tokens suitable for fingerprints of each app. The repository is formed as a matrix in which each row corresponds to a token t, and each column corresponds to a *suggested* app x. The matrix element t, x, denoted as $MAP_{t,x}$, stores the number of instances in which token t was suggestively associated with app x.

Table 1 shows a snapshot of the MAP repository. Note the additional column in the repository which contains the total count of each token's suggested associations to any apps (denoted as column $*$ in Table 1). In the illustrated example, the repository indicates that tokens `angrybirds` and `rovio` are by far most frequently associated to *Angry Birds* app, which qualifies them for *Angry Birds* fingerprints. On the other hand, tokens such as `google` and `mobile` have dispersed associations across numerous apps, thus not being suitable for any app fingerprints.

3.4 SCORE: Probabilistic App Identification

SCORE algorithm determines the most likely app identities in the observed traffic. The algorithm measures similarity between the tokens found in the traffic and all token-to-app associations suggested by the MAP repository, thus identifying the most likely corresponding app. The decisions span flow sets and each decision is referred to as *app identification instance*.

SCORE flow sets: Flow sets are the units of SCORE's decision making. They are formed by bundling traffic in a different manner than MAP's flow grouping.

Table 1. MAP repository example.

tokens/apps	*	Angry Birds	Piggies	Google Maps	...
angrybirds	500	450	0	0	...
rovio	700	600	50	0	...
mobile	3000	50	30	100	...
google	2000	60	40	200	...
...	...	...	...	...	...

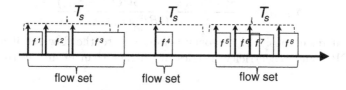

Fig. 3. SCORE grouping of flow sets.

This enables MAP and SCORE to operate independently and if needed simultaneously. The difference stems from the fact that SCORE does not need any flows with explicit app identifiers, because app identity can be readily suggested by the MAP repository. This is one of the key advantages of AppPrint: *The system is capable of identifying apps even when none of the flows (in a flow set) can be a priori characterized individually.*

For flow sets, a simple time slotting mechanism suffices: Flows that originate from the *same source* (*i.e.*, source IP address) and have starting times that fit the same time slot constitute a flow set instance. The duration of each time slot T_S is a configurable parameter. A flow set example is illustrated in Fig. 3.

SCORE and eccentricity metrics: To identify the most likely app for a given flow set, we develop a pair of metrics that leverage indications of the MAP repository. Let S_T be a set of tokens in a flow set F and S_A be the set of all apps in MAP repository. The similarity between the flow set F and an app x is evaluated as:

$$SCORE(x) = \sum_{t \in S_T} \frac{\frac{MAP_{t,x}}{MAP_{t,*}}}{\sum_{a \in S_A} \delta(t,a)}, \tag{1}$$

where $MAP_{t,x}$ is the value of the t, x element in the MAP repository, $MAP_{t,*}$ is the total number of token t's suggested associations to any apps, $\delta(t,a)$ is an indicator of t being associated to an app a in the repository, i.e., $\delta(t,a) = 1$ if $MAP_{t,a} \neq 0$.

The intuition behind the SCORE metric is the following: If tokens in the flow set S_T mostly associate with an app x, the app should score high as provided by the ratio of $MAP_{t,x}$ and $MAP_{t,*}$. Moreover, the token set should not have many other suggested app associations, as accounted by $\sum_{a \in S_A} \delta(t,a)$.

The combination of these two criteria results in a high confidence that a decision about app identity for a flow set can be made unambiguously.

Once the SCORE metric for the flow set F is calculated against all candidate apps in the MAP repository, AppPrint decides whether the flow set can be attributed to the highest scoring app. This decision is based on the *eccentricity* metric. The metric requires that the score of the highest ranking app is significantly different from any other potential apps. Given the top ranked app x_{1st} and the second-best app x_{2nd}, the eccentricity ϕ is a relative difference in their scores:

$$\phi_{SCORE} = \frac{SCORE(x_{1st}) - SCORE(x_{2nd})}{SCORE(x_{1st})} \tag{2}$$

The final result positively associates app x_{1st} to the flow set if and only if the SCORE and eccentricity metrics are higher than Θ and Φ thresholds, respectively.

4   Evaluation

In this section, we evaluate the proposed MAP-SCORE algorithm (MS) against two state-of-the-art approaches for discovery of app identities: (i) one based on the content of HTTP User-Agent fields (*UA*), and (ii) another based on explicit app identifiers found in any HTTP header fields (*HH*). Both of these reference approaches rely solely on explicit app identifiers, which makes them perfectly accurate (although on a limited set of flows).

In preparation, we conducted exhaustive sensitivity testing of the three key MAP-SCORE parameters: (1) flow (set) grouping interval T, (2) threshold Θ of the SCORE metric, (3) threshold Φ of the SCORE eccentricity. We found that app classification is largely consistent over various parameter settings whenever T is around 10 s, Θ is between 0.1 and 0.2 and Φ is around 0.3. The parameters set for our experiments are $T = 10s$, $\Theta = 0.1$ and $\Phi = 0.3$.

4.1   Datasets

Lab Trace: To evaluate AppPrint, we partly use lab traffic generated by running individual apps in order to establish a ground truth. To this end, we downloaded $40K$ Android apps from Google's Play Store and collected their traffic. Each app was run on multiple versions of Android emulators provided by the Android SDK. We use the Android monkey tool [12] to emulate user interaction with the apps. Similarly, we collected $7K$ popular apps from Apple's iTunes App Store. Given that Apple does not provide any emulators for iOS devices, we developed one and enabled it to automatically install and execute apps, as well as collect app traffic.

Real Trace: We also evaluate AppPrint on a large anonymized dataset from a major US cellular provider. The dataset contains 7 days of traffic from about $200K$ anonymous and mostly Android users. This dataset faithfully represents

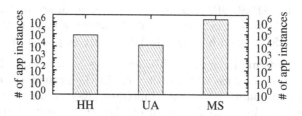

Fig. 4. Number of identified app instances.

actual human usage of mobile apps. However, it does not provide any a priori information of apps behind the traffic, except for a small portion of flows (less than 1 %) whose apps can be determined via User-Agent (UA) or header data (HH) approaches.

4.2 App Identification

We first evaluate the traffic coverage characterized by MAP-SCORE (MS) in the real trace. Due to the lack of comprehensive ground truth in this trace, it is impossible to fully evaluate correctness of MAP-SCORE's results. Thus, we later conduct precision analysis on the lab trace in order to provide a holistic view in AppPrint's capabilities.

Our experiments use the first 6 days of the real trace to provide training for the MAP repository. Our evaluation is based on running SCORE against the flow sets in the 7th day of data. The same evaluation methodology is used for the other two approaches, user agents (UA) and header data (HH), i.e., we evaluate their characterization capabilities only on the 7th day of data.

Coverage of the real traffic: The number of *identified app instances* is used as a coverage comparison metric. For MAP-SCORE, an app-instance identification corresponds to SCORE positively associating an app fingerprint to a flow set. By design, there can be at most one such app identification per flow set. For HH and UA, we count the total number of *distinct* app identifications in each flow set - i.e., depending on the number of different explicit app identifiers found in the flow set, there may be more than one app identified per flow set.

As plotted in Fig. 4, MAP-SCORE (MS) identifies $1,729K$ app instances, while UA identifies close to $13K$ app instances and HH about $86K$ app instances. Coverage-wise, MAP-SCORE performs an order of magnitude better. We also note that UA is not as effective as described in [14]. This is due to the fact that "our" cellular provider mainly supports Android, the platform that doesn't force developers to code explicit app identifies in User-Agents. In contrast, the trace studied in [14] included a significant portion of the traffic from iOS devices, whose apps predominantly include app-identifying information in User-Agents.

Among $1,729K$ positive fingerprint matches of MAP-SCORE, we found that $84K$ are consistent with the indications of UA or HH approaches. This can be used as a hint of MAP-SCORE's accuracy. Further accuracy analysis could not be conducted on the real trace because it does not contain the ground truth for the remaining $1645K = 1729K - 84K$ MAP-SCORE app identifications.

Precision evaluation: In order to further assess accuracy of MAP-SCORE results, we use the lab trace which does contain the ground truth of flow-to-app associations. We built the trace by combining lab-generated traffic of 1000+ apps which appeared in the MAP repository (i.e., the repository trained on the first 6 days of the real trace). Then, SCORE was run against such traffic. To evaluate app-identification precision and coverage, we use the standard ratios of true positive and false positive detections. Our results indicate that MAP-SCORE achieves 81 % flow-set coverage with 93.7 % precision. This supports our claim that AppPrint can identify the most likely apps with a wide flow-set coverage and with a high confidence.

Further, this result supports our assumption about the noise canceling properties of MAP-SCORE fingerprints (stated in Sect. 3.3). Specifically, even though MAP was trained on the noisy real traffic, fingerprint indications were still highly precise when applied on the ground truth of the lab traffic. Thus, the app fingerprinting noise largely dispersed over time and large user population as we expected.

4.3 Effectiveness of Grouping Flows

Next, we evaluate the importance of flow grouping, *i.e.*, the importance of using tokens from multiple flows towards building app fingerprints. We take an extreme

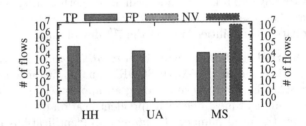

Fig. 5. Number of identified app instances without flow grouping.

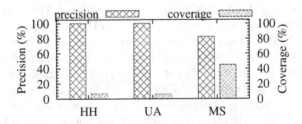

Fig. 6. Precision and coverage of app-instance identifications in the lab trace without flow grouping.

approach by preventing any grouping, i.e., we apply AppPrint on the flow sets containing only single flows. The settings for these experiments are similar to the ones described in Sect. 4.2.

Real traffic: We first evaluate the number of identified app instances on the 7th day of the real traffic. The results for header data (HH) and user agent (UA) approaches do not change significantly; a slight increase in identification is due to counting distinct app identifications per each flow vs. counting them once per flow set. Next, this setting enables us to better qualify MAP-SCORE (MS) results. Specifically, using per-flow indications of deterministic HH and UA approaches, we can classify MS results as (i) true positives (TP) when MS agrees with HH or UA, (ii) false positives (FP) when there is a disagreement, and (iii) non-verifiable characterizations (NV) when HH or UA cannot characterize a flow, but MS can.

The results in Fig. 5 indicate that although MS identifies one order of magnitude more app instances than with flow grouping enabled (compare Figs. 4 and 5), the number of true positives decreases from $85K$ to $26K$. This clearly demonstrates a positive effect of flow grouping on AppPrint's accuracy.

Lab traffic: We use the lab trace to assess the impact of single-flow flow sets on precision (see Fig. 6). Our results indicate that MAP-SCORE (MS) achieves much higher coverage than HH and UA, but its precision drops to 82.3 % (about 10 % less than with flow grouping enabled, see Sect. 4.2). In summary, not leveraging tokens from multiple flows has notable negative effects on both coverage and precision of AppPrint.

4.4 Identifying Apps Without A&A Traffic

To evaluate AppPrint's capabilities on paid apps (without incurring high monetary costs of purchasing the apps), we leverage the key difference between free and paid apps: Paid apps mostly do not exchange ads and analytic (A&A) traffic [7,13], while the rest of their communications are largely similar to free apps. Thus, we can still employ our lab- and real-traffic traces by removing all A&A flows. Also note that our MAP repository still remains representative because most paid apps have their free counterparts developed on the same code base, thus using similar traffic tokens (readily captured by our MAP repository). Our experimental settings are otherwise similar to the ones described in Sect. 4.2.

Figure 7 shows the number of app instances identified by the three techniques on the real trace. In this experiment header data (HH) approach identifies only $3.7K$ app instances, user agent (UA) approach identifies $13K$ (remaining unaffected), and MAP-SCORE (MS) identifies $1,508K$. In comparison with A&A flows included (see Fig. 4), MAP-SCORE identifies only about 11 % less app instances.

For the lab trace, precision and coverage are plotted in Fig. 8. Note that the coverage of HH gets very low because this technique largely relies on A&A traffic for explicit app identifiers. UA still has a low coverage, but it is largely

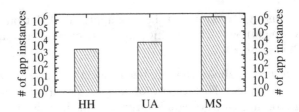

Fig. 7. Number of app instances identified in the real trace without A&A flows.

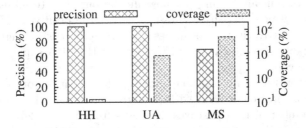

Fig. 8. Precision and coverage of app-instance identifications on the lab trace without A&A flows.

unaffected by the lack of A&A flows. Finally, MAP-SCORE associates apps to about 50 % of flow sets, but its precision drops to around 70 %.

5   Conclusion

The paper proposes AppPrint, a system for automatic identification of mobile apps in arbitrarily small samples of Internet traffic. AppPrint enables network administrators to regain fine grained visibility into their traffic, thus benefiting network management and security. The system achieves this by its unique capability to learn app fingerprints dispersed over multiple and often individually inconclusive traffic flows. We evaluated AppPrint on a trace of a large cellular provider in the United States and on our comprehensive lab trace spanning thousands of apps. The results show that AppPrint outperforms state-of-the-art approaches by identifying over one order of magnitude more instances of apps in the real traffic, while achieving up to 93.7 % precision.

References

1. Apsalar: Data-Powered Mobile Advertising. http://apsalar.com/
2. Choi, Y., Chung, J.Y., Park, B., Hong, J.W.K.: Automated classifier generation for application-level mobile traffic identification. In: Proceedings of Network Operations and Management Symposium (NOMS) (2012)
3. Dai, S., Tongaonkar, A., Wang, X., Nucci, A., Song, D.: NetworkProfiler: towards automatic fingerprinting of Android apps. In: INFOCOM. Turin, Italy, April 2013

4. Falaki, H., Lymberopoulos, D., Mahajan, R., Kandula, S., Estrin, D.: A first look at traffic on smartphones. In: Proceedings of the 10th ACM SIGCOMM Conference on Internet Measurement, IMC 2010, pp. 281–287. ACM, New York (2010)

5. Falaki, H., Mahajan, R., Kandula, S., Lymberopoulos, D., Govindan, R., Estrin, D.: Diversity in smartphone usage. In: Proceedings of the 8th International Conference on Mobile Systems, Applications, and Services, MobiSys 2010, pp. 179–194. ACM, New York (2010)

6. Gember, A., Anand, A., Akella, A.: A comparative study of handheld and non-handheld traffic in campus Wi-Fi networks. In: Spring, N., Riley, G.F. (eds.) PAM 2011. LNCS, vol. 6579, pp. 173–183. Springer, Heidelberg (2011)

7. Leontiadis, I., Efstratiou, C., Picone, M., Mascolo, C.: Don't kill my ads!: Balancing privacy in an ad-supported mobile application market. In: Proceedings of the Twelfth Workshop on Mobile Computing Systems & Applications, HotMobile 2012, pp. 2:1–2:6. ACM, New York (2012)

8. Maier, G., Schneider, F., Feldmann, A.: A first look at mobile hand-held device traffic. In: Krishnamurthy, A., Plattner, B. (eds.) PAM 2010. LNCS, vol. 6032, pp. 161–170. Springer, Heidelberg (2010)

9. Mobile App Usage Further Dominates Web. http://www.flurry.com/bid/80241/Mobile-App-Usage-Further-Dominates-Web-Spurred-by-Facebook#.VAZhp9-c3PE

10. Moore, D., Keys, K., Koga, R., Lagache, E., Claffy, K.C.: The coralreef software suite as a tool for system and network administrators. In: Proceedings of the 15th USENIX Conference on System Administration, LISA 2001, pp. 133–144. USENIX Association, Berkeley (2001)

11. Rastogi, V., Chen, Y., Enck, W.: AppsPlayground: automatic security analysis of smartphone applications. In: Proceedings of the Third ACM Conference on Data and Application Security and Privacy, CODASPY 2013, pp. 209–220 (2013)

12. UI/Application Exerciser Monkey. http://developer.android.com/tools/help/monkey.html

13. Wei, X., Gomez, L., Neamtiu, I., Faloutsos, M.: ProfileDroid: multi-layer profiling of android applications. In: Proceedings of the 18th Annual International Conference on Mobile Computing and Networking, Mobicom 2012, pp. 137–148. ACM, New York (2012)

14. Xu, Q., Erman, J., Gerber, A., Mao, Z., Pang, J., Venkataraman, S.: Identifying diverse usage behaviors of smartphone apps. In: Proceedings of the 2011 ACM SIGCOMM Conference on Internet Measurement Conference, IMC 2011, pp. 329–344. ACM, New York (2011)

Uncovering the Footprints of Malicious Traffic in Cellular Data Networks

Arun Raghuramu[1]($\boxtimes$), Hui Zang[2], and Chen-Nee Chuah[3]

[1] Department of Computer Science, University of California, Davis, USA
araghuramu@ucdavis.edu
[2] Guavus Inc., San Mateo, CA, USA
hui.zang@guavus.com
[3] Department of Electrical and Computer Engineering,
University of California, Davis, USA
chuah@ucdavis.edu

Abstract. In this paper, we present a comprehensive characterization of malicious traffic generated by mobile devices using Deep Packet Inspection (DPI) records and security event logs from a large US based cellular provider network. Our analysis reveals that 0.17 % of mobile devices in the cellular network are affected by security threats. This proportion, while small, is orders of magnitude higher than the last reported (in 2013) infection rate of 0.0009 %. We also perform a detailed comparison of infection rates of various mobile platforms and show that platforms deemed to be more secure by common opinion such as BlackBerry and iOS are not as safe as we think. However, Android still remains the most affected platform with an infection rate of 0.39 %. We present a detailed discussion of the top threat families targeting mobile devices observed in our dataset. Lastly, we characterize the aggregate network footprint of malicious and benign traffic in the cellular network and show that statistical network features can be used to distinguish between these traffic classes.

1 Introduction

The pervasive use of mobile devices such as smartphones to access an array of personal and financial information makes them rich targets for malware writers and attackers. Studies have revealed threats and attacks unique to mobile platforms, such as SMS and phone call interception malware [1]. The claims about prevalence of mobile malware were recently disputed when Lever et. al [2] showed that mobile malware appears only in a tiny fraction (0.0009 %) of devices in their dataset, indicating that mobile application markets are providing adequate security for mobile device users. However, the work in [2] failed to provide a comprehensive view of malicious network traffic since the analysis was limited to threats which issue DNS requests to known malicious domains. Also, [2] did not quantify the prevalence of specific types of threats affecting the network in their characterization study.

© Springer International Publishing Switzerland 2015
J. Mirkovic and Y. Liu (Eds.): PAM 2015, LNCS 8995, pp. 70–82, 2015.
DOI: 10.1007/978-3-319-15509-8_6

In this paper, we performed a detailed characterization of malicious traffic generated by mobile devices using deep-packet flow records and security event logs from a major US-based cellular network. Our analysis revealed that 0.17 % of over 2 million devices in the cellular network triggered security alerts. This fraction, while still small, is *orders of magnitude higher* than the previous infection rate reported in [2] and is in agreement with recent direct infection rate measurements focusing on the Android platform [3]. This alarming infection rate calls for a more careful and thorough study of malicious traffic in the mobile ecosystems.

A second area of our focus deals with the problem of 'detecting' malicious hosts/URLs. Previous studies such as [4,5] treat this as a supervised learning problem where a classifier learns on a combination of DNS, WHOIS, lexical, and other features associated with a given host to decide whether it is malicious or benign with high accuracy. Other studies such as [6,7] exclusively utilize lexical features to achieve similar goals. A different approach, Nazca [8], was proposed recently to detect malware distribution networks by tracking web requests associated with malware downloads and installations.

Instead of focusing on features associated with the malware or hosts (e.g., URL content, WHOIS, etc.), we examined the network-level statistical features of traffic associated with malicious domains. We observed that there are distinctive network access patterns that can be leveraged to distinguish between benign and malicious sites. To the best of our knowledge, this is the first study that applies such network-level features to the malicious host identification problem.

The contributions of our work are two-fold:

(a) We provide a large-scale characterization of malicious traffic by analyzing DPI records and security alerts of over 2 million devices. Apart from revealing higher infection rate, we show that four classes of threats: privacy-leakage, adware, SIP attacks and trojans - are most prevalent in mobile devices. Also, we find that 0.39 % of Android devices are infected, while the infection rates of BlackBerry and iOS devices which are commonly considered more secure are observed to be comparatively high (0.32 % and 0.22 % respectively).

(b) We analyze the aggregate network-level features of user traffic for both malicious and benign domains, and demonstrate that they are sufficiently distinct. This allows us to build a machine learning classifier that identifies malicious domains utilizing statistical properties of network traffic. We believe that this opens up an interesting direction for detection of unknown malicious domains.

The remainder of the paper is organized as follows: Sect. 2 provides an overview of our datasets and methodology. In Sect. 3 we present the findings of our characterization study of mobile threats. Section 4 describes the nature of network footprints of malicious traffic. Section 5 concludes the paper.

2   Data Summary and Methodology

Our dataset, collected at a distribution site operated by a US cellular service provider, is multiple terabytes in size and logs HTTP activities of over two million

Table 1. Security data sources and their alert triggering mechanism

Data source	Alert triggering event(s)
IDS-1	DNS requests seen to known malicious domains
IDS-2	(a) The HTTP request header contains a known malicious user agent string or URI
	(b) Leakage of IMEI, IMSI, phone number or location information through a HTTP header or URI
	(c) Attempts to connect to a known C&C server
	(d) DNS request to a known malicious domain (Utilizes a different set of malicious domains from IDS-1)
	(e) Known malicious behavior. Eg. Attempt to trigger a DDoS, replay attack, etc.
AV-1	Known malware detected on a device through a signature

subscribers for a week-long period in summer 2013. What makes the dataset more interesting is the associated security alert logs generated by commercial systems deployed in the network.

Specifically, the following traces are contained in our dataset:

- Deep Packet Inspection (DPI) Records: These records log HTTP activity of subscribers in the network and contain flow level information associated with each HTTP request, such as, the timestamp, duration, bytes transmitted in each direction, source IP address, URL, and User Agent of the flow.
- Intrusion Detection System (IDS) and Anti-Virus (AV) Alert Logs: These logs contain threatname (usually vendor specific), subscriber IP address, timestamp, destination HTTP domain, and destination port of the alerted activity.
- IP Assignment Records: These records map dynamically assigned IP addresses to anonymized subscriber device IDs.
- VirusTotal, McAfee scan results: We performed additional scans on certain domains and IP's in the IDS and AV logs to obtain additional information about the threats and number of malware detection engines flagging it as positive (malicious).

We perform two processing tasks to help characterize malicious events in the carrier's network. We describe each of these tasks in greater detail below.

(a) *Building Ground Truth for Malicious Traffic:* As mentioned earlier, the carrier deploys two separate commercial IDS's in its premises. Each IDS passively monitors different characteristics of traffic and flags security events without initiating any 'block' actions. We utilize logs produced by these appliances in our characterization study. We also use records logged at AV scanners deployed at select end-client devices as an additional auxiliary source of security evidence. Table 1 describes the alert triggering mechanism of these IDS and AV systems. We collect IP's and URL's associated

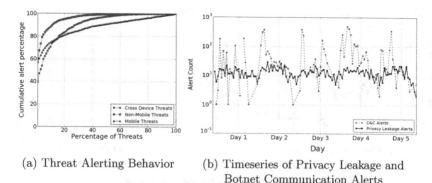

(a) Threat Alerting Behavior   (b) Timeseries of Privacy Leakage and
Botnet Communication Alerts

Fig. 1. Macroscopic characterization of alert data

with the alert events and submit them to commercial URL scanners such as VirusTotal [9] to eliminate false positives and to gather detailed information about the threats associated with these alerts. In addition, we manually group the most prominent threats in the network into four general categories or "Threat classes"as: Trojans, Privacy leakage threats, Potentially Unwanted Applications(PUA) and SIP threats based on the common characteristics and infecting behavior of the threats.

(b) *Identifying Devices and Platforms:* The events in our malicious traffic ground truth database could have been triggered by either mobile devices such as smartphones and tablets or laptops and desktops that connect to the cellular network via hotspots/modem devices. We were provided with the registered make, model and operating system information for about half of the anonymized subscribers in the trace. For the other subscribers, we infer the device type, make, and OS type using the User-Agent fields from their DPI records with the help of an in-house tool[1]. The devices in our alert datasets are then classified manually as one of the four general categories: phones, tablets, hotspots/modems and other devices.

3 Characterizing Mobile Threats

3.1 Prevalence of Malicious Traffic

As described earlier, we do not limit our characterization to web traffic generating DNS requests to malicious domains. Instead, we include non-HTTP malicious traffic such as VoIP security events occurring on ports 5060 and 5061 and a number of security events on non-standard ports such as 8080/8090 in our study. Thus, we capture a more complete view of malicious traffic in the cellular network.

---

[1] This utility analyzes every User-Agent string in the DPI trace associated with the unknown device to make an estimate of its make, model and platform.

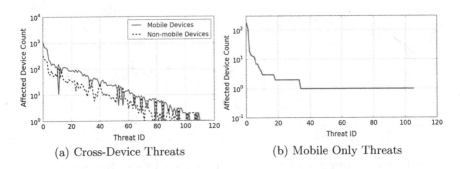

(a) Cross-Device Threats   (b) Mobile Only Threats

Fig. 2. Infection Effectiveness of Threats

In the dataset, 0.23 % of devices were observed to trigger security alerts and 73.2 % of these events originated from mobile devices such as smartphones and tablets while the rest are triggered by devices behind wireless hotspots or modems, and hence cannot be uniquely identified as being mobile or non-mobile. This puts the lower bound of the overall infection rate of mobile devices at 0.17 %, which is orders of magnitude higher than those reported in the most recent work by Lever et al. [2]. Also, our observed infection rate is in agreement with the reported rate in a recent study focusing on direct measurement of Android malware infection rates [3]. We note that our notion of 'infection' is similar to that of [2]. We mark a device as infected when we observe a security alert originating from it. This is reasonable since (a) The IDS systems in the network are passively monitoring threats and do not engage in 'blocking' malicious traffic, (b) We only use alerts which are known true positives and (c) This allows us to do a one-to-one comparison of infection rates with previous work.

Further, we rank the individual infected devices based on the total number of security alerts generated by them over the course of the week, and found that the top 20 % of the devices account for more than 80 % of the security alerts. Interestingly, the top 20 % of the infected devices primarily consisted of Android and iOS based phones/tablets.

Based on the methodology described in Sect. 2, we extracted detailed information about the threat associated with each security event by leveraging commercial virus-scanning tools, and through manual inspections. We found 327 unique threats in our *malicious traffic groundtruth* dataset that spans over the course of one week. After performing device classification, we further categorized these 327 threats into three classes with 75 % confidence intervals as follows: (a) mobile-only threats that infect mobile devices (b) non-mobile threats that infect non-mobile devices, and (c) cross-device threats that infect both types of devices. Figure 1a characterizes the macroscopic alerting behavior of the three classes of threats in the network. The x-axis in this graph represents the top n % of threats in terms of the total number of alerts generated. In general, a small fraction of threats (5–15 %) are responsible for a major proportion (over 80 %) of the observed alert traffic. However, we note that mobile threats in general tend to generate less number of alerts than their non-mobile counterparts. This might

Table 2. Top categories of prevalent mobile malware

Threat class	Threat description	Unique threats	# Mobile	# Non-mobile and un-known	# Associ-ated IPs	Asso-ciated ports
Trojans	Malware which utilizes techniques of social engineering, drive-by download and advanced rootkits to affect user devices	8	1669	470	159	53
Privacy leakage	Leakage of sensitive information such as IMEI number and user location	2	1277	418	77	8080, 80
Adware and PUA	HTTP Requests to known adware domains and requests with known malicious UA strings	3	1179	368	45	80
SIP threats	Illegal session information modification and replay attacks on SIP protocol	2	161	98	21	5060, 5061

indicate that attackers have adapted mobile malware to be stealthier and harder to detect on the network. Moreover, some mobile-specific threats (e.g., privacy leakage) generate less network footprints and hence trigger less number of alerts.

Exploring this further, we see that the number of alerts observed to be generated per threat is a function of the threat family (e.g. botnet, data leakage, etc.) and the number of devices affected by the threat. Privacy leakage threats such as threats responsible for leaking IMEI or location information from a device generally do not generate as many alerts as devices affected by a botnet threat (as shown in Fig. 1b). A 'zombie' bot device makes regular call-backs to command and control servers for downloading instructions, data exfiltration and so on, hence generating a much larger footprint in the security alert logs. This implies that mining alert logs generated by network access activities could be effective in early detection and prevention of botnet-like threats. However, similar methodology will be ineffective for other threats, such as data leakage, that leave very little footprints.

3.2 Top Mobile Threats

Next, we examine the threats that infected the most number of *mobile* devices. Malware writers often aim to infect as many devices as possible in order to maximize their financial or other gains. Therefore we use the number of devices affected by a threat to quantify its success in the cellular network.

Figure 2 plots the infection effectiveness of two categories of threats: cross-device threats and mobile-only threats, respectively. The x-axis plots threat id in decreasing order of rank based on the total number of devices affected (i.e., the first threat id affects the most number of devices). Notice from this graph that only a few threats are able to successfully affect a large number of devices (either

Table 3. Types of Privacy Leakage

Type of data	Affected devices
IMEI number	757
Device location	603
Phone number	14
Call logs	5
SMS logs	1

non-mobile or mobile). To better analyze the nature of these prominent threats, we further classify the top 15 threats (either mobile-only or cross-device threats) affecting the most number of mobile devices in the network into four different classes based on unique characteristics exhibited by each threat as shown in Table 2. We now describe the characteristics of each of these malware categories and how they affect end users:

Trojan Threats: These programs deliberately cause harm to a user device while posing to be a benign application such as a free anti-virus solution. The harm can be either in terms of allowing unauthorized remote access to the device, hijacking device resources, turning the device into a bot/proxy, stealing user information etc. This class of malware is observed to be the most effective form of threat currently affecting mobile devices. Interestingly, through the course of our analysis, we detected instances of the Zeus trojan affecting 82 distinct iOS based mobile devices in the network. Although mobile variants of this threat affecting other platforms such as Windows Mobile and Android have been seen in the wild, to the best of our knowledge, this is the first time a variant of this threat was identified affecting iOS devices [10]. Unfortunately, we were not able to explore characteristics of this malware variant further due to limitations in the dataset.

Privacy Leakage Threats: Threats which maliciously leak IMEI (International Mobile Equipment Identity) number or device location information in the HTTP headers or URI affect over 1200 unique mobile devices, making this one of the most prevailing attacks targeting mobile devices in our dataset. Although traditional desktop malware which leak sensitive user data exist, this problem is more pronounced in the mobile ecosystem. This may be due to the sensitive nature of data stored on mobile devices which attackers deem valuable, issues of application over-privilege in some mobile platforms, and the availability of third party app stores which facilitates deploying such malicious applications. Table 3 categorizes the types of privacy leakage issues revealed in our ground truth data. Clearly, information such as those presented above would potentially allow an attacker to uniquely observe a targeted user and his activities, making this a serious violation user privacy.

Adware and Potentially Unwanted Applications (PUA): This class of applications sneak into a device deceptively and get installed in such a way that

Table 4. Affected mobile platforms

Device platform	% Total devices	% Infection rate	% Mobile alerts
iOS	40.57%	0.22%	53.12%
Android	20.09%	0.39%	45.74%
Windows	0.2%	0.12%	0.76%
RIM OS	0.08%	0.32%	0.15%
Custom Feature Phone OS and Others	39.06%	0.0009%	0.21%

it can be difficult to detect and remove. The primary motive of these programs is to display unwanted advertisements to users, often in the form of pop-up ads. While some of these apps may just be a minor irritant to the user, they may, in some cases, also act as dangerous spyware that monitor user behavior and collect data without consent.

SIP Threats: Session Initiation Protocol (SIP) is widely used for controlling multimedia communication sessions such as VoIP calls over the internet. Our results indicate that vulnerabilities in this protocol is seen to be a popular target for attackers seeking to exploit mobile devices. These are alarming trends since such vulnerabilities can potentially give attackers the ability to listen-in on confidential voice communications or launch denial of service attacks as reported in previous studies [11,12].

3.3   Infection Rates of Popular Mobile Platforms

The question of which mobile platforms are most vulnerable to security threats has been a hot topic of debate for several years. We attempt to answer this question by utilizing ground truth data obtained from the operational cellular network. Table 4 presents the following data points: (a) The proportion of devices belonging to each identifiable mobile platform in our dataset; (b) The proportion of devices of a given platform that are infected, or the infection rate; and, (c) The proportion of alerts observed in the ground truth originating from a given platform.

We observe from the second column of the table that Android is the most vulnerable platform with a 0.39% infection rate. This infection rate is slightly higher than those claimed by the most recent independent study of malware infection rates in Android by Truong et al. [3] who measure it to be in the range of 0.26–0.28% and three times the rate reported by Google [13]. Android is followed closely by Blackberry with an infection rate of 0.32% and iOS with 0.22%. These figures show that the walled garden approach/security through obscurity as employed by these platforms are failing to ensure against malware spread. Blackberry devices are often used for business purposes due to their security capabilities. However, the nature of data stored on these devices may induce attackers specifically target this platform which can explain its high infection rate. Attackers are however failing to affect a large proportion of users with devices running Windows based mobile platforms as noted by recent industry reports [14].

4 Network Footprints of Cellular Threats

In this section, we investigate if network access patterns associated with malicious domains/hosts contacted by infected user devices exhibit distinct statistical features when compared to accesses to their benign counterparts. There are many existing studies that target accurate detection of malicious domains/URL's by using different methodologies. Some of these studies utilize a combination of DNS and WHOIS features, host based features, content of the webpage, etc. in order to achieve their goals [4,5] while some other studies such as [6] and [7] exclusively use lexical features. The motivation of our study however is to investigate if any of the statistical network features can complement the existing detection rules. This can be helpful in situations where other data such as DNS, WHOIS, etc. which are useful for the malicious domain classification task is infeasible to obtain or is otherwise unavailable.

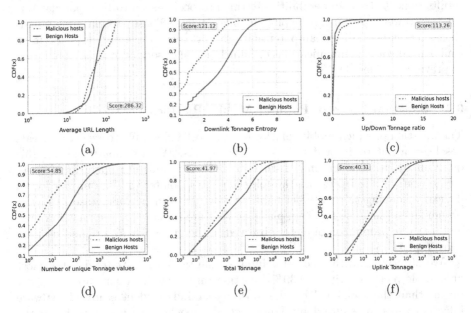

Fig. 3. Network Footprint of Malicious Domains

4.1 Feature Extraction and Selection

In order to perform our classification experiment, we first build a set of known malicious domains using information from the ground truth alert database.

Table 5. Comparing ROC Areas

Data set	ROC area-α	ROC area-β	ROC area-γ
600 malicious 600 benign	0.843	0.744	0.9
540 malicious 600 benign	0.83	0.737	0.897
480 malicious 600 benign	0.838	0.732	0.895
420 malicious 600 benign	0.84	0.73	0.891
360 malicious 600 benign	0.852	0.746	0.897
300 malicious 300 benign	0.84	0.703	0.885
240 malicious 600 benign	0.813	0.703	0.885
180 malicious 600 benign	0.796	0.771	0.857
120 malicious 600 benign	0.824	0.76	0.869
60 malicious 600 benign	0.763	0.728	0.876

We then create a set of benign domains by randomly choosing domains visited by subscriber devices which are otherwise not listed in the ground truth database. We further verify they are benign by running the domains through commercial URL scanners. For these set of known malicious and benign domains, we extract lexical and statistical network features as follows:

(a) *Lexical features:* Each target domain/host name is broken into multiple 'tags' or 'tokens' based on the '.' delimiter. We identify 6,729 such unique lexical tags through this process over a set of 1200 benign and malicious domains. We then utilize the frequency of occurrence of each tag in a given domain name as the lexical features of the target. This approach to represent lexical information is commonly referred to as the bag-of-words model. Variants of this model have been used to generate lexical features for use in detecting malicious URL's in previous studies such as [4,7].

(b) *Statistical Network Features:* Using the DPI records from the cellular carrier we extract the following 12 heuristic features for each target domain: Uplink data transfer volume (or uplink tonnage), downlink data transfer volume (or downlink tonnage), ratio of uplink/downlink tonnage, total tonnage, proportion of failed connections, average URL length, number of connections, number of unique source IP's connecting to the domain, number of failed connections, entropy of destination IP addresses, downlink tonnage entropy and the number of unique tonnage values.

We start our analysis by identifying specific network and lexical features that contribute towards distinguishing between malicious and benign hosts. In order to select such features, we utilize the raw set of attributes described above and apply the Chi-squared statistic evaluation [15]. The Chi-squared score essentially measures the difference between the conditional distributions of a network feature associated with the two classes: malicious vs. benign domains/hosts. On the basis of the results of this exercise, we narrow down our feature set to 53 distinct attributes associated with each malicious/benign domain after removing attributes which have a score of zero. This reduced feature set includes 10 statistical network features and 43 distinct lexical features. Figure 3 shows the cumulative distribution function (CDF) of six selected network features associated with malicious and the benign hosts that exhibited the highest chi-squared scores. It is visually apparent that there is significant difference between the conditional distribution for malicious vs. benign domains/hosts for these network features. Other network features which were selected but not shown include the connection entropy, the destination IP entropy, the downlink tonnage and the number of unique tonnage values.

4.2 Classification of Malicious/Benign Domains

Many of the statistical network features have complex non-linear relationships. This makes the task of classification of domains/hosts into malicious and benign categories non-trivial. To tackle this problem, we use a machine learning approach which can handle such dependent features efficiently. In particular we use the "Random Forest" ensemble learner [16] to create a model with the individual features. This classification method operates by constructing multiple decision trees at a time (15 in our case) and predicts a class by aggregating the predictions of the ensemble. In addition, we use the n-fold cross validation technique to evaluate the accuracy of our model (n=10).

We run our classification experiments on varying proportions of malicious and non-malicious hosts employing (a) Statistical network features alone (α), (b) Lexical Features alone (β) and (c) Statistical network features in addition to lexical features (γ). Figure 4a and b present the receiver operating characteristic(ROC) for two of our cross-validation experiments. The ideal ROC would lie close to the upper-left corner with false positive rate close to 0 % and true positive rate close to 100 %. Note that with the addition of statistical network features to simple lexical features, we obtain a better true positive rate at lower false positive rates for most combinations of malicious and benign hosts.

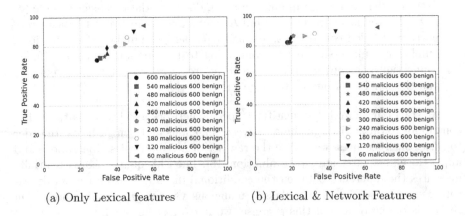

(a) Only Lexical features   (b) Lexical & Network Features

Fig. 4. Cross-Validation Results

We observe from Table 5 that the ROC area is higher in the case where we utilize statistical network features along with lexical features (column 3) to perform classification as compared to using the lexical features alone (column 2) or statistical network features alone (column 1) for all proportions of malicious and benign domains. These preliminary results show that statistical network features are complementary to lexical features and hold promise to add to capabilities of existing detection rules to help solve the malicious domain detection problem. A deeper analysis of this result is warranted and we leave it as an important area of exploration for our future work.

5   Conclusions

In this paper, we present a study of malicious mobile traffic by using data obtained from a major US based cellular carrier spanning a one week period that contains over two million subscribers. Our investigation reveals that 0.17 % of mobile devices are affected by security threats. This infection rate while still small, is orders of magnitude higher than the last reported infection rate of 0.0009 % making this a worrisome problem. We combine multiple disparate data sets to uncover details about the threats affecting mobile devices in the cellular network and their unique characteristics. We also perform a detailed analysis of infection rates in various popular mobile platforms. Our results show that platforms deemed to be more secure by common opinion as iOS and BlackBerry are not as secure as we think. However, Android still remains the most affected platform with an infection rate of 0.39 %. Lastly, we characterized the aggregate network footprint of malicious and benign domains associated with the threats observed in our dataset and showed how statistical network features can be used to potentially aid detection of malicious domains/hosts when used in conjunction with other lexical feature sets. Our preliminary results in this direction are promising and we leave more detailed analysis to future work.

Acknowledgement. We would like to thank Parth H. Pathak for his insightful comments on this work. We are grateful to Theo Pan and Josh Vaughen for their help with obtaining VirusTotal data. This work was supported in part by the the Intel Science and Technology Center for Secure Computing.

References

1. Wei, X., Gomez, L., Neamtiu, I., Faloutsos, M.: Malicious android applications in the enterprise: What do they do and how do we fix it? In: Proceedings of 28th IEEE International Conference on Data Engineering Workshops (ICDEW) (2012)
2. Lever, C., Antonakakis, M., Reaves, B., Traynor, P., Lee, W.: The core of the matter: analyzing malicious traffic in cellular carriers. In: Proceedings of NDSS 2013 (2013)
3. Truong, H.T.T., Lagerspetz, E., et al.: The company you keep: mobile malware infection rates and inexpensive risk indicators. In: Proceedings of 23rd International Conference on World Wide Web, pp. 39–50 (2014)

4. Ma, J., Saul, L.K., Savage, S., Voelker, G.M.: Identifying suspicious URLs: an application of large-scale online learning. In: Proceedings of 26th ACM Annual International Conference on Machine Learning, pp. 681–688 (2009)
5. Choi, H., Zhu, B.B., Lee, H.: Detecting malicious web links and identifying their attack types. In: Proceedings of 2nd USENIX Conference on Web Application Development (2011)
6. Blum, A., Wardman, B., Solorio, T., Warner, G.: Lexical feature based phishing URL detection using online learning. In: Proceedings of 3rd ACM Workshop on Artificial Intelligence and Security, pp. 54–60 (2010)
7. Le, A., Markopoulou, A., Faloutsos, M.: Phishdef: URL names say it all. In: Proceedings of IEEE INFOCOM, pp. 191–195 (2011)
8. Invernizzi, L., Miskovic, S., et al.: Nazca: detecting malware distribution in large-scale networks. In: Proceedings of NDSS 2014 (2014)
9. The virustotal online scanner. http://www.virustotal.com/en/about
10. Maslennikov, D.: Zeus in the mobile - facts and theories (2011). http://www.securelist.com/en/analysis/204792194
11. El Sawda, S., Urien, P.: SIP security attacks and solutions: a state-of-the-art review. In: IEEE Information and Communication Technologies, ICTTA 2006, vol. 2, pp. 3187–3191 (2006)
12. Geneiatakis, D., Dagiuklas, T., et al.: Survey of security vulnerabilities in session initiation protocol. IEEE Commun. Surv. Tutor. 8(1–4), 68–81 (2006)
13. Patterson, S.M.: Contrary to what you've heard, Android is almost impenetrable to malware (2013). http://qz.com/131436/contrary-to-what-youve-heard-android-is-almost-impenetrable-to-malware
14. Cisco 2014 annual security report. http://www.cisco.com/web/offers/lp/2014-annual-security-report/index.html
15. Liu, H., Setiono, R.: Chi2: feature selection and discretization of numeric attributes. In: IEEE 7th International Conference on Tools with Artificial Intelligence, pp. 388–391 (1995)
16. Breiman, L.: Random forests. Mach. Learn. 45(1), 5–32 (2001)

Characterizing Instant Messaging Apps on Smartphones

Li Zhang$^{(\boxtimes)}$, Chao Xu, Parth H. Pathak, and Prasant Mohapatra

University of California, Davis, CA 95616, USA
{jxzhang,chaoxu,phpathak,pmohapatra}@ucdavis.edu

Abstract. Proliferation of smart devices has fueled the popularity of using mobile instant messaging (IM) apps at a rapid pace. While the IM apps on smartphones have become increasingly popular, there has only been a little research on understanding the characteristics of these apps. Because most of the IM apps use proprietary protocols, it is challenging to analyze their internal operations. In this work, we present a comprehensive characterization of mobile IM apps using experiments on LTE cellular network. We decompose the operations of an IM app into multiple independent states which allows us to systematically study them. We characterize the energy and bandwidth efficiency of each of the states and provide numerous insights. Our analysis reveals that typing notification feature of the IM apps is a major contributor to the energy consumption. We also find that the bandwidth efficiency of current IM apps are alarmingly poor compared to other applications such as email and web surfing. These, along with other findings, provided in this work can help improve the energy and network performance of IM apps.

1 Introduction

Recent years have witnessed a fast growing trend of using the new generation of mobile instant message (IM) applications such as WhatsApp, WeChat and Line on the smartphones. WhatsApp, for example, is ranked as the third all-time-popular Android apps in Google's Android app store [1] with a total of 590 million users in 193 different countries [5]. According to [2], the mobile IM apps have overtaken the Short Message Service (SMS) operated by cellular network carriers, with 19 billion messages sent per day compared with 17.6 billion SMS messages.

While the adoption of mobile IM apps are rapidly increasing, very little research has been done in characterizing them. This is because there are numerous challenges in characterizing the IM apps. First, compared to other types of mobile apps studied in [6,10,15,17], the IM apps involves much more user interaction such as typing, reading and user notifications. This makes the automated characterization extremely difficult. The new set of features (e.g. typing and read notifications) offered by the IM apps are much more complex compared to the traditional SMS services. Also, there is a lack of transparency in the application layer protocols used by the popular IM apps. Most of the current IM apps either implement their own protocol or modify existing standard such as XMPP to

© Springer International Publishing Switzerland 2015
J. Mirkovic and Y. Liu (Eds.): PAM 2015, LNCS 8995, pp. 83–95, 2015.
DOI: 10.1007/978-3-319-15509-8_7

customize them. This makes it even more difficult to understand the underlying operations of the apps.

In this work, we present a comprehensive characterization of the popular IM apps for smartphones using experiments on LTE cellular network. We address the challenges listed above by dissecting the operations of IM apps into many different states and then evaluate the energy and the network efficiency of each of them. Some of the main insights provided by our study are as follows:

- We find that sending and receiving typing notifications are major contributors to the total energy consumption when the IM app is running in the foreground. Many IM apps use frequent periodic typing notification messages which result in very poor energy efficiency.
- Today's IM apps have extremely low bandwidth efficiency (average amount of traffic per one character of user message). This is true even when the app is running in the foreground and has minimal requirement of maintaining the "online presence". This shows that while XMPP-like IM protocols offer efficient ways of maintaining "online presence", the current IM apps show poor network efficiency when running in the foreground.
- Because users spend significant amount of time on IM apps compared to other types of apps, simply switching to darker graphical interface can yield surprising energy benefits.
- When the IM apps are running in background, the method used to notify the user about incoming message has a significant impact on the energy consumption.

The rest of paper is organized as follows. We describe the experimental setup and the data collection in Sect. 2. The foreground and the background characterization results are presented in Sects. 3 and 4 respectively. Then we discuss the related works in Sect. 5. Section 6 concludes the paper.

2   Data Collection and Methodology

In this section, we first provide the details of data collection for different IM apps. We represent the operations of an IM app using a state transition diagram. For each of the states, we will test 5 most popular IM apps, and profile the energy consumption and the network traffic generated.

2.1   State Transitions in IM App Usage

As shown in Fig. 1, the operations of an IM app can be divided into 6 distinct states. When the users are in a conversation, the IM app runs in the foreground, occupying the entire screen. When the users are using another app or when the screen is turned off, the IM app runs in the background but still keeps maintaining connections with its remote servers.

Foreground: When the IM app is in the foreground, the user is considered to be "in conversation". There are two "in conversation" states.

- **In Conversation Sending (ICS):** The ICS state is defined as the period from when the user starts her typing of the message to the time when the read notification is received. In this state, there are 4 functions: type, send typing notification, send message and receive read notification.

- **In Conversation Reading (ICR):** The ICR state is from receiving the typing notification to sending the read notification. This state has 3 functions: receive typing notification, receive and display message, send read notification.

Background: There are four background states.

- **Background Idle with Screen On (BION):** BION is a state that the IM app is running in the background while neither occupying the screen nor getting any incoming message. This state has only 1 function: keep maintaining the on-line presence with the server.

- **Background Receive with Screen On (BRON):** The BRON state is from the time when message starts to arrive to the time when its notice is displayed to the user. This state has 2 functions: receive message and display notice. This state ends before the user takes any action for the received message, therefore the IM app will not send out a read notification.

- **Background Idle with Screen Off (BIOFF):** The BIOFF state is the period when the IM app is idly listening in the background and the screen is off. Similar to BION state, the BIOFF state also has only 1 function: keep maintaining the on-line presence.

- **Background Receive with Screen Off (BROFF):** This state starts when the message arrives and the screen is off. This state ends once the user is notified by some form of notification either using sound, vibration or screen turn-on.

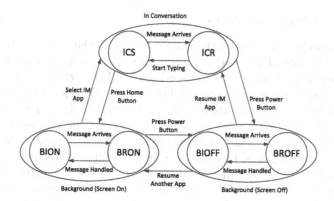

Fig. 1. The state transition diagram of an IM app usage

Table 1. List of selected IM apps; Number of users data from [5]

Apps	Mobile Users	Covered Countries	Originated From	Icon
WeChat	600 million	∼ 200	China	
WhatsApp	590 million	∼ 100	USA	
Facebook Messenger	300 million	Unknown	USA	
Line	300 million	193	Japan	
Viber	200 million	193	Israel	

2.2 Experiment Settings

We select the top 5 mobile IM apps in terms of the number of users by the end of 2013. The names and the statistics of the selected apps are listed in Table 1. Our experimental setup consists of a Samsung Nexus S smartphone (running Android 4.1.2), a Macbook Air, a Dell Latitude E5430 laptop and a Monsoon Power Monitor. We install *tcpdump* on the phone to capture the network traffic. The Macbook Air is used as the phone's SSH console. The Monsoon Power Monitor is employed to measure the power consumption of the smartphone, and the Dell laptop serves as the power monitor console. The sampling frequency of the power monitor is set to 5 KHz.

We conducted all the experiments on AT&T's cellular network data connection. We also turn off the WiFi and Bluetooth radios and fix the volume, brightness, vibration and keystroke feedback settings to avoid any unintended impact on measured energy. To turn off any additional background services on Android, we limit the number of background processes to one and use "Advanced Task Killer Pro" app to kill any additional running processes.

2.3 Methodology and Metrics

To get a comprehensive view of the characteristics of the selected IM apps, we test all the 6 states of the apps, by using a set of the most commonly used IM messaging literacy among college students [7]. In [7], the authors listed the taxonomy of the IM conversation topics. For example, the 5 most popular conversation topics are: emotional support, fictional people, video games, computers and shared interests. We picked one conversation in each kind of the popular topics from the typical examples concluded in [7] and created a database of 70 messages. The length of the messages varies from 4 characters to as many as 125 characters, where the characters may include letters, punctuation marks and metadiscursive markers. To reduce the effect of randomness, the typing of each message in each run of the experiments is repeated 20 times to calculate an average value. We repeat the experiments for two different users to eliminate any user-specific typing characteristics.

The performance of the IM apps in the state with sending/receiving activities are mainly evaluated by two metrics: (i) Energy efficiency: energy consumption per character sent/received (Joule/character) and (ii) Bandwidth efficiency: the amount of network traffic generated per character sent/received (byte/character). In the idle listening states, since there are no user intended messages, we will use the average energy consumption per hour (J) and the average network traffic per hour (KByte) as the evaluation metrics.

3 In Conversation Sending/Receiving (ICS/ICR)

We conducted a total of 12,600 runs of experiments by manually typing, and collected 2.4 GB of energy and network traffic traces. From the network traces, we observed that all the 5 selected IM apps are built on the client/server architecture, where the message sender and the message receiver communicate indirectly through a certain number of servers. Although following the same architecture, the application layer protocols used by each app are quite different. By linking the server port number with the registry of Internet Assigned Numbers Authority (IANA) [8], we found that WeChat, WhatsApp, FB Messenger, Line and Viber use commplex-main, XMPP, HTTPS, SSL and Virtual Reality Modeling Language (VRML) [14] respectively.

As shown in Fig. 2, the ICS state can be divided into two phases: (1) typing the message & sending typing notification, and (2) sending the message & receiving the read notification. Correspondingly, the ICR state is also consisted of two phases: (1) receiving the typing notification, and (2) receiving the message & sending the read notification. Since the typing of a long message needs considerable amount of time, we can observe a time gap between the first and the second phase of the ICR state. During the time gap, the radio will be tuned to the paging channel (PCH) state to save energy.

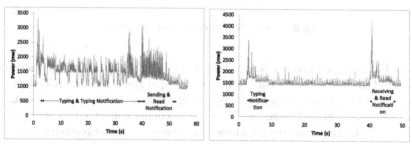

(a) Sending a Message with 120 Char- (b) Receiving a Message with 120 acters   Characters

Fig. 2. Examples of energy traces of in conversation states (WhatsApp)

3.1 Energy Characterization

The energy consumption of "in conversation" states can be attributed to two factors: (1) the Graphical User Interface (GUI) and (2) user operations such as typing or sending messages etc.

GUI. The average values of the energy consumption of the GUIs of the IM apps are shown in Fig. 3(a). It is observed that the GUIs of the ICR states always consume more energy than the GUIs of the ICS states (36.3 % more on an average). This is because the conversation windows of the IM apps are usually in brighter colors, while the default keyboard background of Android is in darker color. In the ICR state, the conversation window usually occupies the entire screen; while in the ICS state, the dark keyboard will occupy about half of the screen which reduces the overall energy consumption. Therefore the GUIs of ICR state will consume more energy than the GUIs of ICS state.

Since the energy consumption of the display is highly dependent on the hardware, there is only a little that can be done from the app development perspective. We observe that Line and Viber (refer Fig. 3(a)) consumes much less energy in ICR and ICS states simply due to the fact that their GUIs use darker colors. Because users spend a large amount of time on the IM apps (very high user residence time [17]), it is advisable to incorporate such modifications. We observe that the GUI consumption of each app in each state is more or less constant (coefficients of variance laying in the range of $(0.0053, 0.0228)$), hence we deduct the GUI energy from the energy measurements shown in the rest of this paper.

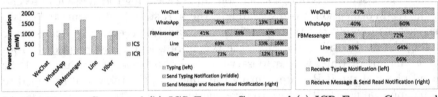

(a) The Energy Consumed by The GUIs   (b) ICS Energy Consumed by User Operations   (c) ICR Energy Consumed by User Operations

Fig. 3. The factors of energy consumption

ICS and ICR User Operations. The characteristics of the energy consumption related to user operations are shown in Fig. 3(b) and (c). In the ICS state, we can see the typing message and sending typing notification time phase consumes much (308 % on average) more energy than the energy consumed by sending the message and receiving the read notification. However, on the receiving side, the difference of the energy consumed by the user operations in the two time phases is relatively small (40 % on average).

Energy for Typing: We first turn off the radio and simply measure the energy of typing. We observe that over 60.2 % of the energy cost is attributed to typing in the ICS state.

Energy for Typing Notifications: We observe that sending the typing notification in ICS state consumes as much energy as sending the actual message and receiving the read notifications combined. In the ICR state, receiving typing notification consumes as much as 37 % (average for all 5 apps) of state's total energy consumption. The high energy consumption is due to the fact that however small the typing notification message is, it requires the radio interface to be turned on. This shows that sending and receiving typing notifications is a major factor of energy consumption (often comparable to sending and/or receiving the actual message). This means significant amount of energy can be saved by simply turning off the typing notifications. This also calls for a more energy efficient solution for enabling typing notifications.

Energy for Read Notifications: Because the sending and receiving read notification is submerged in receiving and sending message respectively, it is difficult to isolate the energy consumption of the read notification. However, we expect the energy consumption of the read notification to be much lesser than that of typing notification. This is because the read notification is only sent once while the typing notification involves many messages (continuously based on when user starts and stops typing until the message send button is pressed). Also, because sending/receiving read notification is mostly submerged with receiving/sending the message, no separate radio wake up is necessary, further reducing its energy overhead.

Energy Efficiency. We now present the results about per character energy consumption as defined in Sect. 2.3. To understand this, we compare the energy consumption for many short messages to fewer long messages. The size of the complete message is chosen to 120 characters which is divided into substrings, each of which is sent individually. As shown in Fig. 4, we consider 1 to 6 as possible number of substrings. When number of substrings is 1, it means that the entire 120 character message is sent at once. On the other hand, when the number of substrings is 6, a total of 6 messages are sent separately each of which is of 20 characters. Figure 4 shows energy consumption per character when different number of substrings are sent.

As shown in Fig. 4(a), the energy spent on sending each character increases as the length of the substrings decreases. This is mainly caused by the overhead of sending typing notifications because an IM app needs to tune its radio to dedicated channel (DCH) state and also suffers the tail energy overhead in the Forward Access Channel (FACH) state. We can also observe the energy efficiency of

Table 2. ICS: the average traffic statistics of 30 character messages

Apps	Number of TCP connections	Number of packets	Average packet size (byte)	Duration (s)
WeChat	1	38	61.4	33.54
WhatsApp	1	14	110.9	21.35
FB messenger	1	28	166.4	22.42
Line	1	12	87	20.74
Viber	1	26	108.5	22.39

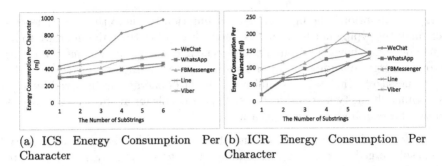

(a) ICS Energy Consumption Per Character

(b) ICR Energy Consumption Per Character

Fig. 4. Energy consumption per character

WeChat is much lower compared to other apps. This is because WeChat aggressively sends typing notifications every 2 seconds. Since typing many shorter messages takes much more time combined than typing one long message, number of typing notifications increase sharply for WeChat, resulting in sharp increase in energy consumption. To further validate this, we present network traffic statistics in Table 2. It shows that WeChat sends more smaller packets for typing notifications. On the other hand, WhatsApp and Line send fewer packets due to fewer typing notifications which also reflects in their per character energy efficiency in Fig. 4(a).

In the ICR state, the energy consumption also follows the same trend that many shorter messages consume more energy as shown in Fig. 4(b). However, we observe some anomaly in case of FB Messenger and Viber where many shorter messages (no. of substrings = 6) are more energy efficient compared to fewer medium sized messages (no. of substrings = 5). This is because both these apps *delay* sending the typing notifications. This allows the typing notification to be received almost at the same time (compared to Fig. 2) with the actual message, which eliminates additional radio wake up and saves energy. This shows that if the typing notification can be delayed towards sending the actual message, it is possible to reduce the energy overhead of sending/receiving the typing notifications, especially for small length messages.

Findings: (1) Sending and receiving typing notification is a major contributor to the total energy consumption of ICR and ICS states. IM apps which periodically send the typing notifications suffer from very high energy consumption. Because most of the IM messages are small in length, delaying the sending of typing notification can save significant energy. Also, an adaptive scheme should be designed that can control when to send the typing notification depending on the length of user's input message. Such a scheme can achieve the correct balance between usefulness of typing notifications and their energy consumption. (2) Because user's residence time on IM apps are much longer compared to other types of apps, simply switching to darker GUI can yield surprising energy benefit.

Table 3. ICR: the average traffic statistics of 30 character messages

Apps	Number of TCP connections	Number of packets	Average packet size (byte)	Duration (s)
WeChat	1	20	280	10.3
WhatsApp	1	12	78.7	11.5
FB messenger	2	26	235.3	16.4
Line	1	8	187.5	12.4
Viber	1	14	122.4	22.6

3.2 Bandwidth Efficiency

We now analyze the bandwidth efficiency (amount of traffic generated per character sent/received) of the IM apps and present the results in Fig. 5(a) and (b). This helps us to understand how much traffic the IM apps generate compared to the amount of useful information (instant message) exchanged. It is observed that network traffic per character is different when receiving or sending the same message. This is expected given that all the apps use client-server architecture and the sent message is first processed at the server before it is delivered to the receiver. It is also observed that network traffic per character is much higher on the receiving side compared to the sending side.

We observe that FB Messenger has the worst bandwidth efficiency for both sending and receiving sides in most cases. On the other hand, WhatsApp and Line achieve very high bandwidth efficiency compared to other apps. Due to the unavailability of their internal design, application layer protocol customization etc., it remains inconclusive why certain apps achieve high or low bandwidth efficiency.

Comparison with Other Types of Applications. We now compare the bandwidth efficiency of IM apps to other kind of applications. We first construct a set of emails and plain HTML pages with the same set of messages tested on the IM apps. For email, we measure the amount of traffic generated by Google Mail and the size of the actual emails. For HTML, we set up a web-server which holds a plain HTML page (without any images) and connect it via a client to measure the traffic and the size of HTML page. The bandwidth efficiency of Email and HTML are compared with IM apps in Fig. 5(c). As we can observe, IM apps have extremely poor bandwidth efficiency which shows that even the modern protocols such as XMPP (used by WhatsApp) are not bandwidth efficient.

Traffic Due to Typing and Read Notifications. It was observed in Sect. 3.1 that typing notifications are a major contributor to energy consumption. We now evaluate how much network traffic is generated due to the typing and read notifications. Figure 5(d) shows the ratio of traffic due to notifications to the total traffic. We observe that the ratio is small for most of the applications. This way, the actual traffic due to notifications is low, however, because the notifications

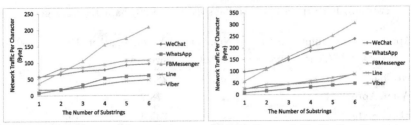

(a) ICS Network Traffic Per Character (b) ICR Network Traffic Per Character

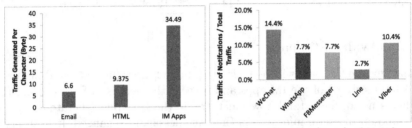

(c) The Bandwidth Efficiency of Different Applications

(d) Ratio of Traffic (Byte) of Notifications to The Total Traffic

Fig. 5. The bandwidth consumption statistics of in conversation states

are sent/received using many small packets (Table 3), it causes frequent radio wake up and results in poor energy efficiency.

Findings: (1) The IM apps have extremely poor bandwidth efficiency compared to other applications such as email and web-surfing. Modern IM protocols such as XMPP which are optimized to reduce traffic in background states demonstrate the same poor level of bandwidth efficiency in the foreground states. Further improvements are necessary to improve the network performance of instant messaging apps and protocols. (2) Typing notification which is a major contributor in energy consumption does not introduce proportionally high network traffic.

4   The Background States

The performance of the IM apps running in the background is now characterized. We show the corresponding results in Figs. 6, 7 and 8. Similar to the ICR state, we can also observe the energy efficiency of the background receiving decreases if the length of the messages decreases, as shown in Fig. 6. However, the reasons behind the phenomenons are quite different. In the background receiving states, we did not observe any typing notification nor read notification from the network traces. The main cause of the energy efficiency reduction is the overhead of notifying the users through certain methods, e.g. banner size notification, pop-up window and icon label. In the BRON state, Viber uses pop-up window, while in the BROFF state, both Line and Viber use pop-up window. The pop-up window results in significant increase of energy consumption for these two apps as seen in Fig. 6.

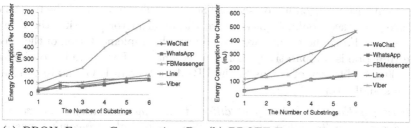

(a) BRON Energy Consumption Per Character

(b) BROFF Energy Consumption Per Character

Fig. 6. The energy efficiency of background receiving

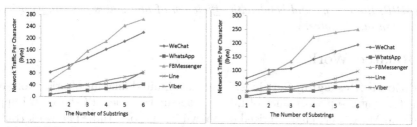

(a) BRON Bandwidth Consumption Per Character

(b) BROFF Bandwidth Consumption Per Character

Fig. 7. The bandwidth consumption of background receiving

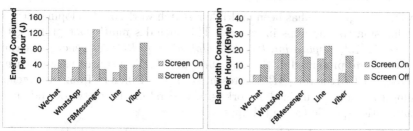

(a) Energy Consumption of Idle States

(b) Bandwidth Consumption of Idle States

Fig. 8. The statistics of idle states

Comparing Figs. 4(b) and 7, we can observe that the bandwidth consumption of the background receiving follows the same trend but is slightly lower than the bandwidth consumption of the ICR state, since there are no typing notifications and read notifications. On average, the BRON and the BROFF states consume 9.6 % and 8.5 % more bandwidth than the ICR state.

The statistics of the idle listening states are shown in Fig. 8. The main function of the idle listening states is to communicate periodically with the server to maintain the online presence. Therefore the number and the frequency of exchanging "keep online" packets are the main factor affecting the energy consumption. From the results, we can observe the implementation of the "keep online" function is comparatively more energy efficient. For example, considering the 1,500 mAh battery of Nexus S, the FB Messenger in BION state can have 172 h of standby time.

Findings: (1) Energy efficiency of different IM apps in background receiving states depends mostly on how the app notifies the user about incoming message. Apps that use pop-up window notification consume drastically more energy than the apps using banner notification or icon label. This sheds light on the potential to improve energy efficiency by simplifying the user notification process. (2) With improved methods of maintaining "online presence" in today's IM protocols such as XMPP, the energy and bandwidth efficiency of idle states are comparatively better than other states.

5   Related Work

Traditional Messaging Services: There is a limited amount of prior work on characterizing the performance of IM apps on smartphones. PC-based IM apps (AIM and MSN) were characterized in [16] where authors studied network traffic related characteristics. Similarly, [9] characterized the users' conversation styles of IM apps in workplace, by analyzing the SMS messages exchanged through AT&T's cellular network. Note that different from both these efforts, we have attempted to characterize smartphone IM apps which have revolutionized the way people connect in today's era.

App Profiling: There has been multiple research works on developing methods to profile smartphone apps in general. This includes multi-layer profiling tool *ProfileDroid* [15], *Application Resource Optimizer (ARO)* [12], energy measurement tool *eprof* presented in [11] and third-party API resource usage measurement tool *API Extractor (APIX)* presented in [18]. Different from these generic profiling tools, our focus in this work is to understand the network and energy characteristics specific to the IM apps.

Mobile IM Apps: Considering the research specific to mobile IM apps, [3,4] modeled user's residence time on IM apps and typical message arrival rate. Based on these models, they derived energy consumption models of IM apps. The provided model, however, only provides a high-level coarse-grained behavioral analysis which is independent of the operation of the underlying IM app. In this paper, our focus is on the operations of different IM apps. In other related work [13], the authors showed the energy consumption of IM apps can be reduced by message bundling. To evaluate their bundling algorithms, the authors implemented a customized IM app and developed a software tool *Energy Box* to estimate the energy consumption of sending/receiving instant messages by analyzing the tcpdump traces. Note that such techniques to improve energy efficiency of IM apps are in line with our effort to quantify the energy consumption of popular IM apps.

6   Conclusions

By decomposing the operations of IM apps into 6 states, we characterized the energy and the bandwidth efficiency of IM apps. We also analyzed various operations of the IM apps, e.g. typing notification, read notification, sending/receiving messages. Our analysis revealed there is still plenty of improvements necessary in the IM apps especially in the "in conversation" and the "background receiving" states to improve their energy and bandwidth efficiency. However, we observe that the background idle states already have comparatively high energy and bandwidth efficiency.

References

1. AppBrain. http://www.appbrain.com/stats/
2. BBC. http://www.bbc.com/news/business-22334338
3. Chung, Y.W.: Investigation of energy consumption of mobile station for instant messaging services. In: ISADS 2011, pp. 343–346 (2011)
4. Chung, Y.W.: An improved energy saving scheme for instant messaging services. In: WiAd 2011, pp. 278–282 (2011)
5. Clifford, C.: Top 10 apps for instant messaging, Entrepreneur, 11 December 2013
6. Falaki, H., Lymberopoulos, D., Mahajan, R., Kandula, S., Estrin, D.: A first look at traffic on smartphones. In: IMC 2010, pp. 281–287 (2010)
7. Haas, C., Takayoshi, P.: Young people's everyday literacies: the language features of instant messaging. Res. Teach. Engl. **45**(4), 378–404 (2011)
8. I. A. N. A. (IANA). https://www.iana.org/assignments/
9. Isaacs, E., Walendowski, A., Whittaker, S., Schiano, D.J., Kamm, C.: The character, functions, and styles of instant messaging in the workplace. In: CSCW 2002, pp. 11–20 (2002)
10. Lee, S.-W., Park, J.-S., Lee, H.-S., Kim, M.-S.: A study on smart-phone traffic analysis. In: APNOMS 2011, pp. 1–7 (2011)
11. Pathak, A., Hu, Y.C., Zhang, M.: Where is the energy spent inside my app? Fine grained energy accounting on smartphones with Eprof. In: EuroSys 2012, pp. 29–42 (2012)
12. Qian, F., Wang, Z., Gerber, A., Mao, Z., Sen, S., Spatscheck, O.: Profiling resource usage for mobile applications: a cross-layer approach. In: MobiSys 2011, pp. 321–334. ACM (2011)
13. Vergara, E.J., Andersson, S., Nadjm-Tehrani, S.: When mice consume like elephants: instant messaging applications. In: e-Energy 2014, pp. 97–107 (2014)
14. VRMLSite. http://www.vrmlsite.com
15. Wei, X., Gomez, L., Neamtiu, I., Faloutsos, M.: Profiledroid: multi-layer profiling of android applications. In: Mobicom 2012 (2012)
16. Xiao, Z., Guo, L., Tracey, J.: Understanding instant messaging traffic characteristics. In: ICDCS 2007, pp. 51–51 (2007)
17. Xu, Q., Erman, J., Gerber, A., Mao, Z., Pang, J., Venkataraman, S.: Identifying diverse usage behaviors of smartphone apps. In: IMC 2011, pp. 329–344 (2011)
18. Zhang, L., Stover, C., Lins, A., Buckley, C., Mohapatra, P.: Characterizing mobile open apis in smartphone apps. In: IFIP Networking Conference 2014, pp. 1–9 (2014)

Do Mobile Data Plans Affect Usage? Results from a Pricing Trial with ISP Customers

Carlee Joe-Wong[1]([⊠]), Sangtae Ha[2], Soumya Sen[3], and Mung Chiang[1]

[1] Princeton University, Princeton, USA
{cjoe,chiangm}@princeton.edu
[2] University of Colorado-Boulder, Boulder, USA
sangtae.ha@colorado.edu
[3] University of Minnesota, Minneapolis, USA
ssen@umn.edu

Abstract. The growing amount of traffic in mobile data networks is causing concern for Internet service providers (ISPs), especially smaller ISPs that need to lease expensive links to Tier 1 networks. Large amounts of traffic in "peak" hours are of especial concern, since network capacity must be provisioned to accommodate these peaks. In response, many ISPs have begun trying to influence user behavior with pricing. Time-dependent pricing (TDP) can help reduce peaks, since it allows ISPs to charge higher prices during peak periods. We present results from the first TDP trial with a commercial ISP. In addition to analyzing application-specific mobile and WiFi traffic, we compare changes in user behavior due to monthly data caps and time-dependent prices. We find that monthly data caps tend to reduce usage, while TDP can increase usage as users consume more data during discounted times. Moreover, unlike data caps, TDP reduces the network's peak-to-average usage ratio, lessening the need for network over-provisioning and increasing ISP profit.

1 Introduction

Mobile data usage is growing at unprecedented rates, with Cisco estimating that global mobile data traffic grew 81 % in 2013 and projecting a compound annual growth rate of 61 % over the next five years [1]. This trend has significantly increased ISPs' capital expenses, as they must provision their network to accommodate peak usage during the day [3,16]. Smaller ISPs are particularly affected, as their network capacity is limited by middle mile links to Tier 1 operators, which are leased at rates based on peak usage [20]. Many ISPs are therefore trying to reduce their peak mobile data traffic [18,22]. In this paper, we focus on the use of pricing as an incentive for users to reduce their peak usage.

Most U.S. ISPs charge fixed fees for limited monthly data caps. Yet data caps may not effectively limit usage peaks, as users can remain under their caps by using less data at off-peak times and not changing their peak-time usage. *Time-dependent pricing* (TDP) allows the ISP to effectively target network peaks by offering higher prices at those times, incentivizing users to consume data

© Springer International Publishing Switzerland 2015
J. Mirkovic and Y. Liu (Eds.): PAM 2015, LNCS 8995, pp. 96–108, 2015.
DOI: 10.1007/978-3-319-15509-8_8

at other times. Yet TDP's effectiveness depends on users' willingness to shift their data usage in exchange for reduced prices, which can vary for different users and applications: business users, for instance, might not wait to download email attachments, but teenagers might wait to download video purchases [8]. To the best of our knowledge, there are no systematic studies of these price-delay tolerances, and no works on TDP have yet accounted for the effect of displaying usage statistics to users: showing users these statistics would make them more aware of their usage and might affect their usage behavior. Previous trials have only focused on university populations [2, 8].

In this paper, we present *results from the first TDP trial with a commercial ISP*. We recruited 27 customers of a local U.S. ISP, dividing users into time-independent pricing (TIP) and TDP groups. The TIP users used a data usage monitoring application with their regular pricing plan. We show that this monitoring induced them to reduce their usage below their monthly data caps, but that they still had very high peak usage. The TDP users both monitored their data usage and received time-dependent prices; we show that the prices induced TDP users to increase their usage at discounted times. Thus, *simple data caps do not effectively reduce ISPs' peak network usage, but TDP does*. Our work makes the following contributions:

- An analysis of the results of the first TDP trial with a commercial ISP, including:
- A study of temporal and per-app WiFi and cellular usage data.
- An analysis of the impact of data usage monitoring apps on cellular and WiFi usage behavior.
- An evaluation of real customers' price sensitivity and delay tolerance for different applications.
- An examination of TDP's cost benefits with empirical price sensitivity and delay tolerance estimates.

In the next section, we give an overview of related work. We then describe the trial structure and our analysis methodology in Sect. 3. We analyze users' pre-trial data usage in Sect. 4 before presenting the trial results in Sect. 5. We conclude in Sect. 6.

2 Related Work

Previous trials in a university setting demonstrated TDP's effectiveness in changing mobile data usage patterns [8]. Others have suggested that data usage and user responses to incentives depend on psychological [2] or socioeconomic [14] factors. Another work on price elasticities for wireline broadband speeds considers a wider population [7]. These trials, however, do not analyze TDP's effects on different apps or account for the effect of simply displaying usage statistics to users. We find that displaying usage statistics generally decreases usage volume, but when combined with TDP can result in increased usage at low-price times.

Many studies have found a significant time-of-day pattern in cellular network traffic [11]. Others have analyzed LTE network performance [9] and compared the performance of different network interfaces (e.g., LTE and WiFi) [19]. Papers focusing on individual users' data consumption show a large diversity in the amount of data used by different users and different apps on mobile and WiFi networks [5,6,13,21]. These lead to distinct temporal usage patterns, which [12] showed can be leveraged to improve users' experience with intelligent WiFi offloading. Similarly, [10] shows that delaying mobile off-screen traffic, which is assumed to be delay-tolerant, can improve energy usage. Another work on Super Bowl traffic shows that short-term delays can be leveraged to eliminate congestion [4]. Our work provides a more nuanced estimation of delay tolerances and examines their monetary value to users by offering price incentives.

3   Methodology

We designed the trial to determine the effects of data usage monitoring and a combination of TDP with usage monitoring. We first outline the trial structure and then describe the data collected and apps distributed to trial participants. We finally present a model for users' price-delay tolerances that allows us to evaluate TDP's benefits for ISPs.

3.1   Trial Participants and Structure

We recruited 27 active trial participants from an ISP's customer base. While our sample size is small, the number of participants was limited by the fact that we changed some of their mobile data plans to TDP, broadening the trial's financial implications beyond those of simply measuring usage. All participants used their own Android devices. They did not use data monitoring apps before the trial, but did have monthly data caps.

All active participants downloaded custom-built apps for the trial, which we describe in more detail in the next section. These participants were divided into two groups: time-independent pricing (TIP) and TDP users. The TIP users installed data monitoring apps, allowing us to estimate the effect of usage monitoring with data caps. The TDP users' app both monitored data and offered time-dependent prices. Thus, their behavior is affected by both data monitoring and TDP. We additionally collected passive network data on more than 5000 "control" users, who did not install any apps. Table 1 summarizes the three groups of users.

The control and TIP users' data caps, which are not shared among devices, ranged from 1 to 10 GB and were the same as before the trial. TDP users were charged hourly time-dependent prices, e.g., \$10/GB from 12 to 1am and \$15/GB from 1 to 2 am. The prices offered ranged from \$10/GB to \$20/GB, and were chosen to be no higher than the ISP's most popular data plan: a monthly 1 GB cap for \$19.99. Prices were randomly determined and shown to the TDP users 24 hours in advance, allowing them to plan their usage over the next day.

Table 1. Three groups of trial participants.

	Recruitment	Data collection	Data plan
Control	Random	RADIUS logs	Unchanged
TIP	Volunteer	Trial app & RADIUS	Unchanged
TDP	Volunteer	Trial app & RADIUS	TDP rates

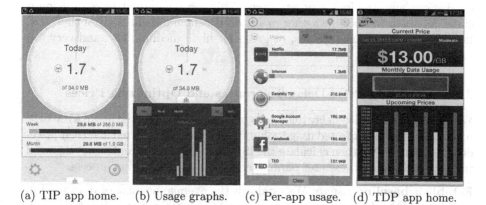

(a) TIP app home.   (b) Usage graphs.   (c) Per-app usage.   (d) TDP app home.

Fig. 1. Screenshots of the TIP and TDP apps. The TIP app's small pie chart indicator on the upper left of the screen indicator bar (1a) shows the approximate portion of a user's monthly data cap used so far. The TDP app's colored price indicator on this bar (1d) indicates the current price range.

3.2 Data Collection

Our dataset consists of two separate types of data: one 21.5 GB set of RADIUS network data, and one 10.5 GB set of application usage data. The RADIUS data was collected from March 2012 to June 2013 for all TIP, TDP, and control group users and contains 140 million session records, including input and output byte counts and start and end timestamps.

The second dataset was collected by TIP and TDP trial participants' apps during the June 2013 trial. This data consists of uplink and downlink cellular and WiFi byte counts for every application, collected every ten minutes, as well as the hourly prices offered to TDP participants.[1] We developed separate TDP and TIP apps for the trial, which collect usage information and display it to users.

The TIP app is a usage monitoring application with screens shown in Fig. 1a, b and c. Users could view their monthly, weekly, and daily usage as a fraction of their data cap (Fig. 1a and b), as well as their per-app usage (Fig. 1c). Daily and weekly data caps were calculated based on the monthly cap and number of

---

[1] We did not collect more detailed data, e.g., packet traces, to maintain users' privacy. Participants fully consented to the data collection, but complete anonymity was not possible as we had to calculate how much to charge the TDP users.

days left in the month. Users could quickly see the remaining fraction of their monthly cap by looking at the pie chart icon on the bar at the top of the screen.

The TDP app allows users to monitor their spending on data and see the future prices. As with the TIP app, users can see their per-app usage (Fig. 1c). However, the main screen has been modified (Fig. 1d) to show the future prices and the amount the user has spent during the month. On the top left of the home screen bar, we show a color-coded price indicator that is visible both inside and outside our app; the indicator lets users easily see the current price, making it easier for them to decide whether or not to consume data at a given time [15]. It is colored red, orange, yellow, or green for high, medium, low, and very low prices respectively.

3.3   Estimating Price-Delay Tolerances and Optimizing Prices

We quantify users' price-delay tolerances by fitting their observed usage with TDP to a model of users' expected usage volume given the prices offered and their price-delay tolerances. We then calculate the ISP's expected profit and users' expected traffic patterns with these user parameters. We use the following process:

Establish baseline usage: We establish the average amount of data used in each hour of the day by extrapolating from TDP users' pre-trial RADIUS data. We divide the usage into different apps using the fraction of data used by each app in each hour by TIP users.[2]

Model users' price-delay tolerances: We use a model adapted from our previous work [8,17]. We define "waiting functions" $w_\beta(d,t)$ that give the probability that a user will wait for time t, given a savings d on the usage price. The waiting functions have the form $w_\beta(d,t) = C(\beta)\max(d,0)(t+1)^{-\beta}$, where $C(\beta)$ is a normalization constant and the β parameter controls the user's "willingness-to-wait:" w_β decreases faster with t for larger β, making users less likely to wait for longer amounts of time. The value of β differs for different applications, e.g., a user is more likely to delay a software update than checking email. We can compare apps' delay tolerances by comparing their β parameters.

Estimate the model parameters: We choose the model parameters that provide the best fit between observed TDP trial usage and the usage predicted by our model, given the prices offered during the trial.

To predict TDP usage, we identify two types of changes in usage relative to the baseline: first, users may shift some usage from higher- to lower-priced times. We use the waiting functions above to calculate the expected amounts shifted for each app. Second, price discounts can induce users to increase their overall usage [15,17]. Since the amount of the increase depends on the app and time of the day (e.g., users are unlikely to increase their usage while sleeping), we parameterize the usage increase with $\alpha_a(t)$, which depends on the app a and hour t. We use

---

[2] We use per-app data for the TIP users since TDP can skew the app distribution [8], and we have no pre-trial per-app data. RADIUS logs do not have per-app data, and distributing apps before the trial would have skewed users' behavior.

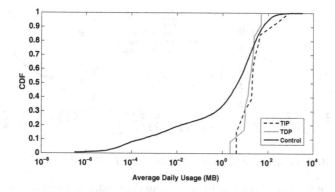

Fig. 2. Average daily usage (March 2012–June 2013).

the form $V_a(t)\left((1 + d(t))^{\alpha_a(t)} - 1\right)$, where $V_a(t)$ is the pre-trial (baseline) usage for app a and $d(t)$ the discount offered (i.e., the maximum price, normalized to 1, minus the offered price) in hour t. In accordance with the economic principle of diminishing marginal utility, we constrain $\alpha_a(t) \in [0, 1]$. Note that if $\alpha_a(t) = 0$, the usage does not increase with $d(t)$. We add this term to the amount of traffic shifted to find the total traffic for each app in each hour as a function of the discounts offered and model parameters β and $\alpha_a(t)$.

Calculate profit-maximizing prices: Given the parameter estimates, we can optimize the prices offered over the day so as to maximize ISPs' profit with TDP, i.e., revenue minus cost. The revenue is simply the sum of the time-dependent prices multiplied by the expected usage under TDP. We model the cost as a piecewise-linear function, with zero marginal cost below a fixed capacity C and a constant marginal cost γ for usage above this capacity. Thus, ISPs will choose time-dependent prices so as to maximize their profit

$$\sum_{t=1}^{T} (1 - d(t)) X(t) - \gamma \max\left(X(t) - C, 0\right), \tag{1}$$

where $X(t)$ is the expected usage at time t after TDP. By continually re-estimating the price-delay tolerances and re-optimizing the prices offered accordingly, the ISP can adapt its prices to changes in user behavior.

4   Traffic Characteristics

In this section, we first construct baseline usage information for TIP, TDP, and control users from our pre-trial RADIUS dataset. We then characterize the major apps used by TIP and TDP users. In all figures, hours given are in local time.

4.1   How Much Data Do Users Consume?

Figure 2 shows the cumulative distribution function (CDF) of all users' average daily usage. We see that the TIP and TDP users use similar amounts of data, ranging from 2 to 100MB, i.e., a few hundred MB to 3 GB per month. While a

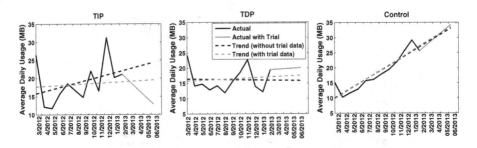

Fig. 3. Average monthly usage for the TIP, TDP, and control users.

Table 2. Usage fraction of the top 10 apps, comprising 63.1 and 78.0 % of total mobile and WiFi usage respectively.

Rank	App (Mobile)	%	App (WiFi)	%
1	com.facebook.katana	15.24	com.facebook.katana	18.93
2	android.process.media	11.39	android.process.media	17.83
3	com.pandora.android	9.05	com.android.browser	11.64
4	com.android.browser	8.71	com.android.email	7.37
5	com.android.email	7.26	mobi.ifunny	6.75
6	mobi.ifunny	3.19	com.android.chrome	4.20
7	com.motorola.motoemail	2.27	com.pandora.android	3.64
8	com.datawiz.tip	2.01	com.rhythmnewmedia.android.e	3.00
9	com.motorola.blur.service.main	1.99	com.alphonso.pulse	2.51
10	com.motorola.contacts	1.99	com.datawiz.tip	2.11

substantial minority (34.1 %) of control users use less than 1MB per day, none of these users volunteered for our TIP or TDP trial groups.

Users' average daily usage changes over time. Figure 3 shows the average daily usage in each month over one year (March 2012–February 2013), fitted with a linear trendline. We see that usage generally increases for TIP and control users, as is consistent with the growing amounts of mobile data traffic, but remains anomalously flat for TDP users. Usage observed during the June 2013 trial period fits this trend for the control group. However, the TIP users see a large decrease and the TDP users a slight increase in usage compared to that predicted by the trendlines. Thus, *TIP users decrease their usage and TDP users increase their usage* during the trial. We examine these findings and their psychological causes in Sect. 5.

4.2 How Is Usage Distributed Among Apps?

Table 2 shows the fraction of mobile (cellular) and WiFi usage corresponding to the top 10 apps. Many of the same apps appear for mobile and WiFi, with

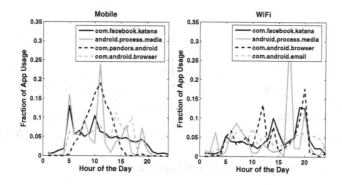

Fig. 4. Mean hourly usage for the top 4 apps.

Facebook and Android's media process the number 1 and number 2 apps for both interfaces. Pandora, web browsing, email, and iFunny also appear in the top 7 apps for both WiFi and mobile usage.[3] Mobile usage is more evenly distributed among apps than is WiFi usage, with the top 10 apps comprising 63.1 % of mobile and 78.0 % of WiFi usage. Apps outside the top 10 each accounted for less than 2 % of usage.

Figure 4 shows the hourly usage of the top four apps for mobile and WiFi. We see that WiFi is generally used more in the evenings, likely because people are at home then and have WiFi connectivity there. While most apps have generally similar usage patterns, there are some differences: Pandora, for instance, is only used between 5am and 3pm on mobile and peaks around 10am. Android's media process, which is used by other apps to stream videos, shows high peaks for mobile and WiFi usage, likely due to its high bandwidth requirements.

5   Pricing Effects

In this section, we present the trial results. Throughout the discussion, we use the peak-to-average ratio (PAR) of hourly usage over a day to measure the degree to which ISPs must over-provision their network. A higher PAR indicates that the ISP's network has more idle capacity, as it is provisioned for higher peak capacity than is needed on average. Before the trial, TIP and TDP users had an average PAR of 1.88, indicating that the peak hourly traffic was almost twice the mean.

We first show that TIP users decrease their total usage to remain below their data caps, but increase their mobile usage's PAR and may increase their overall WiFi usage. TDP users increase their usage in response to price discounts, allowing ISPs to reduce their PAR by up to 31.4 % with profit-maximizing prices.

---

[3] Larger sample sizes with a broader population may yield different top apps.

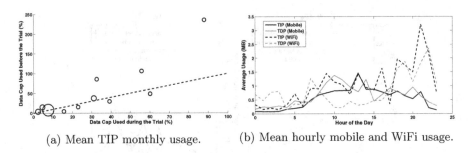

(a) Mean TIP monthly usage.   (b) Mean hourly mobile and WiFi usage.

Fig. 5. Monthly and hourly usage volumes.

5.1 Do TIP Users Decrease Their Usage?

Most TIP users decrease their usage in order to remain below their data caps. However, their PAR increases to 2.67 from 1.88 before the trial.

Figure 5a shows TIP usage as a fraction of users' data caps before and during the trial. Each circle represents a user, and the circle size is proportional to the user's data cap. The dashed line represents equal usage fractions before and during the trial. In general, users' usage amounts are closer to their data cap during the trial. A few users' data points lie above the dashed line, indicating that they used less of their data caps during the trial. These users, all with relatively small 1GB caps, exceeded their data caps before the trial, but no users did so during the trial. Other users' data points lie below the dashed line, indicating that they used more of their data caps during the trial than before. The data monitoring app ensured that they did not have to worry about hitting their data caps.

We conjecture that users reduce their monthly data usage by shifting some of their usage to WiFi. While we do not have pre-trial WiFi statistics (WiFi data was not collected by the network), 65.42 % of TIP users' data was consumed over WiFi, versus 55.39 % of TDP users'. Figure 5b shows the hourly mobile and WiFi usage patterns for TIP and TDP users. WiFi is used more than mobile in the evening, and spikes at these times for TIP users. This spike may indicate unusually large WiFi usage due to users' not using mobile data.

5.2 Do TDP Users Respond to Price Discounts?

TDP users increase their usage more in discounted hours. ISPs' profit-maximizing prices can decrease their peak-to-average hourly traffic ratio by up to 31.4 %.

Price-delay tolerances: We offered four different prices during the trial: $10 (green price indicator), $15 (yellow), $18 (orange), and $20 (red) per GB. Figure 6 shows the % change in usage in different hours for each price, compared to usage in the same hour (e.g., 12 to 1am) for the same user before the trial. While the TIP usage changes are similar for all prices, TDP users have more positive changes for $10/GB versus $20/GB, in both the bottom 90th (Fig. 6a)

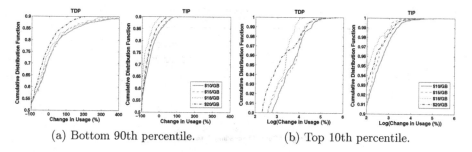

(a) Bottom 90th percentile.   (b) Top 10th percentile.

Fig. 6. Change in hourly usage relative to pre-trial usage for the same user in the same hour of the day.

Table 3. Price-delay tolerance for the top 5 mobile apps.

App	Estimated β	Mean α
com.facebook.katana	2.326	0.503
android.process.media	1.341	0.234
com.pandora.android	0.479	0.141
com.android.browser	0	0.212
com.android.email	3.000	0.979

and top 10th (Fig. 6b) percentiles of usage changes. The difference is less pronounced for the intermediate $15/GB and $18/GB prices, but is still apparent, especially around the 80th percentile. TDP users thus distinguished between very low, moderate, and high prices, perhaps using the colored price indicators. For all prices, TDP users had more positive usage changes than TIP users, likely because they were saving money on some of their usage and felt they could use more data overall. TDP changes above the 97th percentile are less price-dependent, but these are likely outliers occurring when usage increases during hours of very small pre-trial usage.

As explained in Sect. 3.3, we compare the delay tolerances for different apps by fitting our waiting function model to the trial usage. Table 3 shows the resulting β parameters and average α parameters over time for the top five mobile apps (Table 2). We see that while Pandora has a lower value of β, corresponding to higher delay tolerance, email has the lowest delay tolerance (highest value of β). Web browsing, however, has the highest delay tolerance, perhaps reflecting users' use of the web for looking up non-urgent information. Surprisingly, email has the highest α value (i.e., increase at low-price times independent of shifting), likely because users downloaded more email attachments and images when the price was low.

Maximizing ISP profit: Finally, we use the parameters in Table 3 and app usage fractions in Table 2 to calculate the optimal time-dependent prices offered by the ISP, which maximize (1) for different marginal costs of exceeding capacity (γ). To measure TDP's effect on usage peaks, we calculate the PAR with

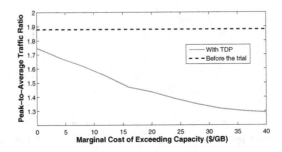

Fig. 7. Peak-to-average hourly traffic ratio with TDP.

these optimized prices. Figure 7 shows the achieved PAR for a range of γ values, compared to that before the trial. Even when $\gamma = 0$, the PAR improves due to discounts in less congested hours, which induce an increase in usage and revenue. Thus, TDP can more effectively increase ISP profit and reduce the network's PAR than can simple data caps.

6   Discussion and Conclusion

Pricing is a unique way of controlling network usage in that it explicitly relies on user attitudes and responses to incentives. Thus, to supplement our measurement results, we conducted three opinion surveys with the TIP and TDP participants before, during, and after the trial.[4] As part of the survey, users were asked their opinions on TDP's viability. Most users–especially TDP users in the mid-trial survey–expressed some concern over TDP's possible complexity. However, nearly all users preferred TDP to forced usage throttling in the mid- and post-trial surveys. Combined with our measurement results, we see that TDP can be more effective than capping or throttling usage, but must be implemented carefully to avoid undue complexity. One possible strategy is to use binary prices, e.g., charging either \$10/GB or \$20/GB in any given hour.

Our work shows that users do change their behavior in response to changes in their pricing plans; in particular, TIP users reduce their usage in response to data caps, possibly increasing their WiFi usage. However, data caps are not sufficient to prevent ISPs' need to over-provision networks according to their peak usage. Time-dependent pricing allows ISPs to reduce their peak-to-average traffic ratio, yet requires more sophisticated understanding from users than monthly data caps. While customers are willing to shift their usage in response to time-dependent prices, a full implementation and deployment of TDP will require more experimentation with a wider range of users.

---

[4] Pre-trial TIP and TDP, mid-trial TIP, mid-trial TDP, post-trial TIP, post-trial TDP surveys: https://www.surveymonkey.com/s/{LPYDGWG, 63PVQCW, ZLLLQ86, CPPBH92, CPZP57Q}.

Acknowledgments. We gratefully acknowledge the assistance of our colleagues at the Matanuska Telephone Association. Part of the work was supported by NSF CNS-1117126.

References

1. Cisco Visual Networking Index: Global mobile data traffic forecast update, 2013–2018 (2014). http://www.cisco.com/c/en/us/solutions/collateral/service-provider/visual-networking-index-vni/white_paper_c11-520862.pdf
2. Dyaberi, J.M., Parsons, B., Pai, V.S., Kannan, K., Chen, Y., Jana, R., Stern, D., Varshavsky, A., Wei, B.: Managing cellular congestion using incentives. IEEE Commun. Mag. **50**(11), 100–107 (2012)
3. El-Sayed, M., Mukhopadhyay, A., Urrutia-Valdés, C., Zhao, Z.J.: Mobile data explosion: monetizing the opportunity through dynamic policies and QoS pipes. Bell Labs Tech. J. **16**(2), 79–100 (2011)
4. Erman, J., Ramakrishnan, K.K.: Understanding the super-sized traffic of the Super Bowl. In: Proceedings of ACM IMC, pp. 353–360. ACM (2013)
5. Falaki, H., Lymberopoulos, D., Mahajan, R., Kandula, S., Estrin, D.: A first look at traffic on smartphones. In: Proceedings of ACM IMC, pp. 281–287. ACM (2010)
6. Falaki, H., Mahajan, R., Kandula, S., Lymberopoulos, D., Govindan, R., Estrin, D.: Diversity in smartphone usage. In: Proceedings of ACM MobiSys, pp. 179–194. ACM (2010)
7. Glass, V., Stefanova, S., Dibelka, R.: Customer price sensitivity to broadband service speed: what are the implications for public policy? In: Sen, S., Joe-Wong, C., Ha, S., Chiang, M. (eds.) Smart Data Pricing. Wiley, New York (2014)
8. Ha, S., Sen, S., Joe-Wong, C., Im, Y., Chiang, M.: TUBE: time-dependent pricing for mobile data. In: Proceedings of ACM SIGCOMM, vol. 42, issue 4, pp. 247–258 (2012)
9. Huang, J., Qian, F., Guo, Y., Zhou, Y., Xu, Q., Mao, Z.M., Sen, S., Spatscheck, O.: An in-depth study of LTE: effect of network protocol and application behavior on performance. In: Proceedings of ACM SIGCOMM, pp. 363–374. ACM (2013)
10. Huang, J., Qian, F., Mao, Z.M., Sen, S., Spatscheck, O.: Screen-off traffic characterization and optimization in 3G/4G networks. In: Proceedings of ACM IMC, pp. 357–364. ACM (2012)
11. Huang, J., Xu, Q., Tiwana, B., Mao, Z.M., Zhang, M., Bahl, P.: Anatomizing application performance differences on smartphones. In: Proceedings of ACM MobiSys, pp. 165–178. ACM (2010)
12. Im, Y., Joe-Wong, C., Ha, S., Sen, S., Kwon, T.T., Chiang, M.: AMUSE: empowering users for cost-aware offloading with throughput-delay tradeoffs. In: Proceedings of IEEE INFOCOM, pp. 435–439. IEEE (2013)
13. Maier, G., Schneider, F., Feldmann, A.: A first look at mobile hand-held device traffic. In: Krishnamurthy, A., Plattner, B. (eds.) PAM 2010. LNCS, vol. 6032, pp. 161–170. Springer, Heidelberg (2010)
14. Rahmati, A., Tossell, C., Shepard, C., Kortum, P., Zhong, L.: Exploring iPhone usage: the influence of socioeconomic differences on smartphone adoption, usage and usability. In: Proceedings of MobileHCI, pp. 11–20. ACM (2012)
15. Sen, S., Joe-Wong, C., Ha, S., Bawa, J., Chiang, M.: When the price is right: enabling time-dependent pricing of broadband data. In: Proceedings of SIGCHI, pp. 2477–2486. ACM (2013)

16. Sen, S., Joe-Wong, C., Ha, S., Chiang, M.: Incentivizing time-shifting of data: a survey of time-dependent pricing for internet access. IEEE Commun. Mag. **50**(11), 91–99 (2012)
17. Sen, S., Joe-Wong, C., Ha, S., Chiang, M.: Smart data pricing (SDP): economic solutions to network congestion. In: Haddadi, H., Bonaventure, O. (eds.) Recent Advances in Networking, ACM SIGCOMM, pp. 221–274 (2013)
18. Sen, S., Joe-Wong, C., Ha, S., Chiang, M.: A survey of smart data pricing: past proposals, current plans, and future trends. ACM Comput. Surv. **46**(2), 15 (2013)
19. Sommers, J., Barford, P.: Cell vs. WiFi: on the performance of metro area mobile connections. In: Proceedings of ACM IMC, pp. 301–314. ACM (2012)
20. Tipmongkolsilp, O., Zaghloul, S., Jukan, A.: The evolution of cellular backhaul technologies: current issues and future trends. IEEE Commun. Surv. Tutor. **13**(1), 97–113 (2011)
21. Xu, Q., Erman, J., Gerber, A., Mao, Z., Pang, J., Venkataraman, S.: Identifying diverse usage behaviors of smartphone apps. In: Proceedings of ACM IMC, pp. 329–344. ACM (2011)
22. Zander, J., Mähönen, P.: Riding the data tsunami in the cloud: myths and challenges in future wireless access. IEEE Commun. Mag. **51**(3), 145–151 (2013)

IPv6

IPv6 AS Relationships, Cliques, and Congruence

Vasileios Giotsas, Matthew Luckie$^{(\boxtimes)}$, Bradley Huffaker, and Kc Claffy

CAIDA, UC San Diego, La Jolla, USA
{vgiotsas,mjl,bradley,kc}@caida.org

Abstract. There is increasing evidence that IPv6 deployment is maturing as a response to the exhaustion of unallocated IPv4 address blocks, leading to gradual convergence of the IPv4 and IPv6 topologies in terms of structure and routing paths. However, the lack of a fully-connected transit-free clique in IPv6, as well as a different economic evolution than IPv4, implies that existing IPv4 AS relationship algorithms will not accurately infer relationships between autonomous systems in IPv6, encumbering our ability to model and understand IPv6 AS topology evolution. We modify CAIDA's IPv4 relationship inference algorithm to accurately infer IPv6 relationships using publicly available BGP data. We validate 24.9 % of our 41,589 c2p and p2p inferences for July 2014 to have a 99.3 % and 94.5 % PPV, respectively. Using these inferred relationships, we analyze the BGP-observed IPv4 and IPv6 AS topologies, and find that ASes are converging toward the same relationship types in IPv4 and IPv6, but disparities remain due to differences in the transit-free clique and the influence of Hurricane Electric in IPv6.

1 Introduction

Depletion of the unallocated IPv4 address pool increases the pressure for widespread adoption of IPv6. IPv6 deployment has long been characterized as largely experimental, dominated by research and education networks [7,16]. However, recent studies suggest that the IPv6 network is maturing, reflected in increasing similarity of the IPv6 and IPv4 networks in terms of topological structure, routing dynamics and AS path congruity [9]. Czyz *et al.* also found the IPv6 traffic mix (set of applications using IPv6) in 2013 much more similar to the IPv4 traffic mix than in the past [8].

Despite these signals of convergence, noticeable differences remain between IPv4 and IPv6 routing relationships. In August 2010, Giotsas *et al.* found disparity in IPv4 and IPv6 AS relationships as inferred from BGP communities and local preference values [13]. Dhamdhere *et al.* showed that while 40–50% of dual-stacked paths observed in public BGP data were identical in 2012, if the ASes followed the same routing policies in IPv4 and IPv6, then 60–70% of paths could have been congruent [9]. They also found significant deviation between the most prominent ASes (those that appeared most frequently in AS paths) in IPv4 and IPv6, with the most prominent AS in the IPv6 topology (Hurricane Electric) appearing in a much larger fraction of IPv6 AS paths than the most prominent AS in the IPv4 topology (Level 3) appeared in IPv4 AS paths.

© Springer International Publishing Switzerland 2015
J. Mirkovic and Y. Liu (Eds.): PAM 2015, LNCS 8995, pp. 111–122, 2015.
DOI: 10.1007/978-3-319-15509-8_9

Because IPv6 deployment did not build on the existing IPv4 network, the IPv6 topology evolved in parallel, and not all assumptions relied upon by IPv4 AS relationship inference algorithms hold in IPv6. Inferring AS relationships is more challenging in IPv6 than in IPv4 for two reasons. First, given its still low deployment and different economics compared to IPv4 [9], IPv6 business policies are less rigorously enforced, leading to more policy violations [14] which impede the accuracy of relationship inference heuristics. Second, the IPv6 graph is not fully connected due to peering disputes between large transit-free providers [17,23]. These challenges have discouraged both research [21] and commercial [22] efforts from inferring IPv6 AS relationships.

We make the following contributions. First, we adapt our IPv4 AS relationship algorithm [18] to accurately infer IPv6 AS relationships by accounting for IPv6-specific realities: in particular, the IPv6 AS topology is still not fully connected due to peering disputes [17]. We use our algorithm to infer AS relationships for January 2004 to July 2014 and publicly release our inferences. Second, we evaluate our algorithm's accuracy by validating 10,357 (24.9 %) of our 41,589 inferences using three sources of validation data, and find our provider-customer and peer-peer inferences have a 99.3 % and 94.5 % positive predictive value (PPV), respectively, in July 2014. We publicly release our validation data, which we derive quarterly between 2004 and 2014. Finally, we use our inferences to understand the growing congruity between IPv4 and IPv6 AS topologies. We show that despite growing congruity between the graphs, IPv6 AS relationships have evolved differently from those in IPv4. Disparate dual stack relationships are decreasing, from 15 % in January 2006 to 5 % in 2014, consistent with previous findings of growing similarity between IPv4 and IPv6 [8,9]. However, Hurricane Electric (HE) is the main contributor of disparate relationships, and over 50 % of their dual stack relationships differed between IPv4 and IPv6 in July 2014.

2   Background on Inferring as Relationships

AS relationships are often abstracted into three conventional classes [10]. In a provider-customer (p2c) relationship, a customer AS buys transit from a better connected AS to expand its reachability. In a peer-peer (p2p) relationship, two ASes provide access to their own and their customers' networks. In a sibling-sibling (s2s) relationship, two ASes under common ownership may provide mutual transit to each other. ASes that can reach every network in the routing system without purchasing transit are known as Tier-1 ASes. Tier-1 ASes maintain p2p links between each other to ensure their global reachability, forming a clique that serves as the backbone of inter-domain routing. AS relationships translate into BGP routing policies that determine the economics of traffic exchange [11]. Accurate knowledge of AS relationships is thus essential to understanding not only inter-domain routing but also Internet economics [18]. Unfortunately, AS relationships are often treated as proprietary by ISPs and controlled by non-disclosure agreements, leading researchers to build algorithms

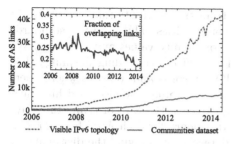 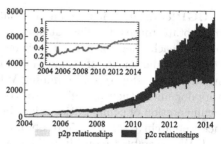

(a) Communities data compared to visible IPv6 topology. The inset graph shows the fraction of links in common.

(b) The composition of the communities data by relationship type. The inset graph shows the fraction of p2c relationships.

Fig. 1. Summary of the communities validation dataset over time. For July 2014 the dataset includes 7,514 relationships that cover 18.1 % of the visible topology, 64 % of which are p2c relationships and the rest p2p.

that heuristically infer AS relationships using publicly available BGP routing data. We recently developed an algorithm for inferring IPv4 AS relationships; we validated 34.6 % of 126,082 p2c and p2p inferences for April 2012 to have a 99.6 % and 98.7 % PPV, respectively [18]. Our approach began by inferring a Tier-1 clique, applied heuristics to infer p2c links based primarily on how neighbors were observed to export routes, and inferred the remainder to be p2p. Section 4 describes how we modified this algorithm to infer AS relationships in the IPv6 topology graph.

Our IPv6 AS relationship algorithm infers conventional p2c and p2p relationships and does not infer complex AS relationships by design. We have developed and validated an algorithm to infer hybrid and partial transit relationships in IPv4 [12]. That algorithm uses conventional AS relationship inferences as input, and it is possible to apply the same heuristics to the output of our conventional IPv6 algorithm to infer complex IPv6 AS relationships.

3 Data

3.1 BGP Paths

We extracted AS paths from every vantage point providing BGP data to Route Views (RV) [4] and RIPE RIS [3] by downloading one RIB file per day between the 1st and 5th of every month between January 2004 and August 2014 and extracting AS paths that announced reachability to IPv6 prefixes.

3.2 Validation Data

For validation, we used three sources of IPv6 AS relationship data: BGP communities, RPSLng, and local preference (LocPref). We had access to BGP community data every month, quarterly RPSLng dumps, and three LocPref collections.

BGP communities are an optional transitive attribute that operators use to annotate routes [6]. The meaning of communities values are not standardized and each operator defines their own community values and meanings. We compiled a dictionary of community values and corresponding meanings that encode relationship types by mining WHOIS records and websites where operators document their specific use of community values; we also used historical documentation of communities values in archived WHOIS records and the Wayback web archive service [15] to obtain a dictionary for each April from 2004 to 2014. We assembled monthly validation datasets by applying the dictionary to corresponding public BGP data; the composition of this set of validation data over time is summarized in Fig. 1. For April 2014, our dictionary included 1,560 communities values defined by 284 ASes, and we used the dictionary to obtain validation data for 7,514 IPv6 links for the July 2014 IPv6 AS topology.

RPSLng is the Routing Policy Specification Language next generation [5], which network operators can use to store routing policies in public databases. The largest source of such data is RIPE's WHOIS database; many European IXPs require operators to register routing policies with RIPE NCC. An import rule specifies which route announcements to accept from neighbors, and an export rule specifies what routes to advertise to neighbors. The special rule ANY is used to import/export all routes from/to a neighbor, and indicates a customer/provider relationship. Using RIPE's WHOIS database from July 2014, we extracted 739 c2p relationships with the following method: if X has a rule that imports ANY from Y, and Y has a rule that exports ANY to X, we infer X is a customer of Y. Because RIPE NCC no longer provides the changed dates in their WHOIS dumps, we were unable to filter by freshness and used all records.

Despite the many links in our communities and RPSLng datasets, they include less than 2 % of the IPv6 links observed in public BGP data for Hurricane Electric (HE), the most prominent AS in the IPv6 graph [9]. To extend our validation dataset to include HE's relationships we use the local preference (**LocPref**) attribute, which does not directly encode relationship information but often reflects it [11]. LocPref is a number that expresses the level of preference an AS gives a route if multiple routes are available for the same prefix. LocPref values are also non-standardized, but many ASes assign the highest value to their customers and the lowest to their providers, which maximizes transit revenue. We collected LocPref values for HE's neighbors by querying its public route server in July 2014, and we used two older datasets from [13]. Figure 2 summarizes the collected LocPref values for HE's IPv6 neighbors; with few exceptions (22/2325 neighbors, marked with red crosses) HE assigns a single LocPref value to all prefixes received by each neighbor. Where HE assigned multiple values for different prefixes received from the same neighbor, we chose the value assigned to the most prefixes, since altering LocPref values is not typical behavior. When comparing HE's LocPref values in IPv4 to inferred IPv4 relationships, we found a consistent mapping between LocPref 140 and HE's customers (2591/2593) and LocPref 100 and HE's peers (601/603). This mapping is HE-specific and not valid for every AS.

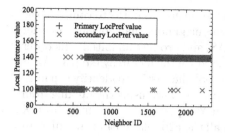

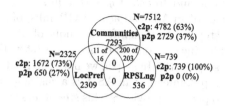

Fig. 2. Summary of HE's LocPref validation dataset. In all three snapshots the LocPref values are concentrated around 100 and 140.

Fig. 3. Summary of agreement across validation data sources (first number inside intersections is number of overlapping relationships that agree). Communities and RPSLng data have the largest agreement, over 98 %.

Algorithm 1. is a summary of our IMC 2013 IPv4 AS relationship inference algorithm. The bold lines were updated to accommodate IPv6.

Require: AS paths, Allocated ASNs, IXP ASes
 1: Discard or sanitize paths with artifacts
 2: Sort ASes in decreasing order of computed transit degree, then node degree
 3: **Infer clique at top of AS topology (updated)**
 4: Discard poisoned paths
 5: Infer c2p relationships top-down using above ranking
 6: Infer c2p relationships from VPs inferred not to be announcing provider routes
 7: Infer c2p relationships for ASes where customer transit degree exceeds provider's
 8: Infer customers for ASes with no providers
 9: **Infer c2p relationships between stub and clique ASes (removed)**
10: Infer c2p relationships where adjacent links have no relationship inferred
11: Infer remaining links represent p2p relationships

Figure 3 shows the overlap between the BGP communities, RPSLng, and LocPref validation data sources for July 2014. The BGP communities and RPSLng data had the largest overlap, and were consistent 98 % of the time.

4   Inference Methodology

4.1   Overview of Existing IPv4 Algorithm

Our IPv6 AS relationship algorithm is based on our IPv4 algorithm [18], with adjustments to account for differences in the routing ecosystems [9,13]. In particular, the IPv6 AS topology lacks a fully connected clique that serves as the transit backbone because of a long-standing peering dispute between Cogent and Hurricane Electric [17].

Algorithm 1 summarizes our IPv4 AS relationship inference algorithm (details in [18]), highlighting the two steps we changed to accurately infer IPv6 relationships. First, we sanitize the input data by removing paths with artifacts, i.e., loops, reserved ASes, and IXPs (step 1). We use the resulting AS paths to compute the node and *transit degree* (the number of unique neighbors that appear on either side of an AS in adjacent BGP links) of each AS, and produce an initial rank order (step 2). We then infer the clique of ASes at the top of the hierarchy (step 3). After filtering out some poisoned paths (step 4), we apply heuristics to identify c2p links (steps 5–10). In step 5, we infer c2p relationships top-down using the ranking from step 2, inferring an AS X is a customer of Y if Y exports routes received from X to peers or providers; this step infers 90 % of all the c2p relationships we infer. In step 6, we infer c2p relationships from VPs we find announcing no provider routes, which we define as VPs that provide paths to fewer than 2.5 % of the ASes. In step 7, we infer c2p relationships for ASes where the customer has a larger tran-sit degree than its provider, to infer c2p relationships for links skipped in step 5. In step 8, we infer customers for provider-less non-clique ASes, which were also skipped in steps 5 and 7 because those steps require a non-clique AS to have a provider in order to infer customers relationships. In step 9, we infer that stub ASes are customers of clique ASes even if we do not observe the clique AS export-ing the customer's route to other peers; in IPv4 stub networks are unlikely to meet the peering requirements of clique members, and are most likely customers. In step 10, we resolve relationships where we observe triplets with adjacent unclassified links. Finally, we classify all remaining unclassified links as p2p.

4.2   Inferring the IPv6 Clique

Our inference algorithm follows a top-down approach starting from the clique members, to avoid relationship cycles and errors caused by stub ASes with high peering visibility. Inferring the IPv4 clique is relatively straightforward, given the maturity of the IPv4 network. In contrast, the IPv6 transit market is still in its early stages, making it more difficult to determine clique ASes. Because the accuracy of the inferred clique impacts the overall accuracy of the inferred relationships, we first focus on challenges of inferring the IPv6 clique.

To infer the IPv4 clique, our algorithm from [18] first sorted ASes by decreas-ing transit degree and then applied the Bron/Kerbosch algorithm to find the clique involving the first ten ASes that has the largest transit degree sum. We label these first ten ASes as the *seed* ASes because inferences for other ASes descend from this initial set. For each remaining AS, we added the AS to the clique if we observed a link with every other clique AS, and the AS did not appear to receive transit from one clique member to reach a second clique mem-ber. This approach works well for inferring the IPv4 clique because the largest transit degree ASes have restrictive peering policies, maintaining a peering clique with only selected transit-free ASes. For April 2014, the largest IPv4 transit degree AS was Level3 which maintains a restrictive peering policy. In contrast, the largest IPv6 transit degree AS is HE, which has an open peering policy, and is part of large peering meshes with ASes that are not transit-free; calculating the clique starting from the ASes with the largest transit degrees returns incor-rect cliques in IPv6. Furthermore, because the IPv6 network is still early in its evolution, the IPv6 network is more dynamic than the IPv4 network, making

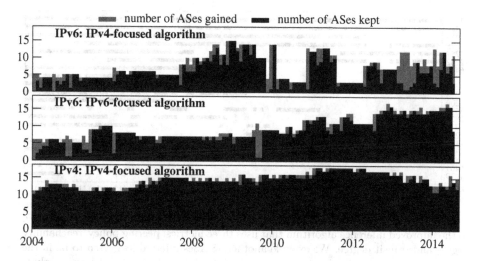

Fig. 4. By improving the way in which we infer the IPv6 transit-free clique, we reduce the average number of ASes that are added or removed between temporally adjacent cliques from 3.4 to 1.8, bringing the IPv6 clique's stability closer to the average of 1.5 seen in IPv4.

transit degree alone an unreliable metric. Figure 4 illustrates the highly dynamic clique membership that results when applying our IPv4-focused algorithm to the BGP-observed IPv6 AS topology over the last decade; on average, 3.4 ASes changed between temporally adjacent cliques. We found that at least 11 of the 20 ASes most frequently inferred to be in IPv6 cliques had at least one transit provider in our validation data, contradicting the notion of the transit-free clique.

We therefore modified step 3 of Algorithm 1 to consider an AS's *peering policy* and *reachability* in addition to the AS's transit degree. An AS with an *open* peering policy will peer with other ASes, with few or no conditions; a *selective* policy requires conditions on traffic volume and symmetry; and a *restrictive* policy limits peering to as few networks as necessary. The peering policy of an AS expresses an important and relatively stable property of the AS, but is not easily inferred from the topology alone because most peering links are invisible in public BGP data [20]. We used the self-reported peering policy data in PeeringDB [2]; for networks with PeeringDB entries but without a registered peering policy, we assumed a restrictive policy, which operators tend not to disclose [19]. We required the seed ASes to follow a restrictive or selective policy; we did not select ASes with open peering policies as seed ASes even if they had the largest transit degree. In addition, we reduced the initial seed set to three ASes for years before 2007, and to five ASes for 2007 and onwards, based on the accuracy of inferences derived from these seed values. As with the IPv4 method, after we find a clique involving the seed ASes, we add other ASes to the clique whose addition

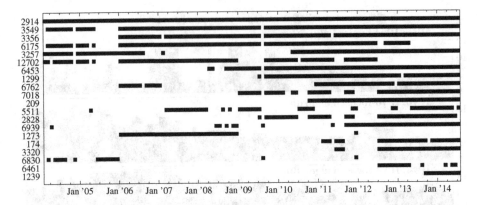

Fig. 5. The top 20 ASes most frequently inferred to be part of the IPv6 clique according to the improved inference algorithm that uses three metrics: peering policy, reachability degree and transit degree. We exclude another 18 ASes inferred less often to be in the clique. The improved algorithm yields a more stable inferred clique, which only include transit-free ASes for most snapshots.

does not result in triplets of consecutive clique members in the BGP-observed paths, implying one of the ASes in the triplet is receiving transit.

The use of a reachability metric is required because some transit-free ASes are partitioned from each other due to peering disputes [17,23]. The use of a partitioned AS as a seed can yield an incomplete clique. To minimize the chance of using a partitioned AS, we required that seed ASes provide direct BGP feeds to RV or RIS and announce routes to at least 90 % of the BGP-visible IPv6 address space. Additionally, if an AS misses just one link from being part of the clique, we considered it a clique member to account for the reality of the currently partitioned IPv6 Internet [17,23], provided that the AS does not receive transit from one clique member to reach a second clique member, i.e. could not be transit-free. As with the IPv4 algorithm, if there are multiple cliques we select the clique with the largest transit degree sum. Note that some ASes previously used different AS numbers in IPv4 and IPv6, most notably Sprint (IPv4 AS1239, IPv6 AS6175) and Verizon (IPv4 AS701, IPv6 AS12702). Both ASes eventually used a single ASN for both IPv4 and IPv6, but when they were transitioning to a single ASN (i.e., the IPv4 ASN) they used both ASNs in the IPv6 AS topology. During the period when they used both ASNs, we merged the IPv6 AS links for both ASNs for these two organizations to capture their full connectivity during the period they were shifting all of their neighbors to their primary ASN.

Figure 5 shows the IPv6 clique inferred using the improved clique inference method. The improved method infers more stable IPv6 cliques that are composed of transit-free ASes with the number of ASes entering or leaving the clique reducing from an average 3.4 ASes with the IPv4-focused method to 1.8 with our IPv6-focused method. This improvement brings the edit distance between temporally adjacent cliques much closer to IPv4's average of 1.5 ASes.

4.3   Inferring Clique-Stub Relationships

After we infer the clique, we apply the rest of the steps in Algorithm 1 without modification until step 9, which infers stub ASes to be customers of clique ASes irrespective of whether we observed a clique AS exporting a stub AS as a customer. In IPv4, this step avoids misinferring backup transit links as p2p, and relies on the fact that no clique members have an open peering policy. Establishing backup transit links is a popular strategy for IPv4 ASes that need to ensure reliable connectivity in the face of failures, but backup transit links appear to be less critical in IPv6 given the low levels of traffic [8] and small size of the topology. Therefore, we skip step 9 of the algorithm.

4.4   Validation

We evaluated the positive predictive value (PPV) of our improved algorithm, defined as the proportion of inferences of a particular type that were correct. Figure 6 shows the PPV over time according to our validation datasets described in Sect. 3.2. Our algorithm achieves high PPV throughout the period of inferences (January 2004–July 2014), with PPV for both p2c and p2p inferences consistently above 96 % after spring 2009 for the communities and after fall 2012 for the RPSLng data. The PPV for inferences validated using the LocPref data is over 96 % for the three points in time

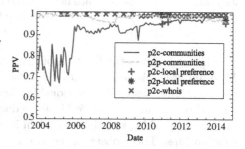

Fig. 6. Validation of our inferences over time using the three validation datasets described in Sect. 3.2. Validation results involving the BGP communities and local preference datasets are in strong agreement despite involving different ASes.

where we have LocPref data. The diversity of validation data sources and high PPV values strengthens our confidence in the suitability of our algorithm and the accuracy of our inferences. Figure 6 shows that both p2c and p2p relationships are inferred with high PPV, except for before 2006 when p2c inferences have a PPV of less than 80 % for many BGP snapshots. However, our validation dataset (and the IPv6 AS topology) is considerably smaller (Fig. 1) prior to 2006.

5   Analysis

We compare IPv6 and IPv4 routing relationships starting from 2006 to avoid artifacts from inference errors on very small early topologies. *Congruent relationships* refer to dual-stack AS links with the same relationship type in IPv4 and IPv6; *disparate relationships* are dual-stack links where the relationship differs from IPv4 to IPv6. The fraction of disparate relationships decreases linearly over time (Fig. 7a), from 15 % in 2006 to 5 % in 2014, because congruent relationships increase in number faster than disparate ones, suggesting convergence.

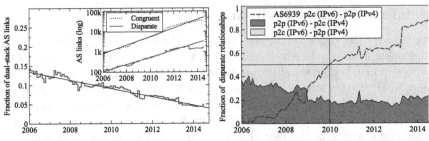

(a) Fraction of disparate relationships for dual-stack AS links. Inset graph plots number of disparate relationships.

(b) The fraction of disparate relationships by type (colored areas), and the contribution of AS 6939 (HE, dashed line).

Fig. 7. The fraction of disparate relationships decreases over time to about 5 % in July 2014, showing convergence between the IPv4 and IPv6 topologies. Most disparate relationships after 2010 are due to HE's free IPv6 transit service.

Figure 7b shows the fraction of disparate relationships by relationship type. Most inferred disparate relationships are p2c in IPv6 and p2p in IPv4, and the remaining disparate relationships are p2p in IPv6 and p2c in IPv4. HE (AS6939) contributes over 50 % of the disparate $IPv6_{p2c}/IPv4_{p2p}$ relationships after 2010, peaking in July 2014 when it contributed 87 % of observed disparate relationships. These observations are consistent with the behavior of the IPv6 tunnel broker service provided by HE, which allows free transit, so that IPv4 peers can be IPv6 customers without cost [1]. This strategy allows HE to acquire many IPv6 (free-transit) customers compared to IPv4, illustrated by comparing HE's IPv4 and IPv6 customer cones. The customer cone is defined as the ASes that an AS can reach by following a customer link (the AS's customers, customers of those customers, and so on) and is a metric of influence of an AS in the transit market. Figure 8 compares the relative size of the customer cones between IPv4 and IPv6 over the last 9 years for the 9 largest providers as of July 2014. HE is the only AS with a significantly larger customer cone in IPv6 than in IPv4 (over

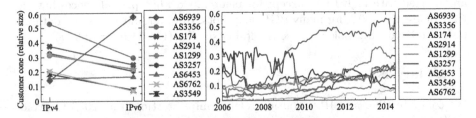

Fig. 8. The fraction of ASes in the customer cones of the largest 9 providers. The left plot compares the customer cones between IPv6 and IPv4 for July 2014. The right plot shows their growth over time. HE (AS6939) has a larger customer cone in IPv6 than in IPv4; most other ASes have smaller, but still growing customer cones (except for AS3549, Global Crossing, which merged with Level3 in 2012).

50 % of IPv6 ASes). However, the relative sizes of customer cones of the largest providers have an increasing trend, in contrast with the trend observed in the IPv4 topology [18]. The only exception is Global Crossing (AS3549), which was acquired by Level3 (AS3356) in 2012.

6 Conclusion

The low level of IPv6 deployment has hindered efforts to accurately infer IPv6 AS relationships. We tackled this challenge by modifying CAIDA's IPv4 relationship inference algorithm, which required a focus on the correct inference of the IPv6 clique. The clique is a crucial component of AS topology, but with fundamental disparities between IPv4 and IPv6, including the extreme peering openness of some IPv6 ASes, and long-lived peering disputes among transit-free IPv6 networks. To overcome these obstacles, we used two new metrics to help filter out topological inconsistencies in IPv6: peering policy and BGP-observed reachability.

We validated ten years of our algorithm's inferences against three data sources: BGP communities, RPSLng, and local preference values, which covered 25 % of the BGP-observed topology for July 2014. Our inferences achieved an overall Positive Predictive Value of at least 96 % for each dataset since 2009, with increasing accuracy over time. We found that dual-stack relationships are increasingly congruent, as disparate relationships decreased from 15 % in 2006 to 5 % in 2014, while the number of nodes and links increased by a factor of 14.5 times and 22 times, respectively. Notably, disparate relationships are now dominated by a single AS, Hurricane Electric, whose long-standing offer of free IPv6 transit has enabled it to become the dominant transit-free provider in IPv6, with the largest customer cone in the IPv6 topology, despite not even being a transit-free network in IPv4.

Our validation and inference data is available at http://www.caida.org/publications/papers/2015/asrank6/

Acknowledgements. The work was supported by U.S. NSF grant CNS-1111449, DHS S&T Cyber Security Division (DHS S&T/CSD) BAA 11-02 and SPAWAR Systems Center Pacific via contract number N66001-12-C-0130, and by DRDC pursuant to an Agreement between the U.S. and Canadian governments for Cooperation in Science and Technology for Critical Infrastructure Protection and Border Security. The work represents the position of the authors and not of NSF, DHS, or DRDC.

References

1. Hurricane electric IPv6 tunnel broker. https://tunnelbroker.net/
2. PeeringDB. http://www.peeringdb.com
3. RIPE Routing Information Service (RIS). http://www.ripe.net/ris
4. Route Views. http://www.routeviews.org/
5. Blunk, Y., Damas, J., Parent, F., Robachevsky, A.: Routing policy specification language next generation (RPSLng). RFC 4012, March 2005

6. Chandra, R., Traina, P., Li, T.: BGP communities attribute. RFC 1997. August 1996
7. Colitti, L., Gunderson, S.H., Kline, E., Refice, T.: Evaluating IPv6 adoption in the internet. In: Krishnamurthy, A., Plattner, B. (eds.) PAM 2010. LNCS, vol. 6032, pp. 141–150. Springer, Heidelberg (2010)
8. Czyz, J., Allman, M., Zhang, J., Iekel-Johnson, S., Osterweil, E., Bailey, M.: Measuring IPv6 adoption. In: SIGCOMM, pp. 87–98 (2014)
9. Dhamdhere, A., Luckie, M., Huffaker, B., claffy, k., Elmokashfi, A., Aben, E.: Measuring the deployment of IPv6: topology, routing and performance. In: IMC, pp. 537–550 (2012)
10. Gao, L.: On inferring autonomous system relationships in the Internet. IEEE/ACM Trans. Netw. **9**(6), 733–745 (2001)
11. Gill, P., Schapira, M., Goldberg, S.: A survey of interdomain routing policies. CCR **44**(1), 28–34 (2013)
12. Giotsas, V., Luckie, M., Huffaker, B., claffy, k.: Inferring complex AS relationships. In: IMC, November 2014
13. Giotsas, V., Zhou, S.: Detecting and assessing the hybrid IPv4/IPv6 AS relationships. In: SIGCOMM Poster, pp. 424–425 (2011)
14. Giotsas, V., Zhou, S.: Valley-free violation in Internet routing - analysis based on BGP community data. In: IEEE ICC 2012 CQRM, pp. 1208–1212, June 2012
15. Internet Archive: Wayback Machine. http://archive.org/web/
16. Karpilovsky, E., Gerber, A., Pei, D., Rexford, J., Shaikh, A.: Quantifying the extent of IPv6 deployment. In: Moon, S.B., Teixeira, R., Uhlig, S. (eds.) PAM 2009. LNCS, vol. 5448, pp. 13–22. Springer, Heidelberg (2009)
17. Leber, M.: IPv6 internet broken, cogent/telia/hurricane not peering, NANOG. http://mailman.nanog.org/pipermail/nanog/2009-October/014017.html
18. Luckie, M., Huffaker, B., claffy, K., Dhamdhere, A., Giotsas, V.: AS relationships, customer cones, and validation. In: IMC 2013, pp. 243–256 (2013)
19. Norton, W.: Restrictive peering policy. DrPeering International. http://drpeering.net/FAQ/What-is-a-restrictive-peer.html
20. Oliveira, R., Pei, D., Willinger, W., Zhang, B., Zhang, L.: The (in)completeness of the observed Internet AS-level structure. IEEE/ACM Trans. Netw. **18**(1), 109–122 (2010)
21. UCLA: Internet AS-level topology archive. http://irl.cs.ucla.edu/topology
22. Zmijewski, E.: A Bakers Dozen, 2013 Edition. Renesys Blog. http://www.renesys.com/2014/01/bakers-dozen-2013-edition/
23. Zmijewski, E.: World IPv6 Day. Renesys Blog. http://www.renesys.com/2011/06/world-ipv6-day/

Measuring and Characterizing IPv6 Router Availability

Robert Beverly[1]([⊠]), Matthew Luckie[2], Lorenza Mosley[1], and Kc Claffy[2]

[1] Naval Postgraduate School, Monterey, CA, USA
rbeverly@nps.edu, ldmosley@cmand.org
[2] CAIDA, UC, San Diego, CA, USA
{mjl,kc}@caida.org

Abstract. We consider the problem of inferring IPv6 router uninterrupted system availability, or *uptime*, from a remote vantage point without privileged access. Uptime inference is important to broader efforts to measure and characterize the availability of critical infrastructure, provides insight into network operations, and has subtle security implications. Our approach utilizes active probes to periodically elicit IPv6 fragment identifiers from IPv6 router interfaces, and analyzes the resulting identifier time series for reboots. We demonstrate the approach's potential by characterizing 21,539 distinct IPv6 router interfaces over a five-month period. We find evidence of clustered reboot events, popular maintenance windows, and correlation with globally visible control plane data. Our results, validated by five ASes, provide initial insight into the current state of IPv6 router availability.

1 Introduction

Significant recent work examines IPv6 adoption [6], usage [23], and performance [8]. Less well-studied is the *reliability* of IPv6 infrastructure. This paper focuses on measuring and characterizing the reliability of one of the most critical components of IPv6 infrastructure: IPv6 routers. Understanding IPv6 router reliability provides insights into not only the current maturity of production IPv6, but also operational properties of IPv6 networks, including vulnerability information.

We develop, analyze, and validate a technique to remotely estimate, without privileged access, the uninterrupted system availability, or *uptime*, of IPv6 devices. Our technique relies on inducing IPv6 fragments from remote endpoints and analyzing the sequence of IPv6 fragment identifiers returned as a result of periodic probing. Importantly, our active probing consists of ICMP6 echo requests and therefore is conducive to characterizing devices that do not permit TCP connections, e.g. routers. As a proof-of-concept, we apply our technique over a five-month period to a collection of 66,471 IPv6 router interfaces on the Internet; our technique made uptime inferences on 21,539 (32%) of these interfaces (≃47% of the interfaces were unresponsive, while 21% did not permit uptime inference). We validate our technique against five providers that positively confirm our reboot inferences. We find that while 68% of interfaces and

© Springer International Publishing Switzerland 2015
J. Mirkovic and Y. Liu (Eds.): PAM 2015, LNCS 8995, pp. 123–135, 2015.
DOI: 10.1007/978-3-319-15509-8_10

78 % of core routers experience no restarts during our measurement period, a few devices experience many restarts. We further discover evidence of correlation between restarts and global BGP events observed in public route collectors. Finally, we show that router restarts occur most frequently on Tuesday and Wednesdays, and least often on weekends. Our contributions include:

1. An active probing method that permits remote IPv6 router uptime inference without privileged access.
2. Real-world deployment and validation of the technique.
3. Insights into how different devices send IPv6 fragments over time, including a previously unstudied cyclic behavior exhibited by Linux-based devices.
4. A five-month study of reboots among 21,539 IPv6 router interfaces where we find that core routers tend to have longer uptimes than border routers.

2   Technique and Data for Inferring IPv6 Router Uptime

We assume that a router's uptime can be estimated by inferring the last time the router rebooted, i.e. a *reboot event*. To infer a router reboot event, we rely on the fact that many routers maintain externally observable state that resets when rebooted. Specifically, the control plane IPv6 stack implementation on many routers maintains monotonically increasing IPv6 fragment identification (ID) counters that are initialized to zero or a random number [2]. By periodically probing routers to obtain and increment their ID field, and segmenting the time-series of IDs into monotonically increasing subsequences, we can infer that reboot events occur in the periods between subsequences.

In this section, we first explain the IPv6 ID field and our technique to obtain the ID time series. We then describe our experimental methodology and data (Sect. 2.2) and our algorithm (Sect. 2.3). We detail how we handle an important subset of interfaces (those that return cyclic ID sequences) in Sect. 2.4, and describe our procedure to identify routers and annotate them with their role and their timezone (Sect. 2.5). We discuss limitations of our technique in Sect. 2.6.

2.1   Obtaining and Using the IPv6 ID Field

Unlike the IPv4 header, the IPv6 header lacks an IP ID field used for fragmentation and reassembly. IPv6 routers perform no in-network packet fragmentation; the IPv6 protocol shifts this burden of fragmentation to the sender. If a sender must fragment a packet, it adds an IPv6 extension header on each packet fragment that includes a 32-bit ID field to facilitate reassembly. While routers primarily perform data-plane forwarding, they also run an IPv6 stack as part of their control plane. Building on our technique in [2], now implemented in speedtrap [16] and integrated into the scamper packet prober [15], we elicit IPv6 IDs by sending ICMP6 packets to a router's control plane via one or more of its interfaces. Specifically, we induce a router's IPv6 stack to originate IPv6 fragment IDs by sending an ICMP packet too big message (PTB) with an MTU value smaller than the size of the packets subsequently solicited from it. We use scamper to first send 1300-byte ICMP echo request packets; when we receive 1300-byte echo replies, we send the router a PTB message with an MTU of 1280 bytes. If the router follows the IPv6 protocol [7], it will subsequently send fragmented echo replies containing fragment IDs in response to our probes.

Note that except for responses to our probes, a router does not typically send fragmented IPv6 traffic, and hence the IPv6 counter has no natural background rate of change (velocity). In contrast, control plane IPv4 packets sent by a router increment the fragment ID counter because every IPv4 packet contains a fragment identification field. In addition, the IPv4 fragment identifier field is 16 bits, but 32 bits in IPv6. Our prior work used IPID-based inferences to infer IPv6 router aliases [16]; in this work we extend this method to enable new inferences, leveraging the monotonicity of IPv6 IDs to infer router uptime.

2.2 Obtaining IPv6 Router Interface Addresses

We assemble a set of candidate IPv6 router interfaces from traceroutes conducted in January and February 2014 by CAIDA's macroscopic IPv6 topology discovery infrastructure [12]. The union of all interfaces discovered in this period across 32 geographically distributed vantage points (VPs) includes 66,471 unique IPv6 router interfaces. Although these interfaces are a subset of the complete IPv6 Internet, the set is sufficiently large and diverse to demonstrate our uptime inference technique, and reveal preliminary insights into IPv6 router availability.

We probed these interfaces every 6 h between March 5th and July 31st 2014 from a single host on the Virginia Tech campus (an educational network on the U.S. east coast with native IPv6). The set of interfaces were randomly permuted before each probing round. For each interface, we sent four ICMP6 echo requests (per Sect. 2.1); probing this set of addresses at 20 packets per second required approximately 2.5 h per run. Our probing host had two multi-day outages: March 18–25 and July 2–9, 2014.

2.3 Uptime Algorithm

For each IPv6 interface k, our periodic probing produces a time series of n IPv6 fragment ID (f_i) and timestamp (t_i) pairs: $F_k = (f_1, t_1), (f_2, t_2), \ldots, (f_n, t_n)$ where $t_i < t_{i+1}$. Some interfaces were unreachable while ICMP6 blocking prevents the PTB from reaching others; in such cases F is the empty set[1]. 31,170 interfaces (46.9 %) either were unresponsive (e.g. due to ICMP6 filtering, address changes, network changes) or did not return fragment IDs (e.g. due to PTB or fragment filtering).

For the remaining 35,301 interfaces that returned IDs, we observed a variety of router implementation-specific behavior. In total, 20.1 % of the interfaces returned random IDs; our prior work [16] found that random IDs were attributable to BSD-based devices, including Juniper routers. Because random IDs are

---

[1] A small fraction of the interfaces return only a small number of IDs over the experiment duration; we exclude those where $n < 20$.

Table 1. Classification of IP-ID behavior. We can infer reboot events for interfaces we classify as monotonic or cyclic, and some events for interfaces we classify as odd.

Classification	Interfaces	
Monotonic	20,429	30.7%
Cyclic	1,110	1.7%
Odd	432	0.6%
Random	13,330	20.1%
Unresponsive	31,170	46.9%
Total	66,471	100.0%

by definition non-monotonically increasing, we cannot form uptime inferences over this set. Thus, before performing uptime inference, we segment the interfaces in our dataset into classes as summarized in Table 1.

The classification logic divides a time series F_k into sequentially increasing subsequences such that $f_i + 1 = f_{i+1}$. This step breaks random ID series into singleton subsequences, while preserving groups of monotonic runs. We infer interfaces with all singleton sequences to be random, and classify each non-random subsequence as monotonic or cyclic. If all labels agree, we classify the interface with that label.

Several factors complicated this classification. When the labels for subsequences did not all agree, we classified the interface as *odd*. For instance, some interfaces changed behavior during the course of our experiment, suggesting a hardware or software change. Other interfaces returned deterministic IDs, e.g. always zero, or returned multiple replies for each probe. In total, 0.6% of the interfaces exhibited odd or inconsistent behavior, and we excluded them from our analysis. Another complicating factor is interfaces that return cyclic IDs with large offsets. We identify cyclic interfaces as those with IDs greater than 10,000 that appear in multiple subsequences. In Sect. 2.4 we discuss root causes of cyclic IDs and how we accommodate them.

Finally, we infer uptimes for the set of interfaces we classify as monotonic. First, we filter noise in the time series. For example, we obtained an f sequence: ..., 405, 406, 407, 850815256, 408, 409, ... At present, we cannot positively identify the cause of these infrequent, but clearly erroneous IDs. We therefore remove element i if and only if $f_{i-1} + 1 = f_{i+1}$, i.e. we remove an outlier in the midst of an otherwise exact sequence. We then form monotonically increasing subsequences such that if $f_{i+1} < f_i$, we know that a reboot event occurred between t_i and t_{i+1}. Because $t_{i+1} - t_i$ is bounded by the frequency at which we probe, as much as six hours in our experiment, there is inherent error. The difference between the last and first sample in a subsequence therefore provides a conservative uptime estimate.

2.4 Cyclic Interfaces

We classified 1.7% of the interfaces in our set as cyclic because they exhibited an incrementing but cyclic pattern of IP-ID values, e.g. $(N, N+1, N+2, N, N+1, N+2)$.

This interface IP-ID behavior is consistent with some versions of the Linux kernel. The last version of the Linux kernel that used a single central counter was 3.0, released Jul 21, 2011. For Linux kernel versions 3.1 (released Oct 24, 2011) through 3.9 (released Jun 30, 2013) the kernel uses a counter per destination IP address, with the initial value computed as a function of (1) the destination IP address and (2) a randomly generated secret obtained when the system booted. The kernel creates an *inet peer* structure per IP address, where it stores information including the next IP-ID value to use when sending a packet. These *inet peer* structures are discarded when the route times out or is garbage collected (the kernel is limited to 65,664 inet peer structures). When the structure is later recreated for the same destination IP address (for instance during our next probing round) it will use the same initial IP-ID value if neither the secret value (initialized on system boot) nor the destination address value (which we control) changed. As a real world example, a particular interface in our dataset returned the same sequence $f = $ 0x28c2c283, 0x28c2c284, 0x28c2c285 on each probing cycle until it rebooted and then returned a different sequence with the same period: $f = $ 0x415bd0cc, 0x415bd0cd, 0x415bd0ce.

For these cyclic interfaces, we detect a reboot event as an abrupt change in IP-ID value, which indicates the secret has changed. We empirically define an abrupt change as either an IP-ID value that is lower than the range of previous values or at least 2000 higher.

2.5 Inferring Routers, Their Roles, and Their Location

We used speedtrap [16] to resolve aliases (i.e. map multiple IP addresses to the same physical router) for the set of 66,471 monitored interfaces. The speedtrap resolution was performed between Sept 19th 16:00 UTC and Sept 20th 07:00. Speedtrap also exploits IPv6 fragmentation identifiers: two interfaces are aliases for the same router if they produce a sequence of non-overlapping IPID samples whose IPID values strictly increase, suggesting the IPID samples are derived from the same counter. Because we ran speedtrap from a different vantage point than from where the uptime IPID samples were collected, and after our data collection completed, our inferred aliases do not perfectly overlap with the interfaces probed. Our speedtrap alias resolution run observed 19,103 interfaces that assign ID values from a monotonically increasing counter. Using speedtrap to find aliases, these interfaces correspond to 12,866 routers. For 9,035 interfaces (70.2%), speedtrap inferred no aliases, and we treat these as routers with a single interface. 20.1% of the remaining routers had two interfaces, leaving approximately 10% of the routers with three or more aliases. For the remaining monotonic and cyclic interfaces that were unresponsive to speedtrap probes, we did not infer aliases and treat each as a router with a single interface.

A well-known limitation of mapping IP addresses to ASes is that an interface may be mapped to a different AS than the AS that owns and operates the router. For example, network service providers frequently allocate one of their own IP addresses to an interface on a customer router. This ambiguity affects our uptime analysis because the reboot of an interface with an address of provider A may actually be a reboot event within customer B's network.

We therefore classify some routers as being *core AS routers* if we believe they represent a router within an AS (intra-AS) as opposed to a border router connecting to other ASes (inter-AS). We examined the AS origin of each IPv6 hop in the corresponding Ark traceroute data for Jan and Feb 2014. We classified a router with interface B_2 as a core router for AS B if we observed a traceroute IPv6 address sequence $A_1B_1B_2B_3C_1$ where AS B originates BGP prefixes for B_1, B_2, and B_3. In contrast, neither B_1 nor B_3 would be classified as a core AS router with this path because they are preceded and succeeded by interface hops belonging to different ASes. This conservative definition of a core AS router allows us to better characterize the origin of reboot events for some large networks with many customers. We inferred 20,093 interfaces as belonging to core routers in their respective ASes.

Finally, we annotated each router with an inferred local timezone, based on its offset from GMT reported by Digital Envoy's NetAcuity commercial geolocation database [9]. This database reported GMT offsets for 65,451 of 66,471 (98.5 %) of the interfaces probed. For routers with more than one observed address, we mapped all interfaces to the same timezone, i.e. we discovered no disagreement among timezones of the interfaces belonging to routers. The quality of IPv6 geolocation databases for individual router interfaces is unknown, and we only probed interfaces every six hours, so we were wary of inferring fine-grained temporal patterns of rebooting. However, we use timezones to estimate the aggregate distribution of reboots across days of the week (Sect. 3.4).

2.6   Limitations

Our uptime technique has several limitations. First, inferences are only possible for those interfaces that return IPv6 fragments, and only for the subset of those with non-random IDs. In addition, because of potential security vulnerabilities introduced by fragmentation, future IETF guidance may deprecate IPv6 fragmentation [4], thereby invalidating our technique. However, in practice we are able to elicit fragments from a large fraction of production routers and do not expect this ability to change in the near-term.

Second, our technique depends on periodic probing. The granularity of our uptime inferences is governed by the rate of probing the remote interface; obtaining high-fidelity uptime inferences may induce unwanted traffic load, especially as the IPv6 Internet grows. Further, we cannot detect multiple reboots of an interface that occur between probing samples. Third, we cannot discern the root cause of a reboot, e.g. a power failure, natural disaster, human error, software fault, or intentional maintenance upgrade.

We currently focus our effort on IPv6 routers. While similar IP-ID behavior is found in IPv4 routers, there are three important differences. First, the IPID counter behavior in IPv4 is much more erratic because routers increment the ID counter every time they create a packet, causing the counter's velocity to be large for routers with chatty routing protocols or SNMP reporting [1,13]. Second, the counter itself only has a range of 65536 values, requiring more frequent probing than in IPv6 to prevent a counter wrap from being interpreted as a reboot.

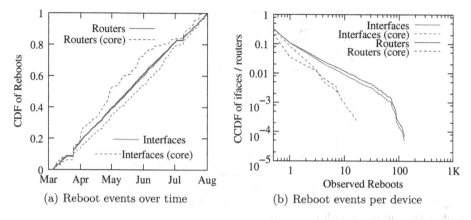

Fig. 1. Distribution of reboots in time and frequency for interfaces and routers measured over five-months. Core interfaces and routers refer to intra-AS devices.

Finally, there are many more router interfaces in the IPv4 topology than in the IPv6 topology; even conducting Internet-scale IPv4 alias resolution on >2M IP addresses is challenging due to the volume of probes required. Sampling router interfaces to infer reboot events would require even more frequent probing than Internet-scale alias resolution. We leave IPv4 uptime inference to future work.

3   Results

We used our uptime inference algorithm to characterize the availability of IPv6 interfaces and routers. Figure 1(a) shows the cumulative distribution of reboot events for the duration of our experiment. The overall rate of interface reboots is relatively uniform – indicating a constant background rate of IPv6 interface reboots without the presence of individual events affecting many interfaces. In contrast, the set of core routers exhibits more variation, suggesting correlated reboot events among routers within a provider or organization.

Figure 1(b) depicts the complementary cumulative distribution of interface and router reboots. The distribution is heavy-tailed: most routers and interfaces experienced no reboots while a few experienced many reboots. Overall, 68 % of the interfaces we monitored experienced no reboots over the measurement period, while ~22 % of interfaces had a single reboot. 99 % of interfaces had 10 or fewer reboots, but three interfaces reboot more than 100 times. Core interfaces and routers were more stable than the broader set. 78 % of core routers did not reboot during our experiment, but 98 % rebooted two or fewer times.

Figure 2 shows the distribution of uptimes, inclusive of only those devices that experienced a reboot. Only 15 % of observed uptimes were less than a day; the median interface uptime was approximately 23 days. Reboots among core interfaces and routers are again relatively more stable, with a median uptime of approximately 50 days, while 10 % had an uptime of 125 days or more.

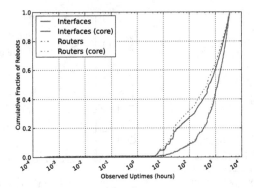

Fig. 2. Distribution of observed uptimes across all observed reboot events (excluding routers and interfaces with no restarts).

The largest uptime, approximately 150 days, corresponds to our full measurement period and represents an interface that rebooted at the beginning of our probing.

3.1 Linux Router Behavior

As described in Sect. 2.4, Linux kernels between 3.1 and 3.9 use a separate counter per source IP address, and the counter appears to wrap to the same initial ID value when the state associated with the source IP address is removed. We detect reboots when we observe an abrupt change in IP-ID value that implies the randomly generated secret used to set the initial ID value has changed. In total, we detected 2,312 reboot events involving the 1,110 cyclic-ID interfaces. The events were evenly distributed throughout the five months of our probing.

3.2 Validation

We solicited validation data from operators of 12 ASes who had previously provided feedback on our AS relationship inferences [17]. Five replied with evidence that supported our inferences of reboot events for 15 routers, either direct validation from system logs, or implicit validation by correlating the event with a BGP session closing. Operators could not confirm all reboots we asked them about, since some routers were using the operator's address space but belonged to customers, so the operator could not verify uptime. Through operator feedback we also learned that the two reboot events we detected for one router on May 18 and June 1 2014 were because the router ran out of TCAM to store the routing table; these reboots occurred before the publicity in August 2014 where individual provider tables reached 512K [5].

3.3 Reboot Event Correlations with BGP

We manually searched public BGP data for BGP prefix withdrawal events that correlated with our inferences of a reboot event. To rule out confounding factors

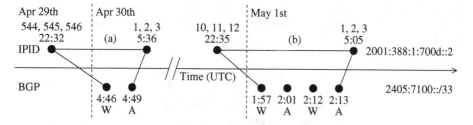

Fig. 3. Timeline of IPID events for 2001:388:1:700d::2 (assigned to a router owned by AS36474) and BGP events for the 2405:7100::/33 prefix announced by AS38474. The time of each event is represented by a dot with inferred uptime events above observed BGP events. The reboot events labeled (a) and (b) correlate in time with the withdrawal (W) and announcement (A) of the prefix as observed at routeviews. No other BGP events involving this AS occurred during this time.

involving events from upstream networks, we searched BGP data provided by the AS where we observed an event involving a customer router, as labeled in DNS. Figure 3 illustrates an example involving two detected reboot events in two days between April 29 and May 1 UTC. The interface 2001:388:1:700d::2 has a DNS PTR record of gw1.er1.aad.cpe.aarnet.net.au, i.e. a customer premises equipment (cpe) router at the Australian Antarctic Division (aad) which is a customer of AARNet, AS7575. AAD is AS38474 in BGP, and announced two IPv6 prefixes: 2405:7100::/33 and 2405:7100:8000::/33. We downloaded all update messages archived from AS7575 by Routeviews' Sydney collector between April 29 and May 1 UTC, and then searched for BGP events involving these two prefixes. The reboot events labeled (a) and (b) in Fig. 3 that occurred between our probing correlate with prefix withdrawal and announcement events, and no other BGP events for AS38474 occurred during this time window. We saw the same behavior involving other customers of other networks in BGP. An open question is the degree to which reboot events in core AS routers result in a BGP event; we hypothesize that neighbors of a network where a core AS router reboots are much less likely to propagate a BGP event than the case in Fig. 3 where a provider propagates a BGP event caused by a customer-edge router reboot. Previous work on pinpointing the cause of a routing change [25] suggested a coordinated approach, where ASes maintain a view of routing changes within their own network, which can be queried when an event occurs. Our results demonstrate the potential to correlate customer edge router reboot events with BGP routing events.

3.4   When Do Routers Reboot?

Table 2 reports the day of the week, in the router's local time zone, when we detect a reboot event. In our data, router reboots were more than twice as prevalent on Tuesday and Wednesday than on Saturday, Sunday, and Monday, regardless of the router classification we made. We found the reduction in reboots

Table 2. Router reboots by day-of-week and router type (Sect. 2.5). Router reboot events were twice as common on Tuesday and Wednesday as on Saturday, Sunday, or Monday.

	Core		All	
Monday	110	9.7%	925	11.2%
Tuesday	226	20.0%	1684	20.4%
Wednesday	227	20.0%	1553	18.8%
Thursday	197	17.4%	1313	15.9%
Friday	157	13.9%	1120	13.5%
Saturday	115	10.2%	864	10.4%
Sunday	101	8.9%	813	9.8%
	1133		8272	

over the weekend relative to the rest of the week surprising. We hypothesized that reboots due to maintenance would occur on the weekend when the network demand and thus potential impact of any disruption is lower. Instead, our data suggests that maintenance occurs during the middle of the week, perhaps due to the difficulty and expense of having a network team available during the weekend. We restrict ourselves to day-of-week granularity because of the relatively coarse (6 h) probing we used to collect the data. In the future, we would like to optimize our probing algorithm to obtain a finer granularity that would allow us to pinpoint reboot events to within one hour. For example, maintenance events might occur in early morning during weekdays, to minimize disruptive impact.

4   Applications and Implications

Despite the Internet's critical importance, relatively little quantitative data exists on its service availability or reliability. A precise definition of Internet infrastructure reliability has yet to solidify [14], although the U.S. FCC has supported efforts to measure reliability from a consumer's perspective [3,24]. At the provider-level, the FCC mandates reporting of significant outages for voice networks, including VoIP networks [10], but there are no outage reporting requirements for broadband network services.

While anyone with management access to a router (e.g. SNMP, ssh) can determine its uptime, our technique uses ICMP6 and requires no privileged access to infer the uptime of a remote router, enabling Internet-wide study of IPv6 router availability and reliability. Prior work has sought to infer reliability indirectly. For instance, Paxson introduced metrics of routing reliability such as route prevalence and persistence [20,22], while Feamster et al. analyzed operational mailing lists to characterize the frequency of faults [11]. More recently, Quan et al. used active probes to infer edge network availability [21]. In contrast, we restrict our attention to the availability of IPv6 routers, but obtain uptime data directly from the routers via active measurement.

Closely related to our technique are uptime inferences using TCP timestamps. For example, nmap [18] gathers remote TCP timestamps to determine the rate at which timestamps increase, and extrapolates to estimate uptime assuming the timestamp resets to zero upon boot. Netcraft uses this technique to infer the uptime of Internet web servers, but notes that uptimes cannot be determined for hosts running modern operating systems due to their use of high-frequency clocks [19]. More importantly, routers rarely listen on any TCP port, rendering active-open TCP-based uptime methods infeasible.

Inferring device reboots also has important security implications. An attacker able to observe when a remote device last rebooted can infer whether that device has installed certain security patches; devices that have not rebooted since a vulnerability announcement are more likely vulnerable. Attackers can also gain knowledge of the likely maintenance windows for different networks, as well as when an attack designed to crash a router is successful.

5 Conclusions

To our knowledge, we have developed, validated, and demonstrated the first remote uptime inference technique applicable to routers. While our method is currently limited to routers supporting IPv6, and only works for 61 % of the responsive routers in our study, it is a first step toward broader insights into Internet infrastructure reliability and operational practices.

While we have demonstrated evidence of correlation between our inferred reboots and BGP events visible in the global routing table, in future work we hope to systematically investigate the relationship between reboots and both IPv4 and IPv6 routing system events. We observed instances of correlated reboots among IPv6 interfaces that are not aliases, implying that multiple routers rebooted within the same time window. Careful analysis of such correlations can reveal hidden relationships among not only routers, but also providers, and potentially reveal hidden correlations such as co-located routers rebooting due to a common power failure.

We focused on IPv6 routers, but our technique applies to any IPv6 device that responds with monotonic fragment IDs, including Linux and Windows machines serving as infrastructure, e.g. web servers, DNS resolvers, etc. A more ambitious longitudinal study, using a higher probing rate, would enable unprecedented macroscopic characterization of the availability of critical IPv6 infrastructure.

Acknowledgments. We thank Stefan Savage for the uptime idea, and to the networks that validated our inferences. This work supported by NSF grants CNS-1111445 and CNS-1111449 and Department of Homeland Security (DHS) contracts N66001-2250-58231 and N66001-12-C-0130. Views and conclusions are those of the authors and should not be interpreted as representing the official policies, either expressed or implied, of the U.S. government.

References

1. Bender, A., Sherwood, R., Spring, N.: Fixing Ally's growing pains with velocity modeling. In: ACM SIGCOMM IMC, pp. 337–342, Oct 2008
2. Beverly, R., Brinkmeyer, W., Luckie, M., Rohrer, J.P.: IPv6 alias resolution via induced fragmentation. In: Roughan, M., Chang, R. (eds.) PAM 2013. LNCS, vol. 7799, pp. 155–165. Springer, Heidelberg (2013)
3. Bischof, Z.S., Bustamante, F.E.: A time for reliability: the growing importance of being always on. In: Proceedings of ACM SIGCOMM, pp. 131–132 (2014)
4. Bonica, R., Kumari, W., Bush, R., Pfeifer, H.: IPv6 Fragment Header Deprecated. Internet Draft, Jul 2013
5. Cowie, J.: Internet touches half million routes: Outages possible next week, Aug 2014. http://research.dyn.com/2014/08/internet-512k-global-routes/
6. Czyz, J., Allman, M., Zhang, J., Iekel-Johnson, S., Osterweil, E., Bailey, M.: Measuring IPv6 adoption. In: Proceedings of ACM SIGCOMM, pp. 87–98 (2014)
7. Deering, S., Hinden, R.: Internet Protocol, Version 6 (IPv6) Specification. RFC 2460, Dec 1998
8. Dhamdhere, A., Luckie, M., Huffaker, B., claffy, k., Elmokashfi, A., Aben, E.: Measuring the deployment of IPv6: topology, routing and performance. In: ACM SIGCOMM IMC, pp. 537–559, Nov 2012
9. Digital Element: NetAcuity Edge. http://www.digitalelement.com/solutions/
10. FCC: Outage reporting to interconnected voice over internet protocol service providers (2012). https://apps.fcc.gov/edocs_public/attachmatch/FCC-12-22A1.pdf
11. Feamster, N., Balakrishnan, H.: Detecting BGP configuration faults with static analysis. In: Proceedings of NSDI, pp. 43–56 (2005)
12. Hyun, Y., claffy, k.: Archipelago measurement infrastructure (2014). http://www.caida.org/projects/ark/
13. Keys, K., Hyun, Y., Luckie, M., claffy, k.: Internet-scale IPv4 alias resolution with MIDAR. IEEE/ACM Trans. Netw. **21**, 383–399 (2013)
14. Lehr, W., Bauer, S., Heikkinen, M., Clark, D.: Assessing broadband reliability: measurement and policy challenges. In: Research Conference on Communications, Information and Internet Policy (2011)
15. Luckie, M.: Scamper: a scalable and extensible packet prober for active measurement of the internet. In: ACM SIGCOMM IMC, pp. 239–245 (2010)
16. Luckie, M., Beverly, R., Brinkmeyer, W., claffy, k.: Speedtrap: internet-scale IPv6 alias resolution. In: ACM SIGCOMM IMC, pp. 119–126, Oct 2013
17. Luckie, M., Huffaker, B., Dhamdhere, A., Giotsas, V., claffy, k.: AS relationships, customer cones, and validation. In: ACM SIGCOMM IMC, pp. 243–256, Oct 2013
18. Lyon, G.F.: Nmap Network Scanning: The Official Nmap Project Guide to Network Discovery and Security Scanning. Insecure (2009)
19. Netcraft: Which operating systems provide uptime information? June 2014. http://uptime.netcraft.com/accuracy.html#uptime
20. Paxson, V.: End-to-end routing behavior in the internet. IEEE/ACM Trans. Netw. **5**(5), 601–615 (1997)
21. Quan, L., Heidemann, J., Pradkin, Y.: Trinocular: understanding internet reliability through adaptive probing. In: Proceedings of ACM SIGCOMM (2013)
22. Rexford, J., Wang, J., Xiao, Z., Zhang, Y.: Bgp routing stability of popular destinations. In: Proceedings of the 2nd ACM SIGCOMM IMW, pp. 197–202 (2002)

23. Sarrar, N., Maier, G., Ager, B., Sommer, R., Uhlig, S.: Investigating IPv6 traffic. In: Taft, N., Ricciato, F. (eds.) PAM 2012. LNCS, vol. 7192, pp. 11–20. Springer, Heidelberg (2012)
24. Sundaresan, S., De Donato, W., Feamster, N., Teixeira, R., Crawford, S., Pescapè, A.: Broadband internet performance: a view from the gateway. ACM SIGCOMM Comput. Commun. Rev. **41**, 134–145 (2011)
25. Teixeira, R., Rexford, J.: A measurement framework for pin-pointing routing changes. In: ACM SIGCOMM NetTs Workshop, Aug 2004

UAv6: Alias Resolution in IPv6 Using Unused Addresses

Ramakrishna Padmanabhan[✉], Zhihao Li, Dave Levin, and Neil Spring

University of Maryland, College Park, MD, USA
{ramapad,zhihaoli,dml,nspring}@cs.umd.edu

As the IPv6 Internet grows, alias resolution in IPv6 becomes more important. Traditional IPv4 alias resolution techniques such as Ally do not work for IPv6 because of protocol differences. Recent techniques adopted specifically for IPv6 have shown promise, but utilize source routing, which has since been deprecated, or rely upon sequential fragment identifiers supported on only a third of router interfaces. As a result, IPv6 alias resolution remains an open problem.

This paper introduces *UAv6*, a new alias resolution technique for IPv6. UAv6 finds aliases in two phases. The first "harvest" phase gathers potential alias pairs, and is based on our empirical observation that addresses adjacent to router interface addresses are often unused. UAv6 probes these unused addresses, eliciting ICMPv6 Address Unreachable responses. The central assumption of this work is that the source address of such a response belongs to a router directly connected to the prefix containing the unused and router interface addresses. The second "disambiguation" phase determines which interface address is an alias of the Address Unreachable's source address. UAv6 uses both new and established techniques to construct proofs or disproofs that two addresses are aliases.

We confirm the accuracy of UAv6 by running the Too-Big Trick test upon the aliases we find, and by comparing them with limited ground truth. We also show that the classic address-based technique to resolve aliases in IPv4 works for IPv6 as well, and show that the address-based technique, UAv6, and the Too-Big Trick are complementary techniques in resolving IPv6 aliases.

1 Introduction

With the impending exhaustion of IPv4 addresses, IPv6 adoption has seen steady growth [8], and particularly robust growth in the last two years [7]. As IPv6 deployment increases, knowledge of its topology becomes valuable to researchers and commercial providers. Traceroutes are the traditional tool for inferring network topology [5,18], but using traceroutes alone for topology-mapping does not suffice. Traceroutes discover multiple interfaces of a router, but do not reveal which interfaces belong to the same router. *Alias resolution* is the process of grouping interfaces onto their corresponding routers, thereby rendering a more accurate picture of the actual network topology.

Numerous alias resolution techniques exist for IPv4 [2,17,18], but protocol differences prevent their straightforward application to IPv6. Researchers

---

The first two authors contributed equally to this work.

© Springer International Publishing Switzerland 2015
J. Mirkovic and Y. Liu (Eds.): PAM 2015, LNCS 8995, pp. 136–148, 2015.
DOI: 10.1007/978-3-319-15509-8_11

have come up with several IPv6-specific techniques over the last decade. Early techniques used the source routing feature in IPv6 to resolve aliases [14,15,19], but source routing in IPv6 has since been deprecated [1]. Another successful approach to resolve aliases is the shared counter method: Ally [18] and Radargun [2] use this technique in IPv4, and recently, the Too-Big Trick (TBT) applied this approach to find aliases in IPv6 [3,12]. However, Speedtrap [12] reports that 68 % of router interfaces do not respond to the Too-Big Trick. Thus, alias resolution in IPv6 remains an open problem.

In this paper, we describe a new alias resolution technique, *UAv6*, which operates in two phases. The first phase, called the *harvest phase*, collects candidate aliases by probing unused addresses in IPv6 router interface prefixes. The IPv6 address space is large enough that addresses for point-to point links are not typically assigned out of 127-bit prefixes which have only two addresses; rather, point-to-point links typically use only two of the four addresses in a /126 prefix. By sending a packet to an address that is within a prefix but not assigned to an interface, we solicit an ICMPv6 Address Unreachable (AU) error. Only a router directly connected to the prefix is likely to respond with an AU. Therefore, the source address of the AU is an alias for one of the used addresses within the prefix. This results in two possible alias pairs, but the harvest phase does not determine which of them is the true alias.

UAv6's second phase, called the *disambiguation phase* determines which of the harvest's candidate aliases are true aliases. Because one of the two candidate aliases produced by the harvest phase must be a true alias, we can either prove one of them to be true, or we can disprove one and conclude the other must be true by process of elimination. We provide tests of both types and show that they are complementary. The first test uses traceroutes to *disprove* one of the candidate aliases: If one of the addresses in the pair appears on the path to the other, they are unlikely to be aliases of one another. The second test uses shared Path MTU (PMTU) caches in some router implementations to *prove* one of the alias pairs true: If an address pair shares PMTU caches, it is a true alias pair, as only aliases share PMTU caches.

The contributions of this work are:

- We observe the presence of unused addresses in router interface address prefixes. We present UAv6, a two-phase alias resolution technique in IPv6 that uses these partially used prefixes.
- We verify UAv6's accuracy by running the TBT test [3] where possible. TBT could be applied to 23.2 % of the alias pairs we found and it confirmed 99.86 % of them. We also compare the aliases we find against limited ground truth from the Internet2 dataset and verify all the Internet2 aliases we discover.
- We demonstrate that a classic IPv4 alias resolution technique, the address-based technique [9,13,18], works in IPv6, in spite of recommendations in RFC 4443 [6]. We show, however, that UAv6 finds almost twice as many aliases as the address-based technique within router interface addresses derived from traceroutes sent by the Ark project [4].

2 Related Work

Alias resolution schemes can be broadly classified into the following categories:

Address-based: In IPv4, some routers are configured to use the outgoing interface's address as the source address for certain ICMP response types. Pansiot and Grad [13] harness this to obtain aliases by checking when the source address in a response is different from the destination probed. Some researchers [12,19] have been discouraged from applying a similar approach in IPv6, because the ICMPv6 specification [6] states that IPv6 routers must use the address to which the packet was sent as the source address in ICMPv6 responses, if the address belongs to the router. We demonstrate in Sect. 5 that, contrary to the specification, the address-based approach finds aliases in IPv6.

Source routing-based: In the early 2000s, only 8 % of IPv4 routers supported source routing [9], but the IPv6 Internet supported the feature in most routers [19]. Early IPv6 alias resolution techniques used source routing-based methods to find aliases [14,15,19]. However, source routing in IPv6 has been deprecated because of security concerns [1] and support is likely to decline further.

Shared counter-based: In IPv4, Rocketfuel [18] introduced Ally, an alias resolution scheme that determines aliases by checking if the "IP-ID" fields on two interfaces are generated from a shared counter. IPv6 dispensed with the IP-ID field because routers do not fragment packets in IPv6 when forwarding. Instead, if an interface obtains a too-large packet, it sends an ICMP Packet Too Big (PTB) message to the source. The source then sends subsequent too-large packets as fragments and inserts a common Fragment ID into fragments for reassembly.

The "Too-Big Trick" (TBT) technique introduced by Beverly et al. [3] found that many IPv6 routers use a counter that is shared among all of its interfaces, from which these fragment IDs are obtained. To solicit fragmented packets, TBT sends a large Echo Request packet (1300 bytes) to both addresses in a candidate alias pair, followed by a PTB message to each of them. Next, it sends large Echo Requests alternately to each address. If the returned fragments have sequential fragment IDs, then TBT declares the pair to be aliases.

Given a set of router interface addresses obtained from traceroutes, TBT requires a number of probes proportional to the number of pairs of addresses, since TBT is a pairwise test. Speedtrap [12] obtains the same aliases that TBT would have obtained, but does so more efficiently. It probes interface addresses in parallel and groups together candidate alias pairs into smaller sets before performing TBT's pairwise test upon members of the set. However, only 32 % of router interfaces in the IPv6 Internet provide fragments from a shared sequential counter [12].

Prefix-based: UAv6 does not depend upon shared sequential counters, support for source routing, or on ICMPv6 responses from different source addresses. Instead, it relies upon the presence of prefixes that contain unused addresses adjacent to router interface addresses. The next section shows that such partially used prefixes are common in IPv6.

3   Unused Addresses in IPv6 Prefixes

Since the IPv6 address space is immense, we expect that IPv6 router interface addresses on point-to-point links are assigned out of /126 prefixes, or larger, leaving some addresses unused. This is similar to the existing practice of using /30s in IPv4 [17]. However, two conflicting RFCs for IP address assignment in IPv6 create uncertainty. RFC 3627 [16], published in 2003, finds that /127 prefix lengths in IPv6 are harmful and recommends the use of /64 prefixes instead for point-to-point links. RFC 6164 [11], published in 2011, recommends the use of /127s for point-to-point links.

We investigate if IPv6 router interface addresses are allocated from /126 or larger prefixes by studying the distribution of their last digits. We extracted 68,474 router interface addresses from traceroutes sent by the Ark project in July 2014 [4]. Figure 1(a) shows the distribution of router interface addresses across the last hex digits for these addresses. Most (59 %) addresses end in hex digits "1" or "2". Further, 82 % end in the binary digits "01" or "10".

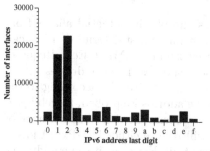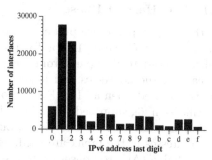

(a) Addresses from CAIDA traceroutes   (b) Addresses that responded to probes

Fig. 1. Distribution of the final hex digit of router interfaces' IPv6 addresses.

We believe that this distribution is a result of ISPs assigning addresses out of /126s, or larger, to point-to-point links. In such networks, one end of the point-to-point link is assigned an address ending with the binary suffix "01" and the other end is assigned an address with the binary suffix "10". The other addresses in the /126 prefix, with suffixes "00" and "11", are unused, or assigned as broadcast addresses.

CAIDA's traceroutes may have recovered addresses in only one direction of a path, if the path had not been probed in the reverse direction. To address this potential bias, we send ICMPv6 Echo Request probes to the rest of the addresses in each address' enclosing /126. In total, we sent probes to 227,212 addresses and received ICMPv6 Echo Replies from 89,756 (39.5 %) of them. We plot the frequency of the last hex digit for these responsive addresses in Fig. 1(b). Unlike Fig. 1(a), we find that the peak for addresses ending in "1" is higher than "2" and the peak for "0" is higher than the other last digits. We speculate that this may be due to some ISPs using hexadecimal "1"s and "0"s on opposite ends of a link.

The peaks for {"5", "6"}, {"9", "a"} and {"d", "e"} are of comparable heights, suggesting that these addresses are used for end-points of a link. Overall, we find that 80.3 % of addresses that responded to our probes with ICMPv6 Echo Replies end in binary suffixes "01" or "10". This supports our belief that IPv6 point-to-point link prefixes are /126s or larger. Only the two addresses assigned to opposite ends of a link are in use and the remaining addresses in the prefix are unused.

4   UAv6 Design

In this section, we describe how UAv6 resolves aliases by using unused addresses. UAv6 consists of two phases, the *harvest* phase and the *disambiguation* phase. In the harvest phase, we obtain Address Unreachable responses from unused addresses and obtain potential alias pairs. In the disambiguation phase, we use established and new methods to prove which potential pairs are truly aliases.

4.1   The Harvest Phase

In the harvest phase, we probe /126 prefixes and obtain potential aliases from the responses. Given a /126 prefix, the harvest phase first determines if we can collect candidate alias pairs from this prefix by sending ICMPv6 Echo Requests to each of the addresses and inspecting the responses. If all addresses in the prefix are used, then all ICMPv6 Echo Replies we receive are, according to the specification [6], supposed to originate from the address we probed, thereby providing no information about aliases. Likewise, we learn no new aliases if none of the addresses in the prefix are used, as we will receive either ICMPv6 Address Unreachable (AU) responses or no responses at all. However, if some addresses in the prefix are used and some are not, then we receive ICMPv6 Echo Replies from the used addresses and AU responses from potential aliases of the used addresses. The harvest phase uses this combination of responses to obtain candidate alias pairs.

Figure 2 shows an example of how the harvest phase works. In this example, there are two routers connected by a point-to-point link; one of the end-points has address X1[1] and the other has X2. The harvest phase sends probes to each address in the /126 prefix "X" viz. X0, X1, X2 and X3. Because X1 and X2 are in use, they will respond with ICMPv6 Echo Replies. As for the unused addresses X0 and X3, we assume that the AU response is sent by an interface (Y) that belongs to one of the routers that is directly connected to the X prefix. We make this assumption because in general, only the routers directly connected to prefix X know that X0 and X3 are unused. Since X1 and X2 are the addresses from this prefix that responded with ICMPv6 Echo Replies, we infer that Y is an alias of X1 or X2. We define (Y, X1) and (Y, X2) to be the two members of a candidate alias pair set, exactly one of which is a true alias pair. For each /126 or larger prefix with used and unused addresses, we obtain one candidate alias pair set at the end of the harvest phase.

---

[1] We use XN as notational shortcut for X::N.

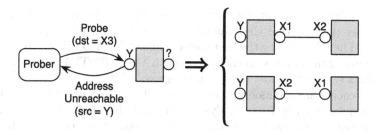

Fig. 2. In its harvest phase, UAv6 sends probes to each address in a given /126 beginning with the prefix "X". A probe for X3, which is likely unused, will probably elicit an ICMPv6 Address Unreachable (AU) message—we assume that this message will be sent from a router that has an interface from the X prefix. In this example, interface Y responded to our probe for X3 with an AU message, so we can deduce that Y is likely an alias for X1 or X2, but not both. The disambiguation phase determines which is the true alias.

4.2 The Disambiguation Phase

In the disambiguation phase, we find the correct alias pair in a candidate alias pair set provided by the harvest phase. We apply two tests which either prove that an alias pair is correct, or prove that one is *not* and thus the other must be. While some candidate alias pair sets can be disambiguated by either test, we show in Sect. 5 that these two tests are complementary, as they rely on different router behaviors.

4.2.1 Traceroute Test

We use traceroutes to obtain disproofs about candidate alias pairs by checking if one of the addresses lies on the route to the other. We expect that a typical IPv6 router first checks if the destination address in the packet belongs to it before decrementing the Hop Limit. An alias of a traceroute destination should thus never send an ICMPv6 Hop Limit Exceeded message, which implies that it should never appear on the route to the destination. We send ICMPv6 traceroutes to X1 and X2, and if Y appears on the route to one of them, we use that as proof that Y is *not* an alias of that address.

The Traceroute test cannot disambiguate all candidate alias pair sets. For instance, traceroute probes may be blocked by some ISPs. Alternately, traceroutes to X1 and X2 may both not find Y on the route if the traceroutes traverse different paths. Therefore, we introduce a complementary technique, which we call the SPMTU test.

4.2.2 Shared PMTU Cache (SPMTU) Test

In the SPMTU test, we use the presence of fragmentation to provide proofs about which of (Y, X1) and (Y, X2) is the true alias pair. By default, IPv6 routers do not fragment packets. However, an IPv6 router can be induced to fragment packets it originates if a host sends a Packet Too Big (PTB) message to the router claiming that the response from the router is too big for its link to handle [3]. The PTB sent by the host contains the claimed MTU, M, of the host's link. The router then makes an entry in its Path MTU (PMTU) cache, indicating that packets sent to the host need to be fragmented if their size exceeds M.

PMTU caches are commonly shared across all interfaces of a router, including routers manufactured by Huawei, Vyatta, HP, and Mikrotik [12]. When a router with a shared PMTU cache receives a PTB message from host h with stated MTU M, it inserts an entry (h, M) into its shared cache. As a result, all interfaces on the router will fragment subsequent packets that exceed M to that host. We use evidence of shared PMTU caches as proof that a candidate alias pair is correct.

We determine which address pair in the candidate alias pair set shares PMTU caches by using the following procedure:

1. **Initialize:** The prober sends an ICMPv6 Echo Request of size S to each of Y, X1, and X2, and verifies that all of them respond with an unfragmented Echo Reply. This step is necessary to ensure that none of the addresses has the prober's address in its PMTU cache.
2. **Populate cache:** If all addresses responded with an unfragmented Echo Reply in Step 1, the prober sends a PTB message with MTU $M < S$ to Y alone. If Y shares its PMTU cache with its aliases, all of them will fragment a packet of size S sent to the prober.
3. **Resolve:** The prober sends an ICMPv6 Echo Request of size S to each of Y, X1, and X2 again. If Y and X1 respond with a fragmented Echo Reply, and X2 responds with an unfragmented Echo Reply, we infer that Y and X1 share a PMTU cache, and must therefore be aliases. Conversely, if Y and X2 fragment and X1 does not, we infer that Y and X2 are aliases.

The SPMTU test is generic and can be applied to *any arbitrary pair* of IPv6 addresses to determine if they are aliases. However, it uses state in routers' caches and hence cannot be repeated with the same prober address until the PMTU cache entry for that prober address expires. We repeat tests using different prober addresses and rely on routers utilizing per-destination PMTU caches; thus a response from the router to a different prober address will not be fragmented. We own a /64 prefix, and use different addresses from the prefix for each test.

Although the SPMTU test can in theory be used as an all-pairs test, we are careful to use it only on candidate alias pairs from the harvest phase, as varying prober addresses may fill routers' caches with addresses from our tests. Since we send one PTB message per candidate alias pair set, the number of prober addresses in the PMTU cache will be at most the number of interfaces on the router.

5   Evaluation

In this section, we evaluate the accuracy of UAv6 against existing IPv6 alias resolution techniques and against limited ground truth from the Internet2 dataset [10].

We also show that a classic IPv4 alias resolution technique, the address-based technique (Sect. 2), works in IPv6, in spite of recommendations in RFC 4443 [6]. Finally, we combine the alias pairs found by UAv6 and the address-based technique and resolve 5,555 aliases in the Ark dataset [4].

5.1   Data Collection

We extracted 68,474 router interface addresses from traceroutes sent by CAIDA's IPv6 Ark project in July 2014 [4]. We found 56,803 /126 prefixes in total, and fed them into the harvest phase.

Recall that the harvest phase discards prefixes wherein the used addresses do not respond to our probes with ICMPv6 Echo Replies or the unused addresses do not elicit AU responses. Sometimes, AU responses do not arrive for the first ICMPv6 Echo Request; we therefore retransmit requests up to 3 times and each request has a timeout of 3 s. Of the 56,803 prefixes, we did not receive ICMPv6 Echo Replies from X1 or X2 for 27,014 (47.6 %) prefixes. For 7935 (14.0 %) prefixes, we did not get AU responses from probes sent to X0 or to X3.

The remaining 21,854 (38.5 %) prefixes are UAv6-applicable. We applied the harvest and disambiguation phases to them and found 15,260 alias pairs.

5.2   The Address-Based Technique in IPv6

We discover that the address-based technique, a classic method of resolving aliases in IPv4 [9,13,18], works in IPv6, too. The address-based technique finds aliases in IPv4 by testing if UDP responses to high-numbered ports contain a different source address from the destination probed. The ICMPv6 specification states that if a message is sent to an address that belongs to a router, the source address of the ICMPv6 response must be that address [6]. If the specification is followed, the address-based technique would not work for IPv6.

However, we find that there exist routers that do not follow the specification: while running UAv6's harvest phase, we observed that some of the ICMPv6 Echo Replies to our probes had a different source address from the probed destination. This implies that the address-based technique also works in IPv6, so we investigated how often it applies. We sent UDP probes with high port numbers to all the addresses we probed in the harvest phase. UDP probes to 227,212 addresses provided 72,457 responses with ICMPv6 Port Unreachable responses. Among them, 8729 (12 %) of the responses had a different source address from the destination of the UDP probes. Of the 89,756 ICMPv6 Echo Replies we received, 1450 (1.6 %) had a different source address. In 1030 cases, both UDP and ICMP probes had a different source address in their response. In total, we discovered 9,143 alias pairs using the address-based technique.

Although it is encouraging that the address-based technique works in IPv6, it has two drawbacks: first, it can only be applied to a small portion of the addresses, and second, it may not work in the future since it does not comply with the ICMPv6 specification. This serves as motivation for complementary techniques like UAv6.

5.3   Accuracy of UAv6

Alias resolution demands very high accuracy, as an incorrectly inferred alias may group two independent routers together, significantly altering the inferred topology. We next turn to evaluate UAv6's accuracy. For alias pairs to which the Too-Big Trick (TBT) is applicable, we use it for cross-validation. We also run UAv6 on the addresses from the Internet2 dataset [10] and verify the aliases it finds against ground truth.

5.3.1   Comparison with TBT

We first evaluate the accuracy of the SPMTU test and the Traceroute test against TBT. We can apply TBT to an address pair if both addresses' routers draw their fragment IDs from sequential counters. For aliases found by the Traceroute and SPMTU tests, we find TBT-applicable pairs and run TBT on them. Table 1 compares the accuracy of our tests against TBT.

Table 1. Comparison of UAv6's accuracy against TBT for alias pairs where both addresses draw fragment IDs from sequential counters.

	Aliases discovered	TBT-applicable	TBT verified
Traceroute	11,128	2,810 (25.3 %)	2,806 (99.86 %)
SPMTU	8,422	1,264 (15.0 %)	1,263 (99.92 %)
Union	15,260	3,539 (23.19 %)	3,534 (99.86 %)

Traceroute test: Using the Traceroute test, we find 11,128 alias pairs from 21,854 UAv6-applicable prefixes. Of them, 2810 pairs (25.3 %) are TBT-applicable. All but 4 of these pairs (0.14 %) are verified by TBT. We manually inspected these pairs and found that, although TBT indicates they have non-sequential fragment IDs, all 4 pairs are verified by the address-based technique. In future work, we plan to examine in greater depth why these established techniques contradict each other in some cases.

Recall that our central assumption is that if Y is the source of an AU response to a packet for X0 or X3, then Y is directly connected to the prefix containing X1 and X2. The Traceroute test provides us with some instances where this assumption is violated. For example, in 527 cases (2.41 %), Y appears on the paths to both X1 and X2. In 55 other cases (0.25 %), Y is more than one hop away from X1 or X2, which indicates that Y is not directly connected to the prefix. We detect these cases and discard them.

SPMTU test: The SPMTU test finds 8422 alias pairs. For the 1263 (15.0 %) alias pairs where TBT could be applied, TBT verified all the alias pairs found by SPMTU except one. We manually inspected this case and found that SPMTU no longer identified the pair as aliases. We recovered the fragment IDs that we had obtained when we first ran SPMTU upon them, and found that the fragment IDs for both addresses in that run had been sequential. We believe that one of the addresses from the pair was reassigned to another router in the sub-24 h gap between our SPMTU run and our TBT run, causing the results to conflict.

Comparison between disambiguation tests: We now compare the aliases found by our disambiguation tests against each other. The union of alias pairs found by the SPMTU and Traceroute tests contains 15,260 pairs, and the intersection has 4289 pairs. There is one alias pair where the two tests conflict. The alias pair chosen by the traceroute test was confirmed by the address-based method, whereas the pair chosen by SPMTU was confirmed by TBT. We believe that this behavior is caused by a misconfigured router responding to probes not addressed to it.

UAv6 is complementary to TBT: We observe that 11,721 (76.8%) alias pairs found by UAv6 are not TBT-applicable, demonstrating that UAv6 is a complementary technique to TBT. For aliases found by the Traceroute test, we find that 74.7% are not TBT-applicable. 54% of these alias pairs do not respond with fragments after a PTB message and 46% respond with random fragments.

Like TBT, the SPMTU test also relies upon fragments received from the addresses. Yet SPMTU differs from TBT in that it relies upon shared PMTU caches in routers while TBT relies upon shared sequential counters from which the fragment ID is drawn. The majority of aliases found by the SPMTU test (85.0%) are not TBT-applicable. This implies that at least one of the addresses in the pair returned fragments not derived from a sequential counter. However, Speedtrap [12] had found in their tests that all routers which implemented shared PMTU caches also used sequential counters. We believe that at least one main router manufacturer is now implementing shared PMTU caches and non-sequential counters on its routers.

5.3.2   Comparison with Ground Truth

We next study UAv6's accuracy using ground truth data from the Internet2 network [10]. We obtained ground truth aliases from Internet2 routers' configuration files. We believe these aliases to be correct, although we omitted some interfaces that are not physical interfaces. The Internet2 topology consists of 579 interface addresses on 11 routers. We obtain the /126 prefix of each interface address and run the harvest phase upon the prefix. Of the 500 /126 prefixes from the Internet2 dataset, we find 62 (12.4%) candidate alias pair sets. The number is small since many prefixes in Internet2 did not respond in the harvest phase.

For each candidate alias pair set, we apply the disambiguation phase and show the results in Table 2. Not all aliases found by the tests could be verified: some aliases are aliases of routers *connected* to Internet2 routers, but not of the Internet2 routers themselves. For these aliases, we do not have ground truth, and thus cannot verify them. The Traceroute test found 31 such aliases and the SPMTU test found 22 of them. The Traceroute test found 6 alias pairs that belonged to Internet2 routers, and the SPMTU test found 15 such pairs. All of these aliases were verified by ground truth, demonstrating UAv6's accuracy.

Table 2. Comparison of UAv6's accuracy against Internet2.

	Aliases discovered	Aliases verifiable	Alias verified	Accuracy
SPMTU	37	15	15	100.00%
Traceroute	37	6	6	100.00%

5.4   Alias Resolution with UAv6 and the Address-Based Method

We close this section by investigating how many aliases each technique finds within the 68,474 router interface addresses extracted from the Ark project in July 2014 [4]. For this comparison, we use the *number of aliases* that each technique finds instead of comparing the number of alias pairs, because a router with n interfaces has $\binom{n}{2}$ alias pairs, but only $n-1$ aliases. We believe this is an unbiased way of measuring the completeness of an alias resolution technique.

We combine the alias pairs we found using UAv6 and the address-based technique and show the results in Table 3. Though UAv6 found only 67% more alias pairs than the address-based technique, it found nearly double the aliases within the addresses already discovered by Ark. Of course, both UAv6 and address-based methods may discover new addresses that were not present in a traceroute measurement. Resolving aliases of interfaces already discovered by traceroute contributes accuracy to an inferred router-level map, while discovering new addresses yields additional detail. However, there were 1407 aliases that the address-based technique alone resolved. Combining the approaches yielded 34% more aliases than the use of UAv6 alone.

Table 3. Number of aliases found by the UAv6 and Address-Based techniques.

	Discovered alias pairs	Routers with aliases	Resolved Ark aliases	Discovered aliases
UAv6	15,259	5,711	4,148	14,760
Address-based	9,143	5,477	2,091	9,118
Combined	22,080	9,307	5,555	21,415

6   Conclusions

IPv6 deployment is on the rise and alias resolution techniques are vital in mapping its topology. In this work, we augmented existing alias resolution methods with UAv6: a new technique that uses partially used IPv6 prefixes to find aliases. We found potential alias pairs by probing /126 prefixes and introduced two tests to disambiguate potential alias pairs. Existing alias resolution techniques and ground truth from the Internet2 topology confirmed UAv6's accuracy. UAv6 is complementary to the address-based technique and to TBT, finding alias pairs that other techniques do not.

The disambiguation tests we employ in this work helped UAv6 recover aliases from 70 % of applicable prefixes, and we believe this can be increased further. For instance, one area of future work is to employ other disambiguation tests, such as the Hop Limit on received packets, to find more aliases. Additionally, we believe that, through the use of multiple vantage points, UAv6 can harvest more applicable prefixes.

Acknowledgments. We thank Matt Lentz and our anonymous reviewers for their comments and suggestions. This work was partially supported by NRL Grant N00173131G001.

References

1. Abley, J., Savola, P., Neville-Neil, G.: Deprecation of type 0 routing headers in IPv6. RFC 5095 (2007)
2. Bender, A., Sherwood, R., Spring, N.: Fixing Ally's growing pains with velocity modeling. In: ACM IMC (2008)
3. Beverly, R., Brinkmeyer, W., Luckie, M., Rohrer, J.P.: IPv6 alias resolution via induced fragmentation. In: Roughan, M., Chang, R. (eds.) PAM 2013. LNCS, vol. 7799, pp. 155–165. Springer, Heidelberg (2013)
4. CAIDA's IPv6 Ark Topology Data. http://www.caida.org/data/active/ipv6_allpref_topology_dataset.xml
5. Claffy, K., Monk, T.E., McRobb, D.: Internet tomography. Nature **7**, 11 (1999)
6. Conta, A., Gupta, M.: Internet Control Message Protocol (ICMPv6) for the Internet Protocol Version 6 (IPv6) Specification. RFC 4443 (2006)
7. Czyz, J., Allman, M., Zhang, J., Iekel-Johnson, S., Osterweil, E., Bailey, M.: Measuring IPv6 adoption. In: ACM SIGCOMM (2014)
8. Dhamdhere, A., Luckie, M., Huffaker, B., Elmokashfi, A., Aben, E., et al.: Measuring the deployment of IPv6 Topology, routing and performance. In: ACM IMC (2012)
9. Govindan, R., Tangmunarunkit, H.: Heuristics for Internet map discovery. In: INFOCOM (2000)
10. Internet2 Topology. http://noc.net.internet2.edu/i2network/live-network-status/visible-network.html
11. Kohno, M., Nitzan, B., Bush, R., Matsuzaki, Y., Colitti, L., Narten, T.: Using 127-Bit IPv6 Prefixes on Inter-Router Links. RFC 6164 (2011)
12. Luckie, M., Beverly, R., Brinkmeyer, W., et al.: Speedtrap: internet-scale IPv6 alias resolution. In: ACM IMC (2013)
13. Pansiot, J.-J., Grad, D.: On routes and multicast trees in the Internet. ACM SIGCOMM CCR **28**(1), 41–50 (1998)
14. Qian, S., Wang, Y., Xu, K.: Utilizing destination options header to resolve IPv6 alias resolution. In: GLOBECOM (2010)
15. Qian, S., Xu, M., Qiao, Z., Xu, K.: Route positional method for IPv6 alias resolution. In: ICCCN (2010)

16. Savola, P.: Use of/127 Prefix Length Between Routers Considered Harmful. RFC 3627 (2003)
17. Sherwood, R., Bender, A., Spring, N.: Discarte: a disjunctive internet cartographer. In: ACM SIGCOMM (2008)
18. Spring, N., Mahajan, R., Wetherall, D.: Measuring ISP topologies with Rocketfuel. In: ACM SIGCOMM (2002)
19. Waddington, D.G., Chang, F., Viswanathan, R., Yao, B.: Topology discovery for public IPv6 networks. ACM SIGCOMM CCR **33**(3), 59–68 (2003)

Server Siblings: Identifying Shared IPv4/IPv6 Infrastructure Via Active Fingerprinting

Robert Beverly[1]([⊠]) and Arthur Berger[2]

[1] Naval Postgraduate School, Monterey, CA, USA
rbeverly@nps.edu
[2] MIT CSAIL/Akamai, Cambridge, MA, USA
awberger@csail.mit.edu

Abstract. We present, validate, and apply an active measurement technique that ascertains whether candidate IPv4 and IPv6 server addresses are "siblings," i.e., assigned to the same physical machine. In contrast to prior efforts limited to passive monitoring, opportunistic measurements, or end-client populations, we propose an *active* methodology that generalizes to all TCP-reachable devices, including servers. Our method extends prior device fingerprinting techniques to improve their feasibility in modern environments, and uses them to support measurement-based detection of sibling interfaces. We validate our technique against a diverse set of 61 web servers with known sibling addresses and find it to be over 97 % accurate with 99 % precision. Finally, we apply the technique to characterize the top ∼6,400 Alexa IPv6-capable web domains, and discover that a DNS name in common does not imply that the corresponding IPv4 and IPv6 addresses are on the same machine, network, or even autonomous system. Understanding sibling and non-sibling relationships gives insight not only into IPv6 deployment and evolution, but also helps characterize the potential for correlated failures and susceptibility to certain attacks.

1 Introduction

While significant prior research has characterized the evolution, routing, and performance of IPv6 [5,6,15], less attention has been given to understanding whether IPv6 infrastructure is being deployed using separate hardware or by adding IPv6 to existing machines. I.e., are providers using separate IPv4 and IPv6 servers to host the same web content, or using single "dual-stacked" servers?

Given an IPv4 and IPv6 address, we seek to infer whether they belong to interfaces on the same physical machine. We term such cross-protocol associated addresses server "siblings." To accurately determine sibling and non-sibling relationships, we leverage prior work on device fingerprinting to perform active measurements of TCP option signatures (coarse-grained) [10] and TCP timestamp clock skew (fine-grained) [9].

The prevalence of shared IPv6 infrastructure has important policy and Internet evolution implications [3]. Moreover, for network operators and researchers,

© Springer International Publishing Switzerland 2015
J. Mirkovic and Y. Liu (Eds.): PAM 2015, LNCS 8995, pp. 149–161, 2015.
DOI: 10.1007/978-3-319-15509-8_12

the way in which IPv6 is deployed has particular impact on measurement and security. A potential, future application for the methods herein is for IPv6 geolocation, where prior knowledge of the corresponding IPv4 sibling can be leveraged. Note that making such inferences based on a common Domain Name System (DNS) name can be dubious. As shown in Sect. 4, a DNS name in common does not imply that the IPv4 and IPv6 addresses are on the same interface, machine, or even autonomous system (AS).

A second area of interest is IPv6 security, as the deployment and maintenance of firewalls, filtering, and intrusion detection systems on IPv6 lags, while tunnels and transition mechanisms facilitate alternate data paths for application-layer attacks. Furthermore, not only are many old IPv4 network-layer attacks feasible in IPv6, IPv6 introduces new attack vectors [7]. The extent to which IPv4 infrastructure depends on IPv6, and vice-versa, therefore has unknown security implications. Whether an attack against the IPv6 address of an Internet web or DNS server impacts an organization's corresponding service for IPv4 depends on whether it is dual-stacked. Further, dual-stacked servers imply the potential for *correlated failures* that impact survivability.

Toward identifying shared IPv4/IPv6 infrastructure, our contributions are:

1. A reappraisal of the current feasibility of Kohno's 2005 physical device fingerprinting [9] method using TCP clock skew.
2. Integration to, and enhancement of, various fingerprinting methods to actively, rather than passively, associate IPv4 and IPv6 server addresses.
3. Evaluation on ground-truth data, with >97% accuracy and 99 % precision.
4. Real-world measurements of siblings and non-siblings among the Alexa top websites, characterizing a portion of Internet IPv6 infrastructure.

2   Background

Inferring IPv4 and IPv6 host associations has largely been confined to client populations using passive, opportunistic measurements. For instance prior projects have used web-bugs, javascript, or flash object to determine the prevalence of IPv6 connectivity and associate IPv4 and IPv6 addresses of connecting clients [14,17]. In contrast our technique is active and we study servers.

Our prior work also examines IPv4/IPv6 associations, but is limited to DNS resolvers [2]; the techniques herein are more general and can be performed actively, on-demand. By operating at the transport layer we can actively probe any listening TCP service to test whether a candidate IPv4 and IPv6 address belong to the same device.

At its heart, our work relies on the rich history of prior research in network fingerprinting. Network fingerprinting is a common technique that relies on implementation and configuration-specific characteristics to uniquely identify devices. We leverage the fact that any application or transport-layer fingerprint will be common to the lower level network protocol, whether IPv4 or IPv6. We use coarse-grained active operating system (OS) fingerprinting, e.g. [10], to eliminate clearly unrelated IPv4 and IPv6 addresses. However, OS fingerprinting alone does not provide sufficient granularity to accurately classify true siblings as the set of possible OSes is small relative to the set of possible addresses.

We therefore leverage previous work on physical device fingerprinting [9]. Kohno's technique measures a machine's clock drift by obtaining TCP-layer timestamps from the remote machine. While this technique has been used in the past, we apply it in a new context and reappraise its feasibility 10 years later. More importantly, skew-based fingerprinting has been primarily used on network clients, rather than servers. We find several interesting server-specific behaviors, e.g. load-balancing, that we take into account. Second, we enhance and combine the technique with other fingerprinting methods. We then evaluate the accuracy of our technique on a distributed set of ground-truth web servers. Last, we apply the method to the new problem of actively interrogating remote IPv4 and IPv6 endpoints over TCP to determine if they are server siblings.

3   Methodology

Our methodology uses active fingerprinting at the TCP layer, as a host's TCP stack is common to both the underlying IPv4 and IPv6 stack. We combine several of such fingerprinting techniques to achieve the best accuracy. Our resulting active method can be run on-demand to provide a server sibling test.

A networked server may have one or more interfaces, each with one or multiple addresses. An interface's addresses can be IPv4, IPv6, or a combination. Our TCP fingerprinting techniques attempt to determine whether a given IPv4 and IPv6 address share a common TCP stack. If the determination is "yes," then we are confident (see Sect. 4 on ground truth) that the two address are on the same server (and in practice likely the same interface), and we classify the address pair as siblings. If the determination is "no," then we are confident that the addresses are on separate interfaces, and most likely separate machines, and we classify the address pair as non-siblings.

3.1   Datasets

This work considers four datasets shown in Table 1. First, a ground-truth dataset (1) where the IPv4 and IPv6 addresses are known to be co-located on the same

Table 1. Properties of the four datasets probed

	Dataset	Hosts	# v4 AS	# v6 AS	Countries	# Option Signatures
(1)	Ground Truth	61	34	34	19	13
(2)	Alexa embedded	1050	85	80	31	30
(3)	Alexa non-CDN	1533	629	575	69	73
(4)	Alexa CDN	230	59	55	18	29

dual-stacked host. Then, for the subset of the Alexa [1] top 100,000 sites with both A and AAAA records in the DNS, we partition into set (2) sites where the IPv4 address is embedded in the corresponding IPv6 address. And for sites not in (2), partition into datasets: (3) those not part of a Content Distribution Network (CDN), and (4) those part of a CDN.

To develop and refine our association inference algorithm, we utilize ground-truth data consisting of 61 hosts with known IPv4/IPv6 association. While this set is relatively small, it spans 34 ASes and 19 countries. Importantly, it allows us to test not only our algorithm's recall (ability to identify true siblings), but also its precision (ability to identify ~1,800 possible combinations of non-siblings).

We query the DNS for the A and AAAA records of the Alexa hosts as retrieved in April, 2014. If the query returns multiple DNS records, we retain only the first. We perform the DNS resolution only once in order to obtain the IPv4 and IPv6 addresses. The remainder of our experimentation involves directly probing IPv4 and IPv6 addresses; the DNS is not subsequently consulted as to avoid dynamics due to DNS or DNS load-balancing.

A total of 6,387 sites in the Alexa top 100,000 have both IPv4 and IPv6 addresses. We remove 22 sites that return non-global IPv6 addresses, e.g. "::.." Because multiple sites can be hosted on one server, we reduce this set to 3,986 unique IPv4/IPv6 address pairs. Further, since the Alexa list is comprised of popular web sites, these sites are frequently part of a CDN. We observe that many sites use anycast, as inferred by collecting RTTs from geographically dispersed vantage points and finding those sites with RTTs that are not physically possible without anycast. We remove these sites from our analysis as to not conflate the effects of anycast with our inferences, leaving 2,813 unique address pairs.

When part of a CDN, the same website is often hosted on multiple machines distributed across sites or geographic regions. We therefore separate the Alexa hosts into those that are part of a CDN versus those that are not. To distinguish CDN site, we query the DNS for the site from five geographically dispersed vantage points. If we obtain different A or AAAA records from multiple vantage points, we label the site as belonging to a CDN. In addition, if the site's DNS CNAME corresponds to a well-known CDN, we place it in the CDN dataset.

Last, we create the "embedded" dataset. In practice, IPv4 addresses are frequently embedded in IPv6 addresses in different ways. We include instances where the IPv4 address is embedded as four bytes, e.g. 162.159.243.37 and 2400:cb00:2048:1::a29f:f325, or where the IPv4 base-10 representation is used as a base-16 sequence, e.g. 142.8.72.175 and 2a01:f1:d0:dc0:142:8:72:175.

Table 1 characterizes the distribution of hosts in each dataset, including the number of IPv4 and IPv6 ASes they represent as inferred from the routeviews global BGP table [12] from the same day as our Alexa site list (April 14, 2014), as well as the geographic distribution as determined by maxmind [11].

3.2   TCP Option Signature

Modern TCP stacks make common use of TCP options, especially options in [8]. While options are standardized, the order and packing of those options is implementation dependent, thereby providing a well-known operating system-granularity fingerprint [10]. For example, FreeBSD in our dataset returns: `<mss 1460, nop, wscale 3, sackOK, TS>` whereas a Linux machine returns: `<mss 1460, sackOK, TS, nop, wscale 4>`.

To form the signature, we preserve the option order, and strip the integer value of the MSS and timestamp options. While the IPv6 MSS is frequently 20 bytes less than the IPv4 MSS (to accommodate the extra 20 bytes of IPv6 header), this is a loose rule in our ground-truth. Some hosts connect via tunnels, with a lower IPv6 MSS, while some hosts support jumbo-grams only for IPv4.

While coarse-grained, the variability of the TCP options signature provides a good first-order filter. Table 1 reports the number of unique TCP option signatures observed for each of the datasets.

3.3   TCP Timestamp Skew

Define a candidate pair as (I_4, I_6). We periodically connect to a running TCP service on I_4 and I_6 and negotiate the TCP timestamp option [8]. We receive a sequence of time-stamped packets along with their arrival time relative to our prober. Let t_i^4 be the time at which the prober observes the i'th IPv4 packet from I_4 and t_i^6 be the observed time of the i'th IPv6 packet from I_6. Similarly, let T_i^4 and T_i^6 be the timestamp contained in the TCP options of the i'th packet from I_4 and I_6 respectively. Following the technique in [9], for each IPv4 packet we compute the *observed offset* or *skew*: $s_i^4 \equiv (T_i^4 - T_0^4) - (t_i^4 - t_0^4)$ and likewise for each IPv6 packet, $s_i^6 \equiv (T_i^6 - T_0^6) - (t_i^6 - t_0^6)$.

Given a sequence of skews, we compute drift via the linear programming solution in [13] to determine a line that is constrained to be under the data points, but minimizes the distance to the data points. We obtain:

$$y_4 = \alpha_4 x + \beta_4 \text{ and } y_6 = \alpha_6 x + \beta_6$$

I.e., two lines, one corresponding to the interrogation of I_4 and one to I_6 that lower-bounds the set of offset points observed. The angle θ between them is:

$$\theta(\alpha_4, \alpha_6) = \tan^{-1} \left| \frac{\alpha_4 - \alpha_6}{1 + \alpha_4 \alpha_6} \right|$$

If $\theta < \tau$, then I_4 and I_6 are inferred to be siblings, where τ is a threshold. Empirically, we find that $\tau = 1.0$ degree is sufficiently discriminating.

Figure 1(a) and (b) illustrate the approach using two hosts for which we know their ground-truth interface addresses. Figure 1(a) displays the observed drift from interrogating Host A's IPv6 interface as compared to Host B's IPv4 interface. We observe not only different drift, but see that the clocks on the

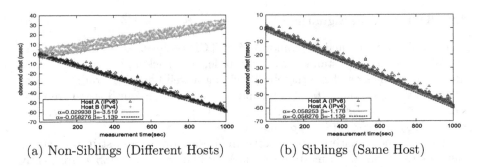

(a) Non-Siblings (Different Hosts)   (b) Siblings (Same Host)

Fig. 1. Timestamp drift of candidate siblings.

respective host are drifting in opposite directions and have different resolutions. Hence, we infer that the IPv4 and IPv6 interfaces are *non-siblings* ($\theta \geq \tau$).

In contrast, Fig. 1(b) displays a *sibling* relationship. In this experiment, we probe the same host (A) via its IPv4 and IPv6 interfaces. We observe nearly identical inferred skew (the linear programming solution determined as $\alpha_4 = -0.058253, \beta_4 = -1.178$ and $\alpha_6 = -0.058276, \beta_6 = -1.139; \theta = 1.3 \times 10^{-3}$).

3.4   TCP Timestamp Point Distance

In our ground-truth testing of the TCP timestamp skew, we make three general observations: (i) some machines now have clocks with negligible drift (e.g. Fig. 2(a)); (ii) some clocks we observe exhibit non-linearity in their skews (e.g. Fig. 2(b)); and (iii) the observed skew of two distinct machines, but with the same OS and located in the same rack, can be very similar (e.g. Fig. 2(c)).

These complicating factors, which Kohno did not observe in 2005, motivate a second test on the TCP timestamps: pair-wise point distance. For each IPv4 packet, with arrival time t_i^4, we find the IPv6 packet whose arrival time is closest (either before or after), say it is packet j, with arrival time t_j^6. We define the absolute value of difference in skews of these two packets to be the pair-wise point difference for IPv4 packet i: $diff(i) = |s_i^4 - s_j^6|$.

After some experimentation, we find that the median of the $diff(i)$'s to be most useful. Figure 2(c) illustrates the merit of the point distance method. The plotted IPv4 and IPv6 skews are from two different, but identical, physical machines in the same data center. The timestamp drifts appear very similar and yield $\theta = 0.358$ degrees, which is less than the τ threshold. Thus, with the skew inference alone, these two addresses would erroneously be inferred to be siblings. However, the point distance correctly rejects them: the median difference is above a chosen threshold of 100 msec.

3.5   Full Algorithm

Algorithm 1 presents pseudocode for the logic to infer whether I_4 and I_6 are siblings. First, we probe I_4 and I_6 over time to obtain the TCP option signatures

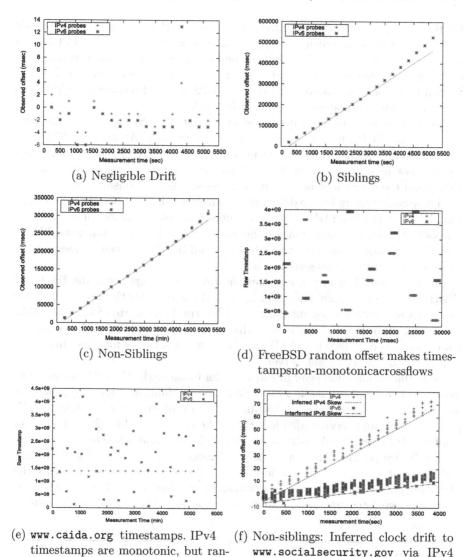

(a) Negligible Drift

(b) Siblings

(c) Non-Siblings

(d) FreeBSD random offset makes times-tampsnon-monotonicacrossflows

(e) `www.caida.org` timestamps. IPv4 timestamps are monotonic, but random for IPv6 due to a proxy.

(f) Non-siblings: Inferred clock drift to `www.socialsecurity.gov` via IPv4 and IPv6

Fig. 2. Examples of insufficient drift angle, necessitating point distance (Sect. 3.4) (a–c) and complicated association inferences (d–f).

$Signature^{4,6}$ and vectors of skew measurements $s^{4,6}$. The first condition (line 3) is to test whether the option signatures differ (Sect. 3.2), in which case we infer that the addresses are non-siblings and terminate.

We observe that the options returned by various TCP stacks can be divided into five cases: (1) no options returned; (2) timestamp not present in options; (3) timestamps non-monotonic between connections; (4) timestamps are random;

(5) timestamps are monotonic. Lines (4–8) tests for these cases. Non-monotonic timestamps can occur when I_4 or I_6 are addresses of a front-end load balancer and the clocks of the machines behind the load balancing are not precisely synchronized. In this case, the timestamps of a single flow are monotonic, but can be non-monotonic across connections. In addition, we also observe TCP stacks where the timestamp always starts at 1 for each connection.

Next are random timestamps. Some TCPs, notably BSD-based [16], randomize the initial TCP timestamp values on a per-flow basis. As shown in Fig. 2(d), the timestamps increase linearly from some random offset for each connection and are not monotonic across flows. When one addresses presents randomized values and the other does not, we infer a non-sibling relationship.

These cases present both a difficulty and an opportunity. When the timestamps from both the IPv4 and IPv6 address are non-monotonic, missing, or random, we cannot infer a definitive relation and classify their association as "unknown." However, if one protocol matches one of the cases and the other protocol does not, we conclude that the addresses are not related.

As a real-world example, consider the raw timestamps from the IPv4 and IPv6 addresses of www.caida.org in Fig. 2(e). While the IPv4 timestamps increase monotonically with a constant skew, the IPv6 timestamps are random. In addition, the TCP option signatures were different. Correspondence with the system administrators revealed that the IPv6 address was a separate machine that acted as a proxy for the IPv4 web server.

Note that application layer fingerprints, for instance the HTTP headers in our experiment, are not a reliable sibling detection mechanism. Figure 2(f) presents one example in our dataset to highlight our use of granular fingerprints. We probe the site and receive identical HTTP headers via either IPv4 or IPv6 in response. However, the drift-based inference clearly shows these as non-siblings.

Lastly, we perform the skew-based inference (Sect. 3.3), lines 9–12. When testing Algorithm 1 against ground truth, we find corner cases where either the algorithm could not make a determination, or was incorrect. With some experimentation, we determine some additional, simple logic that improved the results.

Algorithm 1. Siblings(I^4, I^6)

1: $(s^4, Signature^4) \Leftarrow probe(I^4)$
2: $(s^6, Signature^6) \Leftarrow probe(I^6)$
3: **if** $Signature^4 \neq Signature^6$ **then return** false
4: **for** case in 'missing', 'non-mono', 'rand' **do**
5:     **if** $case(s^4) = True$ and $case(s^6) = True$ **then**
6:         **return** unknown
7:     **if** $case(s^4) = True$ or $case(s^6) = True$ **then**
8:         **return** false
9: $(\alpha_4, \alpha_6) = slopes(s^4, s^6)$
10: $\theta = angle(\alpha_4, \alpha_6)$
11: **if** $\theta < \tau$ **then return** true
12: **else return** false

However, this logic relies on some rather arbitrary parameter values. We include it here as an optional enhancement, Algorithm 2. We believe that further refinement is possible.

Algorithm 2. Optional, enhancement to Algorithm 1

10: *median* $\Leftarrow$ point distances $diff(i)$'s
11: *range* $\Leftarrow$ max minus min of observed skews
12: **if** *range* < 100 **then return** unknown
13: **if** $(|\alpha_4| \leq 0.0001)$ or $(|\alpha_6| \leq 0.0001)$ **then**
14:     **if** *median* $\leq$ *range*/10 **then return** true
15:     **else return** false
16: **if** *median* > 100 **then return** false
17: return to Algorithm 1 at step 10.

The core reason the drift inference works is that, in the common-case, the remote server's TCP timestamp clock is less accurate than the prober host's packet capture clock. However, in contrast to prior work, we find that for a subset of the machines we probe, the TCP timestamps are set by a clock that is as stable as that of the probing machine, such that the only source of skew comes from probing latency variation (e.g. Fig. 2(a)). As an alternative, we compute the median of the point distances (Sect. 3.4) in line 10 of Algorithm 2, and the *dynamic range* of the skews, defined as: the largest skew observed over time, for either IPv4 or IPv6, minus the smallest skew, line 11. (In the plots of skew, the range is the largest y-coordinate minus the smallest.) If the dynamic range is below a threshold, we cannot obtain a reliable skew fingerprint, as in Fig. 2(a), and classify the relationship as unknown, line 12. Similarly, if either the IPv4 or IPv6 slope (α_4 or α_6) is below a threshold *minslope* $= 0.0001$, we consider the skew-based inference unreliable, line 13. In this case, if the median point distance is an order of magnitude less than the dynamic range we associate the IPs (lines 14–15). Last, if the median point distance is >100 ms, we infer non-siblings.

A limitation of our technique is that we require the ability to negotiate a TCP connection with the remote device, i.e. the remote machine must be listening on a publicly accessible TCP port. As applied to common server infrastructure, e.g. remote web or DNS servers, this does not present a practical limitation.

4 Results

This section analyzes results from deploying the aforementioned technique on our datasets, including ground-truth and the larger IPv4 and IPv6 Internet.

4.1 Ground Truth Validation

To validate the accuracy of our technique, we examine the ground truth dataset described in Sect. 3.1. We perform multiple rounds of testing. While the data provides us with true associations, for evaluation purposes, we also test false associations in each round. These known non-siblings are formed by randomly associating a non-associated IPv6 site with each IPv4 site. In this fashion, we test both type I and type II errors.

Table 2. Relative Ground Truth Performance of Sibling Classifiers

Algorithm	Accuracy	Precision	Recall	Specificity	Unknown
TCP Opts	82.2%	74.1%	98.2%	66.8%	0.0%
Kohno	90.6%	82.3%	97.0%	86.4%	27.8%
Alg 1	94.2%	93.6%	91.4%	96.0%	22.4%
Alg 1&2	97.4%	99.6%	93.1%	99.8%	29.4%

We wish to understand discriminative power of both the original Kohno timestamp skew algorithm, as well as our enhancements, in distinguishing siblings from non-siblings. First, we look at using TCP options as a classifier alone. As shown in Table 2, TCP options yield an accuracy of 82.2% with 74.1% precision, 98% recall, and 67% specificity. (Where precision is the fraction of identified siblings that are truly siblings, recall is the fraction of all ground-truth siblings classified as siblings, and specificity measures the ability to identify non-siblings). Thus, while the option signature alone does not provide sufficient granularity, it eliminates non-siblings with minimal overhead (just a single TCP ACK packet from the IPv4 and IPv6 target).

We next examine Kohno's original timestamp skew algorithm alone, without consideration of TCP options. Over ten rounds, we obtain an accuracy of 90.6% with 82.3% precision, 97.0% recall and 86.4% specificity. We then examine Algorithm 1 and the combined Algorithms 1 and 2 as detailed in Sect. 3.5. We see that each provides increasingly accurate sibling classification, with the full algorithm yielding an accuracy of 97.4%, with 99.6% precision, 93.1% recall, and 99.8% specificity over the ten rounds of testing. However, some of this accuracy comes at the expense of our full algorithm labeling 29.4% of the hosts as "unknown" as it cannot make a definitive determination.

4.2   Web Server Machine Siblings

As an initial application of our sibling detection technique, we characterize sibling relationships among a subset of important Internet infrastructure, Alexa [1] top 100,000 websites as gathered, resolved, and probed in April, 2014 (details of dataset in Sect. 3.1). We perform our probing from a host with high-speed, native IPv6 connectivity. To remain inconspicuous, we probe at a low rate. We fetch the root HTML page from each site's IPv4 and IPv6 interfaces once every ~3.5 h over ~17 days.

We then apply our inference Algorithm 1 and 2 to the datasets in Table 1. As described in Sect. 3, there are a variety of potential outcomes. For each of

Table 3. Alexa Machine-Sibling Inferences

	Dataset (Table 1)		
Inference	non-CDN	CDN	Embedded
Siblings			
- v4/v6 drift match	816 (53.2%)	55 (23.9%)	978 (93.1%)
Non-Siblings			
- v4 and v6 opt sig differ	229 (14.9%)	14 (6.1%)	22 (2.1%)
- v4 or v6 missing	70 (4.6%)	11 (4.8%)	7 (0.7%)
- v4 or v6 random	23 (1.5%)	13 (5.7%)	1 (0.1%)
- v4 or v6 non-monotonic	52 (3.4%)	47 (20.4%)	1 (0.1%)
- v4/v6 drift mismatch	35 (2.3%)	13 (5.7%)	0 (0.0%)
Unknown			
- v4 and v6 missing	196 (12.8%)	6 (2.6%)	26 (2.5%)
- v4 and v6 random	32 (2.1%)	25 (10.9%)	6 (0.6%)
- v4 and v6 non-monotonic	78 (5.1%)	45 (19.6%)	9 (0.9%)
- v4 or v6 unresponsive	2 (0.1%)	1 (0.4%)	0 (0.0%)
Total	1533 (100%)	230 (100%)	1050 (100%)

the three Alexa datasets, we divide the inferences into three major categories in Table 3: siblings, non-siblings, and unknown.

In aggregate, we find 53.2% of the IPv4/IPv6 addresses of non-CDN, 23.9% of CDN, and 93.1% of embedded are siblings via the full Algorithm 1 and 2. Fully 42.6% of the CDN, and 26.7% of the non-CDN have addresses we infer to be non-siblings. While we expect a high proportion of siblings among sites with embedded addresses, 3.0% are non-sibling underscoring the fact that addresses alone do not imply the same machine. And we cannot definitively determine 20% of the non-CDN, 33.5% of the CDN, and 3.9% of the embedded sites.

The largest contributing subset of non-monotonic timestamps are CDN sites – as we might expect due to the various forms of load balancing inherent in CDN architectures. A non-trivial fraction of non-CDN and CDN sites have missing timestamps. We learned via personal communication with an operator that missing timestamps in one case were due to a front-end load balancing device; similar middlebox issues [4] likely cause the missing timestamps observed here.

Among the sibling and non-sibling populations, we examine the origin AS of the prefixes to which the addresses belong from the routeviews [12] BGP table. The origin AS of the corresponding IPv4 and IPv6 addresses of a website allow us to determine whether non-siblings are within the same network, if not the same host. As shown in Table 4, 21.8% of the non-siblings in our non-CDN dataset are in different ASes, as compared to 10% of the siblings. Siblings may be in different ASes when an organization uses IPv6 tunnels or a different AS for IPv6. By contrast, 97.3% of the inferred siblings among the embedded sites are

Table 4. Alexa Machine-Sibling AS Agreement

Inference	Fraction of matching (I^4, I^6) ASNs		
	non-CDN	CDN	Embedded
Siblings	90.0 %	83.6 %	97.3 %
Non-Siblings	78.2 %	51.0 %	87.1 %
Unknown	91.6 %	62.3 %	78.0 %

within the same AS. Only 51 % of the non-siblings among the CDN sites reside within the same AS. Manual investigation of some of the siblings in different ASes reveals that the ASes belong to the same organization.

5   Conclusions and Future Work

We developed, validated, and applied a method for using TCP-layer fingerprinting techniques to identify IPv4 and IPv6 addresses that belong to the same machine. By combining coarse and fine-grained TCP-layer fingerprinting, we identify server "siblings." We can imagine several other applications of sibling interface identification: predicting correlated failures or similar behaviors under attack (and whether the IPv4 and IPv6 interfaces share fate); IPv6 geolocation that leverages knowledge of the corresponding IPv4 address; and comparing IPv4 and IPv6 path performance, by providing certainty as to whether a measurement end-point is common; and more generally, understanding how IPv6 and IPv4 network infrastructures are co-evolving at a macroscopic level. Although we applied our technique to web servers, it generalizes to any device with a listening TCP service, including DNS, email, and peer-to-peer services.

Although our technique validated surprisingly well for our diverse set of ground truth, we see at least three areas for improvement. First, the optional enhancement algorithm (Algorithm 2) we used to classify problematic cases contains parameters and thresholds that may overfit our data. A larger ground-truth dataset would support further refinement and higher confidence in our inferences. Second, although we detect certain instances of TCP load-balancing by observing multiple monotonic sequences with different initial offsets, it would be better to use reverse-proxy detection techniques to discern cases where a TCP-splitting proxy sits in front of the interrogated web server.

Last, our preliminary sensitivity results show that our inferences are stable even with fewer data points and over shorter time frames. Our technique can make some sibling inferences quickly, with only a few TCP observations, whereas others require samples across longer time periods. We leave a complete temporal sensitivity analysis to future work.

Acknowledgments. Thanks to kc claffy, Justin Rohrer, Nick Weaver, and Geoffrey Xie for invaluable feedback. This work supported by in part by NSF grant CNS-1111445 and Department of Homeland Security (DHS) S&T contract N66001-2250-58231. Views and conclusions are those of the authors and should not be interpreted as representing the official policies, either expressed or implied, of the U.S. government.

References

1. Alexa: Top 1,000,000 sites (2014). http://www.alexa.com/topsites
2. Berger, A., Weaver, N., Beverly, R., Campbell, L.: Internet nameserver IPv4 and IPv6 address relationships. In: Proceedings of the ACM Internet Measurement Conference. pp. 91–104 (2013)
3. Claffy, K.: Tracking IPv6 evolution: data we have and data we need. SIGCOMM Comput. Commun. Rev. **41**(3), 43–48 (2011)
4. Craven, R., Beverly, R., Allman, M.: A middlebox-cooperative TCP for a non end-to-end internet. In: Proceedings of ACM SIGCOMM, pp. 151–162 (2014)
5. Czyz, J., Allman, M., Zhang, J., Iekel-Johnson, S., Osterweil, E., Bailey, M.: Measuring IPv6 adoption. In: Proceedings of ACM SIGCOMM, pp. 87–98 (2014)
6. Dhamdhere, A., Luckie, M., Huffaker, B., Elmokashfi, A., Aben, E., et al.: Measuring the deployment of IPv6: topology, routing and performance. In: Proceedings of the ACM Internet Measurement Conference, pp. 537–550 (2012)
7. Heuse, M.: Recent advances in IPv6 insecurities. In: Chaos Communications Congress (2010)
8. Jacobson, V., Braden, R., Borman, D.: TCP Extensions for High Performance. RFC 1323 (May 1992)
9. Kohno, T., Broido, A., Claffy, K.C.: Remote physical device fingerprinting. In: Proceedings of IEEE Security and Privacy, pp. 211–225 (2005)
10. Lyon, G.F.: Nmap Network Scanning: The Official Nmap Project Guide to Network Discovery and Security Scanning (2009)
11. Maxmind: IP Geolocation (2014). http://www.maxmind.com
12. Meyer, D.: University of Oregon RouteViews (2014). http://www.routeviews.org
13. Moon, S., Skelly, P., Towsley, D.: Estimation and removal of clock skew from network delay measurements. In: Proceedings of INFOCOM, vol. 1 (Mar 1999)
14. Ripe, NCC: World IPv6 day measurements (2011). http://v6day.ripe.net
15. Sarrar, N., Maier, G., Ager, B., Sommer, R., Uhlig, S.: Investigating IPv6 Traffic. In: Taft, N., Ricciato, F. (eds.) PAM 2012. LNCS, vol. 7192, pp. 11–20. Springer, Heidelberg (2012)
16. Silbersack, M.J.: Improving TCP/IP security through randomization without sacrificing interoperability. In: Proceedings of BSDCan (2006)
17. Zander, S., Andrew, L.L., Armitage, G., Huston, G., Michaelson, G.: Mitigating sampling error when measuring internet client IPv6 capabilities. In: Proceedings of the ACM Internet Measurement Conference, pp. 87–100 (2012)

Internet-Wide

On the Power and Limitations of Detecting Network Filtering via Passive Observation

Matthew Sargent[1]([✉]), Jakub Czyz[2], Mark Allman[3], and Michael Bailey[4]

[1] Case Western Reserve University, Cleveland, OH, USA
matthew.sargent@case.edu
[2] University of Michigan, Ann Arbor, MI, USA
[3] Intl. Computer Science Institute, Berkeley, CA, USA
[4] University of Illinois at Urbana-Champaign, Champaign, IL, USA

Abstract. Network operators often apply policy-based traffic filtering at the egress of edge networks. These policies can be detected by performing active measurements; however, doing so involves instrumenting every network one wishes to study. We investigate a methodology for detecting policy-based service-level traffic filtering from passive observation of *traffic markers* within darknets. Such markers represent traffic we expect to arrive and, therefore, whose absence is suggestive of network filtering. We study the approach with data from five large darknets over the course of one week. While we show the approach has utility to expose filtering in some cases, there are also limits to the methodology.

1 Introduction

In this paper we develop a methodology for broadly understanding policy-based network filtering across the Internet. We begin with three observations from previous work:

Policy-based Filtering Happens: We understand from experience and anecdote that network operators apply policy-based filters to traffic leaving their networks. These filters are used for myriad reasons, including (*i*) because particular traffic types are not meant to traverse wide-area networks (e.g., internal file sharing), (*ii*) to prevent services from being leveraged by external devices (e.g., using an internal mail server as an open relay), (*iii*) to funnel all user traffic through some proxy (e.g., to implement capacity-saving caching or content-based filtering) and (*iv*) to prevent propagation of malware. The community has previously taken modest steps to empirically understand such filtering. For instance, the Netalyzr [12] tool determines whether 25 popular services are blocked or not via active probing from within the network under study.

Missing Traffic Illuminates Network Behavior: Previous research shows that we can detect broad network outages by monitoring dark address space for the *curious absence* of traffic. In other words, when a large darknet suddenly receives no background radiation from a previously active network, we can conclude there is a change in policy. This has been studied in the context of both

© Springer International Publishing Switzerland 2015
J. Mirkovic and Y. Liu (Eds.): PAM 2015, LNCS 8995, pp. 165–178, 2015.
DOI: 10.1007/978-3-319-15509-8_13

political events [10] which cause authorities to sever ties with the Internet, as well as natural disasters [3] which have the same impact on network traffic, even if these do not share the goal of policies that thwart communication of political adversaries.

Malware is Ubiquitous: A wealth of compromised devices on edge networks try to indiscriminately propagate using a set of vulnerabilities that span services [1,18].

We believe the above suggests we can leverage the ubiquity of background radiation to form an expectation that specific *marker traffic* should arrive from a given origin network. When the expectation fails to hold, we are left with the strong suggestion of a policy-based filter hindering the specific kind of traffic in a given origin network. As a concrete exemplar, we study this technique in the context of over 96 billion Conficker packets that arrive at our darknet to form a broad understanding of TCP port 445 filtering in origin networks across the Internet.

By studying one week of traffic arriving at five /8 darknets—roughly 2.25 % of the IPv4 address space—we find evidence that both supports and refutes our hypothesis. We find that in the case of Conficker—a large malware outbreak— detecting silence from a given origin network for a given kind of traffic does in fact allow us to understand the policy filters in place across the Internet. On the other hand, while we observe much malware in our datasets, we find each specific kind of traffic rarely spans enough of the origin networks to broadly develop an expectation that the given traffic should be present and thus develop conclusions based on the absence of such traffic. Therefore, we also learn that searching for silence in darknet traffic is limited to only significant events—i.e., full outages or large malware outbreaks. However, even with the limitations, we will show that the general approach does increase our broad understanding of policy-based traffic filtering.

2   Related Work

We leverage a number of technologies and techniques that have been developed by the community, including observing background radiation (e.g., [14,18]), and using darknets as an observatory (e.g., [2]). None of this previous work addresses the topic of inferring service-level network policy via passive observation, which we tackle in this paper.

Meanwhile, studying policy-based network filtering of various kinds has previously been conducted via active measurements from the edge network under study (e.g., [4,5,8,12]). The policies the previous work addresses are myriad— from the impact of bogon filtering to the ability to spoof packets to service-level policies. The wealth of work illustrates the interest in this topic. Our goals are similar to some of this previous work; however, our approach is to leverage passive measurements to understand the Internet broadly without the need to instrument every edge network, which is at best a large logistical undertaking.

The closest work to ours is in using the lack of background radiation from a given network to detect large scale outages that stem from natural disasters [3] or political events [10]. Our work shares their general notion that a lack of background radiation destined to a darknet can illuminate events within the network. We take this notion a step further and detect service-level policies applied to network traffic.

3   Data Collection

We use two primary sources of data for this study. The first dataset is a list of known Conficker infected hosts obtained via the Conficker domain sinkhole [13]. The Conficker worm [15] has been plaguing the Internet since 2008 and, six years later, continues to be the top globally-detected worm in the first half of 2014 [11]. It propagates via several vulnerabilities in Microsoft Windows, as well as via dictionary attacks on passwords. Propagation via the network vector involves scanning random IPs on TCP port 445 [6]. A flaw in the random number generator results in Conficker only targeting IP addresses with both second and fourth octets less than 128, which effectively excludes more than three-quarters of addresses from ever being scanned [16]. One of the main ways that Conficker has been disabled by researchers is to pre-emptively determine and register botnet-related domain names—which are generated algorithmically—that the malware uses for command and control. Subsequently, by observing communication to these domains, we are able to discover IP addresses of Conficker-infected hosts [13]. The list of infected IP addresses we use in this study was collected at the same time as our darknet data (described below) and contains 17.5M Conficker infected hosts from 1.6M/24 networks.

The second dataset is a set of packet traces of traffic arriving at five unallocated IPv4 darknets: 23.0.0.0/8, 37.0.0.0/8, 45.0.0.0/8, 100.0.0.0/8, and 105.0.0.0/8. We obtained permission from the Regional Internet Registrars (RIRs) to simultaneously announce these network blocks for one week, January 14–20, 2011. We validated that our routes for these prefixes were globally visible to the majority of Route Views' [17] 121 peers during the week of our data collection. In aggregate, our darknet observes traffic to nearly 84M IPv4 addresses or roughly 2.25 % of the usable IPv4 address space. While using darknets is a well-known technique (e.g., [18]), to our knowledge, this is the largest simultaneous IPv4 darknet collection to date.

In total, our darknet data comprises roughly 96.1B packets from 4.1M/24 address blocks in the Internet. Table 1 gives a broad characterization of our darknet data. Due to the lack of two-way traffic, we are unable to directly estimate how much measurement-based packet loss impacts our dataset. However, we have previously used the monitor to capture traffic at 1 Gbps without significant loss and the average rate of the darknet data is less than 98 Mbps. Therefore, we do not believe the amount of traffic our monitor failed to collect rises to the point of impacting our high-order conclusions.

Next, we classify the darknet data into five categories: (*i*) *Conficker* traffic represents TCP SYNs to port 445 from a known Conficker-infected host;

Table 1. Darknet data characterization.

Address Block	Packets (billions)	Bytes (trillions)	Rate (Mbps)	Rate (Kpps)	Source/24s (millions)
100/8	22.1	1.7	22.5	36.7	3.1
105/8	17.1	1.1	15.0	28.2	2.1
23/8	16.9	1.8	23.4	28.0	2.6
37/8	21.7	1.5	20.3	35.9	2.4
45/8	18.2	1.3	16.6	30.1	2.3
All	96.1	7.4	97.8	159	4.1

(*ii*) *Likely Conficker* traffic includes TCP SYNs to port 445 from hosts not on the Conficker-infected host list but to an IP address that Conficker is known to target; (*iii*) *Scanning* traffic represents TCP SYNs that could not be produced by Conficker processes; (*iv*) *Backscatter* traffic represents SYN+ACK packets that are likely the result of SYNs spoofed to be from our darknet; and (*v*) *Other* traffic, which includes all traffic not falling into one of the other categories. Figure 1 shows the breakdown of the traffic captured to each /8 we monitor. We note that the amount of Conficker traffic is relatively uniform across the /8 blocks we monitor.

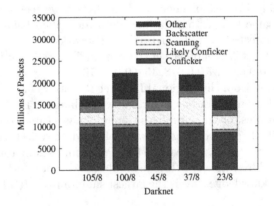

Fig. 1. Traffic volume by category for each darknet.

A final caveat is that we cannot verify the source addresses in packets arriving at our monitor. We know spoofing is both possible and likely present—e.g., see the amount of backscatter in Fig. 1 as an indication of the prevalence of spoofing. Therefore, in the remainder of the paper we take care to include this ambiguousness in our interpretation of the results.

4   Preliminaries

As we discuss in Sect. 1, our hypothesis is that we can use the background radiation from malware to infer filtering policies across the Internet. In this section we offer several comments on the efficacy of this approach in general and also for specifically detecting policy-based TCP port 445 filtering.

General Coverage: A natural first question is whether we in fact observe traffic in our darknet from a broad spectrum of Internet endpoints. To quantify the fraction of the Internet that transmits traffic to our darknet we use routing tables from Route Views at the beginning of our darknet collection (January 13, 2011) to determine that 2.43B addresses are routed. The set of /24 networks we receive traffic from corresponds to 2.40B IP addresses when taking into account routed prefix size—or, 98.8 % of the routed IP addresses. Some of this traffic is no doubt spoofed, so we compute the number of addresses belonging to /24s that send at least five scanning or backscatter packets[1]. We find 1.85B such addresses—or, 76.1 % of the routed IP addresses. This analysis leads us to conclude that background radiation—and the lack thereof—arrives at our darknet from a broad spectrum of the Internet and therefore is a potential source of information about policy-based filtering in the Internet.

Conficker Coverage: While the amount and breadth of background radiation offers hope that we can broadly detect filtering policy, Conficker is an imperfect marker. As we note above, Conficker-infected endpoints are known to inhabit 1.6M of 4.1M /24 address blocks we observe sending traffic to our darknet. This partially stems from the error in Conficker that prevents it from scanning three-quarters of the network. While the footprint of the marker scopes the amount of the network we can assess, we are unaware of any other technique that achieves this level of coverage. While not ideal, we believe even an imperfect marker can provide a better understanding than we have today.

Conficker Behavior: Another preliminary question we must tackle pertains to the behavior of Conficker. Before we can infer that we are missing some marker traffic, we must have an expectation about how much such traffic we should observe. In order to remain undetected, Conficker infectees only scan after five minutes of keyboard inactivity on a given host [7]. Further, Conficker has four scanning modes—a number of them localized in scope. Finally, an infected host obviously cannot scan when the host is powered off. Given these constraints, we cannot simply compute an expectation based on a model of each host scanning continually and uniformly.

We can determine a rough idea of whether we should expect to observe traffic from each infectee, as follows. We know that, when scanning, each infected machine pauses between 100 ms and 2 s between probes [7]. Given that we observe nearly 84M IP addresses, we would expect to observe one out of every 52 probes—or, one probe every 104 s if we assume the slowest scanning rate.

---

[1] Five is a somewhat arbitrary choice that weeds out /24 address blocks that send exceedingly little traffic for illustrative purposes.

Or, if we are to observe 10 probes from a given infected machine on each /8 we monitor, the host would have to scan for 86 min over the course of the week—or less than 1 % of the week. Therefore, our first order assumption—which we revisit in Sect. 5—is that we should observe Conficker activity from all infected hosts.

5   Validation

While the cursory analysis in Sect. 4 suggests inferring policy-based filtering of TCP port 445 should be possible given both the proliferation of Conficker and our broad vantage point, this section tests our assumptions and frames the confidence we can gain from the results. We note that given the breadth with which we aim to develop understanding, we have no ground truth. Therefore, we cannot absolutely prove our inferences correct, but aim to illustrate that they are likely to be so.

An Anecdote: Comcast provides a list of ports that are subject to policy filtering for its residential customers—including TCP/445 [9]. In our darknet data we find nearly 3M packets from Comcast's 76.102.0.0/15 address block. As expected, we find no TCP/445 traffic even though our list indicates 81 Conficker-infected hosts within the given address block. While this is an obviously anecdotal case, it is illustrative of our goal to detect policy from the absence of specific traffic from given address blocks.

Conficker Sending Behavior: The preliminary analysis in Sect. 4 suggests our darknet is big enough to observe all Conficker-infected hosts scanning with high probability based on what we know about Conficker's behavior. To check this we consider all Conficker infectees from /24 address blocks where we observe some traffic to TCP port 445. In this case, we do not believe there is a general policy against TCP/445 traffic at the /24 level. However, we find TCP/445 traffic from only 51 % of the infected hosts across these cases. Our data does not shed light on why we do not observe 49 % of the Conficker hosts. The reasons could be many, including policy at finer granularity than a /24 (even to the host granularity), reactive filtering in response to scanning and removal of Conficker from the machine. We combat this situation by requiring multiple Conficker infectees per address block to overcome the seeming failure of some Conficker hosts to send scanning traffic.

Active Measurement: As part of its suite of active measurements, Netalyzr [12] attempts to establish a TCP/445 connection to a known server. We have obtained the Netalyzr test results starting one month before and ending one month after our darknet data collection. We find 1,555 hosts in the Netalyzr data that are also infected with Conficker. We therefore can evaluate our technique using the Netalyzr results as ground truth. First, we find 176 hosts (11 %) where Netalyzr is run multiple times and shows inconsistent results. This shows that filtering policy and end-host behavior are not consistent across two months and therefore that the Netalyzr data is at best an approximation of ground truth with respect to the darknet data. For another 647 hosts, Netalyzr concludes a port-based filter is in place. The darknet data agrees with this assessment in 97 % of the cases. In the 3 % of the cases where Netalyzr concludes port filtering, we find a minimum of 17 TCP/445 packets from each host, with a median of 1,369 TCP/445 packets—and therefore we conclude that no filter is in place. We believe the likely cause for this is a policy change. Finally, Netalyzr finds 732 hosts to be unfiltered. However, we only observe 279 (38 %) send traffic to our darknet, seemingly leaving our method with a large error. However, we note that the analysis in the last paragraph shows that we can only expect traffic from roughly half the infected Conficker hosts. Applying that expectation, the accuracy of the inference from the darknet data increases to 76 %. As we note previously, the error can come from myriad places. Further, we show below that using multiple infected hosts can increase our confidence in our inferences.

Broad Comparison: Finally, we again compare our darknet observations with Netalyzr's results, but instead of using single IP addresses we will now aggregate results across /24 address block, routed block (determined from Route Views) and autonomous system. This allows us to bring multiple infected hosts to bear on our inference, but at the expense of possibly observing multiple policy domains.

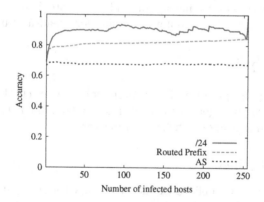

Fig. 2. Accuracy of the three methods when varying the number of infected hosts required before making comparisons with Netalyzr.

Figure 2 shows the accuracy of our inference with respect to the Netalyzr results as a function of the number of Conficker infected hosts for the given aggregate block.[2] This plot first illustrates that regardless of level of aggregation the accuracy roughly levels off once a handful of Conficker infectees are present within the block. Second, the tighter we scope the block the better the accuracy, with /24 blocks showing the best accuracy, followed by routed blocks and then

---

[2] There are more Conficker infected hosts in some of the routed blocks and ASes, however, we truncate the plot at 255 for comparison with /24 blocks.

autonomous systems. We believe this is because as we increase the aggregation the instances of multiple policy domains also increases. Therefore, trying to treat the entire block the same leads to incorrect inferences.

We find that approximately half the hosts that contact the Conficker command and control structure ultimately show up in our darknet data. We see this manifests in the accuracy rate in Fig. 2. Requiring five infected hosts per /24 should mean one of the Conficker infectees sends traffic with a 96 % likelihood. When applying this threshold and comparing with the Netalyzr results we find an accuracy of 80 %. In approximately 6 % of the cases Netalyzr determines the network is filtering traffic while we observe Conficker from the given /24 in our darknet data. Finally, in 14 % of the cases Netalyzr is able to establish a TCP/445 connection while we find no Conficker in our darknet collection and hence infer the given /24 is filtering TCP/445. While the reason for this discrepancy is not clear, we note that it will cause an over-estimate of the amount of filtering in the network.

Summary: As we show in this section, looking for the curious absence of traffic to understand fine-grain network filtering policy is not a clean process. We clearly need to understand the signal we expect to find. However, our conclusion is that, while this process is not perfect, we can use it to gain an approximate understanding of policy filtering in the network. Finally, while active measurements may be more precise, they are much more difficult to obtain on a large scale basis and therefore we are trading absolute precision for breadth of understanding.

6   Data Analysis

After establishing the promise of our methodology in Sects. 4 and 5, we now return to our high-level goal from Sect. 1 to understand network filtering of TCP port 445 traffic using Conficker as a marker.

6.1   /24-Based Policy

As we develop above, we believe Conficker is a marker that will illuminate network filtering policy for the broad regions of the network where it is known to exist—even if the marker is less than ideal in some situations. As a starting point, we aggregate and label traffic based on the source /24 address block, our expectations of Conficker, and the traffic that arrives in our darknet.

First, as we sketch in Sect. 4, we do not expect Conficker from roughly 60 % of the /24 blocks observed at our darknet monitors. For roughly 0.2 % of the /24 blocks from which we do not expect Conficker traffic we do in fact observe Likely Conficker at our darknet. This shows that the list of Conficker-infected hosts is comprehensive and not missing a significant portion of hosts infected with the malware. We do not further consider address blocks where we do not expect Conficker as we can infer nothing from its absence in these cases.

This leaves us with Conficker infectees in roughly 40 % of the /24 address blocks in our darknet data. We now need a process to label each /24 address block by its filtering policy. Given our validation work in Sect. 5, we proceed in two steps. First, when we observe Conficker traffic from a /24 block we determine there is no general TCP/445 filtering. Second, we know we cannot expect Conficker from all infectees, and so the absence of the marker does not necessarily indicate a network filter. Rather, we determine a /24 block is filtering TCP/445 when (*i*) we find no TCP/445 traffic in our darknet data and (*ii*) the /24 block has at least five infectees. As we develop in Sect. 5 the second criteria gives us at least 96 % confidence that Conficker should arrive and therefore when it does not we infer a policy-based filter.

We find 434K (27 %) of the 1.6M/24 blocks with Conficker infectees are not imposing TCP/445 filtering on their traffic. Meanwhile, we infer that 448K/24 blocks (28 %) filter TCP/445 traffic. That is, we are able to confidently characterize the filtering policy of 882K /24 networks—or 9.3 % of all the routed address space. This is, by far, a larger portion than previous methodologies can claim—e.g., Netalyzr runs from the month surrounding our data collection cover 23K/24 networks. Our analysis leaves 747K/24 blocks (45 %) from which we do not observe TCP/445 traffic but which do not contain five infectees. These are cases where we have an indication of possible filtering, but cannot develop high confidence in this determination.

6.2   Routed Prefix-Based Policy

We next turn to a larger aggregation of address blocks to better understand filtering policy at a coarser granularity. We leverage routed prefixes as found in Route Views at the time of our darknet data collection for this analysis. Our general method to infer whether filtering happens for an entire prefix is to look for consistent behavior from the /24 blocks within the prefix. Since we tackle /24 address blocks above, in this section we only study the 140 K routed prefixes that are at least a /23 (out of 254 K total routed prefixes).

Of the 140 K prefixes we consider, we find no Conficker infectees and no TCP/445 traffic for 61 K of the prefixes. We cannot further study these prefixes as we have no expectation of TCP/445 traffic and therefore the absence of such traffic does not inform our assessment of filtering. This leaves roughly 79 K prefixes on which we have some expectation of observing TCP/445 traffic. We summarize our results in Table 2.

First, when each /24 block containing at least one Conficker infectee within the routed prefix produces TCP/445 traffic we conclude the network applies no general TCP/445 filtering. Table 2 shows 13 % of the prefixes do not filter TCP/445. Similarly, when we observe no TCP/445 traffic for each /24 block containing at least one infectee across a prefix with at least five total infectees we conclude filtering is in place for the entire prefix. We find prefix-wide filtering in 35 % of the prefixes. We also find cases where no TCP/445 traffic arrives at our darknet, but the routed prefix contains fewer than five infectees. We cannot confidently determine that these prefixes filter TCP/445—even if the data suggests this may be the case. We denote these cases "low signal" in the table and find 28 % of the prefixes fall into this category.

Table 2. Labels assigned to routed prefixes /23 or larger based on their component /24s.

Classification	Amount	Percentage
No Filtering	10,084	13 %
Filtering	27,351	35 %
Multiple Policies	14,536	18 %
Low Signal	22,075	28 %
Muddled/No Filtering	5,178	7 %

Finally, we are left with prefixes that have indications of both no filtering—i.e., we observe TCP/445 traffic—and filtering—i.e., the infectee list suggests we should observe more TCP/445 traffic than we do. For cases where we observe traffic from at least five infectees we conclude that the prefix has multiple policies. In other words, we are confident in our determination that filtering is occurring within the prefix and yet we still observe TCP/445 traffic from the prefix. We find this happens in 18 % of the cases. As the size of the address blocks we consider increases this is a natural finding that follows our intuition—i.e., that the block would be split up into multiple policy domains. Finally, we have cases where we observe TCP/445 traffic and there are also indications we should see additional traffic, but from less than five infectees. In this case, we know filtering is not in use across the entire prefix and, even though we have some indication that filtering may be happening, we cannot conclude it is with confidence. We find 7 % of the prefixes in this "muddled" state.

We next consider the fraction of each prefix we use to determine its filtering policy. For each routed prefix, we calculate the fraction of the constituent /24 blocks (i) with a known Conficker infectee and (ii) where we conclusively determine that filtering is or is not present. Figure 3 shows the distribution of prefixes according to these fractions. The "all" distribution in the plot shows the expected prefix coverage based on the Conficker infectee list, whereas the "classified" distribution shows the fraction of /24 blocks we actually use in concrete prefix classifications. Comparing the distributions shows that, when making a classification, we generally use more of the prefix (i.e., more /24s) than the expectation predicts, which adds to our confidence in the classifications.

Next, we examine the size of the routed prefixes we are able to concretely classify. The distribution of the size of all routed prefixes we consider, as well as the distributions of the routed prefix sizes for each concrete classification we make are given in Fig. 4. The figure shows that the distribution of network size for networks we can concretely detect filtering policy is similar to the distribution of the size of all origin networks. In other words, neither our detection nor results are biased by prefix size. Further, we find that networks that filter TCP/445 are slightly larger than networks that do not filter TCP/445. This perhaps indicates that operators of larger networks are more diligent about security policy than

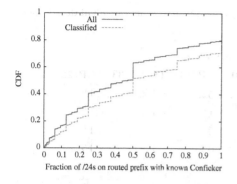

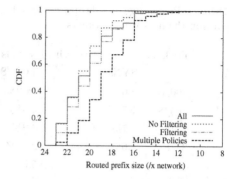

Fig. 3. CDF of the fraction of /24s on a routed prefix with known Conficker.

Fig. 4. CDF of the routed prefix sizes on which we make judgements.

those of smaller networks. Finally, we find that networks with multiple policies are larger than networks with a single policy. As we note above, this is natural because as network sizes increase the tendency to have multiple administrative and policy domains to cope with a variety of situations arises.

Finally, we note that we are able to confidently determine a single filtering policy in roughly half of the /23 and larger routed prefixes. This corresponds to 699M IP addresses or 28 % of the routable addresses during the week of our darknet data collection.

7 Limitations

From previous research we understand that full network outages—whether caused by policy decisions or natural disasters—can be detected by the absence of traffic arriving at darknets. Further, in the previous sections we illustrate that we can use similar strategies to infer finer-grained policy such as port blocking. As developed thus far, both the course- and fine-grained policy discovery requires big events— i.e., a broad swatch of the Internet becoming unreachable or malware that is both prevalent and energetically propagating.

A natural next question is whether the aggregate background radiation that appears at darknet monitors provides enough information to form further general understanding of policies across the Internet. To address this question we first determine the top TCP ports arriving at our darknet.[3] We then calculate the number of origin /24 networks that source each kind of traffic and compare this to the total number of origin /24s we observe. Table 3 shows the results. In the best case—port 80—we find SYNs from only 18 % of origin /24s we observe. This either means 82 % of the /24s either (*i*) are subject to policy blocking or (*ii*) do not source radiation to port 80. We believe the latter is far more likely

---

[3] We included UDP in our analysis, but elide it from this discussion due to space constraints and its similarity with the TCP results.

Table 3. Percentage of /24s observed sending TCP SYNs to other prevalent destination ports in the measured darknets.

Darknet	# /24s Receiving SYNs	% /24s w/SYN for			
		TCP/80	TCP/139	TCP/1433	TCP/22
100/8	2.0M	14.2%	1.5%	<1%	<1%
105/8	1.5M	4.0%	1.1%	<1%	<1%
23/8	1.7M	6.2%	1.0%	<1%	<1%
37/8	1.6M	21.6%	1.0%	<1%	<1%
45/8	1.6M	5.6%	1.1%	<1%	<1%
All	3.1M	18.2%	1.3%	<1%	<1%

than the former. That is, background radiation does not in general energetically target our darknet enough to develop a solid expectation that the traffic should be there and hence draw conclusions about its absence. Further, for the other top ports the prevalence is even smaller than for port 80 and, hence, makes any conclusions about policy even more tenuous.

Therefore, our conclusion is that while the general technique of searching for the absence of traffic can be useful, it has its limits.

8   Conclusions

This paper makes several high-order contributions:

Methodology: We develop a novel methodology for detecting service-level network filtering based on passive observation of traffic markers. While this aspect of the Internet has been previously studied, our passive observation-based technique allows for developing an understanding at a breadth previously unattainable. Using Conficker as our exemplar, we are able to conclusively determine the network filtering policy of 699M IP addresses or roughly 28% of the routed IPv4 address space. Although this is a modest fraction of the Internet, it is much larger than previous attempts. For instance, the original Netalyzr study [12] reports results from 100 K test runs. Even if each Netalyzr run represents a /24 network our results cover 27 times as much of the Internet.

State of TCP/445: Of the address space we can conclusively assess, we find filtering of outgoing TCP/445 traffic occurs in two-thirds of the cases. We also note that as the size of the routed prefix under study increases the chance of finding multiple service-level filtering policies within the prefix also increases. While we believe it is a natural and expected result that larger networks would encompass more than one administrative and policy domain, we believe this offers a cautionary note in that aggregating too much of the network can dilute any understanding we derive.

Methodological Limitations: Finally, we illustrate that there are limits to the methodology of using the absence of background radiation to infer policy. In particular, we can leverage large events to infer policy, but more run-of-the-mill instances of background radiation are not energetic and wide-spread enough to allow us to form the expectation of traffic and hence draw conclusions when the expectation fails.

Acknowledgments. We would like to thank Christian Kreibich for the Netalyzr data, Phillip Porras for the Conficker sinkhole data, and Vern Paxson for comments on an earlier draft. This work is sponsored by NSF grants CNS-1213157, CNS-1237265, CNS-1505790 and CNS-1111699.

References

1. Allman, M., Paxson, V., Terrell, J.: A brief history of scanning. In: Proceedings of the ACM SIGCOMM Conference on Internet Measurement, IMC'07 (2007)
2. Bailey, M., Cooke, E., Jahanian, F., Nazario, J., Watson, D.: The internet motion sensor: a distributed blackhole monitoring system. In: Proceedings of Network and Distributed System Security Symposium, NDSS'05, pp. 167–179 (2005)
3. Benson, K., Dainotti, A., claffy, k., Aben, E.: Gaining insight into AS-level outages through analysis of internet background radiation. In: Traffic Monitoring and Analysis Workshop, TMA'13 (2013)
4. Beverly, R., Berger, A., Hyun, Y., claffy, k.: Understanding the efficacy of deployed internet source address validation filtering. In: Proceedings of the ACM SIGCOMM conference on Internet Measurement, IMC'09 (2009)
5. Bush, R., Hiebert, J., Maennel, O., Roughan, M., Uhlig, S.: Testing the reachability of (new) address space. In: Proceedings of the SIGCOMM workshop on Internet Network Management, INM'07, pp. 236–241. ACM, New York (2007)
6. CAIDA: Conficker/Conflicker/Downadup as seen from the UCSD Network Telescope. http://www.caida.org/research/security/ms08-067/conficker.xml (2013)
7. Chien, E.: Downadup: attempts at smart network scanning. http://www.symantec.com/connect/blogs/downadup-attempts-smart-network-scanning (2009)
8. Choffnes, D.R., Bustamante, F.E., Ge, Z.: Crowdsourcing service-level network event monitoring. In: Proceedings of the Conference on Applications, Technologies, Architectures, and Protocols for Computer Communications, SIGCOMM'10 (2010)
9. Comcast: Blocked ports list. https://customer.comcast.com/help-and-support/internet/list-of-blocked-ports/
10. Dainotti, A., Squarcella, C., Aben, E., Claffy, K.C., Chiesa, M., Russo, M., Pescapé, A.: Analysis of country-wide internet outages caused by censorship. In: IMC '11 (2011)
11. F-Secure: Threat Report H1 2014. http://www.f-secure.com/documents/996508/1030743/Threat_Report_H1_2014.pdf (2014)
12. Kreibich, C., Weaver, N., Nechaev, B., Paxson, V.: Netalyzr: illuminating the edge network. In: Proceedings of the ACM SIGCOMM Conference on Internet Measurement, IMC'10 (2010)
13. Kristoff, J.: Experiences with conficker c sinkhole operation and analysis. In: Proceedings of Australian Computer Emergency Response Team Conference (2009)

14. Pang, R., Yegneswaran, V., Barford, P., Paxson, V., Peterson, L.: Characteristics of internet background radiation. In: Proceedings of the ACM SIGCOMM conference on Internet Measurement, IMC'04 (2004)
15. Porras, P., Saidi, H., Yegneswaran, V.: An analysis of conficker's logic and rendezvous points. Technical report, SRI International (2009)
16. Richard, M., Ligh, M.: Making fun of your malware. In: Defcon 17 (2009)
17. University of Oregon: Route Views project. http://www.routeviews.org/
18. Wustrow, E., Karir, M., Bailey, M., Jahanian, F., Houston, G.: Internet background radiation revisited. In: Proceedings of the ACM SIGCOMM Conference on Internet Measurement, IMC'10 (2010)

Distilling the Internet's Application Mix from Packet-Sampled Traffic

Philipp Richter[1]([✉]), Nikolaos Chatzis[1], Georgios Smaragdakis[1,2],
Anja Feldmann[1], and Walter Willinger[3]

[1] TU Berlin, Berlin, Germany
prichter@inet.tu-berlin.de
[2] MIT, Cambridge, USA
[3] NIKSUN, Inc., Princeton, USA

Abstract. As the Internet continues to grow both in size and in terms of the volume of traffic it carries, more and more networks in the different parts of the world are relying on an increasing number of distinct ways to exchange traffic with one another. As a result, simple questions such as "What is the application mix in today's Internet?" may produce non-informative simple answers unless they are refined by specifying the vantage point where the traffic is observed, the networks that are involved, or even the type of interconnection used.

In this paper, we revisit the question of the application mix in today's Internet and make two main contributions. First, we develop a methodology for classifying the application mix in packet-sampled traces collected at one of the largest IXPs in Europe and worldwide. We show that our method can classify close to 95 % of the traffic by relying on a *stateful* classification approach that uses payload signatures, communication patterns, and port-based classification only as a fallback. Second, our results show that when viewed from this vantage point and aggregated over all the IXP's public peering links, the Internet's application mix is very similar to that reported in other recent studies that relied on different vantage points, peering links or classification methods. However, the observed aggregate application mix is by no means representative of the application mix seen on individual peering links. In fact, we show that the business type of the ASes that are responsible for much of the IXP's total traffic has a strong influence on the application mix of their overall traffic and of the traffic seen on their major peering links.

1 Introduction

Knowing the Internet's application mix is important for tasks such as identifying the emergence of new trends in Internet usage, optimizing application performance, and provisioning network resources. As a result, there exists a growing body of literature on inferring the Internet's application mix, with the different papers typically relying on different data sources and deploying different traffic classification techniques (e.g., see [13,25,29] and references therein).

© Springer International Publishing Switzerland 2015
J. Mirkovic and Y. Liu (Eds.): PAM 2015, LNCS 8995, pp. 179–192, 2015.
DOI: 10.1007/978-3-319-15509-8_14

However, due to the heterogeneity of the Internet and its complex topology and global scope, there are no simple answers to questions like "What are the most popular applications in today's Internet?" or "What is the application mix in today's Internet?" In fact, as more and more networks consider factors such as cost, performance, security, ease-of-use, and flexibility when deciding about which kind of traffic to send over which type of peering links, the application mix can be expected to differ from link to link.

In this paper, we are primarily interested in how representative commonly-reported aggregate statistics concerning the Internet's application mix are in view of the network's enormous heterogeneity. To this end, we first develop a new methodology to classify traffic from packet-sampled traffic traces. Packet sampling is a widely employed technique when monitoring high-bandwidth infrastructures and is commonly used by large ISPs and IXPs. We then rely on traffic traces collected at such a large IXP and apply our traffic classification methodology to infer the application mix on tens of thousands of public peering links at this IXP.[1] Our results show that the heterogeneity of the Internet extends directly to the application mix of its traffic, and we illustrate the observed heterogeneity by providing insight into how and why the application mix can differ from interconnection to interconnection and among different types of networks.

Our contributions can be summarized as follows:

- We develop a traffic characterization methodology that is able to classify up to 95 % of the traffic in our dataset (i.e., peering traffic exchanged at a large IXP, see Sect. 2). The novelty of our methodology is that it uses a *stateful* classification technique (i.e., it keeps track of classified connection endpoints) that is by and large able to overcome the challenges posed by random packet sampling (see Sect. 3).
- We apply our new methodology to a set of traffic traces collected at a large European IXP over a period of 2.5 years and provide details about the aggregate application mix seen at this IXP, including pronounced diurnal cycles as well as trends that become visible when monitoring the application mix over time (see Sect. 4).
- We compare the aggregate application mix observed at our IXP to that reported in other recent studies, which use different techniques and vantage points. We find that when aggregated over all of the IXP's peering links, the observed application mix is comparable to the application mix reported in these studies. However, we also show that the aggregate application mix is by no means representative of the application mix seen on an individual peering link and that the business type of the networks on either side of these peering links has a strong influence on the application mix of the traffic that traverses those links (see Sect. 5).

---

[1] Traffic traversing the IXP's private peering links is not collected and not considered here.

2 Dataset Characteristics

In this paper, we rely on packet-sampled traffic traces captured from the public switching fabric of a large European IXP. We use five snapshots (selected from a period that spans 2.5 years), each covering a full week (168 consecutive hours). Table 1 lists the pertinent properties of these traces. Unless mentioned otherwise, we use the most recent snapshot (i.e., 09-2013) as default dataset.

During the most recently monitored period in September 2013, the IXP had close to 500 members and a peak traffic rate close to 2.5 Tbps. Our traces consist of sFlow [28] records, captured using a random packet sampling rate of 1-out-of-16K (2^{14}) packets. For more details on the sampling process and the IXP's peering link characteristics, see [7,27]. sFlow captures the first 128 bytes for each Ethernet frame. Thus, each packet includes the full link layer (Ethernet), network layer (IP), and transport layer (TCP/UDP) protocol headers, as well as a limited number of payload bytes. In the most common case, where the IPv4 and TCP protocols are used, this leaves 74 bytes worth of payload information (if TCP option fields are set, the available payload is further reduced by a few bytes).

Table 1. Overview of dataset characteristics. The number of packets/bytes refer to the number of packets collected i.e., after sampling.

Name	Timerange	Sampling	Packets	Bytes	IPv4/IPv6	TCP/UDP
09-2013	2013-09-02 to 2013-09-08	1/16 K	9.3 B	5.9 TB	99.36/0.63	83.7/16.3
12-2012	2012-12-01 to 2012-12-07	1/16 K	8.5 B	5.5 TB	99.64/0.36	83.1/16.9
06-2012	2012-06-04 to 2012-06-10	1/16 K	7.3 B	4.6 TB	99.80/0.20	80.7/19.3
11-2011	2011-11-28 to 2011-12-04	1/16 K	6.4 B	4.2 TB	99.93/0.07	79.8/20.2
04-2011	2011-04-25 to 2011-05-01	1/16 K	5.3 B	3.5 TB	99.94/0.06	79.2/20.3

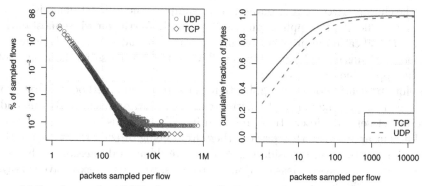

(a) Samples per flow (1200s timeout).

(b) Fraction of total bytes related to number of packets sampled per flow.

Fig. 1. IXP data sampling characteristics relevant for traffic classification.

In the following, we consider only IPv4 traffic, as the fraction of IPv6 is still below 1 % in all our snapshots.

The sampled nature of our datasets poses significant challenges when trying to apply traditional traffic-classification approaches (see Sect. 3 for details). To assess the impact of sampling on the visibility of "full" flows, we aggregate the packets sampled at our IXP using the typical 5-tuple aggregation consisting of source and destination IP addresses, source and destination port numbers, and the transport protocol. Figure 1(a) shows the number of packets that are sampled for each flow, using a 1200 s timeout. It shows that we see only a single packet for some 86 % of the sampled TCP flows (76 % for sampled UDP flows). We also observe flows for which we sample several hundreds of thousands of packets over the course of one week. Surprisingly, UDP flows dominate the heavy-hitter flows and closer inspection reveals that most of the large UDP flows are related to recursive DNS interactions between name servers. Accordingly, Fig. 1(b) shows the cumulative total number of bytes related to flows for which we sample less or equal than x packets. It shows that in case of TCP, more than 45 % of the bytes are sampled from flows for which we sample only a single packet (27.5 % for UDP). Since we only observe packets, we cannot rely on any per-flow properties nor can we expect to sample packets at any specific position of a flow e.g., the first packet(s). Moreover, we cannot expect to have any visibility into the bidirectional nature of any of the flows–all that sampling gives us is a "random set of packets."

3   Classification Approach

3.1   Related Work

Application classification has attracted the attention of researchers for many years and has resulted in a large number of different methods and studies. However, the characteristics of our datasets (i.e., sampling, no bidirectional visibility) pose new challenges for application classification. In particular, since most of the existing classification approaches require information that is not available in our datasets(e.g., unsampled packet traces, flow statistics), these methods are not directly applicable in our context.

Before presenting our new application characterization method, we first provide a condensed taxonomy of existing classification approaches. To this end, we follow closely the description presented in [20] and focus on those aspects of the different approaches that prevent them from being directly applicable to the types of datasets we are considering. For a more detailed discussion of the various existing application classification approaches, we refer to extensive surveys such as [10,13,20,25,29].

Port-based approach: Many applications typically run on fixed port numbers which can be leveraged to classify packets to their corresponding applications. The drawbacks of port-based classification are that (i) applications can rely on random port numbers (e.g., as Peer-to-Peer (P2P) applications) and *(ii)* applications might use well-known port numbers to obfuscate traffic (e.g., see [24]). On the positive side, port-based classification has been shown to be still effective [23], is robust to sampling and can be applied to our dataset in a straight-forward manner. Note that port-based classification was already performed for the sFlow data captured at this IXP in [7].

Payload-based approach: Also referred to as Deep Packet Inspection (DPI), payload-based classification produces very accurate results by relying on application-specific signatures (i.e., known byte patterns of known protocols). Application signatures are typically based on protocol handshakes and can often be assembled using only the first few payload-carrying packets that are exchanged between the communicating hosts (i.e., an HTTP GET request followed by an HTTP/1.{0,1} reply). The payload-based approach is often used to establish ground truth for the application mix of traffic traces (see e.g., [11] for a comparative study). While we have access to the initial bytes of the payload of each sampled packet, we do not necessarily sample the first packet(s) of flows that contain application signatures. In addition, we cannot inspect bidirectional payload patterns of flows using our datasets.

Flow features-based approach: By utilizing flow properties (e.g., the total number of packets, average packet size), several approaches focus on classifying flows as belonging to specific applications without inspecting the payload of packets. Since we do not have per-flow information, these approaches are not applicable to our datasets.

Host behavior-based approach: This class of approaches classifies traffic by profiling the detailed network interaction of hosts (e.g., which destinations are contacted on which ports [19] or the network-wide interactions of hosts [17]). The various approaches in this class have been shown the be particularly effective for characterizing P2P applications [18]. While we are not able to perform fine-grained profiling of hosts due to the sampled nature of our data, we do make use of properties inferred from the *social* behavior of hosts to uncover parts of Peer-to-Peer traffic.

3.2 Building Blocks

The foundation of our classification approach outlined below is the ability to attribute *some* of the sampled packets to their respective applications by mainly using payload signatures and partly relying on port numbers. In particular, we rely on signatures which we derived from the *L7-filter* [3] and the *libprotoident* library [8] for well-known protocols such as HTTP, SMTP, POP3, IMAP, NNTP and SSH. We also make use of application signatures derived from protocol specifications [1,6] for BitTorrent. We also used available signatures to detect other P2P protocols (e.g., eDonkey) but their contributions in terms of classifying packets were insignificant. We verified all application signatures using manually generated traffic traces. For SSL-based protocols (we focus on HTTPS, NNTPS,

POP3S, and IMAPS), we use signatures indicating an SSL handshake and consider SSL handshake packets on the well-known port number of the respective application (e.g., 443 for HTTPS) as belonging to that application.

To ensure the accuracy of our application signatures (i.e., keeping the false positives low by limiting the number of signatures), we restrict our set of application signatures and port numbers and only consider applications that *(i)* generate significant traffic and *(ii)* are reliably detectable using application signatures and, if needed, port numbers. For example, we do not try to classify Skype traffic because its detection remains unreliable unless specialized approaches are used [9].

3.3   Classification Method

Figure 2 illustrates our classification pipeline. In particular, our classification approach requires that the given traffic trace be processed twice, first in a *pre-classification* phase and then in a *classification* phase. The purpose of the first phase is to derive *state*, which will then be leveraged in the *classification* phase to attribute packets to their respective endpoints, revealing the corresponding application.

I. Pre-classification phase

The goal of the pre-classification step is to extract server *endpoints* and IP addresses of clients, which will be used as state in the subsequent classification phase. In this phase, we rely solely on payload-based classification using our validated signatures (as well as SSL signatures on well-known ports). For each packet that belongs to a client-server application, we save the server endpoint, i.e., its (IP, port) tuple. To identify the server-side of a packet, we rely on directed signatures (e.g., HTTP request vs. HTTP reply). For packets matching a BitTorrent signature, we save the SRC and DST IPs but not the port numbers. Since most BitTorrent traffic that matches our signatures is UDP-based which, due to its connectionless nature, is more susceptible to spoofing as well as other phenomena such as BitTorrent DHT poisoning for control traffic (e.g., [30]), we only count an IP address as BitTorrent speaker if we sample at least 2 packets that originate from/are sent to that IP address matching our signatures. Additionally, we save IP addresses of HTTP clients. In this pre-classification, we identify more than 2.7 M HTTP server endpoints (1.43 M unique IP addresses), and 210 K HTTPS endpoints. On the client side, we identify 37.7 M HTTP client IPs, as well as 38.9 M BitTorrent speakers, where the overlap between HTTP client IPs and BitTorrent speakers is 12.4 M IP addresses.

II. Classification phase

We next process that same trace again and ensure that each packet proceeds through the classification pipeline shown in Fig. 2. Once a packet can be attributed to an application, no further processing will be done for that packet.

Step 1: Payload signature matching. We match our previously extracted application signatures on each packet. Just by matching application signatures,

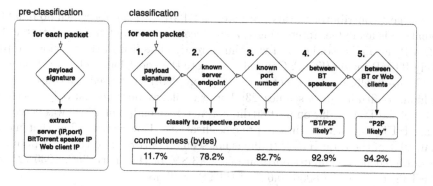

Fig. 2. Classification pipeline.

we are able to classify 11.7 % of the bytes exchanged at our IXP. This unexpected high number (recall that application signatures typically occur only in the first packets of a flow) is mainly the result of a proliferation of UDP-based BitTorrent data transfers, i.e., μTP [6]. μTP is a transport protocol based on UDP and includes its own header in every single packet. Thus, its classification is robust to sampling – in stark contrast to TCP traffic. The proliferation of μTP has also been reported in earlier studies [14,22], as well as the rise of UDP-based applications using own headers in every packet [15]. In total, 11.3 % of the packets matched a signature, of which 84.5 % matched the BitTorrent UDP signature, another 11.7 % matched an HTTP signature, 2.4 % an SSL handshake on port 443, 0.94 % a BitTorrent TCP signature, and 0.46 % other signatures.

Step 2: Server endpoint matching. If a packet does not contain a valid application signature, we then check if the source or the destination (IP, port) tuple of the respective packet is a known server endpoint, as identified in our pre-classification step. If so, we classify the packet as belonging to the specific application. In this step, we classify 66.5 % of bytes! This result highlights the efficiency of using a stateful application characterization approach. While we cannot sample application signatures on a per-flow basis, aggregating the information on a per (IP, port) endpoint basis largely overcomes the challenge posed by packet sampling. At the same time, we achieve a high confidence by relying on strong payload-based classification. This method works particularly well for popular client-server based applications, most prominently HTTP, where a large number of connections is destined to a comparably small number of server endpoints. To assess the impact of possibly stale endpoints (e.g., hosts that do not run the classified application on their server endpoint after some time), we repeated the classification by only using server endpoints that were identified within a time frame of 24 (12) h, which reduced our completeness by only 1 % (2 %) of the bytes.

Step 3: Port-based classification. We next use a short list of 15 known port numbers (mapping to 13 applications) to classify respective packets as belonging to the corresponding application. In this step, we classify another 4.5 % of all bytes.

The largest contributor to this third step is RTMP (1.7 %), for which no reliable signature is available. Interestingly, a significant fraction of traffic on port 1935 (RTMP) is HTTP traffic (and was thus already classified in the previous step), likely RTMP-inside-HTTP. Generally, we note that port-based classification can still be used reliably (but is not necessarily complete) when used in a conservative fashion, confirming prior studies [23]. For example, we observe that only less than 0.3 % of the TCP traffic on port 80 did not match an endpoint which was detected using HTTP signatures (in the pre-classification). However, we find that more than 10 % of the total HTTP traffic is not seen on port 80, and the most popular encountered non-standard ports are 8080 (3.8 % of HTTP traffic), 1935 (2.9 % of HTTP traffic) and 8000 (0.6 % of HTTP traffic).

Step 4: Packet exchanged between BitTorrent speakers. In this step, we consider packets that were not classified in a prior step and classify them as "BT/P2P likely" if they are exchanged between two previously identified BitTorrent speakers. This step enables us to classify an additional 10.2 % of the IXP's traffic. Depending on the individual client's configuration and capabilities, BitTorrent relies on TCP and UDP as transport protocol for data exchange as well as for exchanging control messages (e.g., DHT queries). While we are able to classify the bulk of BitTorrent UDP traffic (recall that we classified more than 11 % of the traffic just using signatures), we are not able to classify the bulk of TCP traffic exchanged between BitTorrent speakers. In this step we account for this portion of the traffic. To provide further empirical support for this approach, we inspected partly sampled TCP messages of the peer-wire protocol [1] which corresponds to the transfer of *chunks*. By extrapolating the number of *piece* messages of the BitTorrent peer-wire protocol and multiplying it with the observed chunk size (16 K in 99 % of all cases), we can estimate that the pure content volume (excluding headers and control traffic) exchanged via BitTorrent TCP peer-wire connections is around 8 %. Thus, we are convinced that the majority of the traffic classified in this step is indeed BitTorrent traffic. To acknowledge the lowered confidence and the possibility of other protocols contributing to this class, we classify these packets as "BT/P2P likely".

Step 5: Packet exchanged between Web clients or BitTorrent speakers. As a tie-breaking criteria, we classify all packets that are exchanged between either Web clients or BT speakers as "P2P likely". We only classify another 1.3 % of the IXP's total traffic by using this heuristic. This small number suggests that most P2P likely traffic is indeed exchanged between BitTorrent speakers and was already classified in the previous step.

Using this classification approach, we are able to attribute 82.7 % of the IXP's overall traffic directly to its corresponding application (Steps 1–3). More than 78 % of the traffic can be classified either directly using payload signatures or by matching the packet to server endpoints identified using payload signatures – we only fall back to port-based classification for 4.5 % of the traffic. Another 11.5 % of the traffic is classified as "BT/P2P likely" using our heuristics based on the social behavior of hosts.

4   The Internet's Application Mix Seen at an IXP

In this section, we discuss properties of the observed application mix. Figure 3 shows the result of our classification method when applied to the IXP's traffic, both in terms of packets and bytes (flow statistics are not obtainable from our packet-sampled traces). We observe that HTTP(S) clearly dominates the application mix with a share of more than 65 % of the bytes. While the increasing dominance of HTTP for a multitude of applications has been reported in prior studies (e.g., [26]), the other significant share of traffic is composed of the BitTorrent UDP and BT/P2P likely class, accounting for some 20 % of the exchanged bytes. Other protocols such as email, newsgroups, RTMP etc. account for roughly 6 % of the bytes exchanged at the IXP.

Figure 4(a) shows a timeseries of the contributions of the various applications for the 09-2013 trace. While we see that HTTP(S) always dominates (its share never drops below 55 %), we observe a typical diurnal pattern indicating more pronounced HTTP(S) usage in the busy hour in the late afternoon. The share of BitTorrent/P2P peaks in the off-hours. Interestingly, we observe a second peak of BT/P2P activity each day, which is likely due to BitTorrent users in various time zones. Also the protocols in the "other known" category dominate in the off-hours. NNTP(S) is the largest contributor to this category and is reportedly used for file-sharing [23].

Next, we use five snapshots to infer the application mix as observed at this IXP during the last 2.5 years. The results for the exchanged bytes are shown in Fig. 4(b). We observe that while the IXP's aggregate application mix is relatively stable, there is a significant increase of HTTPS traffic during these 2.5 years, from 1.9 % in April 2011 to 11.1 % in September 2013. Note that while in the snapshots from November 2011 to December 2012, both the share of HTTPS and HTTP traffic increased, there is a simultaneous decrease in HTTP and steep increase in HTTPS in 2013, suggesting a widespread switchover from HTTP to HTTPS in 2013.

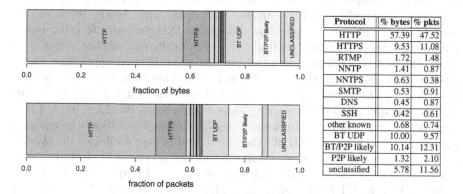

Protocol	% bytes	% pkts
HTTP	57.39	47.52
HTTPS	9.53	11.08
RTMP	1.72	1.48
NNTP	1.41	0.87
NNTPS	0.63	0.38
SMTP	0.53	0.91
DNS	0.45	0.87
SSH	0.42	0.61
other known	0.68	0.74
BT UDP	10.00	9.57
BT/P2P likely	10.14	12.31
P2P likely	1.32	2.10
unclassified	5.78	11.56

Fig. 3. Application mix (September 2013) for packets and bytes.

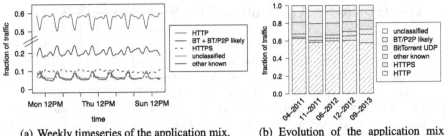

(a) Weekly timeseries of the application mix.

(b) Evolution of the application mix over the last 2.5 years.

Fig. 4. Application mix over time.

Table 2. Reported application mix in other studies (fixed, IPv4).

Study	Network type	Method	Bytes				
			Year	HTTP(S)	Other known	BT/P2P	Unclassified
[21]	5 large ISPs	Payload-based	2009	52.1 %	24 %	18.3 %	5.5 %
[21]	110 Networks	Port-based	2009	52 %	10 %	1 %	37 %
[23]	Large ISP	Payload-based	2009	57.6 %	23.5 %	13.5 %	10.6 %
[16]	Large ISP	Payload-based	2010	60 %	28 %	12 %	N/A
[12]	260 Networks	Port-based	2013	69.2 %	4 %	<7 %	20 %
[4]	Various	Payload-based [5]	2014	≈70 %	N/A	6 %	N/A
[4]	Various	Payload-based [5]	2014	≈65 %	N/A	15 %	N/A
[4]	Various	Payload-based [5]	2014	≈60 %	N/A	30 %	N/A
[4]	Various	Payload-based [5]	2014	≈65 %	N/A	9.4 %	N/A

5   The Application Mix: A Moving Target

5.1   The Aggregate View

The Internet's application mix has been the topic of numerous past studies by networking researchers and commercial companies alike. In the following, we report how the observed application mix at our IXP compares to other recent studies that not only relied on traffic data from different vantage points (and hence different types of peering links) but also used different application classification methods. Recall that in this study, we are only considering traffic that traverses the IXPs public peering links and have no visibility into the traffic that is sent over the private peering links established a this IXP. Table 2 lists some of the pertinent prior studies and provides information about the reported application mix, the type of traffic data used, and (where available) the classification method used.[2] A cursory comparison of the results of these studies with our findings suggests that the application mix of the Internet is rather homogeneous. That is, HTTP(S) dominates with a share of roughly 60 %, no matter

---

[2] Note that the applications belonging to the "other known" traffic class vary across studies.

where in the network and with what methodology the application mix was measured. Other protocols such as BitTorrent or P2P seem to vary by region from around 10 % to 30 %, but these variations could also be in part due to varying classification approaches.

5.2 Beyond the Aggregate Application Mix

Next, we take a closer look at the apparent homogeneous nature of the Internet's application mix and examine in detail the application mix of the traffic that traverses the peering links of specific networks.

Figure 5 shows the application mix for each of the top-15 traffic-contributing member ASes of our IXP and top-3 traffic-contributing transit providers that are also IXP members. The type of the top-15 traffic-contributing IXP members is either *Content/CDN*, *Hoster/IaaS* or *Eyeball/Access*, and together they are responsible for 59 % of the all the traffic (in bytes) seen at this IXP. We see that for all networks of type *Content/CDN* HTTP(S) traffic clearly dominates, with shares close to 100 %. While most of these networks still rely mainly on HTTP, we notice one prominent network (third bar from the left) that has almost a 50/50 ratio of HTTP and HTTPS traffic. This example suggests that the earlier reported growth in HTTPS is mainly driven by some big content providers switching over to HTTPS. Overall, for networks of type *Content/CDN* we observe little or no application-mix heterogeneity on their individual links. Networks of the type *Hoster/IaaS* show a more diverse profile when it comes to their application mix. While HTTP still dominates, we see surprisingly no significant amount of HTTPS traffic. At the same time, these networks also see other types of traffic of various protocols as well as significant shares of BitTorrent traffic and unclassified traffic. Note that BitTorrent is also increasingly used to deliver video content or software [2]. In short, the diverse application mix contributed by Web hosters reflects the fact that they offer infrastructure services to a wide variety of companies and individuals, which in turn make different use of the provided resources. The results for *Eyeball/Access* networks show that the application mix of networks connecting end-users to the IXP also

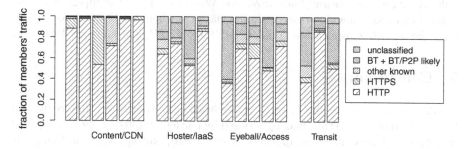

Fig. 5. Application mix of the top-15 traffic-contributing non-transit member ASes (grouped by business type) and the top-3 traffic-contributing member ASes that are transit providers.

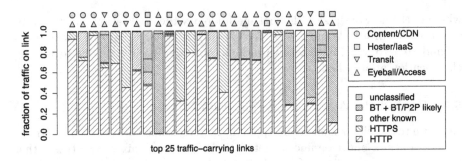

Fig. 6. Application mix of the top-25 traffic-carrying links.

varies significantly. While for some of them, HTTP(S) (along with small fractions of other traffic such as email, RTMP, news) clearly dominates, we also see eyeball networks with more than 50 % of BitTorrent traffic — the two networks with significant BitTorrent contributions are serving eastern European countries, while the other three networks are serving users in central Europe. This observation suggests that the differences in BitTorrent usage also reflect geographic properties (i.e., varying application popularity). The application mix seen for *Transit* networks is in general quite diverse as they typically carry traffic from a wide range of different networks.

The picture of the Internet's application mix sharpens even more when we look at the application mix seen on individual peering links. Figure 6 shows the application mix for the top-25 traffic-carrying bidirectional links at our IXP. The figure also includes the business types of the networks on either side of these peerings. Based on this set of links which see significant traffic, we observe a variety of different application mixes. While all Content-to-Eyeball links carry exclusively HTTP(S) and few other known applications, BitTorrent is the clear winner on two links between Eyeball networks. Thus, when taking into account the business types of two networks associated with a peering link, we notice a strong dependency on the resulting applications mix. The few links that show a more heterogeneous application mix are usually transit links or, interestingly, links involving Hosters and IaaS providers. When looking at the top-25 unidirectional links (not shown), we see a similar pattern, where for Content-to-Eyeball links the resulting application homogeneity (i.e., HTTP) is even more dominant.

6   Conclusion

In this paper we developed a traffic classification methodology that is by and large able to overcome the challenges posed by packet-sampled traffic through the use of a *stateful* classification approach based on endpoint-aggregation. Using our new methodology we can attribute more than 78 % of the bytes exchanged over the public switching infrastructure of a large IXP to their respective application by relying on strong payload-based classification. We attribute another 11.5 %

when including a heuristic based on communication patterns and classify an additional 4.5 % using port-based classification. In the process, we observe that the aggregate application mix as seen at our IXP is largely consistent with that reported in other recent studies. However, when dissecting the traffic and examining the application mix of Internet traffic that traverses individual public peering links, we show that the application mix becomes heterogeneous but is strongly influenced by the business type of the networks on either side of a peering link.

Acknowledgements. We want to express our gratitude towards the IXP operators for their generous support and feedback. We thank the anonymous reviewers for their helpful feedback. Georgios Smaragdakis was supported by the EU Marie Curie IOF "CDN-H" (PEOPLE-628441).

References

1. BitTorrent Protocol Specification v 1.0. https://wiki.theory.org/BitTorrent Specification
2. Digital Trends article, 12 October 2013. http://www.digitaltrends.com/opinion/bittorrents-image-problem/
3. L7-filter. http://l7-filter.sourceforge.net/
4. Sandvine Global Internet Phenomena, 1H 2014. https://www.sandvine.com/downloads/general/global-internet-phenomena/
5. Sandvine Traffic Classification. https://www.sandvine.com/technology/traffic-classification.html
6. uTorrent Transport Protocol Specification. http://www.bittorrent.org/beps/bep_0029.html
7. Ager, B., Chatzis, N., Feldmann, A., Sarrar, N., Uhlig, S., Willinger, W.: Anatomy of a large European IXP. In: ACM SIGCOMM (2012)
8. Alcock, S., Nelson, R.: Libprotoident: Traffic classification using lightweight packet inspection. University of Waikato, Technical report (2012)
9. Bonfiglio, D., Mellia, M., Meo, M., Ritacca, N., Rossi, D.: Tracking down skype traffic. In: IEEE INFOCOM (2008)
10. Callado, A., Kamienski, C., Szabo, G., Gero, B., Kelner, J., Fernandes, S., Sadok, D.: A survey on internet traffic identification. IEEE Commun. Surv. Tutor. **11**(3), 37–52 (2009)
11. Carela-Español, V., Bujlow, T., Barlet-Ros, P.: Is our ground-truth for traffic classification reliable? In: Faloutsos, M., Kuzmanovic, A. (eds.) PAM 2014. LNCS, vol. 8362, pp. 98–108. Springer, Heidelberg (2014)
12. Czyz, J., Allman, M., Zhang, J., Iekel-Johnson, S., Osterweil, E., Bailey, M.: Measuring IPv6 adoption. In: ACM SIGCOMM (2014)
13. Dainotti, A., Pescape, A., Claffy, K.: Issues and future directions in traffic classification. IEEE Netw. Mag. **26**(1), 35–40 (2012)
14. Finamore, A., Mellia, M., Meo, M., Munafo, M., Rossi, D.: Experiences of Internet traffic monitoring with Tstat. IEEE Netw. **25**(3), 8–14 (2011)
15. Finamore, A., Mellia, M., Meo, M., Rossi, D.: KISS: Stochastic packet inspection classifier for UDP traffic. IEEE/ACM Trans. Netw. **18**(5), 1505–1515 (2010)
16. Gerber, A., Doverspike, R.: Traffic types and growth in backbone networks. In: OFC/NFOEC (2011)

17. Iliofotou, M., Gallagher, B., Eliassi-Rad, T., Xie, G., Faloutsos, M.: Profiling-by-association: A resilient traffic profiling solution for the internet backbone. In: ACM CoNEXT (2010)
18. Karagiannis, T., Broido, A., Faloutsos, M., claffy, Kc.: Transport layer identification of P2P traffic. In: ACM IMC (2004)
19. Karagiannis, T., Papagiannaki, K., Faloutsos, M.: BLINC: multilevel traffic classification in the dark. In: ACM SIGCOMM (2005)
20. Kim, H., Claffy, K., Fomenkov, M., Barman, D., Faloutsos, M., Lee, K.-Y.: Internet traffic classification demystified: Myths, caveats, and the best practices. In: ACM CoNEXT (2008)
21. Labovitz, C., Lekel-Johnson, S., McPherson, D., Oberheide, J., Jahanian, F.: Internet inter-domain traffic. In: ACM SIGCOMM (2010)
22. Lee, C., Lee, D.K., Moon, S.: Unmasking the growing UDP traffic in a campus network. In: Taft, N., Ricciato, F. (eds.) PAM 2012. LNCS, vol. 7192, pp. 1–10. Springer, Heidelberg (2012)
23. Maier, G., Feldmann, A., Paxson, V., Allman, M.: On dominant characteristics of residential broadband internet traffic. In: ACM IMC (2009)
24. Moore, A.W., Papagiannaki, K.: Toward the accurate identification of network applications. In: Dovrolis, C. (ed.) PAM 2005. LNCS, vol. 3431, pp. 41–54. Springer, Heidelberg (2005)
25. Nguyen, T.T.T., Armitage, G.: A survey of techniques for internet traffic classification using machine learning. IEEE Commun. Surv. Tutor. **10**(4), 56–76 (2008)
26. Popa, L., Ghodsi, A., Stoica, I.: HTTP as the narrow waist of the future Internet. In: ACM HotNets (2010)
27. Richter, P., Smaragdakis, G., Feldmann, A., Chatzis, N., Boettger, J., Willinger, W.: Peering at peerings: On the role of IXP route servers. In: ACM IMC (2014)
28. InMon–sFlow. http://sflow.org/
29. Valenti, D., Rossi, D., Dainotti, A., Pescapè, A., Finamore, A., Mellia, M.: Reviewing traffic classification. In: TMA (2013)
30. Wang, L., Kangasharju, J.: Real-world sybil attacks in BitTorrent mainline DHT. In: IEEE GLOBECOM (2012)

Enabling Internet-Wide Deployment of Explicit Congestion Notification

Brian Trammell[1]([✉]), Mirja Kühlewind[1], Damiano Boppart[1],
Iain Learmonth[2], Gorry Fairhurst[2], and Richard Scheffenegger[3]

[1] Communication Systems Group, ETH Zurich, Zurich, Switzerland
trammell@tik.ee.ethz.ch
[2] University of Aberdeen, Aberdeen, Scotland, UK
[3] NetApp, Inc., Vienna, Austria

Abstract. Explicit Congestion Notification (ECN) is an TCP/IP extension to signal network congestion without packet loss, which has barely seen deployment though it was standardized and implemented more than a decade ago. On-going activities in research and standardization aim to make the usage of ECN more beneficial. This measurement study provides an update on deployment status and newly assesses the marginal risk of enabling ECN negotiation by default on client end-systems. Additionally, we dig deeper into causes of connectivity and negotiation issues linked to ECN. We find that about five websites per thousand suffer additional connection setup latency when fallback per RFC 3168 is correctly implemented; we provide a patch for Linux to properly perform this fallback. Moreover, we detect and explore a number of cases in which ECN brokenness is clearly path-dependent, i.e. on middleboxes beyond the access or content provider network. Further analysis of these cases can guide their elimination, further reducing the risk of enabling ECN by default.

1 Introduction

Explicit Congestion Notification (ECN) [1] is a TCP/IP extension that allows congestion signaling without packet loss. Even though ECN was standardized in 2001, and it is widely implemented in end-systems, it is barely deployed. This is due to a history of problems with severely broken middleboxes shortly after standardization, which led to connectivity failure and guidance to leave ECN disabled. The authors revisited this question in [2], finding an increase in the number of servers which successfully negotiate and use ECN, but with nearly no use of ECN within a national-scale access network.

In this paper we show that server-side support for ECN negotiation has further increased. Unfortunately, server-side support is only the first step. Since TCP clients initiate ECN negotiation, it is client-side support and negotiation by default that is necessary to complete deployment on end-systems. While ECN must also be enabled on routers together with an Active Queue Management (AQM) scheme in order to be useful, the lack of deployment on end-systems reduces the incentive to deploy on routers and vice-versa. In the past two years,

© Springer International Publishing Switzerland 2015
J. Mirkovic and Y. Liu (Eds.): PAM 2015, LNCS 8995, pp. 193–205, 2015.
DOI: 10.1007/978-3-319-15509-8_15

there has been increasing deployment of AQM [3] in the Internet; we expect this trend to continue and to drive router support for ECN. We therefore choose to focus on end-system deployment to break this loop, in the context of supporting on-going research in this area [4] to define more beneficial signaling. Specifically, this work aims to answer the following questions:

- What is the marginal risk of enabling ECN by default at the client-side?
- How can we detect and localize connectivity/signaling issues related to ECN?

To do so, we performed the following active measurements on nearly 600,000 popular web servers[1] taken from the Alexa top million list:

- Connectivity dependency: can ECN negotiation cause connectivity issues?
- ECN readiness: how many webservers will negotiate ECN if asked?
- ECN signaling anomalies: is ECN signaling viable to use end-to-end?

Specifically, the key focus of this work is on connectivity issues caused by ECN, in order to provide operational guidance and an answer to our most important question: is it now safe to use ECN-by-default on the client side to drive ECN deployment in the Internet? On this point we conclude that enabling ECN by default on client devices carries with it a low marginal risk of increased connection latency when fallback as recommended in RFC 3168 [1] is properly implemented; more measurement is necessary to localize the rare devices within the Internet that may lead to path-dependent failure of ECN-enabled connections. We provide a patch for Linux at http://ecn.ethz.ch/ecn-fallback; work to incorporate fallback into the Linux kernel mainline is ongoing.

All tools used in this study are available as open-source software, as are the raw data and intermediate results listing servers by ECN support status, from http://ecn.ethz.ch. We intend this work to introduce an ongoing ECN and middlebox impairment observatory which will support an effort to deploy ECN on an Internet-wide scale.

1.1 Overview of Explicit Congestion Notification (ECN)

ECN uses two bits in the IP header to mark traffic as ECN-capable or as having experienced congestion along the path, and when used with TCP it uses two flags, ECE and CWR, to negotiate the use of ECN in the TCP handshake and subsequently to echo congestion marking back to the sender during the connection. To review, a client sends an initial SYN ECE CWR to the server to negotiate ECN; to confirm negotiation, the server responds SYN ACK ECE, or to deny, simply SYN ACK. Section 6.1.1.1 of RFC 3168 [1] recommends falling back to non-ECN support if the initial SYN ACK ECE connection attempt fails.

After successful negotiation, data packets from each side can be marked using one of the ECN-Capable Transport codepoints (ECT(0)/ECT(1)) in the

---

[1] We examine HTTP in this study for comparison with related work, and because large-scale probing of HTTP is less likely to be regarded as abuse than other services.

IP header, which is replaced with the CE codepoint if a router's AQM along the path determines the link is congested. This congestion signal is echoed back to the sender marking all acknowledgments with the ECE flag until the sender acknowledges the receipt of the congestion signal with the CWR flag.

This describes the case where everything goes well. The negotiation and signaling in ECN can however go badly for various reasons. First, the two bits in the IPv4 and IPv6 header used for ECN were previously part of the Type of Service (ToS) byte, and there are still middleboxes and firewalls deployed in the Internet that use the old definition of these bits, interfering with ECN signaling. Second, firewalls may be configured to strip the ECN bits in the IP or TCP header, leading to negotiation and signaling errors; or to drop SYN ACK ECE, specifically to disable ECN, leading to connection failure. Third, end hosts and TCP proxies may have design or implementation faults in their handling of the semantics of the ECN bits.

1.2 Related Work

This work follows directly our previous work [2] and from [5], which sought to measure the state of ECN deployment as of August 2014 and September 2011, respectively. Our numbers for ECN capability and non-capability of webservers, being taken from the Alexa top million and using a comparable methodology, are therefore directly comparable to those in [2,5]. We show that ECN support in webservers continues to increase, and reached the majority of the top million by the middle of 2014. Methodologies for packet mangling and marking are also comparable to those in [5]. More generally, this work follows from the continuing history of measurements of the Internet to estimate the ability to deploy new featues at the endpoints (e.g. Honda et al [6], Medina et al [7]), and contributes a data point to the continuing effort to improve the situation (e.g. the IAB Stack Evolution program[2] [8], or middlebox cooperation schemes such as [9]).

2 Methodology

2.1 Measurement Setup and Data Set

All measurements in this paper were performed from vantage-points running Ubuntu 14.04 (kernel 3.13.0 without SYN retry fallback as in RFC3168 [1]), run by commercial hosting provider Digital Ocean, in London, New York, and Singapore. Initial investigation showed that all ECN signaling works properly on this provider's networks, and all sites have native dual-stack connectivity. We ran trials on three seperate occasions, on 27 August, 4 September, and 9 September 2014.

As with previous work on testing ECN readiness of webservers [2,5], we select our targets from Alexa's publicly available top million websites list. We then resolve these to at most one IPv4 and one IPv6 address per site. Duplicate IP

---

[2] http://www.iab.org/activities/programs/ip-stack-evolution-program.

addresses are eliminated, taking the highest-ranked website for each address. Name resolution was performed on 27 August 2014 from the London vantage point using Google's public DNS server (8.8.8.8), resulting in 581,737 unique IPv4 addresses and 17,029 unique IPv6 addresses.

2.2   ECN-Spider and QoF

We built an active measurement tool atop the operating system's ECN implementation, to test ECN negotiation and negotiation-linked connectivity. This tool, called ECN Spider, is implemented in Python 3. ECN Spider takes as input a list of IP addresses along with the associated domain name and a number as a label to be used in later analysis; in this work, we use the Alexa rank. For each unique address, the tool then simultaneously opens one connection without attempting to negotiate ECN and one connection attempting to negotiate ECN, and reports the connection status for each, along with timing and HTTP status information.

ECN Spider's design is based on utilizing Linux's system-level configuration of ECN negotiation using the sysctl facility, using the implemented TCP stack instead of packet injection. For each site, we must therefore:

1. disable ECN using sysctl
2. open a socket to the target (attempts a SYN 3WHS)
3. enable ECN using sysctl
4. open a socket to the target (attempts a SYN ECE CWR 3WHS)
5. perform HTTP requests via both sockets.

To make it possible to test a half million websites in a reasonable amount of time, the sysctl calls are performed in their own thread, which synchronizes with several hundred worker threads, amortizing the cost (about 10ms) of changing the system-wide setting. Each connection attempt is given 4 seconds to succeed, which can lead to transient connection failures on slower websites, but is necessary to keep slow and disconnected sites from delaying testing.

ECN Spider always tests connectivity without ECN first, in order to eliminate the possibility that sending an ECN negotiation packet down a path changes the result of the non-ECN SYN. When performing HTTP requests, ECN Spider does not follow redirects or otherwise crawl resources on the retrieved page.

While ECN Spider can detect whether or not a connection failed in the presence or absence of ECN negotiation, it cannot detect whether or not ECN was actually negotiated or observe negotiation anomalies, since this information is not available in userland. Therefore, we simultaneously observe the traffic with the QoF [10] flow meter to evaluate the traffic generated by ECN Spider providing TCP flags and ECN signaling information on a per-flow basis.

2.3   IPtables Packet Mangling

We also combined ECN Spider with the Linux iptables connection tracking and packet-mangling facilities in order to test the three following cases:

1. ECE response: mark all outgoing packets with CE to verify that we see ECE
2. CWR response: mark all incoming packets with CE to verify that we see CWR in response to ECE-marked ACKs
3. CE and ECT blackhole testing: mark SYN with CE/ECT(0)/ECT(1) to verify that marked packets are not dropped on path.

In all cases the TCP MSS was set to 300 bytes, in order to split HTTP requests into multiple packets. For the ECE and CWR response testing, we used QoF for data analysis; for the CE and ECT blackhole testing, we analyzed ECN Spider's connectivity logs assuming that a path that drops marked SYNs would also drop other marked packets.

3   The Marginal Risk of Enabling ECN by Default

In our previous work [2], we found a multiple order-of-magnitude difference between the proportion of webservers supporting ECN negotiation and marking, and passively-measured flows on a university network actually negotiating and using ECN. Since webserver support is largely driven by the default configuration of the server operating system, the question naturally arises of whether client-side support could be driven by the same mechanism.

This is not a viable strategy if there still exist many paths through the Internet where attempting to negotiate ECN causes connectivity issues. Note that even with RFC3168 fallback, ECN-dependent connectivity can lead to additional connection setup latency, which depends on the client operating system. So we turn our attention to the question of marginal risk: how many additional connectivity issues can we expect if we turn ECN on by default?

3.1   Connectivity Dependency and Anomalies

Table 1 shows that for the vast majority of sites we probed, connectivity is clearly independent of whether ECN is requested or not. 578,433 (99.43 %) of IPv4 and 16945 (99.50 %) of IPv6[3] exhibit no ECN-dependent connectivity.

In 2443 cases for IPv4 and 16 cases for IPv6, connectivity apparently depends on ECN not being requested.The vast majority of these (2193 IPv4 and 13 IPv6 hosts) exhibit stable connectivity dependency at or near the host itself: every attempt to connect to the host with ECN failed, and every attempt to connect without succeeded.

This leaves us with the anomalous cases. We observe stable ECN dependency on the path in 15 cases for IPv4. Here, every connection attempt requesting ECN fails from one vantage point but succeeds from another. 6 of these sites are within a single AS (26496, GoDaddy.com LLC), and occur on servers used to park domain names. The remaining 9 may be more problematic, as they could represent ECN-disabling devices on path. A further 34 IPv4 and 3 IPv6

---

[3] Note that the relatively high prevalence of permanent IPv6 connection failure (nearly 10 %) indicates continued limited operational experience with IPv6.

Table 1. Connectivity statistics, of 581,737 IPv4 hosts and 17,029 IPv6 hosts, all vantage points, 27 Aug – 9 Sep 2014

IPv4		IPv6		Description
Hosts	pct	Hosts	pct	
553805	95.20 %	14889	87.43 %	Always connected from all vantage points
3998	0.69 %	1594	9.36 %	Never connected from any vantage point
8631	1.48 %	138	0.81 %	Single transient connection failure
11999	2.06 %	324	1.90 %	Non-ECN-related transient connectivity
578433	**99.43 %**	**16945**	**99.50 %**	**Total ECN-independent connectivity**
2193	0.38 %	13	0.08 %	Stable ECN dependency near host
15	0.00 %	0	0.00 %	Stable ECN dependency on path
34	0.01 %	3	0.02 %	Potential ECN dependency on path
201	0.03 %	0	0.00 %	Temporal ECN dependency
2443	**0.42 %**	**16**	**0.09 %**	**Total ECN-dependent connectivity**
862	0.15 %	69	0.41 %	Inconclusive transient connectivity

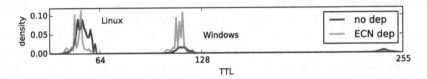

Fig. 1. TTL spectrum of ECN-dependent and -independent connectivity cases

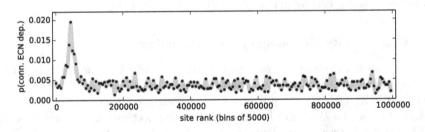

Fig. 2. Proportion of sites failing to connect when ECN negotiation is requested

hosts exhibit *potential* ECN dependency: no connection attempt requesting ECN succeeds from one vantage point, and at least one connection attempt with ECN from another vantage point succeeds, though we cannot rule out transient connectivity effects here. We also observed time-dependent anomalies: 201 cases for IPv4 where connectivity was ECN-independent from all vantage points during one trial, but ECN-dependent during another. This probably represents changes in network or host configuration during the time we ran our trials.

A further 862 cases for IPv4 and 69 for IPv6 cannot be definitively classified as either ECN-dependent or transient, leading us to estimate an upper-bound "blackhole" rate of 0.57 % for IPv4 and 0.50 % for IPv6. This is comparable to [5], suggesting that boxes that break connectivity when ECN is requested are not being replaced quickly.

Connectivity dependency can be linked to the operating system of the web-server by estimating the initial TTL. As shown in Fig. 1, sites with initial TTL 64 (Linux) and 128 (Windows) are roughly equally represented among hosts exhibiting ECN-dependent connectivity, while Linux servers are far more common among the majority where connectivity is ECN-independent. ECN-dependent connectivity failure also depends slightly on website rank as shown in Fig. 2: as many as 2 % of websites with an Alexa rank between 50,000 and 55,000 fail to connect when ECN is requested, compared to a background rate of about 0.5 %. The distribution of these sites by rank is shown in Fig. 2.

3.2   RFC 3168 Fallback Testing

Based on our RFC3168 ECN fallback Linux patch applied to single Ubuntu 14.04 machine at ETH Zurich running the 3.13 kernel we reran ECN Spider against the hosts which showed some evidence of connectivity depending on ECN and, as expected, we found that this patch eliminated connection failures attributable to ECN negotiation, at the cost of increased connection setup latency[4]. Therefore the implementation of ECN fallback as the default behavior in all operating systems will restore connectivity and is an important step for wide-scale deployment of ECN.

3.3   Conclusions

Our analysis therefore indicates that enabling ECN by default would lead to connections to about five websites per thousand to suffer additional setup latency with RFC 3168 fallback. This represents an order of magnitude fewer than the about forty per thousand which experience transient or permanent connection failure due to other operational issues. Comparison with [5] indicates this situation is likely unchanged in its magnitude since 2011.

As not all websites are equally popular, failures on five per thousand *websites* does not by any means imply that five per thousand *connection attempts* will fail. While estimation of connection attempt rate by rank is out of scope of this work, we note that the highest ranked website exhibiting stable connection failure has rank 596, and only 13 such sites appear in the top 5000.

4   An Analysis of ECN Signaling

We then analyzed the traces taken from our three ECN Spider runs using QoF to determine the extent of server-side support for ECN, and to investigate the prevalence of the different ways in which the ECN mechanism can fail today in the Internet.

---

[4] Fallback latency is a function of client implementation. We note anecdotally that additional latency is on the order of seconds on Windows 7, and barely noticeable on Mac OS X Mavericks.

Table 2. ECN negotiation statistics, of 581,711 IPv4 hosts and 17,028 IPv6 hosts, all vantage points, 27 Aug – 9 Sep 2014, compared to previous measurements.

IPv4		IPv6		2011	2012	Description
Hosts	pct	Hosts	pct	pct[5]	pct[2]	
326743	**56.17 %**	**11138**	**65.41 %**	11.2 %	29.48 %	**Capable of negotiating ECN**
324607	55.80 %	11121	65.31 %	–	–	...and always negotiate
2136	0.37 %	17	0.11 %	–	–	...sometimes negotiate, of which...
107	0.02 %	1	0.01 %	–	–	negotiation depends on path
27	0.02 %	0	0.00 %	–	–	sometimes reflect SYN ACK flags
248791	43.23 %	3961	26.23 %	82.8 %	70.52 %	Not capable of negotiating ECN
2013	0.35 %	83	0.48 %	–	–	...and reflect SYN ACK flags
6177	1.06 %	1929	11.33 %	–	–	Never connect with ECN (see Sect. 3.1)

4.1 ECN Negotiation

As seen in Table 2, the majority of the top million web servers (56.17 % of those connecting for IPv4, 65.41 % for IPv6) are now capable of negotiating ECN, continuing a more or less linear trend since 2008. We attribute this to the decision to negotiate ECN if requested by the client by default in common server operating systems. Indeed, there continue to be large differences in ECN support per operating system, as shown in Fig. 3: note here that almost no initial-TTL 128 (i.e. Windows) or 255 (Solaris; also Google) hosts negotiate ECN. Considering only initial-TTL 64 (Linux) hosts, 326,720 of 468,555 or 69.73 % are ECN capable.

As with connectivity, the proportion of hosts negotiating ECN depends slightly on the rank of the site, as shown in Fig. 4. The highest ranked website that will negotiate ECN has rank 6 (www.wikipedia.org). We note that websites of higher rank generally use custom networking software, and are therefore not affected by ECN negotiation by default. The top 100,000 sites are less likely to support ECN negotiation than the remaining 900,000.

Troubling are the 107 IPv4 hosts and one single IPv6 host for which ECN negotiation appears to be dependent on the vantage point. This indicates a device on path which mangles the ECN TCP flags. There are also 2029 IPv4 and 16 IPv6 hosts which sometimes negotatiate and sometimes do not, indicating either path or temporal instability in ECN signaling. Further, there are 2047 IPv4 hosts and 83 IPv6 hosts which reflect the ECN TCP flags on the SYN ACK (i.e., answering SYN ECE CWR with SYN ACK ECE CWR), indicating poorly implemented end-host stacks or TCP proxies. Of these, 693 IPv4 hosts and one IPv6 host go on

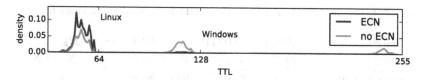

Fig. 3. Comparison of TTL spectrum between ECN-capable and -incapable hosts

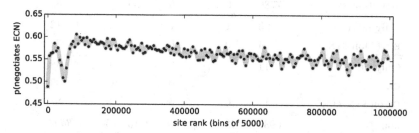

Fig. 4. Proportion of sites negotiating ECN by rank

to send ECT(0) marked packets, indicating that the end host may believe it has negotiated ECN correctly.

4.2 IP Signaling Anomalies

Assessing middlebox mangling of IP ECN signaling, we see in Table 3 that 315,605 (97.2 %) of the IPv4 hosts and 8998 (80.9 %) of IPv6 hosts that always negotiate ECN mark all subsequent packets ECT(0) which is the expected signaling; we would expect ECN to work in these cases. On the other hand, there are 6939 (2.1 %) IPv4 and 2013 (18.1 %) IPv6 hosts which always negotiate ECN but never send an ECT marked packet in any trial from any vantage point. While it is acceptable for hosts which have negotiated ECN not to mark every data packet, this could also indicate a middlebox along the path that does not interfere with the ECN TCP signaling but does with ECP IP signaling. We note that this anomaly is less common for IPv4 than reported in [5], but it is not clear to what to attribute this change.

We can observe various interesting anomalies here which indicate possible mangling. 1995 IPv4 hosts do not appear to negotiate ECN but send ECT(0) marked packets anyway. 46 of these set ECT(0) on the SYN ACK which indicates a middlebox overwriting the former ToS field. The other 1849 cases indicate either a broken TCP stack, or ECN TCP flag mangling on the downstream path wherein the server believes ECN has been negotiated, but the client does not, i.e. the ECE bit is cleared from the SYN ACK ECE sent by the server. We note that the magnitude of this anomaly is comparable with that reported in [5], indicating little if any improvement in middlebox mangling of ECN on this point. Conversely, Table 4 gives insignt on hosts and paths using the ECN IP bits for non-ECN purposes, showing statistics for ECN marking by servers on connection attempts without ECN negotiation.

Table 3. Relationship between ECN IP and TCP flags (*expected cases in italics*)

Marking	IPv4 (N = 581711)			IPv6 (N = 17028)		
	ECN	Reflect	No ECN	ECN	Reflect	No ECN
Only ECT(0)	*315605*	693	1995	*8998*	1	46
ECT(0) + ECT(1)	0	0	0	4	1	7
ECT(0)on SYN ACK	7780	0	46	89	0	82
Only ECT(1)	3	1	17	0	10	12
ECT(1)on SYN ACK	4	0	16	7	0	31
Only CE	11	1	7	0	0	48
CE + ECT	5	2	0	23	66	39
CE on SYN ACK	11	0	5	22	0	87
none	6939	1343	*243150*	2013	5	*3694*

Table 4. Marking on flows without ECN negotiation attempt

Codepoint	IPv4 (N = 581711)			IPv6 (N = 17028)		
	Once	Always	SYN ACK	Once	Always	SYN ACK
ECT(0)	4592	104	68	179	2	101
ECT(1)	21	18	18	116	76	39
CE	21	17	17	162	12	94

There are a few additional anecdotes to take from this analysis. The incidence of IPv6 negotiation anomalies (15.20 %) is an order of magnitude higher than in IPv4 (1.93 %), indicating that, although negotiation is supported by a higher proportion of IPv6 than IPv4 servers, ECN support in IPv6 in hosts and middleboxes is less mature. Many of these can be traced to specific providers: a single ISP in the Netherlands, for instance, is responsible for all 22 of the hosts that mark CE on the SYN ACK for IPv6 when negotiating ECN. Of five IPv4 hosts which send both CE and ECT marked packets, indicating the potential presence of a CE-marking router, there is only one (www.grandlyon.com, 213.162.51.7, as seen from London on 4 September and Singapore on 9 September 2014) for which we cannot rule out this hypothesis. In neither trial was the connection long enough to observe a CWR acknowledging the resulting ECE.

4.3   IP ECN Connectivity and ECN Echo Tests

To further verify correct ECN signaling end-to-end, we ran CE and ECT blackhole experiments on 24 September, and ECE and CWR response tests on 23 September 2014, both from the London vantage point.

In the blackhole experiment, 4791 (0.82 %) IPv4 hosts and 104 (0.61 %) IPv6 hosts fail to connect when at least one ECN codepoint is set on the SYN. Of these,

2006 IPv4 and 12 IPv6 hosts are among those which also failed to connect from all vantage points when ECN was requested (see Sect. 3.1). 287 IPv4 and 17 IPv6 hosts fail to connect regardless of the ECN codepoint set. In this experiment, the magnitude of transient failure is comparable to that in Sect. 3.

The ECE response test succeeded for IPv4 in 94.8 % (309,842 hosts) of all ECN-enabled cases in Table 2. In contrast, the CWR response test succeeded only in 44.3 % (144,290 hosts) of the cases. Further, we found 690 IPv4 hosts responding with ECE and 351 hosts responding with CWR even though ECN was not successfully negotiated. There also appears to be significant impairment or implementation error in ECN signaling for IPv6, with only 7 hosts responding ECE and 9 CWR.

Reasons for ECE response test failures include clearing of the CE codepoint along the forward path or clearing of the ECE flag along the reverse path. Reasons for CWR test failures include clearing of the ECE flag along the forward path, clearing of the CWR flag along the reverse path, or termination of the flow before CWR could be sent by the sender. As the median size of responses from hosts that did set CWR in the test was 3168 bytes, while the median size from those that did not was only 864 bytes (i.e., smaller than MSS), we do not consider our CWR results as a reliable indication of impairment on path.

Therefore, while the ECN IP-related connectivity risk is proportional to that related to ECN TCP signaling, the correct handling of ECE and CWR signaling after negotiation seem to be more impaired. Even worse, signaling is significantly more impaired on IPv6 than on IPv4.

5   Conclusions, Outlook, and Future Work

We have shown that while webservers support for ECN continues to increase, there does not appear to have been any appreciable reduction in the proportion of potential connectivity failure linked to ECN since 2011. The vast majority of connectivity problems we found with ECN negotiation were close to the server, i.e., cases in which routing changes during a connection would not lead to connection failure in the middle of an ECN-enabled flow. The fallback behavior defined in RFC 3168 eliminates connectivity risk for these cases, such that enabling ECN by default would lead only to increased connection latency when attempting to connect to about five of every thousand websites.

Verifying and localizing ECN path dependency in the remaining cases proves to be quite difficult. Bauer et al [5] used a tomography-based approach (as in e.g. Tracebox [11]) for localizing ECT mark clearing to an Autonomous System (AS); an approach that is unfortunately not applicable to our case. The ICMP Time Exceeded message contains no TCP flag information, making it impossible to verify path-dependent negotiation failures. Traceroute artifacts and on-path blocking of traceroute make it similarly impossible to differentiate connectivity issues from traceroute issues. Correlation of data-plane and control-plane routing information (e.g. from http://stat.ripe.net/) is a promising approach, but in none of our path-dependent connectivity cases did it yield a most-likely

AS for the connectivity failure. We therefore leave further investigation of path dependency to future work, potentially leveraging existing wide-area distributed measurement platforms such as RIPE Atlas[5] to probe the set of paths through the Internet more comprehensively, using the volume of data to make up for the drawbacks of the traceroute-based tomography methods.

Our study shows that while it is safe for operating system vendors to activate ECN on the client-side by default presuming they implement RFC 3168 fallback, we cannot yet unreservedly recommend doing so. For a tiny minority of sites (15 of 598,766, or about 1 in 40,000) we cannot rule out path-dependent connectivity issues. A similar proportion of sites exhibit indiscriminate CE marking, which would cause throughput degradation with use of ECN. These numbers are small enough that targeted collaboration with the operations community based on additional measurement is a viable way forward. We encourage other researchers to use the tools and dataset made available at http://ecn.ethz.ch to continue these investigations, and to guide the eventual elimination of ECN-unfriendly middleboxes, in order to move toward full deployment of ECN.

Acknowledgments. This work was materially supported by the European Commission though the Seventh Framework Grant Agreements mPlane (FP7-318627) and Reducing Internet Transport Latency (RITE) (FP7-317700); no endorsement of the work by the Commission is implied. Thanks to Stephan Neuhaus for his guidance during the development of ECN Spider, to Daniel Borkmann and Florian Westphal for discussions on Linux kernel modifications for RFC 3168 Fallback, and to Stuart Cheshire for his feedback.

References

1. Ramakrishnan, K., Floyd, S., Black, D.: The Addition of Explicit Congestion Notification (ECN) to IP. RFC 3168, IETF (2001)
2. Kühlewind, M., Neuner, S., Trammell, B.: On the state of ECN and TCP options in the internet. In: Proceedings of the Passive and Active Measurement 2013, Hong Kong SAR, China (2013)
3. Baker, F., Fairhurst, G.: IETF Recommendations Regarding Active Queue Management: draft-ietf-aqm-recommendation-08. Internet-draft, IETF (2014) (Work in Progress)
4. Kühlewind, M., Wagner, D.P., Espinosa, J.M.R., Briscoe, B.: Using data center TCP (DCTCP) in the internet. In: Proceedings of the third IEEE Globecom Workshop on Telecommunication Standards: From Research to Standards (2014)
5. Bauer, S., Beverly, R., Berger, A.: Measuring the state of ECN readiness in servers, clients, and routers. In: Proceedings of the Internet Measurement Conference, pp. 171–177 (2011)
6. Honda, M., Nishida, Y., Raiciu, C., Greenhalgh, A., Handley, M., Tokuda, H.: Is it still possible to extend TCP? In: Proceedings of the Internet Measurement Conference, pp. 181–194 (2011)
7. Medina, A., Allman, M., Floyd, S.: Measuring the evolution of transport protocols in the Internet. SIGCOMM Comput. Commun. Rev. **35**(2), 37–52 (2005)

---

[5] https://atlas.ripe.net/.

8. Trammell, B., Hildebrand, J.: Evolving transport in the internet. IEEE Internet Comput. **18**(5), 60–64 (2014)
9. Craven, R., Beverly, R., Allman, M.: Middlebox-cooperative TCP for a non end-to-end Internet. In: Proceedings of ACM SIGCOMM 2014 Conference, Chicago, IL, USA (2014)
10. Trammell, B., Gugelmann, D., Brownlee, N.: Inline data integrity signals for passive measurement. In: Proceedings of the Sixth International Wksp on Traffic Measurement and Analysis, London, England (2014)
11. Detal, G., Hesmans, B., Bonaventure, O., Vanaubel, Y., Donnet, B.: Revealing middlebox interference with Tracebox. In: Proceedings of the 2013 Internet Measurement Conference IMC '13, pp. 1–8, Barcelona, Spain (2013)

Internet Outages, the Eyewitness Accounts: Analysis of the Outages Mailing List

Ritwik Banerjee[1], Abbas Razaghpanah[1(✉)], Luis Chiang[1], Akassh Mishra[1], Vyas Sekar[2], Yejin Choi[3], and Phillipa Gill[1]

[1] Stony Brook University, New York, USA
arazaghpanah@cs.stonybrook.edu
[2] Carnegie Mellon University, Pittsburgh, USA
[3] University of Washington, Seattle, USA

Abstract. Understanding network reliability and outages is critical to the "health" of the Internet infrastructure. Unfortunately, our ability to analyze Internet outages has been hampered by the lack of access to public information from key players. In this paper, we leverage a somewhat unconventional dataset to analyze Internet reliability—the outages mailing list. The mailing list is an avenue for network operators to share information and insights about widespread outages. Using this unique dataset, we perform a first-of-its-kind longitudinal analysis of Internet outages from 2006 to 2013 using text mining and natural language processing techniques. We observe several interesting aspects of Internet outages: a large number of application and mobility issues that impact users, a rise in content, mobile issues, and discussion of large-scale DDoS attacks in recent years.

1 Introduction

As an increasing number of critical services rely on the Internet, network outages can cause significant societal and economic impact [10,18]. Indeed, this importance can be seen when network failures such as cloud computing outages [9], BGP interceptions [14], and large scale DDoS attacks (e.g., [1,3]) make headlines in the popular press. By some estimates, data center network outages can lead to losses of more than $500,000 per incident on average [34], while costs of WAN failures are more challenging to quantify [8]. Thus, there are a large number of past and ongoing efforts to detect and mitigate network outages, including work on novel root cause analysis techniques [24,27], and better network debugging tools [5,11,20,30,41].

While there are several efforts, as mentioned above, to minimize the impact of network outages, there is unfortunately a critical dearth of studies that systematically *understand* network outages. In part, our understanding of outages and network reliability is hampered by the reluctance on the part of network operators to release data due to policy requirements; e.g., even though the FCC maintains a network outage reports system and mandates that network operators provide true estimates, the data is confidential given its sensitive nature [2].

© Springer International Publishing Switzerland 2015
J. Mirkovic and Y. Liu (Eds.): PAM 2015, LNCS 8995, pp. 206–219, 2015.
DOI: 10.1007/978-3-319-15509-8_16

Furthermore, providers have natural economic concerns that such studies may reflect poorly on them and thus impact revenues. As such, the few studies that obtain data from networks are only able to offer insights from a single vantage point such as an academic WAN [43], data center [22] or backbone ISP [32].

Our work is an attempt to bridge this critical gap in our understanding of network reliability. For instance, we would like to understand if specific Internet service providers (e.g., access vs. tier-1), protocols (e.g., DNS vs. BGP), network locations (e.g., specific PoPs or co-location points), or content providers (e.g., web hosting services) are more likely to be involved in network outages. Such an understanding can help network operators and architects focus their resources on making Internet services more robust. For example, providers who know that specific hosting services or protocols are prone to outages can proactively work around these known hotspots.

Toward this goal, we leverage an underutilized dataset: the *outages mailing list* [38] to answer the above types questions. The mailing list serves as a venue for operators to announce and debug network failures. The outages list tends to have some bias towards North American network operators self-reporting outages perceived as 'high impact'. Despite this bias, the dataset also has attributes that are lacking, or only met in isolation in other data sets which can help illuminate different facets of network failures:

Semantic context. Posts contain rich semantic information about what happened during the outage, in contrast to technical data which often requires starting from low-level measurements and inferring whether an event incurred real-world impact.

Interdomain coverage. The mailing list provides an overview of network failures that transcend network boundaries rather than focusing on the point-of-view and failures experienced by a single network.

Longitudinal view. The outages list has been maintained since 2006 offering an unprecedented view of Internet reliability issues discussed by operators over time.

The rich semantic and natural language information contained in the list also presents a challenge in terms of analyzing the outages mailing list. To address this challenge, we turn to natural language processing (NLP), text mining, and machine learning (ML) techniques in order to automatically categorize the posts and threads in the mailing list. However, naively applying these techniques "out of the box" does a poor job of identifying useful semantic information (e.g., Level 3 would naively be considered two words). Thus, we use a careful synthesis of domain knowledge and NLP/ML techniques to extract meaningful keywords to build a classification algorithm to categorize content along two dimensions: (1) type of outage (e.g., attack vs. congestion vs. fiber cut) and (2) the type of entity involved (e.g., cloud provider vs. ISP).

Our analysis reveals the following insights:

User issues dominate. The list is dominated by issues with user-facing components such as misconfigurations and issues with application servers and mobile networks. In terms of entities, networks providing service to users such as access and mobile networks are also prevalent.

Content and mobile issues are on the rise. Starting in 2009, we see a large fraction of threads related to application server problems and content provider networks. These issues tend to relate to common service providers such as Google, Facebook, Netflix. Mobile-centric issues have also increased by 15 % over the past 7 years.

Attacks and censorship are relatively rare. There is less discussion of security issues and censorship in the dataset. However, notable incidents like censorship in Syria and large DNS-amplification-based DDoS attacks (*e.g.*, [35]) did get the attention of the community with a significant increase in posts containing the keyword DNS spiking in 2012–2013.[1]

Contributions and Roadmap: This paper makes the following contributions: (1) Performing an initial analysis of the outages mailing list to understand Internet outages (Sect. 2); (2) A careful application of text mining, NLP, and machine learning techniques to extract useful semantic information from this dataset (Sects. 3, 4); (3) Shedding light on the types of outages and the key entities involved in these outages over time (Sect. 5). Finally, we discuss related work in Sect. 6 and conclude in Sect. 7.

2   Dataset

In this section, we provide background about the mailing list and our dataset (Sect. 2.1), and limitations of using the mailing list to analyze network failures (Sect. 2.2).

2.1   About the Outages Mailing List

The outages mailing list reports outages related to failures of major communications infrastructure components. It intends to share information so that network operators and end users can assess and respond to major outages. The list contains outage reports as well as post-mortem analysis and discussions on troubleshooting.

We analyze a snapshot of the outages mailing list taken on December 31, 2013 containing threads since its inception in 2006. Our dataset is summarized in Table 1. It contains over seven years of discussion on the mailing list. This discussion is organized into 2,054 threads, with a total of 6,566 individual posts. Note that the number of posts is higher than the number of threads and replies combined since it also includes emails that are not part of a thread (e.g. "unsubscribe" emails). A total of 1,194 individuals (identified by e-mail addresses) contributed to the discussions.

---

[1] DNS was used to amplify botnet attacks over this period.

Table 1. Summary of the Outages Mailing List Dataset

First email	Sep 29, 2006
Last email (in dataset)	Dec 31, 2013
Number of posts	6,566
Number of threads	2,054
Number of replies	4,163
Number of contributors	1,194

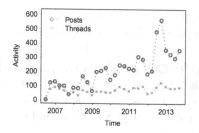

Fig. 1. Outages Mailing List Activity per Quarter.

Activity on the mailing list shows an upwards trend since it was started in 2006. Figure 1 shows quarterly activity on the list in terms of the number of threads and posts. The amount of activity on the list shows a periodic trends with less activity in Q4 which includes the holiday season. We also observe a spike in posts towards the end of 2012 which can be attributed to discussions arising from Hurricane Sandy.

2.2 Limitations

While the mailing list provides a unique view of failures which had observable impact over the past seven years, it also has some limitations. The data is biased towards North American operators and Internet providers since many of the users are US-based system administrators and the forum itself is hosted in North America. Moreover, we are biased towards incidents which transcend network boundaries as incidents which remain internal to a network are unlikely to be posted. Further, the list does not contain technical information about the underlying root cause, and indeed some posts lack a clear root cause. Finally, while the list contains failures that impacted users, there is some selection bias in terms of failures that users report to the list (*e.g.*, the aforementioned North American bias, and bias towards networks upstream of networks whose operators are more active in the list). Despite these limitations, the data contained in the mailing list is valuable because it presents a longitudinal and cross-provider view of failures that had real world impact on the Internet.

3 Keyword Analysis

In this section, we discuss how we extract keywords from the e-mail postings (Sect. 3.1) and present preliminary analysis of topics over time (Sect. 3.2).

3.1 Data Preprocessing

The fact that e-mail postings are comprised of natural language text means that they are rich with semantic information underlying the failure, but also presents a challenge in terms of automatically parsing and processing the data. To address this challenge we employ techniques from text mining and natural language processing (NLP).

Step 1: Collate threads. In general, we consider the dataset at the level of *threads*. Each thread consists of the set of e-mail messages (posts) in the thread. For each thread we extract relevant terms and phrases after removing quoted text (text from previous emails in the thread included in each email) from its posts.

Step 2: Remove spurious data and stop-words. We first discard spurious data contained in the posts. This included identifying e-mail signatures used by posters which contributed to terms and phrases unrelated to the content of the thread. We also extract traceroute measurements which are often contained in posts at this point. While traceroutes are useful for debugging, it is difficult to identify the root cause of an incident via automated analysis of the traceroutes, since the list contains posts on a variety of topics. Thus, we focus on the natural language content of the messages in this paper. We leverage a list of 572 stop words (*e.g.*, articles, prepositions and pronouns) obtained from the SMART information retrieval system [37]. Punctuations are also removed.

The remaining words are lemmatized (the process of grouping together the different inflected forms of a word) using the Stanford CoreNLP toolkit [4] so they can be analyzed as a single item. For example, determining that "walk", "walked" and "walking" are all forms of the same verb: "to walk". Note that the simple stemming (i.e., walking → walk) does not suffice as it cannot differentiate the parts of speech based on context: *e.g.*, when the term "meeting" acts as a verb: "we are meeting tomorrow" *vs.* a noun "let's go to the meeting". Lemmatization, on the other hand, can identify these contextual differences. Additionally, we filter out words with term-frequency inverse document frequency (*tf-idf*) values less than 0.122. Low *tf-idf* indicates that the word is very common throughout the dataset [36]. The threshold was chosen such that it filtered out the bottom 25 % of terms in terms of tf-idf value.

Step 3: Extract nouns and named entities. To obtain additional information about terms contained in the e-mail messages, we use the Stanford part-of-speech tagger [42] and named-entity recognizer [21]. These tools allow us to identify nouns as well as named entities (*e.g.*, identifying "Los Angeles" as a single entity). This process, however, is incomplete for domain-specific entities found in networking-related e-mails. This problem is particularly acute for organization names (*e.g.*, "Level 3"). Instead of retraining the named entity recognition system – a process that would have required extensive human annotation – we leverage Wikipedia to improve named entity recognition for networking entities. We use the simple heuristic that if a term is a capitalized noun, we search for this term or phrase in Wikipedia. If we identify a page which contains this term as the title, we check that the page is a subcategory of the "Telecommunications companies" category. If the page is in this category, we determine that the term is likely the name of a relevant organization. For multi-word entities such as "Time Warner Cable", we consider noun sequences instead of a single term to search for Wikipedia titles.

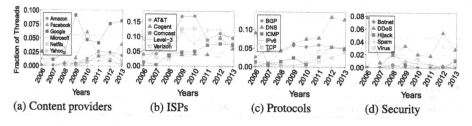

Years   Years   Years   Years

(a) Content providers   (b) ISPs   (c) Protocols   (d) Security

Fig. 2. Keyword trends over the years in the outages mailing list.

3.2 Keyword Trends

As a first step, we consider keyword trends to understand failures discussed in the list (Fig. 2). We focus on keywords in four categories: content providers, ISPs, protocols, and security. For each category we select 5–6 potentially interesting keywords. Among content providers, Google being the most popular, is more heavily discussed than others. In terms of ISPs, AT&T, Verizon and Level-3 are the most frequently discussed, with an upward trend in ISP-related discussion over time. In terms of protocols, BGP and DNS dominate, with DNS experiencing a sharp uptick in discussions in 2012–2013. Our analysis based on binary classifiers (explained in Sect. 4) shows that this is due to a more than twofold increase of DNS-related issues among access (from 3.3 % in 2011 to 7.0 % in 2012) and content providers (0.9 % in 2011 to 2.2 % in 2012). Finally, we observe DDoS as the most prevalent term related to security. It comprises nearly 8 % of posts in 2006 (note that we only have two months of data in 2006) and surges again to 5.5 % in 2012 as a result of large DDoS attacks which occurred that year (*e.g.*, [35]).

4 Classification Methodology

The terms and phrases extracted in our initial processing give a high-level view of the discussions on the mailing list. In this section, we discuss a classification methodology to help us systematically categorize the outages over time.

Conceptually, we can categorize a network outage along two orthogonal dimensions: (1) *type of the outage* (e.g., fiber cut), and (2) *entities involved in the outage* (e.g., access ISPs). Table 2 summarizes the specific categories of types and entities of interest.[2] Thus, our goal is to automatically characterize each outage e-mail thread into categories along these dimensions. Next, we describe how we designed such a classifier.

Labeling: As a first step toward automatic classification, we created a simple website to enable us and our collaborators to manually label a small random

---

[2] We do not claim that this list is exhaustive; it represents a pragmatic set we chose based on a combination of domain knowledge and manually inspecting a sample of the dataset.

Table 2. Summary of categories

Root cause of outage
Congestion, Censorship, Fiber Cut, Device Failure, Natural Disaster, Routing, App. Misconfiguration, Mobile Data Network, DNS Resolution, App. Server Down, Attack, Power Outage

Entities involved
ISP, Cloud Provider, Content Delivery Network, Mobile, Email, Access, Content

sample of the posts along the above two dimensions. We had 5 volunteers, each labeling around 30 threads. To validate that our manual annotations were consistent, we use the Fleiss' κ metric [29]; the κ value was 0.75 for entities and 0.5 for the outage types. To put this in perspective, 0.748 is considered very good and 0.48 is considered a "moderate agreement" [29]. Given this confidence, we use these manual labels to bootstrap our learning process described below.

Choice of algorithm: Our initial intuition was to formulate this as a semi-supervised clustering problem [6,17,46]. That is, we use the labeled data to bootstrap the clustering process, learn features of the identified clusters, and then iteratively refine the clusters. However, we found that the *training error* was quite high (i.e., low F-score on the labeled set). The primary reason for this is the well-known *class imbalance* problem — most real-world datasets are skewed with a small number of classes contributing the most "probability mass". The small number of training samples meant this problem was especially serious in our context.

Given this insight, we reformulated the semi-supervised clustering as a *classification* problem. While classification by itself is not immune to class imbalances, it can be made robust using two well-known ideas: (1) learning multiple binary classifiers and (2) suitable resampling [23,28,44]. For (1), instead of partitioning the dataset into N categories, we learn a "concept" for each category independently; i.e., a binary classifier trying to determine whether a thread belongs in a particular category or not. For (2), we setup the training with undersampling the majority class and/or oversampling the minority class to make the training data more balanced.

We chose a linear-kernel SVM for classification using the LibLINEAR toolkit [19] which performed well in terms of both accuracy and speed. We evaluate the goodness of the learning step using a standard leave-one-out cross-validation and compute the F-score, which is the harmonic mean of precision and recall values [31]. Next, we describe the features provided to the machine learning algorithm.

Feature selection and refinement: The naïve way to set up a NLP classification is to use a standard "bag-of-words" approach—extract words appearing in the entire dataset and create a binary feature vector for each thread indicating whether a specific keyword appears in it. This approach, however, yields very poor results on two fronts. First, while natural language text contains some terms relevant to the outage, it mostly contains English words which are not relevant to the topic and simple filtering steps such as removing stop words (e.g., "the") do not alleviate this problem. Second, this naïve set of features produces a high-dimensional feature space creating more noise.

Thus, we had to take further care in selecting the *feature set* using a combination of domain knowledge and manual inspection as described below. First, since most terms associated with our labels are likely to be nouns, we used a part-of-speech tagger [42] to filter out verbs and adjectives. Second, based on manual inspection, we found that terms in the title of the thread, or near the end of the thread were more informative and thus we experimented with weighing these terms higher. The reason is that the issues are mostly resolved towards the end of the discussion and the terms used are more pertinent to the issue. Third, to identify the entities involved, we further prune the features using a named-entity recognition system [21]. While this step retains good features (*i.e.,* words or phrases recognized as entities), it does not provide any semantic information about them. To this end, we used Wikipedia category information to glean such semantic associations. We collected 20,105 Wikipedia pages under the category "Computer Networking", and weighted the features according to whether they occur in pages under relevant subcategories (*e.g.,* "Akamai" under "Content Delivery Network"). We thus designed feature vectors with relevant entities, and weighted them according to their type. (Note that these three steps are in addition to the preprocessing in Sect. 3 that was less analysis-specific).

Table 3. Summary of feature sets used to improve the performance of the classifiers

Root cause of outage	Entities involved
1. Unigrams	1. Unigrams + bigrams (nouns)
2. Unigrams + bigrams	2. Unigrams + bigrams (nouns) + positional weights
3. Nouns	3. Nouns + named entities
4. Unigrams + bigrams (nouns)	4. Named entities
5. Unigrams + bigrams (nouns) + positional weights	5. Named entities + Wikipedia category information

Table 3 summarizes the different sets of terms we used and Fig. 3 shows how the F-score improves as we add better features. The final features selected differ between the type and entity classifiers; i.e., nouns weighed by their position in the thread performing best for *root cause* and a combination of named entities+Wikipedia category information for the *entities involved*. With these features the mean F-score of the classifiers was 78.8% for *root cause* and 82.9% for *entities involved*. For multi-class classification tasks for which human annotation κ scores are in the range of $0.5 - 0.78$, these results can be considered as reasonably high. Given the relatively small training data set and the succinct nature of the mailing list posts, the resulting performance is very promising, especially

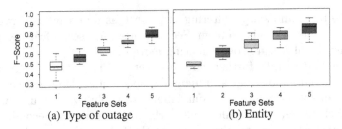

(a) Type of outage   (b) Entity

Fig. 3. F-score of classification results using different feature sets. A higher F-score implies better accuracy and the result shows the effect of our iterative feature refinement process. Table 3 summarizes the feature sets.

for domains for which a large number of user contributed posts are available for analysis.

Finally, one concern with our binary classification approach is the risk that a given thread falls in multiple classes. Fortunately, we found that the majority (>80 %) of threads had at most 1 label (not shown).[3]

5   Characterizing the Causes of Failures

Next, we use the classification methodology from the previous section to analyze common causes and types of outages discussed in the mailing list. Figure 4 shows the fraction of threads classified based on their outage and entity types.

Outage types are dominated by user-observed issues. We find that the majority of threads are placed in categories that indicate user impact. For outage type, mobile data network issues, application server, and application configuration issues dominate, comprising 28 %, 20 %, and 23 % of the data respectively. Upon closer inspection we find common terms in the application clusters related

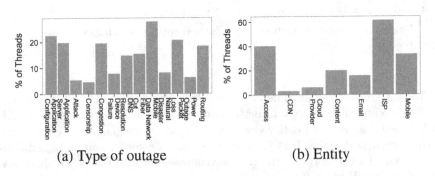

(a) Type of outage   (b) Entity

Fig. 4. Percentage of threads classified into each class

---

[3] The few threads with multiple labels were often related; e.g., congestion and packet loss or mobile + ISP.

to load balancing, server errors, and browsers (along with common applications like Facebook). For mobile, we found mobile network operators like AT&T, Sprint, and Verizon were common keywords. After issues faced by users, topics tend to be related to more operational issues such as congestion, packet loss, and routing. Issues related to attacks, censorship, natural disasters, and power outages are less common.

Dominant entities are access, ISP and mobile networks. Figure 4 highlights the prevalence of ISPs, access networks and mobile networks as entities involved in the outages. Overall, errors in application-specific entities like CDNs, e-mail, cloud and content providers were less prevalent in the mailing list discussions. Keywords in the access category tended to include access network providers like Verizon, Comcast, and Time Warner as well as issues like latency, time outs, and fiber cuts.

Content and mobile issues are on the rise. Figure 5 shows the breakdown of topics by year for outage and entity types, respectively. Starting in 2009 we see the emergence of Content providers as an entity that is commonly discussed in the mailing list. That same year we begin to see more posts related to application misconfigurations. We also observe a corresponding increase in issues related to mobile data.

Correlating keywords and associated outage types. We revisit some of the keywords observed in Fig. 2 and consider the top outage types for threads containing these keywords in Table 4. We consider keywords related to specific entities in three broad classes: ISP (Level 3), content provider (Facebook), and mobile ISP (AT&T). We find that threads containing Level 3 (and other ISPs we consider), tend to relate to operational issues for the network such as congestion, packet loss and routing incidents. In contrast, Facebook and AT&T tend to be discussed in relation to application server/misconfiguration issues and mobile data network issues. Interestingly, we also observe Facebook in threads related to mobile data network issues, possibly related to mobile users having trouble reaching the site. Similarly, AT&T is mentioned in threads related to application

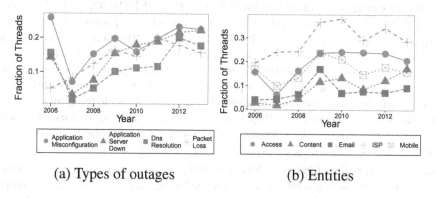

(a) Types of outages   (b) Entities

Fig. 5. Distribution of topics over time for topics that change by at least 10 %

misconfigurations *e.g.*, application specific CDN configurations that may impact users on a specific ISP.

High impact events. Finally, we investigate two incidents which explain spikes in posting in 2012. Among threads with the longest duration and most replies, are those related to a series of large-scale DNS amplification DDoS attacks in September 2012 [1,3]. Threads related to the issue reported performance problems in DNS servers that, as a result of misconfiguration, were acting as open resolvers. These servers were inadvertently flooding targets with large DNS responses, which in turn degraded performance for legitimate DNS queries [40].

Another spike in activity is related to a widespread outage in late October 2012, experienced by users of Windstream, a large ISP in the United States. Users in multiple areas (mainly in the north and northeastern US) experienced outages due to a fiber-cut caused by Hurricane Sandy [45]. Many outages around that time–related to Hurricane Sandy–also contributed to the increase in mailing list activity during fall 2012 [15]. We manually verified that these high-impact events were correctly classified by the machine learning method in terms of both the type of outage and the entities involved.

Table 4. Correlation between entity keywords, and cause of outage

ISP: level 3 Class label (% of threads)	Content: facebook Class label (% of threads)	Mobile: AT&T Class label (% of threads)
Congestion (15.1)	App. server (14.5)	Mobile data networks (26.0)
Packet loss (14.7)	Mobile data netw. (12.9)	App. misconfiguration (12.0)
Routing (14.2)	App. misconfiguration (12.1)	Packet loss (9.6)

6   Related Work

Intradomain reliability. Network reliability has been considered in a variety of networks ranging from an academic WAN [43] and ISPs [32,47] to data centers [22,39] using a variety of data sources. Some monitor properties of intradomain routing protocol such as OSPF Link State Advertisements (LSAs), which can indicate instability or unavailability of network links, or IS-IS messages which require specialized infrastructure for monitoring. More recently, there has been interest in using syslog–which is ubiquitous in many networks–to infer and study network failures. Because these studies rely on protocol and logging messages to infer the state of the network, they have a hard time inferring real user impact. Further, in many cases the network is an important part of the business which makes revealing failures unattractive.

Interdomain reliability. A variety of techniques have been employed to understand reliability at the interdomain level, including ongoing probing and monitoring efforts [26] and crowdsourcing measurements from a large population of P2P users [13]. However, characterization of the Internet's reliability at this level has been hindered by the limited view of the system provided by publicly available datasets (*e.g.*, BGP feeds).

Application layer and user-reported reliability. Network level failures do not always imply application layer or user-observed impact. There have been some studies that specifically try to address this using different techniques. Web application reliability was measured by monitoring Web client connections [33] to determine if failures were primarily client or server-related. Netmedic [25] analyzes correlations between application servers that fail in an enterprise network to understand root cause. In the context of cloud computing, Benson *et al.* attempt to mine threads from customer forums of an IaaS cloud provider [7] to identify problems users face when using cloud computing. This work is similar to our own in that it attempts to gather data from naturally arising user discussions, however, their work takes a more focused view considering only failures of a specific cloud provider.

Concurrently to our study, Dimitropoulos and Djatmiko also recognized the potential of mailing lists as a dataset [16]. However, their analysis is orthogonal to ours, which focuses more on how to apply NLP to exploit the semantics of these datasets and understand them at-scale.

7 Conclusions

In this paper, we explore an operator-run mailing list to understand reliability issues spanning multiple networks over a period of 7 years. Our main observations are that the list is primarily used for discussing issues raised by users (*e.g.*, application and mobile data issues) and that content services are on the rise in terms of discussion threads.

The mailing list data presents only one of many natural language resources that can be used to understand network reliability and the methodology applied in this paper will hopefully inspire further analysis of natural language network datasets (*e.g.*, forums [7] and trouble shooting tickets [12]) and mailing lists such as NANOG. Text-based analysis may also be combined with empirical troubleshooting approaches (*e.g.*, Hubble [26], LIFEGUARD [27]) to provide a more complete view of network reliability when directly measured data is scarce, incomplete, or unavailable.

References

1. Deep inside a DNS amplification DDoS Attack. http://blog.cloudflare.com/deep-inside-a-dns-amplification-ddos-attack
2. FCC network outage reporting system (NORS). http://transition.fcc.gov/pshs/services/cip/nors/nors.html
3. Spamhaus DDoS grows to internet-threatening size. http://arstechnica.com/security/2013/03/spamhaus-ddos-grows-to-internet-threatening-size/
4. Stanford corenlp. http://nlp.stanford.edu/software/corenlp.shtml

5. Alimi, R., Wang, Y., Yang, Y.R.: Shadow configuration as a network management primitive. In: SIGCOMM (2008)

6. Basu, S., Banerjee, A., Mooney, R.J.: Semi-supervised clustering by seeding. Int. Conf. Mach. Learn. **2**, 27–34 (2002)

7. Benson, T., Sahu, S., Akella, A., Shaikh, A.: A first look at problems in the cloud. In: HotCloud (2010)

8. Brandenburg, M.: Determining the impact of wide area network outages. http://searchenterprisewan.techtarget.com/feature/Determining-the-impact-of-wide-area-network-outages

9. Brodkin, J.: Amazon ec2 outage calls 'availability zones' into question. http://www.networkworld.com/news/2011/042111-amazon-ec2-zones.html (2011)

10. Growing business dependence on the internet: new risks require CEO action. http://businessroundtable.org/sites/default/files/200709_Growing_Business_Dependence_on_the_Internet.pdf (2007)

11. Chen, X., Mao, Y., Mao, Z.M., van de Merwe, K: Declarative configuration management for complex and dynamic networks. In: CoNEXT (2010)

12. Cheng, Y.-C., Bellardo, J., Benko, P., Snoeren, A., Voelker, G., Savage, S.: Jigsaw: solving the puzzle of enterprise 802.11 analysis. In: SIGCOMM (2006)

13. Choffnes, D., Bustamante, F., Ge. Z.: Crowdsourcing service-level network event detection. In: SIGCOMM (2010)

14. Cowie, J.: Renesys blog: China's 18-minute mystery. http://www.renesys.com/blog/2010/11/chinas-18-minute-mystery.shtml

15. Darrow, B.: Superstorm Sandy wreaks havoc on internet infrastructure. https://gigaom.com/2012/10/30/superstorm-sandy-wreaks-havoc-on-internet-infrastructure/ (2012)

16. Dimitropoulos, X., Djatmiko, M.: Analysis of outage posts in the nanog and outages mailing lists. https://tnc2013.terena.org/core/presentation/146 (2013)

17. Ding, C., Li, T., Peng, W., Park, H.: Orthogonal nonnegative matrix t-factorizations for clustering. In: Proceedings of KDD (2006)

18. Dynes, S., Andrijcic, E., Johnson, M.E.: Costs to the US economy of information infrastructure failures: estimates from field studies and economic data. In: WEIS (2006)

19. Fan, R.-E., Chang, K.-W., Hsieh, C.-J., Wang, X.-R., Lin, C.-J.: Liblinear: a library for large linear classification. J. Mach. Learn. Res. **9**, 1871–1874 (2008)

20. Feamster, N., Balakrishnan, H.: Detecting BGP configuration faults with static analysis. In: Sigcomm (2005)

21. Finkel, J.R., Grenager, T., Manning, C.: Incorporating non-local information into information extraction systems by gibbs sampling. In: Proceedings of ACL (2005)

22. Gill, P., Jain, N., Nagappan, N.: Understanding network failures in data centers: measurement, analysis, and implications. In: SIGCOMM (2011)

23. Japkowicz, N.: The class imbalance problem: significance and strategies. In: Proceedings of the International Conference on Artificial Intelligence, Citeseer (2000)

24. Javed, U., Cunha, I., Choffnes, D.R., Katz-Bassett, E., Anderson, T., Krishnamurthy, A.: PoiRoot: investigating the root cause of interdomain path changes. In: SIGCOMM (2013)

25. Kandula, S., Mahajan, R., Verkaik, P., Agarwal, S., Padhye, J., Bahl, P.: Detailed diagnosis in enterprise networks. In: SIGCOMM (2010)

26. Katz-Bassett, E., Madhyastha, H., John, J., Krishnamurthy, A., Wetherall, D., Anderson, T.: Studying black holes in the internet with hubble. In: NSDI (2008)

27. Katz-Bassett, E., Scott, C., Choffnes, D.R., Cunha, I., Valancius, V., Feamster, N., Madhyastha, H.V., Anderson, T., Krishnamurthy, A.: LIFEGUARD: Practical repair of persistent route failures. In: SIGCOMM (2012)
28. Kubat, M., Matwin, S., et al.: Addressing the curse of imbalanced training sets: one-sided selection. Int. Conf. Mach. Learn. **97**, 179–186 (1997)
29. Landis, J.R., Koch, G.G., et al.: The measurement of observer agreement for categorical data. Biometrics **33**(1), 159–174 (1977)
30. Mahimkar, A., Song, H.H., Ge, Z., Shaikh, A., Wang, J., Yates, J., Zhang, Y., Emmons, J.: Detecting the performance impact of upgrades in large operational networks. In: Sigcomm (2010)
31. Manning, C.D., Raghavan, P., Schütze, H.: Introduction to Information Retrieval, vol. 1. Cambridge University Press, Cambridge (2008)
32. Markopoulou, A., Iannaccone, G., Bhattacharyya, S., Chuah, C.-N., Ganjali, Y., Diot, C.: Characterization of failures in an operational IP backbone network. IEEE/ACM ToN **16**(4), 749–762 (2008)
33. Padmanabhan, V., Ramabhadran, S., Agarwal, S., Padhye, J.: A study of end-to-end web access failures. In: CoNEXT (2006)
34. cost of data center outages. http://www.emersonnetworkpower.com/documentation/en-us/brands/liebert/documents/white%20papers/2013_emerson_data_center_cost_downtime_sl-24680.pdf (2013)
35. Prince, M.: How to launch a 65Gbps DDoS, and how to stop one. http://blog.cloudflare.com/65gbps-ddos-no-problem (2012)
36. Ramos, J.: Using TF-IDF to determine word relevance in document queries. In: Proceedings of the International Conference on Machine Learning (ICML) (2003)
37. Rocchio, J.J.: Relevance feedback in information retrieval. http://jmlr.org/papers/volume5/lewis04a/a11-smart-stop-list/english.stop (1971)
38. Rode, V.: Outages - outages (planned & unplanned) reporting. https://puck.nether.net/mailman/listinfo/outages
39. Shaikh, A., Isett, C., Greenberg, A., Roughan, M., Gottlieb, J.: A case study of OSPF behavior in a large enterprise network. In: ACM IMW (2002)
40. Sophos user bulletin board. https://www.astaro.org/gateway-products/general-discussion/44500-ddos-attack-via-dns.html
41. Tariq, M.B., Zeitoun, A., Valancius, V., Feamster, N., Ammar, M.: Answering "what-if" deployment and configuration questions with WISE. In: Sigcomm (2008)
42. Toutanova, K., Klein, D., Manning, C.D., Singer, Y.: Feature-rich part-of-speech tagging with a cyclic dependency network. In: Proceedings of NAACL (2003)
43. Turner, D., Levchenko, K., Snoeren, A.C., Savage, S.: California fault lines: understanding the causes and impact of network failures. In: SIGCOMM (2010)
44. Veropoulos, K., Campbell, C., Cristianini, N., et al.: Controlling the sensitivity of support vector machines. In: Proceedings of the International Joint Conference on Artificial Intelligence, vol. 1999, pp. 55–60. Citeseer (1999)
45. Vielmetti, E.: http://goo.gl/ODnq5q (2012)
46. Wagstaff, K., Cardie, C., Rogers, S., Schrödl, S., et al.: Constrained k-means clustering with background knowledge. Int. Conf. Mach. Learn. **1**, 577–584 (2001)
47. Watson, D., Jahanian, F., Labovitz, C.: Experiences with monitoring OSPF on a regional service provider network. In: ICDCS (2003)

Transparent Estimation of Internet Penetration from Network Observations

Suso Benitez-Baleato[1,2]([✉]), Nils B. Weidmann[1], Petros Gigis[3],
Xenofontas Dimitropoulos[3], Eduard Glatz[4], and Brian Trammell[4]

[1] Department of Politics and Public Administration,
University of Konstanz, Konstanz, Germany
`jesus.benitez-baleato@uni-konstanz.de`
[2] University of Santiago de Compostela, Santiago de Compostela, Spain
[3] Foundation of Research and Technology Hellas (FORTH), Heraklion, Greece
[4] Computer Engineering and Networks Laboratory (TIK),
ETH Zurich, Zurich, Switzerland

Abstract. The International Telecommunications Union (ITU) and the
Organization for Economic Cooperation and Development (OECD) provide Internet penetration statistics, which are collected from official
national sources worldwide, and they are widely used to inform policymakers and researchers about the expansion of digital technologies. Nevertheless, these statistics are derived with methodologies, which are often
opaque and inconsistent across countries. Even more, regimes may have
incentives to misreport such statistics. In this work, we make a first
attempt to evaluate the consistency of the ITU/OECD Internet penetration statistics with an alternative indicator of Internet penetration,
which can be measured with a consistent methodology across countries
and relies on public data. We compare, in particular, the ITU and OECD
statistics with measurements of the used IPv4 address space across countries and find very high correlations ranging between 0.898 and 0.978 for
all years between 2006 and 2010. We also observe that the level of consistency drops for less developed or less democratic countries. Besides, we
show that measurements of the used IPv4 address space can serve as a
more timely Internet penetration indicator with sub-national granularity,
using two large developing countries as case studies.

1 Introduction

How has the usage of the Internet technologies increased in different countries?
How has that growth affected economic and societal changes? A main source
of empirical evidence to address these questions are the Internet penetration
statistics provided by the ITU and the OECD. Those statistics are influential
in debates about global technological development, Internet governance and its
societal effects. Moreover, social scientists rely on these datasets to understand

---

Baleato and Weidmann gratefully acknowledge funding from the Alexander von
Humboldt Foundation.

© Springer International Publishing Switzerland 2015
J. Mirkovic and Y. Liu (Eds.): PAM 2015, LNCS 8995, pp. 220–231, 2015.
DOI: 10.1007/978-3-319-15509-8_17

the impact of technology on social and political systems [22]: Is the Internet really a catalyst of popular protest that can topple dictators? Or does it rather play into the hands of autocrats, increasing opportunities for surveillance and censoring?

While important both for policy-making and scientific research, these statistics exhibit some key shortcomings. The ITU and the OECD do not measure Internet penetration directly, but they rather collect and standardize information provided by different governments and their regulatory agencies. Each of these agencies has its own protocol for collecting these numbers at the national level. Thus, the final statistics that are ultimately included in the main datasets may be subject to error due to poor data collection standards, or even systematic inflation due to some countries' incentives to exaggerate economic progress because of aid conditionality. Similarly, differences in data collection across countries may significantly limit comparability and thus impede the main purpose of the data. Also, these statistics become available with significant delay (oftentimes a year or more). Last, only national-level statistics are provided, which makes analysis of variation in Internet penetration *within* countries impossible.

In this work, we make a first attempt to use Internet measurement techniques to independently verify and supplement existing penetration statistics. We introduce a reproducible methodology that uses publicly available data and circumvents the limitations of transparency, comparability availability and resolution. We derive Internet penetration estimates from geolocated network measurements of the globally used IPv4 address space using two different approaches, and then compare our estimates with the official ITU/OECD statistics between 2006 and 2010. We find that our estimates exhibit very high correlation (ranging between 0.898 and 0.978) with the official data for all studied years, which however drops for less developed or democratic countries. In addition, we show that our estimates are consistent with official statistics at the subnational level for two large developing countries. These observations are encouraging, because they suggest that readily available data (e.g. from RouteViews [29]) can be used to cross-check official statistics and derive Internet penetration estimates more timely and with finer geographical resolution than the ITU/OECD statistics.

Our paper is structured as follows. First, we discuss the importance of the Internet penetration statistics for debates on technological development, Internet governance and its societal effects. Then we describe the methods and the datasets that we use to map and geo-localize the used IPv4 address space. After that, we compare them with the official statistics both at the country and the regional level. Finally, we discuss the results, the limitations, and the potential uses of our estimates.

2   Data and Research on Internet Penetration

The ITU is the United Nations telecommunications agency in charge of the global radio spectrum and satellite orbits allocation, the development of technical standards and the fostering of ICT deployment in developing countries [9].

As part of its role in technological development, the ITU collects, verifies and harmonizes ICT statistics. The outcome of this work is disseminated through the World Telecommunications/ICT Indicators Database (WTID), a chronological time series for over 200 countries regularly updated from 1960 on [12]. The WTID is made of more than 150 indicators describing aspects like coverage, traffic, price or quality of several communication technologies, including access and use of the Internet. The Internet penetration indicators are available for 192 countries, starting in 1990. The ITU retrieves this data from questionnaires submitted to the official country contacts. There are two types of national contact points in charge of providing the information to the ITU. The first one is the national telecommunication ministries and regulatory authorities, which provide Internet penetration estimates based on data from fixed and mobile Internet providers. The second source is the national statistical offices, which typically obtain data on access and use of the Internet through surveys. The collected data is then harmonized by the statistical division of the ITU, consistently with a set of guidelines intended to ensure the comparability of the data measurement and collection efforts performed by the respective countries [10,11].

Other organisations providing Internet penetration statistics, such as the Organisation for the Economic Cooperation and Development (OECD), follow a similar procedure. The OECD indicators also rely on data provided by the administrative bodies of the member states and from the EU Community Survey on household use of ICT. They are available for 34 countries starting in 2006 [20]. However, despite the similar data collection method, this does not mean that the values correspond to those in the ITU dataset; the correlation between the two is only 0.705 during our period of analysis (2006–2010). Thus, we will treat the OECD estimates as separate datasets in the analysis below.

2.1 Existing Work

In the following paragraphs, we discuss existing work that relies primarily on the ITU WTID database. Due to the fact that it is the only global cross-national database on ICT penetration, the WTID has been widely used in policy and research. The WTID is the main reference for many other UN agencies, including the Department of Economic and Social Affairs (DESA) and the World Intellectual Property Organisation (WIPO), who use it for their e-Government survey and the Global Innovation Index [27,32]. Also, the ITU data is used to measure the progress of the Millenium Development Goals, a road map adopted by 189 countries to make available the benefits of the ICT for developing countries [26]. Moreover, the WTID is extensively used in the Global Internet Report by the Internet Society (ISOC) [14] and the Global Information Technology Report by the World Economic Forum (WEF) [30], which describe the state of the Internet.

ITU statistics have also been used in research. Economists, for example, have used the WTID to analyze the effect of ICT investment on economic growth [23,24]. In political science, one strand of research has focused on the role of political institutions and economic development for technology adoption [19,21]. Here, again, the methodological approach is cross-national statistical comparison using ITU indicators. Another question political scientists have focused on is the impact of ICT on democratization. Earlier work using ITU data concludes that the Internet fosters democracy through less restrictive channels of communication [2,6]. However, more recent results provide a more cautious view, as they show that closed autocratic regimes are keen adopters of this technology and are no more likely to democratize as a result of ICT introduction [22].

2.2 Limitations of Existing Databases

As the previous section has shown, the ITU indicators are a useful resource both for policy-makers and researchers alike. However, these valuable datasets suffer from a number of shortcomings.

Transparency. The lack of a standardized methodology across countries makes it difficult to understand and verify how the data are generated. For example, many countries will not have systematic data collection routines in place, requiring rough "approximations". Hence, it is not inconceivable that data provided to the ITU is subject to errors and biases in reporting. This may not be a problem affecting ICT statistics alone, but has been shown to be a more general issue with statistics from less developed countries [13].

Comparability. Because of the different quality and accuracy of numbers across countries, comparability in cross-national analyses may be severely hampered. The reason is that differences in Internet penetration across countries as picked up by the WTID can be partly the result of different data collection methodologies. With little information about the procedures employed by each country, it is difficult to even assess the severity of the problem, rather than correct it.

Availability. While the ITU offers semestral updates of their database, these updates are applied only to a selected number of indicators. The final revised edition of the full indicators is only available with one year delay, and is subject of retrospective revision caused by changes either in external datasets (like the population statistics) or by amendments submitted by national agencies. Those delivery times do also affect the other datasets considered; for example, some of the OECD indicators are only delivered with the publication of the Communications Outlook, once every two years [20].

Resolution. The WTID and OECD databases provide national level data only. However Internet penetration does not need to be uniform in a given country; regions of high coverage can exist next to those with low coverage. For many research projects, it would be useful to have indicators at the subnational level (for example, provinces or districts), to study how Internet coverage is provided sub-nationally, and what effects it has. The available statistics are of no use for this.

3   Data Sources and Methodology

In this section we describe the datasets and the processing methodology. First we describe how we use routing data from Border Gateway Protocol (BGP) collectors, namely from RouteViews [29], to estimate Internet penetration. Since not all routed addresses are actually used, we use in addition passive traffic measurements based on NetFlow from an academic Internet Service Provider (ISP) in Switzerland (SWITCH [25]) to estimate the globally active IPv4 address space based on the methodology of [3]. We collapse IPv4 address blocks to /24s which is the longest unfiltered IPv4 prefix; and then geolocalize /24 prefixes in national or large subnational administrative units.

Globally Routed IPv4 Addresses. We first extract routed IPv4 addresses from publicly available BGP tables. In particular, we used a daily routing table snapshot from route-views2.oregon-ix.net for the first 16 days of each February and August between 2004 and 2012. We selected these days to align with the timespan of the NetFlow data that were available to us. We collapsed all prefixes to unique /24s per day. To mitigate the effect of misconfigurations and route leaks, which could pollute our data, we filtered out reserved IPv4 addresses and prefixes larger than /8. In addition, for each 16-day interval we kept the /24 prefixes that were observed in all 16 days. In Fig. 1 we show the number of unique /24 prefixes in each 16-day interval over time with and without our filtering. We observe two large spikes, which were the result of route leaks, which our filtering effectively mitigated. Apart from these two spikes, the effect of filtering is negligible. From 2004 to 2012 the number of routed /24 prefixes doubled.

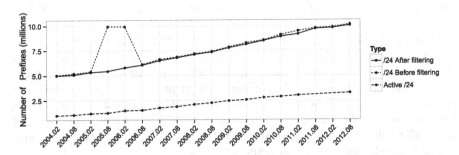

Fig. 1. Routed and active /24 IPv4 address blocks over time.

Active IPv4 Addresses. We also infer active /24 IPv4 address blocks using private network traffic data from an ISP. We use the inferred active addresses as a sanity check on the methodology based on the publicly available routed addresses. Specifically, we used unsampled NetFlow records collected from the border routers of SWITCH the first 16 days of each February and August between 2004 and 2010. For the years 2011 and 2012 we do not use any further the August and February samples due to anomalous or missing data.

We then extracted two-way TCP flows (to eliminate the effect of spoofing) and /24 blocks seen from SWITCH based on the methodology of [3]. Our previous work showed that this approach provides rich visibility (although not complete) into the globally used IPv4 address space [3]. In this paper, we extend our analysis to span a period of 9 years, for which we processed 218 billion flows (corresponding to 8.05 petabytes of traffic) in total. In Fig. 1 we compare how the active address space compares with the routed address space. We observe that on average 27.7 % of the routed address space is seen in the collected netflow data.

Geolocation. We then geo-reference each /24 block using the *Maxmind* GeoIP2 City database [18] and assign it to a country. The GeoIP2 City database is the most accurate geo-database provided by Maxmind, which claims 99.8 % accuracy at the country level and also high levels of accuracy within several different countries worldwide (for more details see [17]). We note though that geolocalization at finer granularity (e.g. the city level) or in cellular networks is still an open research problem and can be inaccurate, which is an issue that may affect our subnational results (cf. Sect. 4.4). We assign the /24 blocks to countries based on their spatial coordinates after removing 13,431 blocks georeferenced to 'EU' with coordinates in Switzerland, which account for approximately 0.05 % of the total active prefixes. We assign coordinates to countries using the CShapes dataset, a Geographical Information Systems (GIS) dataset on international borders that also incorporates border changes over time [31]. Our final indicator of Internet penetration is the number of routed or active /24 blocks in each country.

4   Correlation Analysis of Internet Penetration Estimates

In order to evaluate the consistency between our estimates of Internet penetration and those provided by the ITU and the OECD, we first conduct a bivariate analysis of the correlation of both estimates and how it changes over time. In particular, we correlate the number of routed or active /24 blocks with the number of Internet users according to the ITU or OECD data. For both estimates, we use the logarithm, since the numbers span several scales. We also analyze the agreement between the ITU numbers and our estimates when distinguishing between countries with different levels of economic development and democracy. Lastly, we take our analysis to the subnational level, evaluating the agreement of official and estimated Internet penetration estimates within two large developing countries: India and Turkey. Although we have verified that our findings hold for the entire duration of the studied datasets, we present results primarily for the period between 2006 and 2010 which is covered by all datasets.

4.1   ITU/OECD Statistics vs. Internet Measurements at the Country Level

The scatter plots in Fig. 2 illustrate and quantify the correlation between the proposed and the official Internet penetration indicators for a single time slice

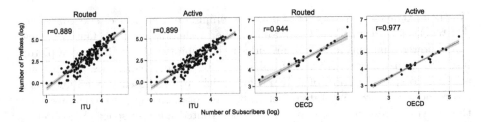

Fig. 2. Scatterplots of the proposed and the ITU/OECD country-level Internet penetration estimates for February 2010. For each scatterplot, we mark the correlation coefficient.

(February 2010). Both for routed and active prefixes, the correlation with the ITU data is very high, i.e. 0.889 or higher, as shown in the first two panels of Fig. 2. This suggests that both the number of routed or active prefixes can serve as good alternative indicators of Internet penetration. This picture improves for OECD statistics, which include more developed countries, as shown in the last two panels of Fig. 2.

The high correlation is also stable over time. The average correlation with ITU across all semi-annual samples between 2006 and 2010 is 0.898 and 0.911 for routed and active prefixes, respectively, and 0.944 (routed) and 0.978 (active) when comparing with the OECD data. Figure 3 shows the evolution over time, both for different validation datasets (ITU/OECD) and different measurement approaches (routed/active).

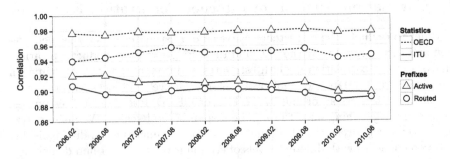

Fig. 3. Correlation over time between official statistics (ITU and OECD) and the number of routed/active prefixes.

4.2 Internet Penetration by Level of Economic Development and Democracy

We have seen that Internet penetration estimates based on network measurements achieve high correlation with the official Internet penetration statistics provided by the ITU and the OECD. However, so far we have treated all countries equally. In order to evaluate how our methods fares in different contexts, we analyze correlations in different types of countries. We conduct this analysis on a global level using the ITU data only. As discussed above, the statistics provided by the ITU may be particularly problematic (i) in less developed countries with poor bureaucracies and (ii) in non-democratic countries where governments are not required or not willing to collect and share data. For these reasons, our analysis aims to establish how the agreement between ITU Internet penetration statistics and our network-based ones varies across different levels of development and different regime types (non-democratic to democratic ones).

Economic development is typically measured using GDP per capita values, which we obtain from [5]. The political regime type is measured using the Polity IV dataset [16]. Polity IV is the most frequently used quantitative database on political regimes, and encodes regime type using a numeric indicator ranging from −10 to 10. Low values correspond to strongly autocratic countries such as North Korea, and high values to established democracies such as the US. We bin the countries in our sample into low-, medium- and high GDP countries (Fig. 4a) and those with low-, medium- and high democracy scores (Fig. 4b). The split is done such that each category includes exactly a third of the countries in our sample. In each category, we compute the correlation between our network-based Internet penetration estimates and the ones from the ITU.

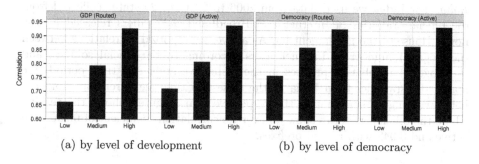

(a) by level of development   (b) by level of democracy

Fig. 4. Correlation between the ITU Internet penetration statistics and the number of routed/active IPv4 /24 prefixes of 192 countries grouped by their GDP and democracy index (Polity IV) into three equal-size groups.

The results show small but distinct trends in the correlations. Figure 4a reveals that the agreement between our estimates and the ITU figures increases for more developed countries, regardless of whether we use estimates based on routed prefixes or active networks. A similar trend can be identified in Fig. 4b for more democratic countries. These trends could have different causes: First, they could be due to limitations of data collection and biases in reporting that affect primarily less developed or less democratic countries. Second, it is possible that our method suffers from a lower accuracy of geo-localization in these countries, which could render it less precise in these contexts. However, due to fairly high accuracy of geo-localization at the country level (see below), we believe that the second reason is probably less influential. This would mean that the trends in the correlations could indeed be due to differences in the quality of the ITU estimates across the different groups of countries.

4.3 Internet Penetration within Countries

Our analysis above compared country-level Internet penetration statistics to those inferred from network observations. In principle, however, the proposed approach can also be applied to the subnational level, by estimating penetration in sub-national units (such as provinces or districts) from the number of routed or active /24 blocks in that unit. Although not the main contribution of this paper, we provide a first analysis here. We focus on two countries for which subnational Internet penetration statistics are publicly available and which have an interesting political profile (India and Turkey). For both countries, the number of routed/active /24 blocks was computed using the geo-localized prefixes as described above, which were assigned to first-tier subnational units (states in India, and provinces in Turkey). The boundaries of these units were taken from the Global Administrative Areas database, a spatial dataset of internal administrative units [28].

India. For India, we used data from 2006 to 2010 for 29 states collected from the official statistics of Internet and Broadband Subscribers released by the Lower House of the Parliament [4]. As above, we reported correlations between the (logged) number of Internet users according to the official sources, and the (logged) number of prefixes in the respective state and time period. We match the statistics from India to the closest in time measurements from the February/August snapshot of the respective year. Figure 5 shows the results, where the official statistics show an average correlation coefficient of 0.956 with active and 0.942 with routed prefixes.

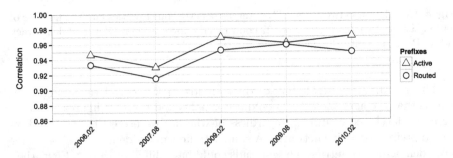

Fig. 5. Correlation over time between official Internet penetration statistics and the number of active/routed prefixes for 29 states within India.

Turkey. In the case of Turkey, we use the statistics of Internet usage for 2010 released for the 81 provinces by the largest ISP (TTNET) and the Information and Communication Technologies Authority [8]. After removing missing cases and matching the administrative units, our final sample includes 65 provinces. Again, we find high correlations. The number of routed /24 blocks correlates with the official number of Internet subscribers at 0.89, which is slightly higher for active networks (0.907).

Thus, our method works well also at the subnational level. A key issue here, however, is the resolution and quality of IP geo-localization. The subnational units we use in this analysis are still fairly large; once we increase resolution down to the level of municipalities or even cities, low geo-localization accuracy becomes a key limitation as discussed next.

4.4 Discussion and Shortcomings

Address Space Over-/Underpopulation. One complication in comparing Internet penetration based on used address space is that an IP address may be used by a different number of subscribers in different regions of the world. Network address translation (NAT) has long broken any assumption of an 1:1 mapping between addresses and users. Further, the causes are not only political and economic, but related to Internet governance as well. IP addresses are allocated by five Regional Internet Registries (RIRs): ARIN for North America, LACNIC for Latin America and the Caribbean, RIPE for Europe and West Asia, APNIC for Asia and the Pacific, and AFRINIC for Africa. Each of these RIRs has a member base made up of Internet service providers and enterprises, a mission to allocate IP address space based on need, and its own framework for deciding policies for allocation of addresses to the members. As global IPv4 space has been exhausted, the different approaches within the different regions [15] have led to regionally linked amounts of pressure to conserve addresses by sharing them more broadly. A complete analysis of this phenomenon is outside the scope of this work, but this should be kept in mind when comparing Internet penetration numbers based on address counting across different RIR regions. Despite these differences, our analysis shows very high correlation coefficients across regions.

IP Address Geolocation. The accuracy of the MaxMind GeoIP database we use for geolocation, and of IP geolocation databases in general, is difficult to evaluate, and generally lacking in good sources of ground truth. Nonetheless, previous research has evaluated the accuracy of a set of these databases, including Max-Mind GeoIP, in 2011 [7]. For national-level data, the MaxMind GeoIP database we use agreed with the majority of other databases 99.1 % of the time, which was the best agreement ratio of any of the evaluated geolocation databases. For subnational data, the authors found that 78 % of the geolocated IP addresses globally were within 40 km of the centroid of the region most probably containing the IP address, with a great deal of regional variation: 75th percentile distances range from about 10 km in the ARIN region, to about 40 km in the APNIC region (containing India), to about 400 km in the LACNIC region. Any analysis of subnational-level IP geolocation data must therefore take the probable error into account, as well as the size of the regions in question. Given the comparison to other databases, however, we have confidence in our selection of MaxMind GeoIP, and in our broad conclusions at both the national and subnational levels.

5   Conclusions

Official statistics about Internet penetration in different countries provided by the ITU and the OECD are widely-used in research studies and policy debates. However, due to the reliance on governments as the source of information, these statistics are derived from opaque methodologies, which may not be comparable. In addition, they are provided with significant delay and only at the national level. In this work, we propose an alternative Internet penetration indicator based on readily available measurements of the routed IP address space per country and show that this approach provides largely consistent results with the official ITU/OECD statistics. This helps both to increase confidence in the ITU/OECD data and to provide an alternative methodology with better data transparency, comparability, resolution, and availability. Furthermore, we showed that the high level of consistency drops for less developed or democratic countries. Finally, we also found that our approach is able to pick up variation in Internet penetration within two large developing countries.

To support our analysis and make our data more broadly accessible to the community, we provide visualisations of the growth of the Internet between 2004 and 2012, measured in terms of globally routed IPv4 addresses, versus the Gross Domestic Product (GDP), the income per capita, the population, and the polity index of 92 large countries in [1].

References

1. Internet growth versus economic and political indicators, October 2014. http://www.ics.forth.gr/tnl/ipen/index.html
2. Best, M.L., Wade, K.W.: The internet and democracy: Global catalyst or democratic dud? Bull. Sci. Technol. Soc. **29**(4), 255–271 (2009)
3. Dainotti, A., Benson, K., King, A., Claffy, K., Kallitsis, M., Glatz, E., Dimitropoulos, X.: Estimating Internet address space usage through passive measurements. ACM SIGCOMM Comput. Commun. Rev. (CCR) **44**(1), 42–49 (2014)
4. Datanet India Pvt. Ltd.: Indiastat.com (2014). http://www.indiastat.com/
5. Gleditsch, K.S.: Expanded trade and GDP data. J. Confl. Resolut. **46**, 712–724 (2002)
6. Groshek, J.: The democratic effects of the Internet, 1994–2003. Int. Commun. Gaz. **71**(3), 115–136 (2009)
7. Huffaker, B., Fomenkov, M., Claffy, K.: Geocompare: A comparison of public and commercial geolocation databases. CAIDA Technical report, May 2011. http://www.caida.org/publications/papers/2011/geocompare-tr/geocompare-tr.pdf
8. ICAT: Turkish electronic communications sector quarterly market reports (2013). http://www.btk.gov.tr/kutuphane_ve_veribankasi/yil_istatistikleri/ehsyib.pdf
9. ITU: Telecommunications development sector. http://www.itu.int/en/ITU-D/

10. ITU: Handbook for the collection of administrative data on telecommunications/ ICT, 2011 (2011). http://www.itu.int/en/ITU-D/Statistics/Pages/publications/ handbook.aspx
11. ITU: Manual for measuring ICT access and use by households and individuals (2011). http://www.itu.int/en/ITU-D/Statistics/Pages/publications/manual2014. aspx
12. ITU: World telecommunication/ICT indicators database (2013). http://www.itu. int/en/ITU-D/Statistics/Pages/publications/wtid.aspx
13. Jerven, M.: Poor numbers: How We Are misled by African Development Statistics and What to Do About It. Cornell University Press, Ithaca (2013)
14. Kende, M.: Global Internet report. Internet Society (2014)
15. Lehr, M., Lear, E., Vest, T.: Running on empty: The challenge of managing Internet addresses. In: Proceedings of the 36th Annual Telecommunications Policy Research Conference (TPRC), Arlington, VA, USA, September 2008
16. Marshall, M.G., Jaggers, K.: Polity IV project: Political regime characteristics and transitions, 1800–2012 (2013). http://www.systemicpeace.org/polity/polity4.htm
17. Maxmind GeoIP2 City Accuracy. https://www.maxmind.com/en/geoip2-city-accuracy
18. Maxmind: GeoIP2 Databases. http://www.maxmind.com/en/geoip2-databases
19. Milner, H.V.: The digital divide: The role of political institutions in technology diffusion. Comp. Polit. Stud. **39**(2), 176–199 (2006)
20. OECD: Key ICT indicators (2013). http://www.oecd.org/internet/broadband/ oecdkeyictindicators.htm
21. Oyelaran-Oyeyinka, B., Lal, K.: Internet diffusion in Sub-Saharan Africa: A cross-country analysis. Telecommun. Policy **29**(7), 507–527 (2005)
22. Rød, E.G., Weidmann, N.B.: Empowering activists or autocrats? The Internet in authoritarian regimes. J. Peace Res. **52**(3), (2015, forthcoming)
23. Roeller, L.H., Waverman, L.: Telecommunications infrastructure and economic development: A simultaneous approach. Am. Econ. Rev. **91**(4), 909–923 (2001). http://www.jstor.org/stable/2677818
24. Sridhar, K.S., Sridhar, V.: Telecommunications and growth: Causal model, quantitative and qualitative evidence. Econ. Polit. Wkly. **41**(25), 2611–2619 (2006). http://www.jstor.org/stable/4418381
25. SWITCH: Swiss National Research and Education Network (NREN). http://www. switch.ch/
26. United Nations: Millenium development goals (2014). http://www.un.org/ millenniumgoals/
27. United Nations Department of Economic & Social Affairs: United Nations e-government survey (2014). http://www.un.org/en/development/desa/publica tions/e-government-survey-2014.html
28. University of California, Berkeley Museum of Vertebrate Zoology and the International Rice Research Institute: Global Administrative Areas Dataset (2012). http://www.gadm.org/
29. University of Oregon: Route Views Project. http://www.routeviews.org/
30. WEF: Global information technology report (2014). http://www.weforum.org/ issues/global-information-technology
31. Weidmann, N.B., Kuse, D., Gleditsch, K.S.: The geography of the international system: the cshapes dataset. Int. Interact. **36**(1), 86–106 (2010). http://dx.doi.org/10.1080/03050620903554614
32. World Intellectual Property Organization: Global Innovation Index (2014). http:// www.wipo.int/econ_stat/en/economics/gii/

Web and Peer-to-Peer

A Quantitative Study of Video Duplicate Levels in YouTube

Yao Liu[1]([✉]), Sam Blasiak[2], Weijun Xiao[3], Zhenhua Li[4], and Songqing Chen[2]

[1] SUNY Binghamton, Binghamton, USA
yaoliu@cs.binghamton.edu
[2] George Mason University, Fairfax, USA
{sblasiak,sqchen}@cs.gmu.edu
[3] Virginia Commonwealth University, Richmond, USA
wxiao@vcu.edu
[4] Tsinghua University, Beijing, China
lizhenhua1983@tsinghua.edu.cn

Abstract. The popularity of video sharing services has increased exponentially in recent years, but this popularity is accompanied by challenges associated with the tremendous scale of user bases and massive amounts of video data. A known inefficiency of video sharing services with user-uploaded content is widespread video duplication. These duplicate videos are often of different aspect ratios, can contain overlays or additional borders, or can be excerpted from a longer, original video, and thus can be difficult to detect. The proliferation of duplicate videos can have an impact at many levels, and accurate assessment of duplicate levels is a critical step toward mitigating their effects on both video sharing services and network infrastructure.

In this work, we combine video sampling methods, automated video comparison techniques, and manual validation to estimate duplicate levels within large collections of videos. The combined strategies yield a 31.7 % estimated video duplicate ratio across all YouTube videos, with 24.0 % storage occupied by duplicates. These high duplicate ratios motivate the need for further examination of the systems-level tradeoffs associated with video deduplication versus storing large number of duplicates.

1 Introduction

User generated video content has exponentially increased in the recent years. For example, *YouTube*, *Dailymotion*, and *Vimeo* are among the most popular websites for uploading and sharing user generated content (UGC). YouTube alone has gained massive popularity: it attracts more than 1 billion users every month, more than 100 h of uploaded video each minute, and more than 1 million creators make money from videos that they have uploaded [3]. We estimate that there are more than 849 million videos on YouTube (Sect. 5.2). According to Sandvine, YouTube generates 13.19 % of all downstream fixed access traffic (e.g., cable network) and 17.61 % of all downstream mobile data traffic in North America during peak hours [2].

© Springer International Publishing Switzerland 2015
J. Mirkovic and Y. Liu (Eds.): PAM 2015, LNCS 8995, pp. 235–248, 2015.
DOI: 10.1007/978-3-319-15509-8_18

Unlike video on-demand service providers such as Netflix, which contracts with a limited number video providers, UGC websites attract large numbers of video uploaders. This high diversity of uploaders poses a unique challenge for these UGC video sharing websites: Videos can be uploaded in different incarnations by different users, leading to duplicates in the video database. While duplicates that occur at the exact byte-level can be captured by the video sharing service using cryptographic hashes, user-generated (near-)duplicate videos are often uploaded in different encodings, have different aspect ratios, can contain overlays or additional borders, or could be excerpted from a longer, original video. As a result, they are assigned their own unique IDs in the video database. Note that duplicates should not be confused with multiple transcoded versions generated by a video sharing service to support streaming at different bandwidths and to different devices. These transcoded versions are associated with a same video ID in the video database.

The proliferation of duplicate videos could impact many aspects of datacenter and network operations and, as a result, have negative effects on the user experience. From the video server's perspective, duplicate videos could increase data storage, power, and therefore overall costs of data center operations. Further, duplicate videos have the potential to harm caching systems, degrading cache efficiency by taking up space that could be used for unique content and increasing the amount of data that must be sent over the network to in-network caching systems. These inefficiencies could be passed on to the user in the form of duplicated search results, longer startup delays, and interrupted streaming [17].

Although it is well known that duplication occurs in today's UGC video sharing websites, little is known about its precise level. Work to more-accurately determine duplicate levels is necessary because, although deduplication procedures can improve the overall efficiency of a video sharing system, deduplication itself could also be costly. Quantifying the level of duplication is therefore critical for determining whether effort to deduplicate, or otherwise mitigate the effect of duplicates, would be worthwhile.

As YouTube is the largest UGC video system today, we choose it as representative of similar services, and measure its level of duplication. In the process of conducting these measurements, we make the following contributions:

- We employ a novel combination of video sampling methods, automated video comparison techniques, and manual validation to estimate duplication levels in large-scale video sharing services.
- Using these methods, we estimate that the duplicate ratio of YouTube videos is 31.7 % and that 24.0 % of YouTube's total video storage space is occupied by duplicates.

The remainder of the paper is organized as follows. Sections 2 and 3 discuss the motivation of this study and related work, respectively. Section 4 describes our duplicate estimation technique. We report our results in Sect. 5. Finally, Sect. 6 concludes this work.

2   Motivation

Anyone who has watched videos on YouTube, or any other video sharing service, has certainly noticed that near-duplicates of the same video often appear in the search results or are recommended as related videos. These impressions, however, are not useful toward making recommendations for taking action to mitigate any potential efficiency loss resulting from unnecessary duplication.

In preliminary work, we performed a small-scale assessment of 50 queries for the titles of 50 popular YouTube videos from a randomly selected set (Sect. 4.1). Manual assessment of these videos produced a rough estimate of a 42 % duplicate ratio.

Viewing a small number of individual search results, however, is unlikely to yield good estimates of the prevalence of duplicates across a video sharing service's entire database. The huge number of videos stored within services such as YouTube also indicates that manually comparing videos to estimate duplicate ratio is infeasible. This intractability motivates the need for a larger scale assessment, assist in determining the necessity of and formulating further systems to conduct video deduplication.

3   Related Work

Data deduplication. Data duplication is common in storage systems. Deduplication operates by detecting duplicates and storing only a single copy of a given chunk of data. It is typically conducted on exact byte-level duplicates [4,6,10, 18,23]. Detecting exact duplicates is often performed using cryptographic-hash based approaches (e.g., SHA1) to create an index for fast lookups. These cryptographic hash-based approaches, however, are inappropriate for detecting near-duplicate videos (i.e., videos that appear the same or very similar to a human viewer). This unsuitability is due to the fact that video files almost always contain significant differences at the byte-level even though the visual content of a video may be replicated (due to changes in encoding, altered resolutions, image-level editing, or temporal editing).

Near-duplicate video detection. The computer vision community has proposed a variety of strategies for detecting near-duplicate videos [5,9,19]. Two main types of tools have been developed. The first is the local image descriptor [13,14,21], which describes small sections within an image/keyframe. The second is the global descriptor [7,16,20,22], which can be used to summarize the entire contents of an image or video. An approach for video duplicate detection that can employ either local or global descriptors is called Dynamic Time Warping (DTW) [15]. DTW is a technique used to measure distance between two sequences where a distance can be defined between sequence elements. DTW operates by aligning elements from a pair of sequences, A and B. Specifically, DTW aligns each element from sequence A to a similar element in sequence B with the constraint that no changes in ordering can occur (see Fig. 1).

Video deduplication. The rapid growth of video content on the Internet and its corresponding storage cost have recently drawn much attention to the task of video deduplication. For example, Kathpal et al. found that multiple copies (versions) of the same video in different encodings and formats frequently exist. The authors proposed to save space by conducting on-the-fly transcoding to only retain the copy with the highest quality [11]. Shen and Akella proposed a video-centric proxy cache, iProxy. iProxy stores the frequency domain information of the video's key frames in an Information-Bound Reference (IBR) table. iProxy improves the cache hit rate by mapping videos with the same IBR to a single cache entry and dynamically transcodes the video during playback [17]. However, both works [11,17] only deal with duplicates introduced by a limited set of transformations, e.g., quantization, resizing, and different formats and encodings. Other forms of transformation, such as excerption, concatenation, and splicing, would not be detected or deduplicated. Katiyar and Weissman proposed ViD-eDup, which uses clustering-based "similarity detection" and performs deduplication by storing the centroid-videos with the highest perceptual-quality [12]. However, since only the centroid of a set of "similar" videos are stored, restored video may no longer represent the original visual content.

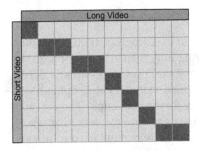

Fig. 1. The standard Dynamic Time Warping algorithm aligns all frames of both videos. Red squares represent aligned video frames.

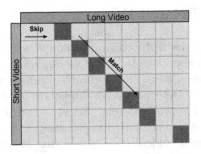

Fig. 2. The modified version of DTW used in this study aligns all elements from the shorter video and can skip frames from the longer video.

4   Methodology

Our set of techniques for video duplicate assessment are applied in the following steps:

Step 1: We use random prefix sampling [8] to sample YouTube videos uniformly and at random. We refer to this set of sampled videos as `sampled videos`.

Step 2: We then search for the title of each `sampled video` using the text-based search engine of YouTube, which returns a list of relevant videos. We refer to these relevant videos as `searched videos`. These `searched videos` are used as a candidate set of duplicates.

Step 3: For each (`sampled video`, `searched video`) pair, we calculate a similarity score which accounts for temporally shifted frames. This score is used to determine whether the `searched video` is a duplicate of the `sampled video`.

Step 4: For each pair of duplicates whose score is below a threshold, we conduct a manual comparison step to eliminate false positives.

In the rest of this section, we explain each step of our technique in detail for assessing duplicate levels in YouTube.

4.1   Random Sampling of Videos

In order to uniformly sample YouTube videos, we use the random prefix sampling method proposed by Zhou et al. [8]. Random prefix sampling involves querying the YouTube search engine with a randomly selected video ID (VID) prefix. The returned query results are existing videos whose VIDs match this random prefix. According to Zhou et al., with a prefix length of five ("-" being the last/fifth symbol in the prefix), all existing VIDs that match the prefix can be returned in one query. Therefore, during the sampling procedure, we randomly generate a fixed number, N_{prefix}, 5-character long prefixes. (In this work, we set N_{prefix} to 1,000.) In the remainder of the paper, we refer to the videos selected by random prefix sampling as `sampled videos`. We make the important assumption that the set of `sampled videos` contains no duplicates. We validate this assumption through both theoretical and experimental analysis in Sect. 5.2.

4.2   Selection of Candidate Duplicate Pairs

The next step involves pruning the number of video pairs that must be assessed with a computationally intensive duplicate detection method. We perform this pruning step by leveraging the metadata-based search engines provided by many video sharing services. In UGC sites, metadata can be an especially good source for retrieving duplicates because uploaders of these duplicates are incentivised to label their videos with metadata to indicate similarity to original popular content, thereby attracting a larger number of views.

We extract each `sampled video`'s title and use it to query the YouTube search engine. This query returns a collection of videos with metadata related to the `sampled video`'s title. Because this set of videos may still be too large to effectively process with DTW, we rely on the ranking capability of YouTube's metadata-based search engine to further filter videos. In particular, we record the top 100 results from each query. Some queries only return fewer than 100 results, and on average, we collected 82 `searched videos` for each `sampled video`. We refer to this set of videos returned from this search procedure as `searched videos`. Pairs of `sampled videos` and `searched videos` are sent to our DTW-based algorithm for duplicate assessment.

4.3   Comparing Sampled and Searched Video Pairs

For comparison, we download both the `sampled video` and `searched video` files from YouTube. YouTube usually encodes videos into multiple versions using different codecs, resolutions, and quantization levels to support streaming at different bandwidths and to different devices. We retrieve only the H.264 Baseline/AAC/MP4/360p version as we find this version is most often available.

After retrieving a set of `searched videos` associated with every `sampled video`, we use FFmpeg [1] to extract images/frames from the video at **one second intervals**. Note that we cannot use keyframes (i.e., I-frames) for comparison, as in related work [20], because the interval between keyframes can vary between videos. To detect pairs of duplicates, we employ a method based on Dynamic Time Warping (DTW) [15]. Like DTW, our duplicate matching system attempts to align frames from pairs of videos. However, we expect shorter videos to align to sub-portions of a longer video. We therefore modified the basic DTW algorithm so that every element of the shorter video must be matched while some elements of the longer video are allowed to remain unmatched (see Fig. 2).

Our variation of DTW operates on pairs of image sequences

$$
\begin{aligned}
A &= a_0,\ a_1,\ \cdots,\ a_i,\ \cdots,\ a_{I-1} \\
B &= b_0,\ b_1,\ \cdots,\ b_j,\ \cdots,\ b_{J-1}
\end{aligned}
\tag{1}
$$

where I and J indicate the number of images in sequence A and B, correspondingly, and we enforce $I >= J$ by swapping videos if necessary.

Figure 3 shows the pseudocode of our adapted DTW algorithm. We use the output of the function *result* to indicate the DTW score between A and B. The smaller the DTW score, the more likely that videos A and B are duplicates.

A key component in the DTW algorithm is the image distance function $d(a_x, b_y)$. Choosing a good image distance function is vital to the accuracy of our duplicate detection method. We used a distance function between image histograms, denoted by $d_h(a_x, b_y)$.

Histogram Distance refers to a distance measurement between images based on the relative frequency of different colors [7,20]. For each image, x, we calculate its color histogram $H_x = (h_x^1, h_x^2, \cdots, h_x^M)$. (The color histogram is a global image descriptor.) We consider images in HSV (Hue, Saturation, and Value) color space because the HSV is more perceptually relevant to human eyes than the RGB representation. The color histogram contains 5 bins for Hue, 8 bins for Saturation, and 16 bins for Value. The total number of bins, M, is therefore $M = 29$. The Value section of the histogram contains a greater number of histogram bins, reflecting the fact that human eyes are more sensitive to light/dark contrast than to color information. As black borders/banners may be introduced during video transcoding and affect our histogram distance metric, we ignore pixels whose $Value = 0$ (black) when calculating histograms.

The `Histogram Distance` between two images x and y is calculated as the squared Euclidean distance between H_x and H_y:

$$d_h(x, y) = \sum_{k=1}^{M} (h_x^k - h_y^k)^2$$

This distance metric can be used to determine if a pair of videos are visually similar. We consider a pair of videos duplicates if their `Histogram Distance` is less than 0.013. This threshold was chosen by calibrating against a precision-recall graph to give a perfect recall (zero false-negative rate) on a set of 100 pairs of videos.

4.4   Manual Validation of Duplicate Pairs

In the pairwise comparison step described above, we deliberately selected a high DTW score threshold to achieve a high recall rate. This high threshold, however, can produce a correspondingly high false discovery rate.

To alleviate this potential problem, we augmented our automated procedure with a **manual duplicate verification** step that has false positive rate near zero. In the manual verification step, for each duplicate pair, a human observer manually viewed both the corresponding `sampled video` and `searched video` to determine if the pair was a true duplicate. Specifically, the human observer considered the `searched video` to be a duplicate of the `sampled video` under any of the following cases:

1: ▷ A, B, I, J are defined in Equation 1.
2: ▷ $d(a_x, b_y)$ denotes distance between image a_x from sequence A and image b_y from sequence B.
3: **function** DTW(A, B)
4:     **assert** $I >= J$
5:     $dtw_{0,0} = d(a_0, b_0)$
6:     **for** $(i = 1; i < I; i + +)$ **do**
7:         $dtw_{i,0} = d(a_i, b_0)$
8:     **for** $(j = 1; j < J; j + +)$ **do**
9:         $dtw_{j,j} = dtw_{j-1,j-1} + d(a_j, b_j)$
10:    **for** $(i = 1; i < I; i + +)$ **do**
11:        **for** $(j = 1; j < min(i, J); j + +)$ **do**
12:            $dtw_{i,j} = dtw_{i-1,j}$
13:            $dist = d(a_i, b_j)$
14:            **if** $(dtw_{i-1,j-1} + dist < dtw_{i,j})$ **then**
15:                $dtw_{i,j} = dtw_{i-1,j-1} + dist$
16:    **return** $result = dtw_{I-1,J-1}/J$

Fig. 3. The DTW algorithm between two image sequences (i.e., videos) A and B.

1. the `searched video` has the same video content as the `sampled video`.
2. the `searched video` is part of the `sampled video`.
3. the `sampled video` is part of the `searched video`.

5   Quantifying Video Duplicate Levels in YouTube

To estimate the number of duplicates in YouTube, we first randomly generated 1,000 prefixes. Using these 1,000 prefixes, we collected 6,365 `sampled videos` and 512,314 associated `searched videos`. For each `searched video` returned by the YouTube search engine, we ran the variation of the DTW algorithm discussed in Sect. 4 to produce a *similarity score*. We set the threshold for duplicate determination high (as discussed in Sect. 4.3) to produce a low rate of false negatives (high recall), then conducted a manual curation step to validate that each candidate pair returned by the DTW algorithm constituted a true pair of duplicates.

Although the manual validation is time and resource intensive, this step was feasible because only the relatively small number of pairs of videos marked as duplicates by the DTW step were manually assessed.

5.1   Results

We present numeric results in Table 1. Out of the 6,365 `sampled videos`, our assessment shows that 631 (10 %) have duplicates within YouTube. Assuming that the 6,365 `sampled videos` were drawn independently and the counts of videos with duplicates and videos with non-duplicates were drawn from a binomial distribution, we can compute a confidence interval around the probability that a `sampled video` has a duplicate using the Beta quantile function. The 95 % confidence interval around this probability is

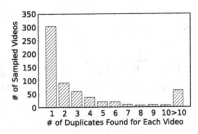

Fig. 4. # of duplicates found for each sampled video with one or more duplicates.

(0.0912, 0.1065). On average, for each `sampled video` associated with one or more duplicates, 4.69 duplicates were discovered. Figure 4 shows the distribution of the number of duplicates for each `sampled video` with one or more duplicates. Out of 631 videos that have duplicates, 304 have only one duplicate found and 63 have more than 10 duplicates found, indicating the high variance of duplicate levels within YouTube. In total, our manually augmented evaluation found 2,960 duplicates of the 6,365 `sampled videos`. Assuming that the number of duplicates associated with each video is drawn from a normal distribution with a standard deviation of 3.38 (the empirical standard deviation), we compute a 95 % confidence interval of (0.382, 0.548) around the average number of duplicates for each video. These measurements indicate that roughly 1/3 of videos on YouTube are duplicates. Of the 2,960 duplicate videos found, only 327 (11 %)

Table 1. Manually augmented assessment of YouTube duplicate levels.

Category	# of sampled videos	Sampled videos that have dups #	Sampled videos that have dups %	# of dups found per category	Avg. # of dups found for sampled videos that have duplicates	Duplicate ratio (%)
Video Category						
Pets & Animals	155	7	4.5%	15	2.14	8.8%
Autos & Vehicles	232	27	11.6%	147	5.44	38.8%
Comedy	462	33	7.1%	169	5.12	26.8%
Education	183	25	13.7%	53	2.12	22.5%
Entertainment	851	59	6.9%	240	4.07	22.0%
Film & Animation	244	29	11.9%	76	2.62	23.8%
Gaming	588	33	5.6%	196	5.94	25.0%
Howto & Style	119	11	9.2%	29	2.64	19.6%
Music	1068	146	13.7%	642	4.40	37.5%
News & Politics	220	42	19.1%	203	4.83	48.0%
Nonprofit & Activism	84	13	15.5%	143	11.00	63.0%
People & Blogs	1477	156	10.6%	767	4.92	34.2%
Shows	7	0	0%	0	0.00	0.0%
Sports	392	32	8.2%	179	5.59	31.3%
Science & Tech	113	9	8.0%	92	10.22	44.9%
Travel & Events	170	9	5.3%	9	1.00	5.0%
Video Duration						
Short [0,240)	4490	418	9.3%	2310	5.53	34.0%
Medium [240,1200]	1743	190	10.9%	596	3.14	25.5%
Long (1200,∞)	132	23	17.4%	54	2.35	29.0%
Video Popularity						
Unpopular (<1000)	5529	513	9.3%	2537	4.95	31.5%
Popular (≥1000)	836	118	14.1%	423	3.58	33.6%
Total						
Total	6365	631	10.0%	2960	4.69	31.7%

have the same byte-level content as the `sampled video`, indicating traditional cryptographic hash-based duplicate detection has only a limited ability to detect duplicate videos.

Table 1 also shows a breakdown of `sampled videos` according to three attributes along the rows: video category, video length, and popularity. The columns of Table 1 give different duplicate statistics. Here "duplicate ratio" is defined as:

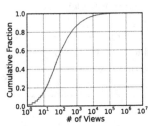

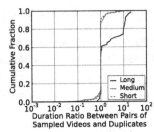

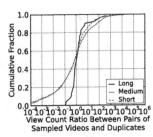

Fig. 5. View count distribution

Fig. 6. $\frac{\text{Duration(sampled video)}}{\text{Duration(duplicate)}}$

Fig. 7. $\frac{\text{ViewCount(sampled video)}}{\text{ViewCount(duplicate)}}$

$$\text{duplicate ratio} = \frac{\#\text{ of duplicates found}}{\#\text{ of sampled videos} + \#\text{ of duplicates found}} \qquad (2)$$

Figure 5 shows the view count (i.e., popularity) of 6,365 `sampled videos`. 5,529 (87%) videos are viewed fewer than 1,000 times (`unpopular`). This statistic is consistent with the findings in Zhou et al. [8] that only 14% of videos in a randomly sampled YouTube dataset have a total view count of more than 1,000.

Figure 6 shows the ratio between the duration of the `sampled video` and the duration of the detected duplicate video. As shown in the figure, most duplicates have the same duration as the sampled video. For `Short`, `Medium`, and `Long` videos respectively, 1,743 out of 2,310 (75%), 375 out of 596 (63%), and 19 out of 54 (35%) have the same durations as the `sampled video`. For `Long` videos, more than 40% of their duplicates are shorter than the `sampled video`. These shorter duplicates are excerpts from longer videos, extracted by users to meet the video duration limits imposed by YouTube. Overall, among all the duplicates found, **72%** have the same duration as the `sampled video`, indicating that excerption occurs less frequently than operations that preserve the length of the video.

We are also interested in determining if sets of duplicates have similar popularities. Figure 7 shows the view count ratios of `sampled videos` versus those of `searched videos`. Approximately 55% of the `searched video` duplicates are watched more frequently than the `sampled video`. These differing frequencies indicate that even if duplicates represent the same or similar visual content, the popularities of individual copies of the same video can vary.

5.2   Uniqueness of Sampled Videos

Given that our duplicate assessment found that approximately one-third of the videos in the YouTube database are duplicates, it seems counter-intuitive that our original assumption holds that each of our 6,365 `sampled videos` is unique. A relatively short analysis, however, shows that this is a reasonable assumption. This analysis is a specialization of the well-known Birthday paradox. Our setting differs from the standard Birthday paradox, where we would assume a uniform distribution over birthdays. In our setting, a large number of people have a unique birthday (i.e., a large number of videos have no duplicates and will be unique in our sample of 6,365). The probability that two or more people in a sample share a birthday, given this highly unbalanced distribution of birthdays, can be computed using a recurrence which we describe below:

$$
R(N,T) = \begin{cases} (1 - q(T)) \times \big((1 - p) \times R(N - 1, T) \\ \qquad\qquad + p \times R(N - 1, T + 1)\big) & \text{if } N > 0 \\ 1 & \text{if } N = 0 \end{cases} \tag{3}
$$

where $R(N,T)$ indicates the probability that a sample of N videos does not contain any duplicates, given that we have already drawn T videos that are associated with copies in the YouTube database (or any video database), where each of these T videos is distinct. The recurrence captures the idea that, if we do not wish to include duplicates in our sample of original videos, we must first draw a non-duplicate given the set of T previously drawn videos associated with a duplicate in the video database with probability $1 - q(T)$. This video must then be selected either from the set of videos with no associated duplicates with probability $1 - p$ or from the set of videos that has at least one duplicate with probability p.

The base case is $R(0,T) = 1$, where have already drawn T videos that are associated with duplicates in the YouTube database, and we have no further videos that need to be selected.

To evaluate this recurrence, we first need to estimate the total number of videos in YouTube. During the random sampling phase, we retrieved 6,365 unique video IDs using 1000 randomly generated prefixes. Using the method proposed by Zhou et al. [8], we estimated the total number of videos on YouTube as $38^4 \times 64 \times \frac{6365}{1000} \approx 849$ million, indicating there were approximately 849 million videos on YouTube at the time we collected the data (July 2013).

Our measurement results indicate that approximately 10 % of the original videos on YouTube have duplicates, meaning that we should set $p = 0.1$ in the computation above. Given our result from the previous section, that each video having one or more duplicates has on average, approximately 4.69 duplicates associated with it, we can estimate the probability of drawing a duplicate for given video as $\frac{4.69}{849 \times 10^6} \approx \frac{1}{181 \times 10^6}$.

Evaluating the above recurrence using a dynamic programming method for $q(T) = \frac{T}{181 \times 10^6}$ and $p = 0.1$ yields $R(6365, 0) = 0.989$. This result means that if we resampled the set of 6,365 videos over 100 separate trials, then we would expect this set of 6,365 sampled videos to contain duplicates in fewer than two of these trials.

Further, we examined the set of sampled videos by first querying the set of searched video VIDs to determine if any match a sampled video VID. For the small set of VIDs that matched, we ran a further DTW comparison. This DTW phase produced much larger DTW distances than the duplicate threshold for all pairs of videos examined, indicating that none of the 6,365 sampled videos were duplicates. We also performed a manual confirmation step, providing further evidence that the 6,365 sampled videos are unique.

5.3   Extra Storage Space Occupied by Duplicate Videos

A direct negative impact of video duplication is the extra storage space consumed by duplicate videos. To estimate the percentage of additional space needed by YouTube to store duplicate videos, we grouped each `sampled video` and its corresponding duplicates into a duplicate set, denoted by D. If no duplicates were associated with a `sampled video`, v, then we constructed the duplicate set, D, to contain only v, i.e., $D = \{v\}$. For each duplicate set, we selected the video with the largest file size to be the `representative video`. We denote the set of all duplicate sets by $\mathcal{D}$ and the `representative video` of set D by D_r. Note that for all videos, we only retrieved the H.264 Baseline/AAC/MP4/360p version, thus encoding rates for all videos in our dataset should be similar. Short videos in D will likely be sub-videos of longer videos in D. Therefore selecting the video with the largest file size as the `representative video` means that the other, shorter, videos in the set are subvideos of the `representative video`. Given these duplicate sets and corresponding `representative videos`, we computed the space used to store duplicates as a percentage of the total storage space as follows:

$$1 - \frac{\sum_{D \in \mathcal{D}} \text{size}(D_r)}{\sum_{D \in \mathcal{D}} \sum_{d \in D} \text{size}(d)} \tag{4}$$

Our results show that the total size of representative videos is 91.9 GB, and the total size of all videos in all duplicate sets is 121.0 GB. These space requirements indicate that roughly 24.0 % YouTube storage is occupied by duplicates.

6   Conclusion

Duplicate videos within large-scale video sharing services have wide ranging potential impacts on data center and network level storage, caching, and energy consumption. A critical first step in determining the true cost of video duplication involves accurate measurement of duplicate levels.

In this work, we proposed a set of techniques for assessing duplicate levels within large-scale video sharing services. These techniques combined video sampling, video search, computing pairwise video similarity through a variation of dynamic time warping, and a manual validation step. Applying these techniques on YouTube produces a duplicate ratio estimate of 31.7 %. Furthermore, we calculate that these duplicates occupy 24.0 % of YouTube's video data storage. These relatively high levels of duplication indicate that further work should be conducted to evaluate specific system-level tradeoffs associated with datacenter costs, as well as network-related concerns such as performance of in-network caching under assessed duplicate levels.

To allow duplicate assessment on ever-increasing video databases, we plan to extend our video duplicate assessment techniques so they can scale to much larger video samples. A potentially necessary step toward scaling this assessment would involve developing a system to index videos by semantic content. This type of indexing system would be essential for reducing the number of video pairs that would need to be evaluated by a computationally-expensive pairwise video comparison technique.

Acknowledgements. We appreciate constructive comments from anonymous referees and our shepherd Dongsu Han. The work is partially supported by High-Tech Research and Development Program of China ("863 China Cloud" Major Program) under grant SQ2015AAJY1595, by China NSF under grant 61471217, by China Postdoctoral Science Fund under grant 2014M550735, and by NSF under grants CNS-0746649 and CNS-1117300.

References

1. FFmpeg. http://www.ffmpeg.org/
2. Sandvine Global Internet Phenomena Report 1H 2014. https://www.sandvine.com/downloads/general/global-internet-phenomena/2014/1h-2014-global-internet-phenomena-report.pdf.
3. YouTube Statistics. http://www.youtube.com/yt/press/statistics.html
4. Bolosky, W.J., Corbin, S., Goebel, D., Douceur, J.R.: Single instance storage in windows 2000. In: Proceedings of USENIX WSS (2000)
5. Douze, M., Gaidon, A., Jegou, H., Marszałek, M., Schmid, C., et al.: Inria-lears video copy detection system. In: TREC Video Retrieval Evaluation (TRECVID Workshop) (2008)
6. Dubnicki, C., Gryz, L., Heldt, L., Kaczmarczyk, M., Kilian, W., Strzelczak, P., Szczepkowski, J., Ungureanu, C., Welnicki, M.: HYDRAstor: a scalable secondary storage. In: Proceedings of USENIX FAST (2009)
7. Hampapur, A., Hyun, K., Bolle, R.M.: Comparison of sequence matching techniques for video copy detection. In: Electronic Imaging 2002, pp. 194–201. International Society for Optics and Photonics (2001)
8. Zhou, J., Li, Y., Adhikari, V.K., Zhang, Z.-L.: Counting YouTube videos via random prefix sampling. In: Proceedings of ACM IMC (2011)
9. Jégou, H., Douze, M., Gravier, G., Schmid, C., Gros, P., et al.: Inria lear-texmex: video copy detection task. In: Proceedings of the TRECVid 2010 Workshop (2010)
10. Jin, K., Miller, E.L.: The effectiveness of deduplication on virtual machine disk images. In: Proceedings of ACM SYSTOR (2009)
11. Kathpal, A., Kulkarni, M., Bakre, A.: Analyzing compute vs. storage tradeoff for video-aware storage efficiency. In: Proceedings of USENIX HotStorage (2012)
12. Katiyar, A., Weissman, J.: ViDeDup: an application-aware framework for video de-duplication. In: Proceedings of USENIX HotStorage (2011)
13. Lowe, D.G.: Object recognition from local scale-invariant features. In: Proceedings of IEEE ICCV, vol. 2, pp. 1150–1157 (1999)
14. Mikolajczyk, K., Schmid, C.: A performance evaluation of local descriptors. IEEE Trans. Pattern Anal. Mach. Intell. **27**(10), 1615–1630 (2005)
15. Sakoe, H., Chiba, S.: Dynamic programming algorithm optimization for spoken word recognition. IEEE Trans. Acoust. Speech Sign. Proces. **26**(1), 43–49 (1978)
16. Shen, H.T., Zhou, X., Huang, Z., Shao, J., Zhou, X.: UQLIPS: a real-time near-duplicate video clip detection system. In: Proceedings of ACM VLDB (2007)
17. Shen, S.-H., Akella, A.: An information-aware QoE-centric mobile video cache. In: Proceedings of ACM MobiCom (2013)

18. Ungureanu, C., Atkin, B., Aranya, A., Gokhale, S., Rago, S., Cakowski, G., Dubnicki, C., Bohra, A.: HydraFS: a high-throughput file system for the HYDRAstor content-addressable storage system. In: Proceedings of USENIX FAST (2010)
19. Wu, X., Ngo, C.-W., Hauptmann, A.G., Tan, H.-K.: Real-time near-duplicate elimination for web video search with content and context. IEEE Trans. Multimed. **11**(2), 196–207 (2009)
20. Wu, X., Hauptmann, A.G., Ngo, C.-W.: Practical elimination of near-duplicates from web video search. In: Proceedings of ACM Multimedia (2007)
21. Yang, J., Jiang, Y.-G., Hauptmann, A.G., Ngo, C.-W.: Evaluating bag-of-visual-words representations in scene classification. In: Proceedings of ACM MIR (2007)
22. Zauner, C.: Implementation and benchmarking of perceptual image hash functions. Master's thesis, Upper Austria University of Applied Sciences, Hagenberg Campus, 43 (2010)
23. Zhu, B., Li, K.: Avoiding the disk bottleneck in the data domain deduplication file system. In: Proceedings of USENIX FAST (2008)

Measuring YouTube from Dual-Stacked Hosts

Saba Ahsan[1]([✉]), Vaibhav Bajpai[2], Jörg Ott[1], and Jürgen Schönwälder[2]

[1] School of Electrical Engineering, Aalto University, Espoo, Finland
{saba.ahsan,jorg.ott}@aalto.fi
[2] Computer Science, Jacobs University Bremen, Bremen, Germany
{v.bajpai,j.schoenwaelder}@jacobs-university.de

Abstract. There is rapid growth in the number of IPv6 users and IPv6 compliant services on the Internet. However, few measurement studies exist about the quality of user experience on IPv6 in comparison to IPv4 for dual-stacked hosts. We present results from a measurement trial consisting of 21 active measurement probes deployed across Europe and Japan connected behind dual-stacked networks, representing 19 different Autonomous System (AS)s. The trial ran for 20 days in September, 2014 and conducted two types of measurements: (a) YouTube performance tests and (b) Speed tests to nearest dual-stacked Measurement Lab (M-Lab) server, both over IPv4 and IPv6. Our results show that a disparity exists in the achievable throughput as indicated by speed tests. We also witness disparity in content delivery servers used for YouTube media for some networks, resulting in degradation of experience over a specific address family.

1 Introduction

The World IPv6 Launch[1] that began in June, 2012 marked its second anniversary this year, reporting an increase in IPv6 usage by 500 % in the past two years. Google reports that as of 2014, over 4 % of their users access Google services over IPv6 in contrast to less than 0.5 % in 2011[2]. With more and more ISPs offering native IPv6 to their customers, there is a need for more measurement studies that can quantify the Internet performance aspects for early adopters of this technology. According to Sandvine Global Internet Phenomena report of 2014, audio and video streaming is the largest traffic category on fixed and mobile networks with YouTube as the largest single source of video streaming around the world[3]. Hence performance of Internet video in general, and YouTube in particular can impact Internet user experience to a great extent.

This paper presents a measurement study carried out in September 2014 that shows a comparison of YouTube performance over IPv4 and IPv6 actively measured over 21 probes distributed over Europe and Japan. To the best of our knowledge, this is the first study to compare YouTube performance over IPv4 and IPv6 from different dual-stacked networks. The probes receive native IPv6

---

[1] http://www.worldipv6launch.org.
[2] http://www.google.com/intl/en/ipv6/statistics.html.
[3] http://www.sandvine.com/trends/global-internet-phenomena.

© Springer International Publishing Switzerland 2015
J. Mirkovic and Y. Liu (Eds.): PAM 2015, LNCS 8995, pp. 249–261, 2015.
DOI: 10.1007/978-3-319-15509-8_19

connectivity and belong to different ISPs, covering 19 different IPv4 and IPv6 ASes. They run two kinds of measurements; speed tests and YouTube tests. Each test is run over IPv4 and then IPv6, giving us a comparison of performance over each. In this paper we make three contributions: (1) We find that there is disparity in the availability of YouTube content caches over IPv4 and IPv6, whereby the content-caches over IPv6 are largely absent, which can affect YouTube performance, (2) The measured YouTube throughput over IPv4 and IPv6 shows significant difference for some probes, resulting in support for better bit rates and thus higher resolution videos over one address family and not the other and (3) We find that Transmission Control Protocol (TCP) connect times over IPv6 are just not high enough for the happy eyeballs algorithm [13] to prefer a connection over IPv4, potentially choosing an IPv6 connection over IPv4, even when the observed throughput over IPv6 is lower. We release[4] the entire dataset to the measurement community.

The paper is organized as follows. We present related work in Sect. 2. Our metric, measurement test, and the methodology describing the measurement setup, trials and decision process is presented in Sect. 3. Insights derived from data analysis are presented in Sect. 4 with conclusions in Sect. 5.

2   Related Work

A number of early studies have focussed on characterization of YouTube videos. For instance, Phillipa Gill *et al.* in [6] (2007) study YouTube workload patterns by measuring local traffic in a campus setting and observing trends of popular videos. Features such as access patterns, file properties, video popularity, reference behaviors, and transfer characteristics are compared against traditional web workloads. Meeyoung Cha *et al.* in [3] (2007) show how YouTube content popularity is driven by truncated power-law distributions. They also study the prevalence and impact of content duplication and illegal uploads on system characteristics. They show how peer-assisted content delivery and caching schemes can offload server-side traffic by as much as 50 %.

These studies have been followed by a number of passive measurement efforts. Vijay Kumar Adhikari *et al.* in [1] (2010) study YouTube traffic dynamics from the perspective of a large tier-1 ISP. Using flow-level data collected at multiple Point of Presence (PoP)s, they show how the employed load-balancing strategy is location-agnostic. They also compare load-balancing strategies employed by YouTube against routing policies used by the ISP and study relationships between them. Alessandro Finamore *et al.* in [5] (2011) compare YouTube experience from mobile and PC-based devices. Using a week-long passively monitored dataset collected from 5 vantage points, they show how user access patterns are device and location agnostic. They also show how YouTube is heavily optimized for PC-based devices and leverages excessive buffering policies. This often leads to more data being fetched than is used for playback. Georgios Dimopoulos *et al.* in [4] (2013) study user-experience from YouTube video sessions. Using a

---

[4] http://www.netlab.tkk.fi/tutkimus/rtc/PAM2015/.

week-long passively collected dataset from within a campus network, they show how redirections to the destination media server is the primary contributor to initial delays. They show how statistical information sent back by the client can be used to identify stall events. They also measured the impact of advertisements on playback abandonment rates.

In recent years, we have witnessed a shift towards actively measuring the playback quality of a YouTube video. For instance, Parikshit Juluri et al. in [7] (2011) introduce the python based `Pytomo`, a tool that models a YouTube client to measure download statistics and estimate playback interruptions. Our YouTube test is inspired but improves upon this tool in three ways: (a) It is written in C, which has allowed us to deploy it on Customer Premises Equipment (CPE)-like devices such as SamKnows, (b) It supports multiple container formats such as MP4, WebM and FLV (unlike `Pytomo` which supports FLV only), and (c) Our test is more aware of available bit rates and resolutions. Vijay Kumar Adhikari et al. in [2] (2012) use PlanetLab vantage points to crawl a finite subset of YouTube videos. They use this dataset to show how: (a) the video ID space is flat, (b) multiple (anycasted) DNS namespaces are used to logically organize media servers and (c) a 3-tier physical cache hierarchy is used to deliver content. Parikshit Juluri et al. in [8] (2013) go further and use `Pytomo` to measure YouTube experience from within three ISP networks. They witnessed noticeable difference in experienced quality across ISPs. They reason that latency is not the primary factor when choosing a video server, but the selection mechanism is largely based on delivery policies and individual agreements with ISPs. Hyunwoo Nam, et al. in [9] (2014) introduce YouSlow, a browser-based plugin that can detect and report live buffer stalling events when watching YouTube videos that are delivered using Adaptive Bitrate Streaming (ABR) technology.

3   Methodology

We utilize two metrics in this study. A Youtube test that measures performance against dual-stacked YouTube media servers, and a SamKnows speed test that measures line rates against dual-stacked Google M-Lab servers. A detailed description of the implementation is given below:

3.1   Metrics

YouTube Performance Test: We have designed a test that can download and mimic playout of YouTube videos. It measures TCP connection establishment times, achievable throughput, and number of stall events as indicators of performance when streaming a YouTube video. The measures are taken over both audio and video streams separately. The test takes a YouTube URL as input, and scrapes the fetched HTML page to extract the list of container formats, available resolutions and URL locations of media servers hosting the streams. The test then locally resolves Domain Name System (DNS) names and establishes two concurrent HTTP sessions to fetch audio and video streams in the desired

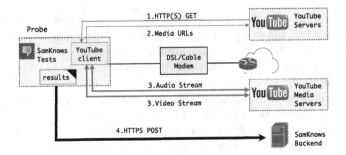

Fig. 1. A measurement setup on top of the SamKnows platform. A dual-stacked probe in addition to the standard SamKnows tests, executes the YouTube test. The YouTube test runs every hour and measures a set of performance indicators to endpoints delivering YouTube audio and video both over IPv4 and IPv6. The locally collected measurement results are pushed every hour to the SamKnows data collection server using HTTP.

format and resolution. The client ensures temporal synchronization between the streams, which means that playout only occurs if both audio and video frames have arrived.

In this process, the test records the time it takes for the `connect(...)` system call to complete as a measure of TCP connect times to both audio and video streams. The DNS resolution time is not taken into account in this measure. The test then measures throughput over the single TCP connection separately (and combined) over both audio and video streams. During playback, a stall event is declared when a frame is not received before its playout time. We use a 2-second prebuffering time, which means that 2 s of audio and video content is downloaded before starting the playout timer. In case a stall occurs, 1 s of media rebuffering is done before resuming the playout timer. The test does not at any time render content, but it only reads the format container to extract frame timestamps. The payload is eventually discarded.

Speed Test: The measurement test is part of the SamKnows' test suite [11] and is used to measure achievable throughput over the line. It uses three simultaneous TCP connections that fetch a portion of a 1 GB, non-zero, randomly generated binary file. Each TCP connection initiates a HTTP GET request to the nearest M-Lab[5] server and the recorded result is an aggregate of the observed values during the measurement. The test was modified to enable throughput measurements over IPv6. We use results from the SamKnows speed test as a baseline to compare the throughput measured from the YouTube test.

3.2   Measurement Setup

We cross-compiled the YouTube test for the OpenWrt platform and deployed it on SamKnows probes. The probes in addition to the YouTube test also run

---

[5] http://www.measurementlab.net.

standard SamKnows tests (which also includes the modified speed test). The YouTube test runs twice, once for IPv4 and subsequently for IPv6 and repeats every hour. For the speed test, each probe selects its nearest dual-stacked M-Lab server based on latency results. The same dual-stacked server is used to measure line rates both over IPv4 and IPv6. The test runs hourly during peak evening hours, and once every six hours after midnight. The data collected is stored on the SamKnows backend as shown in Fig. 1.

Selection of YouTube Videos: We use the YouTube v3 API[6] to generate a list of globally popular videos. We make use of globally popular charts to ensure our measurements become comparable across geographically located vantage points. We also prune out videos from the list that meet any of the three criteria: (a) Video duration is less than 60 s, (b) Video has regional restrictions, or (c) Video is unavailable in Full HD format. The list is generated on the SamKnows backend and is refreshed every 12 h. Each probe pulls this list on a daily basis. This allows us to measure against the same video for the entire day, which enables temporal analysis. On the other hand, cycling videos on a daily basis allows larger coverage of videos with different characteristics.

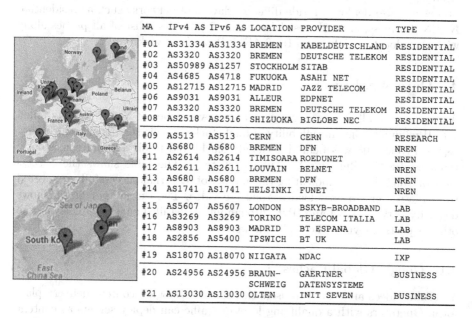

	MA	IPv4 AS	IPv6 AS	LOCATION	PROVIDER	TYPE
	#01	AS31334	AS31334	BREMEN	KABELDEUTSCHLAND	RESIDENTIAL
	#02	AS3320	AS3320	BREMEN	DEUTSCHE TELEKOM	RESIDENTIAL
	#03	AS50989	AS1257	STOCKHOLM	SITAB	RESIDENTIAL
	#04	AS4685	AS4718	FUKUOKA	ASAHI NET	RESIDENTIAL
	#05	AS12715	AS12715	MADRID	JAZZ TELECOM	RESIDENTIAL
	#06	AS9031	AS9031	ALLEUR	EDPNET	RESIDENTIAL
	#07	AS3320	AS3320	BREMEN	DEUTSCHE TELEKOM	RESIDENTIAL
	#08	AS2518	AS2516	SHIZUOKA	BIGLOBE NEC	RESIDENTIAL
	#09	AS513	AS513	CERN	CERN	RESEARCH
	#10	AS680	AS680	BREMEN	DFN	NREN
	#11	AS2614	AS2614	TIMISOARA	ROEDUNET	NREN
	#12	AS2611	AS2611	LOUVAIN	BELNET	NREN
	#13	AS680	AS680	BREMEN	DFN	NREN
	#14	AS1741	AS1741	HELSINKI	FUNET	NREN
	#15	AS5607	AS5607	LONDON	BSKYB-BROADBAND	LAB
	#16	AS3269	AS3269	TORINO	TELECOM ITALIA	LAB
	#17	AS8903	AS8903	MADRID	BT ESPANA	LAB
	#18	AS2856	AS5400	IPSWICH	BT UK	LAB
	#19	AS18070	AS18070	NIIGATA	NDAC	IXP
	#20	AS24956	AS24956	BRAUN-SCHWEIG	GAERTNER DATENSYSTEME	BUSINESS
	#21	AS13030	AS13030	OLTEN	INIT SEVEN	BUSINESS

Fig. 2. Deployment status of our measurement trial as of August 2014. Each vantage point is a SamKnows probe which is part of a larger SamKnows measurement platform. Most of these probes are deployed behind residential networks and receive native IPv6 connectivity from their ISP. A part of these probes are also connected within NREN.

---

[6] https://developers.google.com/youtube/v3/docs/videos/list.

S. Ahsan et al.

Selection of Video Bitrate: YouTube servers provides a list of available resolutions and required bit rates for the requested video. The YouTube test currently does not support Dynamic Adaptive Streaming over HTTP (DASH) [10] during playout, however, it has two modes of operation for dealing with throughput constraints: (a) A *non-adaptive* mode where the test downloads the same video resolution despite video stalls and (b) A *step-down* mode where we step down to a lower resolution if a stall occurs. The test then chooses the next highest bit rate and begins the download from the beginning. The *non-adaptive* mode does not portray the behavior of most YouTube players but is useful in comparing characteristics between IPv4 and IPv6 while keeping conditions identical. The *step-down* mode on the other hand, shows a more user-oriented result in the form of the highest resolution that the client can playout without disruptions over a particular connection. To avoid unnecessary stalling we use results from speed tests to limit the maximum bit rate that the client will attempt to download.

3.3 Measurement Trials

The trial was conducted for 20 days (05th–25th September, 2014) using 21 SamKnows probes deployed behind 19 different ASes across Europe and Japan. These probes are also deployed inside different flavors of networks such as residential, NREN, business, and ISP test labs. Figure 2 provides a list of all probes along with their location, IPv4 and IPv6 AS, ISPs and network types.

4 Data Analysis

A summary of all results is given in Fig. 3. A number of YouTube tests failed over IPv6 due to the unavailability of dual-stacked media servers or connectivity issues. Probe #08 was behind a Google blacklisted resolver[7], and consistently reported 100 % failure for YouTube IPv6 tests. The table shows the *Success Rate* of YouTube tests indicating the number of tests that successfully connected to media servers to download a YouTube video. The throughput graph shows disparity between IPv4 and IPv6 throughput. A detailed analysis, exploring the other aspects shown in the table follows.

4.1 Google Global Caches

YouTube videos are served to users through the Google's content delivery platform. Operators with a qualifying level of traffic can deploy servers as content caches within their networks in order to serve content closer to the users. These caches form Google Global Caches (GGC) and help increase performance and minimize transit bandwidth. Google estimates that 70–90% of their cacheable traffic is served from GGC[8].

---

[7] http://cnds.eecs.jacobs-university.de/users/vbajpai/googleipv6.

[8] https://peering.google.com/about/ggc.html.

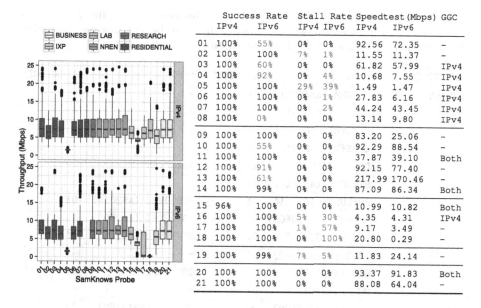

	Success Rate		Stall Rate		Speedtest (Mbps)		GGC
	IPv4	IPv6	IPv4	IPv6	IPv4	IPv6	
01	100%	55%	0%	0%	92.56	72.35	–
02	100%	100%	7%	1%	11.55	11.37	–
03	100%	60%	0%	0%	61.82	57.99	IPv4
04	100%	92%	0%	4%	10.68	7.55	IPv4
05	100%	100%	29%	39%	1.49	1.47	IPv4
06	100%	100%	0%	1%	27.83	6.16	IPv4
07	100%	100%	0%	2%	44.24	43.45	IPv4
08	100%	0%	0%	0%	13.14	9.80	IPv4
09	100%	100%	0%	0%	83.20	25.06	–
10	100%	55%	0%	0%	92.29	88.54	–
11	100%	100%	0%	0%	37.87	39.10	Both
12	100%	91%	0%	0%	92.15	77.40	–
13	100%	61%	0%	0%	217.99	170.46	–
14	100%	99%	0%	0%	87.09	86.34	Both
15	96%	100%	0%	0%	10.99	10.82	Both
16	100%	100%	5%	30%	4.35	4.31	IPv4
17	100%	100%	1%	57%	9.17	3.49	–
18	100%	100%	0%	100%	20.80	0.29	–
19	100%	99%	7%	5%	11.83	24.14	–
20	100%	100%	0%	0%	93.37	91.83	Both
21	100%	100%	0%	0%	88.08	64.04	–

Fig. 3. A summary of all test results. Box plots of the throughputs observed during YouTube tests (left) during the trial. Note that the graph is only used as a show of disparity and not the cause; throughput depends on the selected video, the selected resolution and throttling due to the limited length of the playout buffer, in addition to connection failure and connection bandwidth constraints. The table (right) shows for each probe (i) Success rate, a percentage of YouTube tests that successfully resolved and connected to media servers, (ii) Stall rate, percentage of successful YouTube tests that experienced one or more stall events, (iii) Speedtest (Mbps), the average throughput observed during the entire duration of the trial, (iv) GGC, the availability of GGC over an address family. The table represents results for the data collected in September 2014.

In our analysis, we identified GGC by looking up the Autonomous System Number (ASN) information for the contacted media servers. As expected, many of the GGC served content only over IPv4 and the probes used Google centralized content servers for IPv6. Among residential networks, 6 (out of 8) probes used GGC when using IPv4, but all used central content servers over IPv6. Within lab networks 2 probes used GGC, of which only 1 (#15) also used a GGC over IPv6. NREN and business probes were different in respect that all their IPv4 media servers belonged to a single ASN and this was the same for IPv6 media servers. Subsequently, we observed a degree of stability exhibited in the TCP connection establishment times of these two categories (see Sect. 4.2). Table 1 gives a list of the ASes we observed during our tests along with their categorization and the number of probes they served while the availability of GGC over each address family is shown under GGC in Fig. 3.

Table 1. Categorization of YouTube content (audio and video) delivery by AS as observed over all probes both over IPv4 and IPv6. It can be seen how content-caches and delivery from YouTube CDN is largely absent over IPv6.

CATEGORY	IPV4	n(PROBES)	IPV6	n(PROBES)
CONTENT CACHES	COMHEM (AS39651)	01	-	-
	ASAHI (AS4685)	01	-	-
	JAZZNET (AS12715)	01	-	-
	EDPNET (AS9031)	01	-	-
	DTAG (AS3320)	02	DTAG (AS3320)	02
	BIGLOBE (AS2518)	01	-	-
	ROEDUNET (AS2614)	01	ROEDUNET (AS2614)	01
	NORDUNET (AS2603)	01	NORDUNET (AS2603)	01
	BSKYB (AS5607)	01	BSKYB (AS5607)	01
	SEABONE (AS6762)	01	-	-
	QSC (AS20676)	01	QSC (AS20676)	01
	NG (AS48161)	01	-	-
CDN	GOOGLE (AS15169)	20	GOOGLE (AS15169)	19
	YOUTUBE (AS43515)	03	-	-
	YOUTUBE (AS36040)	02	-	-
	LEVEL3 (AS3356)	01	-	-
IXP	-	-	INTERLAN (AS39107)	01

4.2 TCP Connect Times and Happy Eyeballs

Figure 4 shows the distribution of raw TCP connection establishment times to YouTube media servers both over IPv4 and IPv6 as seen from each probe. These are the TCP connections that are later used to fetch YouTube video and audio streams separately. It can be seen how TCP connect times tend to show more variation for residential (#01–08) and lab (#15–18) probes. Probes deployed behind NREN networks (#09–14) and business lines (#20–21), on the contrary appear to be more stable.

TCP connect times are largely comparable over both address families. This is important to measure because applications (on top of TCP) running on dual-stacked hosts will prefer connections made over IPv6. This is mandated by the destination address selection policy [12]. As such, getaddrinfo(...) tends to resolve DNS names in an order that prefers an IPv6 upgrade path. However, the happy eyeballs algorithm [13] allows these applications to switch to IPv4 in situations where IPv6 connectivity is bad. The connectivity is considered bad when connections made over IPv4 can tolerate the 300 ms advantage imparted to IPv6 and still complete the TCP connection establishment in less time. Figure 5 shows the distribution of TCP connect times across all probes and the values for IPv6 are generally lower than 300 ms. As such, the happy eyeballs algorithm would prefer connections over IPv6.

4.3   Stall Events

Stall events occur due to throughput constraints, which are caused by a bottleneck at any point on the path between the media server and the probe. We observed stall events on 9 probes, 3 of which belonged to lab networks, 1 was in IXP while the remaining were all residential. Some of these cases are discussed below.

In 3 probes #02, #07 and #16, stalling events occurred only during peak hours, however, speed tests showed sufficient throughput values with no degradation during these hours. All 3 probes reported media servers in more than one AS, and the stalling events were specific to a particular AS only. In probe #02, the stall events are specific to servers in AS43515, which is only seen over IPv4 during peak hours and the stalls are also limited to IPv4 only. In case of probe #16, the stall events are seen for servers in AS15169 and the AS appears for both address families, causing stalling events in both cases as well. Figure 6 show hourly trend of YouTube and speed tests for probe #02 and 16. Stall events for probe #07 all occurred for the same video that was downloaded in Ultra HD, with a bit rate of 13 Mbps, which is 4 times the bit rate required during other tests that ran on the probe. While the ASs of media servers used for the video download varied for different hours during the day, all stall events were observed for servers in AS15169. Graphs for probe #07 were not included due to space limitations.

In case of 6 probes (#04–06,17,18,19) the measured throughputs during speed tests indicated insufficient bandwidth and YouTube tests also exhibited stall

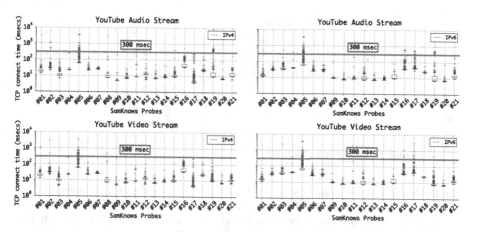

Fig. 4. Boxplots of TCP connection establishment times (in log-scale) to YouTube audio (above) and video (below) streams from each vantage point both over IPv4 (left) and IPv6 (right). The raw TCP connect times to YouTube media servers are comparable over both address family.

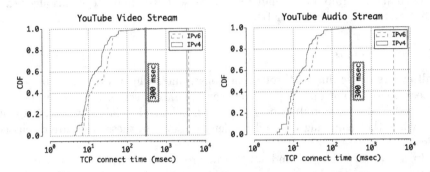

Fig. 5. Distribution of TCP connection establishment times (in log-scale) to YouTube video (left) and audio (right) streams both over IPv4 and IPv6 combined over all probes.

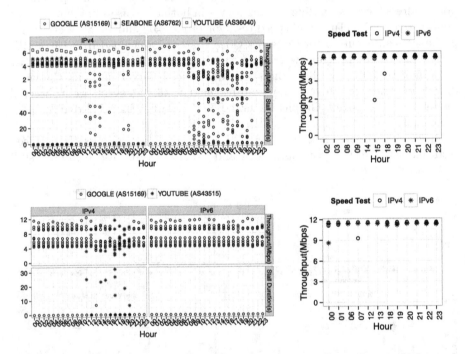

Fig. 6. Hourly trend of stall events, YouTube throughput and speed tests as observed on probe #16 (top) and #02 (bottom) during Trial Phase 1. For both probes, stall events are specific to media servers in a particular AS. We note that the disparity in media servers for each address family leads to stalling only in IPv4 in the bottom graph, while in the top graph it results in more stall events in IPv6 than IPv4. Speed tests, which are run only for specific hours during the day are shown on the right.

events. Figure 7, shows the speed test results for all residential probes, and also the lab probes that exhibit stalling. Note that all 6 of these probes contain some very low throughput measurements. In case of probes #05, #16 and #17, sometimes the competing audio stream consumed too much bandwidth resulting in an insufficient share for the heavier video stream. We identified this as a flaw in our test and noted that pacing audio traffic can help avoid stalls in some cases where the required and available throughput are very close.

4.4   Summary

Among our trial probes, 16 were deployed in home, office or university/research networks and represented real end users with dual-stacked hosts. Disparity in throughput measurements over IPv4 and IPv6 was observed in 10 of them. From the remaining 6, 4 probes showed inconsistent results for YouTube in terms of content delivery, IPv6 connectivity to media servers and/or TCP connect times.

Speed tests revealed a range of achievable throughput for residential networks. 5 out of the 8 residential probes showed disparity in measured throughputs over IPv6 and IPv4, all of them having lower values over IPv6. All these probes used centralized servers for fetching media over IPv6, whereas 6 of them used content caches over IPv4. Half of the probes suffered from connectivity issues to YouTube media servers over IPv6.

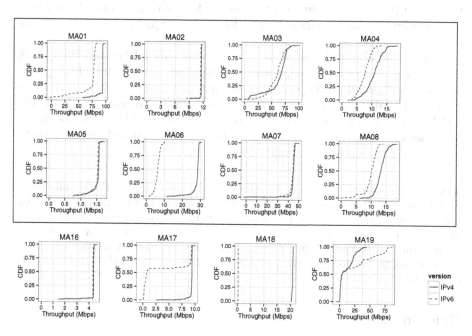

Fig. 7. Distribution of line rates observed by probes wired in behind a residential gateway (boxed) and operator's lab network (unboxed). Line rates are measured using speed test against dual-stacked M-Lab servers.

Office, research and NREN used in the trial were all high-speed networks with even the slowest one reporting an average throughput of over 25 Mbps. YouTube HD content has a typical range of 3–5 Mbps and about 4 times that for 4 K UltraHD, and hence from a required throughput perspective, these networks can easily support YouTube. This was exhibited in the form of 100 % stall-free YouTube tests for these networks. However, networks are typically used by more than one user and even single users run simultaneous tasks. The speed test results in some of these networks show lower throughput values in case of IPv6, which can result in performance degradation for users.

The trial included 4 probes that were deployed in testbeds for ISPs that have not launched IPv6 to customers yet, in order to ascertain network performance before actual IPv6 rollouts. We found erratic results or performance issues on 3 of them, while one showed smooth performance that was consistent over IPv4 and IPv6.

5   Conclusion

We measured YouTube performance from 21 dual-stacked probes deployed in Europe and some parts of Japan and observed two causes of degraded YouTube performance over IPv6 in comparison to IPv4 or vice versa: (i) a disparity in available bandwidth leading to insufficient throughput for a particular address family and (ii) different media content servers for each address family, of which, servers from a certain prefix exhibited lower throughput connections with the probe.

Overall, we observed that network performance over IPv4 and IPv6 is dissimilar in a majority of the networks we studied. From a set of 16 probes deployed in residential, official/educational networks, we observed only 3 probes (MA#11,14,20) with similar network conditions and performance for both IPv6 and IPv4 in terms of speed tests and YouTube delivery. This extent of disparity shows the significance of performance measurements at end points to better understand and improve the quality of services.

Acknowledgements. This work was supported by the European Community's Seventh Framework Programme (FP7/2007-2013) grant no. 317647 (Leone). We would like to thank all the volunteers who hosted a SamKnows probe for us. We would also like to thank Sam Crawford, Jamie Mason and Cristian Morales Vega (SamKnows) for providing us technical support on the SamKnows infrastructure. We also would like to thank Steffie Jacob Eravuchira (Jacobs University Bremen) for reviewing the manuscripts.

References

1. Adhikari, V.K., Jain, S., Zhang, Z.L.: Youtube traffic dynamics and its interplay with a tier-1 ISP: an ISP perspective. In: Proceedings of the 10th ACM SIGCOMM Conference on Internet Measurement, IMC '10. ACM, New York (2010)

2. Adhikari, V., Jain, S., Chen, Y., Zhang, Z.L.: Vivisecting youtube: an active measurement study. In: 2012 Proceedings IEEE, INFOCOM (March 2012)

3. Cha, M., Kwak, H., Rodriguez, P., Ahn, Y.Y., Moon, S.: I tube, you tube, everybody tubes: analyzing the world's largest user generated content video system. In: Proceedings of the 7th ACM SIGCOMM Conference on Internet Measurement, IMC '07, pp. 1–14. ACM, New York (2007)

4. Dimopoulos, G., Barlet-Ros, P., Sanjuas-Cuxart, J.: Analysis of youtube user experience from passive measurements. In: 2013 9th International Conference on Network and Service Management (CNSM), pp. 260–267 (October 2013)

5. Finamore, A., Mellia, M., Munafò, M.M., Torres, R., Rao, S.G.: Youtube everywhere: impact of device and infrastructure synergies on user experience. In: Proceedings of the 2011 ACM SIGCOMM Conference on Internet Measurement Conference, IMC '11, pp. 345–360. ACM, New York (2011)

6. Gill, P., Arlitt, M., Li, Z., Mahanti, A.: Youtube traffic characterization: a view from the edge. In: Proceedings of the 7th ACM SIGCOMM Conference on Internet Measurement, IMC '07, pp. 15–28. ACM, New York (2007)

7. Juluri, P., Plissonneau, L., Medhi, D.: Pytomo: A tool for analyzing playback quality of youtube videos. In: 2011 Teletraffic Congress (ITC) (September 2011)

8. Juluri, P., Plissonneau, L., Zeng, Y., Medhi, D.: Viewing youtube from a metropolitan area: what do users accessing from residential isps experience? In: IFIP/IEEE International Symposium on Integrated Network Management (IM) (May 2013)

9. Nam, H., Kim, K.H., Calin, D., Schulzrinne, H.: Youslow: a performance analysis tool for adaptive bitrate video streaming. In: Proceedings of the 2014 ACM conference on SIGCOMM, pp. 111–112. ACM (2014)

10. Stockhammer, T.: Dynamic adaptive streaming over http: – standards and design principles. In: Proceedings of the Second Annual ACM Conference on Multimedia Systems, MMSys '11, pp. 133–144. ACM, New York (2011)

11. Sundaresan, S., de Donato, W., Feamster, N., Teixeira, R., Crawford, S., Pescapè, A.: Broadband internet performance: a view from the gateway. In: SIGCOMM '11. ACM (2011)

12. Thaler, D., Draves, R., Matsumoto, A., Chown, T.: Default address selection for internet protocol version 6 (IPv6). RFC 6724 (Proposed Standard), Internet Engineering Task Force (September 2012)

13. Wing, D., Yourtchenko, A.: Happy eyeballs: success with dual-stack hosts. RFC 6555 (Proposed Standard), Internet Engineering Task Force (April 2012)

Investigating Transparent Web Proxies in Cellular Networks

Xing Xu[1]([✉]), Yurong Jiang[1], Tobias Flach[1], Ethan Katz-Bassett[1],
David Choffnes[2], and Ramesh Govindan[1]

[1] USC, Los Angeles, USA
{xingx,yurongji,flach,ethan.kb,ramesh}@usc.edu
[2] Northeastern University, Boston, USA
choffnes@ccs.neu.edu

Abstract. People increasingly use mobile devices as their primary means to access the Internet. While it is well known that cellular network operators employ middleboxes, the details of their behavior and their impact on Web performance are poorly understood. This paper presents an analysis of proxy behavior and how transparent Web proxies interact with HTTP traffic in four major US cell carriers. We find that all four carriers use these proxies to interpose on HTTP traffic, but they vary in terms of whether they perform object caching, traffic redirection, image compression, and connection reuse. For example, some transparent proxies unilaterally lower the quality of images, which improves object fetch time but may hurt user satisfaction. We also find that these proxies do not necessarily enhance performance for mobile Web workloads in terms of object fetch times; namely, we observe noticeable benefits only when flow sizes are large and the path between the server and proxy exhibits large latency and/or loss.

1 Introduction

Internet service providers commonly deploy middleboxes inside their networks for security, traffic management, and performance optimization [23]. In the mobile environment, in which resources such as spectrum are scarce, operators have significant incentives to interpose on Internet traffic. Unfortunately, operators are rarely transparent about middlebox policies, and their impact on mobile workloads is poorly understood. Previous work identified that middleboxes exist in cellular networks and characterized several middlebox behaviors [8,11,13,21,24,26]. For example, these studies show that carriers proxy traffic to servers by transparently splitting client TCP connections into two connections: the proxy terminates the client's TCP connection by spoofing as the server, and the proxy establishes a separate connection to the server by spoofing as the client. With split connections, the proxy can configure each segment individually and respond to latency and loss independently, potentially improving performance.

It is widely believed that splitting TCP connections should improve – or at least not worsen – performance for devices in cellular networks, where latencies

© Springer International Publishing Switzerland 2015
J. Mirkovic and Y. Liu (Eds.): PAM 2015, LNCS 8995, pp. 262–276, 2015.
DOI: 10.1007/978-3-319-15509-8_20

and loss can be much larger than in fixed-line paths [9,11,13,21,24]. However, previous studies do not characterize the performance impact for modern cellular networks and workloads.

In this paper, we are the first to conduct a detailed study of transparent proxies in four major US cellular providers (AT&T, Sprint, T-Mobile, and Verizon) across four US metro areas (Boston, Chicago, Los Angeles, and Seattle) and determine their impact on performance. Our measurements indicate that all four carriers use transparent proxies for Web traffic (TCP port 80) which represents a large portion of today's Internet flows. Thus, we focus in particular on transparent Web proxies.

We designed controlled experiments to investigate features of transparent Web proxy implementations including caching, content modification, traffic redirection to preferred servers, and connection persistence. Specifically, we tightly control and monitor the traffic generated by devices, DNS servers, and Web servers to characterize proxy behavior and its impact under varying network conditions and workloads, including representative workloads using a mobile Web browser. We also develop techniques that allow us to infer proxy behavior for communication with servers that we do not control and evaluate proxy impact on popular Web sites. Note that, we conjecture, but do not focus on why do carriers deploy these features.

Key Results. First, each carrier implements proxying policies differently, and they can lead to a different user experience in terms of the speed and quality of downloaded content. For example, image compression can reduce download time by a factor of five, but caching content has little impact on performance in our experiments. Second, we observe that split connections improve performance for larger flows (up to 45%), but have negligible impact on small ones ($\leq$100 KB). We show that proxied connections can provide benefits in lossy and high-latency environments, particularly where the cellular segment is not the dominating factor determining end-to-end performance. We use a mobile Web browser to download replicated Web content from servers we control while approximating the same communication patterns. Under normal network conditions, these proxies do not measurably improve performance, but page load times are 30% faster when we induce loss on the wired segment. Last, we verify that proxying occurs of all of the most popular 100 Web site front pages, but discover that YouTube video servers bypass T-Mobile's proxy, possibly due to special arrangements between the providers [20]. Our results indicate proxies may not necessarily improve performance for mobile users, motivating the need for larger-scale and more in-depth analysis of the performance benefits across networks, devices, locations, and workloads.

2   Background and Related Work

Few studies systematically reveal proxy policies in mobile networks and assess their impact. Early work in this area has focused on understanding, modeling and improving split-TCP designs for proxies in wireless and cellular networks.

An early survey [8] qualitatively characterizes the behavior and role of performance-enhancing proxies for wireless networks in general. Ehsan et al. [11] study the benefits of proxies for satellite networks and describe the benefits of split-TCP connections. Necker et al. [24] explore, through simulation, the impact of proxies on bulk downloads and Web traffic on UMTS networks. Ivanovich et al. [21] discuss advanced ACKing strategies to buffer data at the proxy for increased wireless link utilization. Finally, Gomez et al. [16] show that proxies can improve Web browsing performance, Rodriguez et al. [25] discuss the architecture of a proxy (together with associated TCP optimizations) for a GPRS network, and Baccelli et al. [7] model the performance of split-TCP to understand its asymptotic behavior. In contrast, our work characterizes the behavior and performance impact of *deployed* proxies on *modern cellular networks*, across four major US carriers.

More recently, several pieces of work have explored other aspects of proxy behavior in modern cellular networks. Botta et al. [9] explore how middleboxes can impact measurements, and propose a careful methodology for cellular measurements, some of which we adopt and extend. Farkas et al. [13] use numerical simulations to quantify the performance improvement of proxies in LTE networks, while our work directly measures this improvement. Ehsan et al. [12] study tradeoffs of caching through real user traces. Closest to our work are three measurement studies that have attempted to reveal complementary aspects of proxy behavior. Wang et al. [26] show how cellular middlebox settings can impact mobile device energy usage and how middleboxes can be used to attack or deny service to mobile devices. Michio et al. [19] developed a method for measuring middlebox behavior related to TCP extensions and showed that some proxies remove TCP options and proxy connections, which is supplementary to our works.

Weaver et al. [27] study the prevalence of HTTP proxying using a large dataset of clients and taxonomize the types of HTTP proxying seen in the wild, ranging from transcoding proxies to censoring and anti-virus proxies. Unlike our work, that study does not attempt to enumerate the detailed TCP-level behavior of cellular proxies for various network conditions and Web workloads. Jiang et al. [22] analyze bufferbloat in cellular networks and propose a dynamic window adjustment algorithm to alleviate this. Our work explores proxy behavior, which includes buffers among many other features that impact performance. Finally, Hui et al. [20] confirm our observation that proxies can actually hurt performance instead of improving it. Their proxy bypass experiments with T-Mobile revealed that direct server-client connections have lower retransmission rates, higher throughput, and smaller amounts of bufferbloat.

3   Experimental Testbed

Our testbed design is motivated by three goals. First, we want to conduct controlled experiments to determine how a proxy responds to different Web flow characteristics. Second, for transparently proxied connections, we want to use microbenchmarks to identify under which circumstances the proxy behavior helps or hurts performance in terms of download time. Last, we want to understand how proxy behavior impacts the performance under realistic workloads. We focus on the delivery time of Web sites that include multiple resources from different servers.

With these goals in mind, we set up the following testbed. We use multiple rooted mobile devices (HTC One phones with Android 4.3) and different phone-specific cellular carrier data plans to explore proxy behavior for each of the four major US carriers (comprising 99 % of US subscribers [4]). We control a Web server and a DNS subdomain that resolves to it, allowing us to monitor both endpoints of a connection when we access a URL via one of our mobile devices. Our measurement were conducted in more than 2 months. For each experiment day, we conduct experiments over a wide range of times, including on and off-peak to avoid bias from time-of-day effects. Finally, we run tcpdump on the device and on the server to capture detailed network information, including TCP/IP headers and timestamps (after synchronizing endpoints using NTP).

With full control over the server and client devices, we can explore proxy properties through different experiment configurations, varying parameters such as the content that is fetched, socket properties (e.g. server IP/port), HTTP configuration (including modified headers), and even adjust network conditions. For each given configuration we mention in this paper, we conduct at least 250 trials. When comparing performance results between two configurations, we interleave trials of the two configurations to minimize the probability of signal strength and congestion variation impacting our results. In addition, we monitor signal strength readings to filter out biased results due to poor signal strength.

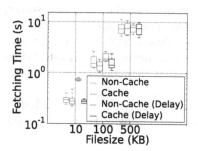

Fig. 1. Fetch times for cached and uncached objects.

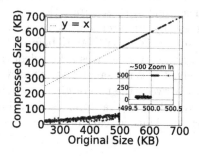

Fig. 2. Impact of Sprint's image compression (original vs. compressed file size).

For all four carriers, we conducted experiments in the metro areas of Boston, Chicago, Los Angeles, and Seattle. In addition, we have measurements for AT&T and T-Mobile in the metro areas of Philadelphia and Washington, DC.

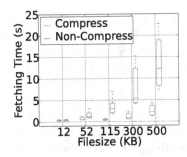

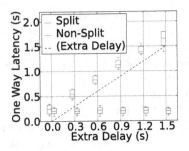

Fig. 3. Fetch times for compressed (left), and original images (right), on Sprint.

Fig. 4. Server-side handshake latency for split (top) and non-split connections, on T-Mobile.

4   Proxy Features

We test a list of well-known proxy features and identify five used in practice: *caching, redirection, content rewriting, connection persistence*, and *delayed server-side handshakes*. We observe different feature sets for each carrier (Table 1), but within each carrier the identified features are consistent across all metro areas we covered.

To observe proxy features, we conduct experiments between the mobile phones and our server. Since we control both endpoints, we can correlate client- and server-side packet traces, and extract features that indicate Web proxy interference. We first establish the presence of a Web proxy by inspecting various connection properties, including the TCP window scaling parameter, receiver window, and sequence and acknowledge numbers. In all four carriers we studied, at least one of these properties was inconsistent between the client and server, suggesting interference by a proxy. In addition, we observe that a client receives the initial TCP SYN-ACK before the server receives a SYN packet, and conversely a server receives acknowledgements for transmitted data packets before the client sees the same data. Thus, we conclude that these proxies split connections between the two original endpoints.

We observe that proxies only intercept traffic on some ports (including port 80). Thus, we can compare data for proxied and unproxied traffic by varying

Table 1. Proxy implementations observed in our study.

	AT&T	T-Mobile	Verizon	Sprint
Caching		✓		✓
Redirection		✓		
Content rewriting				✓
Connection persistence	✓	✓		✓
Delayed handshaking	✓	✓	✓	✓

the server port number. We use port 80 to elicit proxy behavior and port 7777 to bypass the proxy.

To characterize proxy behavior, we parameterize our experiments along multiple dimensions. We vary the server port, to control proxy interference. We analyze traffic observed when accessing different destinations, using both static IPs and DNS names resolvable by our controlled DNS server. We also experiment with multiple content types, flow sizes, packet delay and loss through traffic shaping, and investigate the effect of different HTTP header configurations.

4.1   Caching

Behavior. If a client receives an HTTP response without the request reaching the server, we conclude that the carrier caches content. We use unique resources hosted only on our server to ensure that content can only be delivered by our server or a cache. We observe content caching for T-Mobile and Sprint. They cache most Web objects (*e.g.,* CSS, JavaScript, JPEG, PNG, GIF, and TXT) but they *do not* cache HTML files. Both carriers cache at per-device and per-session granularity. That is, the cache is not shared between users and gets purged whenever the device releases its IP address. We conjecture the reason of doing this is to not cache private or dynamic contents. We observe objects remaining cached for a consistent period of time ($\approx$5 min for Sprint, $\approx$30 min for T-Mobile) across different times of day.

Impact. Object fetch time can decrease since the content is closer to the client. Figure 1 shows the measured fetch time for cached and non-cached objects, and the impact of network latency. From top to bottom, the boxes describe 90th, 75th, 50th, 25th and 10th percentiles (same for subsequent figures). If the cellular link dominates end-to-end latency we observe no noticeable performance gain when accessing cached resources. However, in environments with larger wired latencies (we demonstrate this by introducing delays for outgoing packets on the server side), we see fetch time improvements for small files (10 KB). For larger files (500 KB), TCP throughput is bottlenecked by the carrier capacity, preventing caching benefits. In addition to faster serving time, caching can reduce a carrier's inbound traffic, especially if the carrier segments are lossy.

4.2   Redirection

Behavior. Some proxies redirect traffic based on an independent DNS resolution of the *Host* header field of an HTTP request, ignoring the destination IP in the packet sent by the client. To test for this, we send an HTTP request to our Web server IP (*i.e.,* no client-side DNS resolution required) but provide a third-party domain name in the *Host* field, which triggers an error if handled by our server. If the proxy uses redirection, the request does not reach our server, yet the referenced website renders at the client side. Only T-Mobile elicits this behavior. We confirm it for all of the Alexa top 100 websites.

Impact. We cannot be certain, but this feature could be for traffic engineering considerations, *e.g.,* the carrier can control the destination for HTTP traffic at the proxy instead of relying on devices. In doing so, any server IP mapping based on client-selected DNS servers is silently and transparently overridden by this feature.

4.3   Object Rewriting

Behavior. In this case a proxy modifies file contents, for example to improve performance through mechanisms like whitespace trimming, or image transcoding to reduce the load on the cellular segment. For a variety of Web file types and content patterns, we compared the payloads transmitted by the server with the contents received by the mobile devices to detect this feature. We only observe compression of image files, and only with Sprint up to an original file size of 500 KB (see Fig. 2). We conjecture that the reason of not transcoding large images is to avoid this receiving latency as well as transcoding latency. For text files, we did not observe any trimming of whitespace or comments.

Impact. Compressed files can be fetched faster, as shown in Fig. 3. But, aggressive compression can distort images in ways that are unacceptable to the content provider or user [6]. Further, the proxy must fetch the whole image and transcode it before beginning to forward to the client.

4.4   Connection Persistence

Behavior. Proxies can persist connections to both endpoints. For the server-side segment, some proxies remove a client's `connection: close` directive in the HTTP header (used to inform the server to close the connection upon query response), or add a `connection: keep-alive` entry. To persist the client-proxy connection, some proxies drop the server's TCP FIN packet. We find that AT&T and Sprint proxies keep the connection to the HTTP server alive after each request completes. The keepalive time is ~10 s for AT&T, and ~30 s for Sprint. AT&T, Sprint and T-Mobile drop the TCP FIN from the server to persist the client-proxy connection.

Impact. The advantages of this strategy are that persistent connections avoid the delays that new per-object connections would incur from TCP handshakes and slow start. Reusing a connection can also minimize overhead on NAT table mappings at the edge of the carrier network.

4.5   Delayed Handshaking

Observation. Finally, we confirm that proxies in each carrier delay the initial handshake between themselves and a server until receiving the HTTP request. Proxies wait for HTTP request because information from HTTP request helps caching feature determine whether there is cached version of the request; it also helps redirecting feature to figure out the IP destination. Figure 4 illustrates this behavior. We artificially delay the query which proportionally increases the server-side reception delay for the handshake packet.

Impact. Deferred handshakes can delay end-to-end communication, especially for modern browsers that open a connection early in anticipation of a later query, to avoid incurring the handshake overhead when the query occurs.

5 Split Connection Performance

Intuitively, split TCP connections should offer better client-perceived performance (i.e., faster downloads) than direct connections if the proxy is on the same path. First, splitting the connection reduces the RTTs between connected endpoints, which allows TCP to grow its congestion window faster. Second, it isolates the throughput impact of loss events to an individual segment, and it speeds loss detection and recovery [13, 21, 25].

In practice, splitting TCP connections offers benefits that depend on the size of the flow and the relative performance of the split path segments. For short flows, it is unclear if split connections always result in better client-perceived performance. Likewise, for cases where the cellular segment is substantially worse than the wired segment, reducing RTT and loss have little impact on the fetch time for Web objects.

This section uses controlled experiments to understand the performance impact of split connections for a Web server we host, for alternative network conditions between the server and proxy, and for realistic Web browser workloads. We find that the performance impact varies across carriers, network conditions, or Web sites.

While our experiments cannot be used to compare performance across carriers (since we cannot create identical conditions across them), we can get valuable insights into the conditions under which split-connections do and do not work well, and understand how these insights generalize across carriers. Results from T-Mobile are qualitatively similar to AT&T, and Sprint results are similar to Verizon, so we omit AT&T and Verizon. For full results, see our tech report [28].

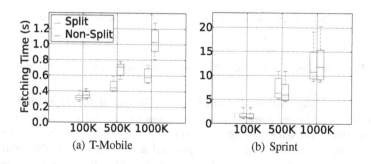

(a) T-Mobile   (b) Sprint

Fig. 5. Fetching times for different file sizes.

Baseline Performance. For each carrier, we fetch objects with different sizes using split and non-split connections. Figure 5(b) shows there is no significant performance difference for Sprint for any file size. In contrast, Fig. 5(a) shows that for T-Mobile, proxied downloads of larger objects finish much earlier (in the 1 MB case, 30 % faster in the median). T-Mobile has much better performance than Sprint, because Sprint has much worse link quality where we conducted our experiments. When we make performance statements about a carrier, say Sprint, that is shorthand for "the performance seen by the mobile device in our testbed connected to the Sprint network", not a blanket statement about the carrier's overall performance.

To understand the reasons for different performance benefits, we analyze the network properties of the cellular and wired path segments. First, we use traces from the server to find that the wired segments (server to proxy) for all four carriers have similar characteristics in terms of latency and bandwidth. For Sprint and Verizon, the limited bandwidth of their cellular segments is the main performance bottleneck, thus limiting the efficacy of split connections. In contrast, AT&T and T-Mobile offer more bandwidth, so transfers benefit from split connections, since shorter latencies enable faster ramp-up of TCP's congestion window.

Interestingly, the TCP congestion window on the server side ramps up slowly in AT&T and T-Mobile due to TCP's Hybrid Start feature used by default in the Linux CUBIC congestion control mechanism [17,18]. The RTT and ACK patterns influenced by the cellular segment result in an early transition to the congestion avoidance phase to prevent heavy losses. Since the connection is sender-limited and never reaches the channel capacity, splitting connections can help to tune features like this for the two path segments independently.

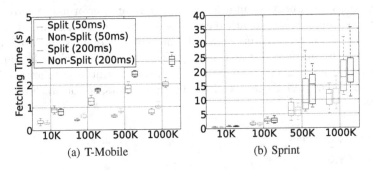

(a) T-Mobile   (b) Sprint

Fig. 6. Fetching times for different file sizes, with varying amounts of delay added.

Impact of Varying Network Conditions. We repeat the experiments above, but emulate high latency wired path segments by having our server introduce 50–200 ms delay on each packet it sends. Figure 6 plots the impact on fetch times for various file sizes, comparing proxied and unproxied traffic. Split connections improve performance in AT&T's and T-Mobile's case for larger files

and delays (*e.g.,* 1 MB and 200 ms delay); we do not observe statistically significant changes with Sprint and Verizon. Performance improvements are similar for
AT&T, Sprint, and Verizon when introducing correlated loss on the wired segment. Interestingly, T-Mobile's performance for proxied traffic is independent of
loss rate in our experiments, because the proxy maintains a large-enough buffer
to compensate for the reduced throughput during loss.

Overall, these experiments show that split connections are most impactful in
environments where the cellular segment is not the dominant factor with respect
to end-to-end performance. Thus, carriers with better cellular links benefit most.

Web Browsing. We now move from characterizing performance for isolated
object fetches to realistic workloads generated by a browser accessing popular Web sites. Since we cannot bypass the proxy when accessing Web servers,
we resort to hosting Web site replicas on our server. For this, we fetch the
original URLs including all embedded resources, even if they are delivered by
third parties. We use a different IP alias for each Web host. We then measure the round-trip time to each real Web host and induce per-alias delay at
our server to approximate the communication patterns between the phone and
the real hosts. We host three qualitatively different types of sites: a news site
(18 objects), a search engine (14 objects), and an image-bound site (8 objects
with 2 large images). We introduce 3 % packet loss on the server side to investigate the impact of congestion. Also, we simulate *follow-up visits*, by fetching the
news site, waiting 10 s, then fetching a link on the page. Thus, proxies that persist connections and cache static content can potentially improve performance
compared to bypassed traffic.

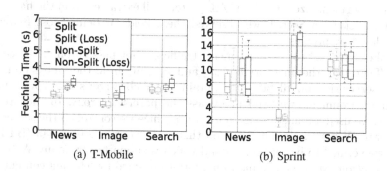

(a) T-Mobile   (b) Sprint

Fig. 7. Fetching times for three Web site types (in loss-free and lossy environments).

Figure 7 shows the Web browsing results. With introduced loss, split connections generally outperform their unproxied counterparts, with up to 30 %
lower completion times in the median. The proxy absorbs losses, thus keeping performance comparable to a loss-free environment. The proxy buffer benefits for T-Mobile mentioned earlier are evident in this experiment as well.
Caching does not provide significant gains on T-Mobile or Sprint in our tests.
In contrast, Sprint's image compression drastically reduces fetch times on the

image-bound site. Finally, we find that T-Mobile and AT&T's persistent connections can improve performance by ~10 % for follow-up visits (not shown).

6   On the Prevalence of Proxying

The experiments above tell us how a cellular proxy interacts with flows to our Web site, but do not necessarily inform how the proxies interact with other, popular sites. For example, a carrier and content provider may have a special agreement to bypass proxies for certain content, or the content provider's servers may be off-path from the proxy. The methodology in the previous sections does not help here because it requires access to the mobile device and server; for popular sites we have access to the former only.

To understand proxying prevalence for commonly accessed servers, we study how many of the 100 most popular websites [1] are proxied. We have no visibility at the server end, so we use a fingerprint analysis technique to identify split TCP connections and determine if the carriers proxy all, some, or none of the sites.

Fingerprinting. The key observation driving our fingerprint-based proxy detection is that proxies use predictable patterns when setting bits in the TCP/IP header, which are different from the ones used by the Web servers. We use the following rules to identify proxying for arbitrary Web sites.

For each Web site, we collect packet traces for four connections with different properties. We fetch content via the cellular (c) and wired connections (w), using HTTP (h), and HTTPS (s). From the traces, we derive connection fingerprints, denoted by $\mathcal{F}_{c,h}$, $\mathcal{F}_{w,h}$, $\mathcal{F}_{c,s}$ and $\mathcal{F}_{w,s}$. The fingerprint for each packet trace is composed of the receiver window, the window scaling option value, advertised maximum segment size, and the IP/ID pattern, all extracted from the handshake response packet. In Sect. 4, we observed these fields as being most frequently manipulated by proxies.

In the wired network environment, traffic cannot pass through the cellular proxy. Therefore, the fingerprints $\mathcal{F}_{w,h}$ and $\mathcal{F}_{w,s}$ are from the Web server (possibly a server-side middlebox). To obtain the Web server's fingerprint in the cellular environment, we need to bypass the potential proxy. In the previous sections, we used a non-standard port (7777) since we controlled the server. But in general, Web sites do not listen on this port, so we use port 443 (HTTPS), which we verified to be un-proxied and which is supported by many Web sites.

In addition, we use a common fingerprint obtained by fetching content from our server, denoted by $\mathcal{F}_p$. We demonstrated earlier that this is the cellular proxy's fingerprint, seen by the client when establishing a connection to our server. Based on these five fingerprints per site, we conclude that the phone communicates with an HTTP proxy to access web resources if the following conditions apply:

$$\mathcal{F}_{c,h} = \mathcal{F}_p \tag{1}$$

$$\mathcal{F}_{c,h} \neq \mathcal{F}_{w,h} \tag{2}$$

$$\mathcal{F}_{c,h} \neq \mathcal{F}_{c,s} \Rightarrow \mathcal{F}_{c,s} = \mathcal{F}_{w,s} \tag{3}$$

First, we check if the phone observes the proxy's fingerprint when establishing a connection to a web server using the cellular network (rule 1). Then, we ensure that the web server is not using the same fingerprint when responding to a client, by accessing the server through a wired connection (rule 2). Finally, we ensure that servers do not simply use different fingerprints depending on the network access type. For this, we check whether the HTTP and HTTPS fingerprints in the cellular environment do not match, indicating that HTTPS traffic bypasses the proxy. If so, we expect that the HTTPS fingerprints should be consistent across network access types (rule 3). Additionally we conclude that the phone always communicates with the same proxy infrastructure for sites w_i if the following additional condition holds:

$$\forall w_1, w_2 : \mathcal{F}_{c,h}(w_1) = \mathcal{F}_{c,h}(w_2) \tag{4}$$

For each of the 100 most popular websites [1], we first obtain the mobile-specific version of the site (if one exists). To control for the fact that fixed-line and cellular networks may resolve DNS names and perform redirection differently, we generate the $\mathcal{F}_{w,*}$ fingerprints by connecting to the same IP address found in the cellular network.

Among these 100 websites, ~20 websites do not support HTTPS. For these websites we cannot check rule 3. For the ~10 websites that always redirect HTTP requests to HTTPS, we use the redirection response as the fingerprint for the HTTP response.

Results. Rule 1 holds for each of the tested websites, and rule 4 holds for all pairs of websites, suggesting that the same proxy handles all of a carrier's Web traffic. Rules 2 and 3 do not hold for a few destinations. In particular, the fingerprints for three websites connecting over the wired network match the fingerprint of the Sprint proxy. For another three websites we observe non-matching HTTPS fingerprints.

Table 2. TCP-based traceroutes show that T-Mobile selectively proxies connections on port 80.

Hop	Test server (port 80)	Test server (port 443)	YouTube (port 80)
1	192.168.42.129	192.168.42.129	192.168.42.129
2	10.170.224.192	10.170.224.192	10.170.224.192
3	10.170.224.138	10.170.224.138	10.170.224.138
4	10.165.54.12	10.165.54.12	10.165.54.12
5	**128.125.121.204**	**10.165.54.1**	**10.165.54.1**
6		10.170.213.11	10.170.213.11
		$\vdots$	$\vdots$
Last		**128.125.121.204**	208.54.39.44

The results above indicate that contents for index pages are proxied, but they do not indicate whether the same is true for all site content. In particular, we suspect that content such as streaming video, which is often heavily optimized based on client performance, could bypass the proxy to avoid interference with these optimizations. To test this hypothesis, we use a similar strategy as above for the video streaming URLs from three popular video streaming websites. For Hulu, we verify that the traffic is proxied for all four carriers. Verizon uses IPv6 for YouTube and NetFlix which we omit from this study. YouTube traffic is proxied for AT&T and Sprint. However, T-Mobile traffic to some YouTube servers bypasses the proxy. We compare paths to YouTube and other hosts with `tcptraceroute`. Table 2 presents our results, indicating that the IP-level path to YouTube servers differs from those passing through the proxy (hop 5), and shares IP hops with paths to our Web server over unproxied connections (hop 6). This observation was subsequently verified when Google and T-Mobile revealed that video bypassed the proxy to improve performance [20].

7   Discussion and Future Work

Limitations. This paper focuses on methodologies and experiments for identifying and characterizing proxies in four US cellular networks using a small number of devices. We measured the impact of proxies for a variety of network configurations, but future work will use a broader set of locations and carriers to generalize our results. Our study characterizes proxies only in IPv4 networks. Only one carrier, Verizon, supported native IPv6 connectivity (in addition to IPv4). Verizon proxies v4 Web traffic but does *not* proxy it when using IPv6, a topic of future work. This study focused on behavior for the 100 most-popular Web sites and one testbed Web site; we found that proxying was consistent for all but YouTube on T-Mobile. We believe that such exceptions to proxying are rare, but we would like to evaluate this on more Web sites.

Selective proxying. We were interested to discover that proxies interpose on connections to almost all major Web sites, but Google's YouTube traffic bypasses T-Mobile proxies. Subsequent to our discovery, Google and T-Mobile revealed that they worked together to enable the bypass [20]. YouTube accounts for significant portions of Internet traffic, and Google has actively developed approaches to improve delivery [3,5,10,14,15]. This suggests that Google sees benefit in maintaining an end-to-end connection to clients, and T-Mobile appears willing to work with (at least some) providers to enable bypassing of the proxy. HTTPS provides another means to bypass the proxy, and providers are increasingly using it to serve Web content. It will be interesting to observe trends over time, to see if the role of proxies diminishes as content moves to HTTPS and, perhaps, as more Web providers negotiate arrangements like YouTube has.

Proxy evolution. Despite evidence of selective proxying and unclear performance benefits from existing proxies, we believe that future proxies can serve an important role in cellular networks. Cellular carriers control the whole transport

segment between the client device and the proxy. As such it is possible to fine
tune connections. For example, connections between the phone and the proxy
can use advanced protocol features which cannot be easily deployed in a public network due to potential third-party interference [14]. With explicit proxies
(*e.g.*, SPDY/compression proxies [2]) a client can use a single connection to the
proxy, which connects to requested sites.

References

1. Alexa Top 100 Websites. http://www.alexa.com/topsites
2. Data Compression Proxy. https://developer.chrome.com/multidevice/data-compre
   ssion
3. Experimenting with QUIC. http://blog.chromium.org/2013/06/experimenting-
   with-quic.html
4. Grading the Top U.S. Wireless Carriers, 8 August 2014. http://www.fiercewireless.
   com/special-reports/grading-top-us-wireless-carriers-second-quarter-2014
5. SPDY Whitepaper. http://www.chromium.org/spdy/spdy-whitepaper
6. Sprint Community. https://community.sprint.com/baw/thread/144305
7. Baccelli, F., Carofiglio, G., Foss, S.: Proxy caching in split TCP: dynamics, stability
   and tail asymptotics. In: Proceedings of INFOCOM (2008)
8. Border, J., Kojo, M., Griner, J., Montenegro, G., Shelby, Z.: Performance enhancing proxies intended to mitigate link-related degradations. Technical report, RFC
   3135 (2001)
9. Botta, A., Pescapé, A.: Monitoring and measuring wireless network performance
   in the presence of middleboxes. In: Proceedings of WONS (2011)
10. Dukkipati, N., Refice, T., Cheng, Y., Chu, J., Herbert, T., Agarwal, A., Jain,
    A., Sutin, N.: An argument for increasing TCP's initial congestion window. In:
    Proceedings of SIGCOMM CCR (2010)
11. Ehsan, N., Liu, M., Ragland, R.J.: Evaluation of performance enhancing proxies
    in internet over satellite. IJCS 16, 513–534 (2003)
12. Erman, J., Gerber, A., Hajiaghayi, M.T., Pei, D., Sen, S., Spatscheck, O.: To cache
    or not to cache: the 3G case. IEEE Internet Comput. 15, 27–34 (2011)
13. Farkas, V., Héder, B., Nováczki, S.: A split connection TCP proxy in LTE networks.
    In: Szabó, R., Vidács, A. (eds.) EUNICE 2012. LNCS, vol. 7479, pp. 263–274.
    Springer, Heidelberg (2012)
14. Flach, T., Dukkipati, N., Terzis, A., Raghavan, B., Cardwell, N., Cheng, Y., Jain,
    A., Hao, S., Katz-Bassett, E., Govindan, R.: Reducing web latency: the virtue of
    gentle aggression. In: Proceedings of SIGCOMM (2013)
15. Ghobadi, M., Cheng, Y., Jain, A., Mathis, M.: Trickle: rate limiting youtube video
    streaming. In: Proceedings of USENIX ATC (2012)
16. Gomez, C., Catalan, M., Viamonte, D., Paradells, J., Calveras, A.: Web browsing
    optimization over 2.5G and 3G: end-to-end mechanisms vs. usage of performance
    enhancing proxies. Wirel. Commun. Mob. Comput. 8, 213–230 (2008)
17. Ha, S., Rhee, I.: Hybrid slow start for high-bandwidth and long-distance networks.
    In: Proceedings of PFLDnet (2008)
18. Ha, S., Rhee, I., Xu, L.: CUBIC: a new TCP-friendly high-speed TCP variant.
    ACM SIGOPS Op. Syst. Rev. 42, 64–74 (2008)
19. Honda, M., Nishida, Y., Raiciu, C., Greenhalgh, A., Handley, M., Tokuda, H.: Is
    it still possible to extend TCP? In: Proceedings of IMC (2011)

20. Hui, J., Lau, K., Jain, A., Terzis, A., Smith, J.: How youtube performance is improved in T-mobile network. In: Proceedings of Velocity (2014)
21. Ivanovich, M., Bickerdike, P., Li, J.: On TCP performance enhancing proxies in a wireless environment. IEEE Commun. Mag. **46**, 76–83 (2008)
22. Jiang, H., Wang, Y., Lee, K., Rhee, I.: Tackling bufferbloat in 3G/4G networks. In:Proceedings of IMC (2012)
23. Kreibich, C., Weaver, N., Nechaev, B., Paxson, V.: Netalyzr: illuminating the edge network. In: Proceedings of IMC (2010)
24. Necker, M.C., Scharf, M., Weber, A.: Performance of different proxy concepts in UMTS networks. In: Kotsis, G., Spaniol, O. (eds.) Euro-NGI 2004. LNCS, vol. 3427, pp. 36–51. Springer, Heidelberg (2005)
25. Rodriguez, P., Fridman, V.: Performance of PEPs in cellular wireless networks. In: Douglis, F., Davison, B.D. (eds.) Web Content Caching and Distribution, pp. 19–38. Springer, Dordrecht (2004)
26. Wang, Z., Qian, Z., Xu, Q., Mao, Z., Zhang, M.: An untold story of middleboxes in cellular networks. In: Proceedings of SIGCOMM (2011)
27. Weaver, N., Kreibich, C., Dam, M., Paxson, V.: Here be web proxies. In: Faloutsos, M., Kuzmanovic, A. (eds.) PAM 2014. LNCS, vol. 8362, pp. 183–192. Springer, Heidelberg (2014)
28. Xu, X., Jiang, Y., Flach, T., Katz-Bassett, E., Choffnes, D., Govindan, R.: Investigating transparent web proxies in cellular networks. Technical report 14-944, University of Southern California (2014)

TrackAdvisor: Taking Back Browsing Privacy from Third-Party Trackers

Tai-Ching Li[1]([✉]), Huy Hang[1], Michalis Faloutsos[2],
and Petros Efstathopoulos[3]

[1] University of California, Riverside, USA
{tli010,hangh}@cs.ucr.edu
[2] University of New Mexico, Albuquerque, USA
michalis@cs.unm.edu
[3] Symantec Research Lab, Culver, USA
petros_efstathopoulos@symantec.com

Abstract. Even though most web users assume that only the websites that they visit directly become aware of the visit, this belief is incorrect. Many website display contents hosted externally by third-party websites, which can track users and become aware of their web-surfing behavior. This phenomenon is called third-party tracking, and although such activities violate no law, they raise privacy concerns because the tracking is carried out without users' knowledge or explicit approval. Our work provides a systematic study of the third-party tracking phenomenon. First, we develop TrackAdvisor, arguably the first method that utilizes Machine Learning to identify the HTTP requests carrying sensitive information to third-party trackers with very high accuracy (100 % Recall and 99.4 Precision). Microsoft's Tracking Protection Lists, which is a widely-used third-party tracking blacklist achieves only a Recall of 72.2 %. Second, we quantify the pervasiveness of the third-party tracking phenomenon: 46 % of the home pages of the websites in Alexa Global Top 10,000 have at least one third-party tracker, and Google, using third-party tracking, monitors 25 % of these popular websites. Our overarching goal is to measure accurately how widespread third-party tracking is and hopefully would raise the public awareness to its potential privacy risks.

1 Introduction

Would you feel that your privacy is violated if someone knew which websites you visited last night? Most people would feel uneasy and want to ensure their personal browsing information is not revealed to anyone else but the opposite is exactly what has been happening thanks to a phenomenon called **third-party tracking**. As a user visits a website of interest, third-party websites linked to that website become aware of the user's browsing activities and due to the ubiquitous use of cookies, these third-parties can uniquely identify the user[1]. Although

---

[1] In general, it is more accurate to say that third party tracking can track and identify web-browsers and not end users. In the rest of this document, we will use the term "tracking a user" to imply tracking the browser that is being used.

© Springer International Publishing Switzerland 2015
J. Mirkovic and Y. Liu (Eds.): PAM 2015, LNCS 8995, pp. 277–289, 2015.
DOI: 10.1007/978-3-319-15509-8_21

this can be appalling for privacy-sensitive users, there is no violation of laws. The third-party tracker is legitimately contacted by the user's browser, because it hosts resources required by the website that the user wants to visit.

It is natural to ask why the third-party tracking phenomenon is occurring and how. The answer to the "why" question is money, marketing, and advertising. It is easy to see that knowing how many users watch golf scores and search for luxury cars can help one place ads more effectively. With third-party tracking, ads on a website can be customized based on the user's visits to other websites. If you searched for yachts on one site, you could be shown yacht insurance ads on another site. The answer to the "how" question is the widespread use of: (a) embedded links on a webpage (think Facebook "Like" or Google+ "+1" button) or content being pulled from another site, and (b) cookies. Cookies turn any browser into a silent accomplice as the browser voluntarily provides cookies to the third-party websites. These cookies could have been obtained from a tracking website at an earlier time (e.g. when we logged in to Facebook). The obvious solution would not work: not sending cookies at all will often degrade the user experience or even "break" the interaction with websites.

In our work, we want to answer two main questions: (a) *How can we identify cookie-based third-party tracking accurately?* and (b) *How widespread is the phenomenon of third-party tracking?* To address both questions, we need a method that, when given a website and the HTTP interactions between users and that website, can identify third-party trackers. The challenge lies in identifying features of cookies and of the user interaction in general that can accurately identify third-party trackers. This is non-trivial and there exists no such method in the literature, as we discuss below. For the remainder of this paper, we use the term **privacy** to refer to the right of a web-browsing user to not have a third-party website become aware of websites that the user visits. We focus on cookie-based tracking, because it is still the most prevalent form of tracking, as we discuss in Sect. 7.

There has been very little attention on measuring the pervasiveness of third-party tracking activities, which is our focus here. To the best of our knowledge, the most widely-used approaches to combat the third-party tracking problem rely on black lists of third-party trackers, which are maintained by corporations or communities. Microsoft's **Tracking Protection Lists (TPL)** [7] is one such prominent black list, which aggregates many others. As we show later, these efforts are far from perfect, as they are geared towards blocking the more well-known third-party trackers. We discuss related and complementary research efforts in Sect. 7.

The contribution of this paper is a systematic study of the third-party tracking phenomenon and its extent. We also briefly discuss practical countermeasures to enable users to protect their web-browsing privacy. First, we propose TrackAdvisor, an effective method to detect third-party trackers that surpasses existing third-party tracking lists in terms of both accuracy and detection. Second, we use TrackAdvisor to study the prevalence of third-party tracking among Alexa's Global Top 10 K websites. We outline our key contributions and results below.

a. We develop TrackAdvisor, a supervised learning approach that identifies third-party trackers with high accuracy. A key novelty of our approach is that it does not rely on a blacklist of websites; TrackAdvisor focuses on the collective statistics of all cookies inside an outgoing third-party HTTP request to infer whether the third-party website that receives those cookies is tracking the user. Using Machine Learning techniques and carefully selected features, our method exhibits a Precision of 99.4 and a Recall of 100 %.

b. We evaluate the accuracy and completeness of TPL and show it yields a relatively low Recall of 72.2 %. Microsoft's Tracking Protection Lists (TPL), which combines many existing blacklists, achieves a Recall of 72.2 % although with a high Precision of 96.3 %. TPL is incorporated in Internet Explorer and can therefore be thought of as the protection that is readily available to users. As a result, its low Recall is somewhat disconcerting.

c. We show that third-party tracking is prevalent: 46 % of Alexa's Global top 10 K sites being tracked. We find that close to 46 % of the *home pages* of the websites in Alexa's Top 10,000 websites have at least one third-party tracker and on average, one out of every three HTTP requests sent to third-party websites is sent to a third-party tracker. More worrisomely, Google is monitoring 25 % of the Alexa sites as a third party tracker through its ad and analytics services. As expected, Facebook and Twitter are also prominent third-party tracking, as Facebook "Like" and Twitter's "Tweet" widgets have become very common, especially on blogs and news-related websites. Interestingly, two lesser known companies, Scorecard Research and QuantServe, are among the top five third-party trackers in our dataset.

2   Background

A. Cookies. In the context of the HTTP protocol and web browsing, a cookie is a small, **local** file (about 4KB in size) that helps a website identify a user and their preferences and it is intended to quickly provide the remote website with information such as language (for rendering the content in the correct language) or geographic location (maybe for nearest store location). Cookies are created by the website and stored on the device by the browser the first time the user visits the website. During every subsequent visit, the browser volunteers the saved information to the website.

There are two main components to the structure of a cookie.

1. A **Name** and **Value** pair, which is explicitly set by the website. The pair can be used to save a user's language preference or geographic location. In the case of a third-party tracker, the value portion will be assigned a string that represents a user's unique ID.
2. **Attributes**, which tell the browser how to handle the cookies. The most common attributes of the cookies are: (a) the **domain** that instructs the browser which cookies to send to which websites upon visit and (b) the **expiration**, which is a timestamp specifying to the browser when to a cookie is to be discarded.

B. Third-party tracking. There are three parties involved in a user's visiting a website: the target website w (the first party) the user wants to visit, the user u (the second party), and the entities (the third party) hosting content external to the website w. Third parties, in this case, are generally transparent to the users and not all of them are third-party trackers.

As the browser needs to download third-party content, it must send an HTTP request to each of the third parties. We call the ones that collect information about the user at this stage **third-party trackers**.

Tracking mechanism: Although HTTP cookies are not the only means with which third-party trackers keep track of users, they are the most popular. There are three reasons to this. Firstly, all browsers can accept and send cookies. Secondly, other non-HTTP cookies exist and can be used for tracking, but they are inefficient or will create legal issues for the entities who utilize them. Finally, even though third-party websites can track a user by their browser fingerprint [13], this method incurs a much higher overhead, thus is unlikely to adopted widely. We will discuss browser fingerprinting and other tracking mechanisms in more details in Sect. 7.

3   Methodology

In this section we will: (1) discuss characteristics of HTTP requests going to trackers and (2) provide an overview of our solution for the problem of detecting third-party trackers.

A. HTTP Requests going to third-party trackers. The key question to ask is whether there are characteristics that differentiate between: (1) HTTP requests carrying information to third-party trackers that can uniquely identify the user, and (2) HTTP requests that carry no such information.

We answer this question positively. The requests going to trackers contain **tracker cookies**, which we define as a cookie that contains a name-value pair that can uniquely identify a user. One such cookie, for instance, may have the name-value pair: UID=163fkcs65bz where the value is simply a unique identifier given to the browser by the website. In contrast, there are **non-tracker cookies**, which are used capture user preferences (e.g. display language, timezone), and the browser provides to them to the website in each visit. Because tracker cookies are meant to identify a user, they bear the following characteristics:

1. Their Lifetimes tends to be much longer than non-tracker cookies. A cookie's Lifetime is the time between its creation time and its expiration time.
2. The value part of the name-value pair inside each cookie (recall that each cookie contains only one such pair) must have sufficient **length** to be able to distinguish one user from many others.

In Fig. 1(a), we show the difference in the lifetime values between tracker cookies and non-tracker cookies that we collected and manually labeled (see Sect. 4 for more details on data collection). We can see that while less than 10 %

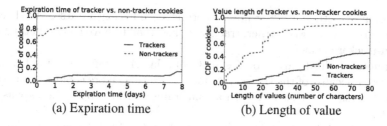

Fig. 1. Difference between tracker and non-tracker cookies

of tracker cookies have a lifetime of a single day or less, at least 80 % of non-tracker cookies have such short lifetime. Furthermore, Fig. 1(b) shows that the length of the value is at least 35 characters for 80 % of the tracker cookies, while 80 % of the non-tracker cookies have values that are shorter than 35 characters.

The next important question to answer is, then, how we can exploit these characteristics in an effort to correctly classify HTTP requests as either going to third-party trackers and carrying user-identifiable information or harmless and carrying no sensitive information.

B. TrackAdvisor: Identifying trackers, one HTTP request at a time.
We present TrackAdvisor, our solution for the problem of identifying third-party trackers. TrackAdvisor looks at *all of the cookies* carried by each outgoing HTTP request, extract collective statistics, and performs classification to determine whether it is heading for a tracker.

TrackAdvisor is a supervised Machine Learning-based application that we envision to reside inside the browser, where it can inspect each outgoing HTTP request and inform the user if the HTTP request carries information that may be able to uniquely identify the user. TrackAdvisor takes as input the cookies exchanged between the browser and the remote websites and identifies the websites that are third-party trackers.

Feature selection: First, we define CookieJar(A, B) as the group of all third-party cookies exchanged between the host A and the remote website B. Note that we exclude the Session cookies because Session cookies are created during a browsing session and are destroyed once the browser is closed. Because of their short-lived nature, Session cookies are unlikely to be used as a tracking mechanism.

Instead of looking at the cookies in CookieJar(A, B) individually, TrackAdvisor looks at CookieJar(A, B) in its entirety, extracts relevant statistics, and performs classification.

We started with considering a large number of features, including maximum Lifetime, minimum ValueLength, mean ValueLength, maximum ValueLength, as well as others. This set of features is then reduced to only three by the Recursive Feature Elimination (RFE) functionality of WEKA [19] which, at a high level, recommends a subset of features that achieves the best accuracy. In our case, the final three features are:

(a) Minimum lifetime: $L_{A,B}^{\min} = \min_c [\text{Lifetime}(c)]$. This feature is selected because trackers, as discussed earlier, tracker cookies tend to have longer lifetime than non-tracker cookies.

(b) Number of third-party cookies in CookieJar(A, B): $N_{A,B}$. This feature is selected because of the trackers' tendency to utilize more cookies than benign third-parties in order to record as much information about the user as possible.

(c) Augmented Lifetime: $L_{A,B}^{\text{aug}} = \sum_c [\text{ValueLength}(c) \times \text{Lifetime}(c)]$. The Augmented Lifetime captures at once captures two important characteristics of tracker cookies: long Lifetime and long ValueLength, and it is also crucial to future-proofing TrackAdvisor's performance against two possible evasive tactics from third-party trackers: **cookie chunking** and **lifetime reduction**. We will discuss the two techniques, as well as how robust TrackAdvisor is against them at the end of Sect. 4.

The steps that TrackAdvisor executes are:

1. Retain only third-party HTTP requests from the browser. A third-party HTTP request is one that is sent toward an URL that does **not** share the same hostname as the website the user intentionally visits. TrackAdvisor achieves this by looking at the referrer of the request and ignoring requests where the hostnames in the referrer and URL fields are the same.

2. For each CookieJar(A, B) representing an HTTP request sent by host A to website B, TrackAdvisor calculates three features of CookieJar(A, B), that we described above: (a) $L_{A,B}^{\min}$, (b) $N_{A,B}$, and (c) $L_{A,B}^{\text{aug}}$.

3. Use a binary classifier to classify the tuple $\langle L_{A,B}^{\text{aug}}, L_{A,B}^{\min}, N_{A,B} \rangle$.
   A positive output from the classifier means that the tuple belongs in an interaction with a third-party tracker and a negative otherwise. We will discuss how to create the classifier from training data in Sect. 4.

4. If the module returns a positive value, we label B as a third-party tracker and add it to a list that will be presented to the user later.

4   Experiments and Evaluation

In this section we will (a) describe our data collection and preliminary labeling processes and (b) compare the performance of Microsoft's Tracking Protection Lists against that of TrackAdvisor.

A. Data Collection. Our dataset is created by visiting the *landing pages* Alexa's Top 10K Global list [2] during the month of July of 2012. We collected our data using **FourthParty** [4], a Firefox extension that collects data in the background as the user browses the Web. The data that we collected are: (a) the header of each HTTP request, (b) the header of each HTTP response, and (c) the cookie log associated with each request and response. We used the automation framework Selenium [9] with FourthParty installed to collect 563,031 HTTP requests and 99,397 cookies. Of all 563,031 requests, 202,556 were sent to third-party websites and 78,213 contain cookies. Out of 99,397 cookies, 22,270 cookies were sent to third-party websites.

B. Creating training and testing data sets. From the set of all HTTP requests to third-party websites, we created a training and a testing data-set as follows:

- D_{train}: includes 500 randomly chosen requests such that roughly half of them were dispatched to third-party trackers and half were meant to retrieve third-party content and containing no tracking information.
- D_{test}: includes 500 HTTP requests that were randomly chosen in a similar fashion to the ones in D_{train}.

D_{train} and D_{test} are mutually exclusive. The former is used to train Track-Advisor and the latter will be used for testing both TrackAdvisor and Tracking Protection Lists.

To establish the ground truth, we label the websites in D_{train} and D_{test} (1,000 in total) as either third-party trackers or benign third-party websites using extensive and careful manual evaluation. In our evaluation, we label a website as a third-party tracker by combining the information gained from the three following processes: (a) a manual inspection the website, (b) a consultation with multiple black lists specifically created for third-party tracker, and (c) a careful inspection of cookie properties. To label something as athird-party tracker, we require significant supporting evidence to that effect. We argue that this method is essentially the same used by the contributors to third-party tracking lists. For transparency, we will make our two labelled sets available to the research community.

C. Reference: Microsoft's Tracking Protection List. We compare our approach against Tracking Protection Lists, which is a black list-based component that is used in Microsoft's Internet Explorer. We selected Tracking Protection Lists because: (a) it uses the same popular black lists (FanBoy, EasyList, EasyPrivacy, etc.) that empower AdBlock Plus and (b) it has been shown that the a combination of the popular black lists achieved comparable performance to Ghostery's [15].

D. Creating a classifier for TrackAdvisor from D_{train}. Recall from the beginning of this section that we have constructed a training dataset and a testing dataset called D_{train} and D_{test}. Also recall that each request in D_{train} is represented by a tuple $\langle L_{A,B}^{\text{aug}}, L_{A,B}^{\text{min}}, N_{A,B} \rangle$. Since each tuple is labeled, we are able to use the WEKA Machine Learning suite [19] to build classifiers. The algorithm that we picked from the suite is Support Vector Machine because it offers the best performance in terms of **Precision** and **Recall**, where $\text{Pr} = \text{TP} / (\text{TP} + \text{FP})$ and $\text{Re} = \text{TP} / (\text{TP} + \text{FN})$. TP is the number of True Positives, FP the number of False Positives, and FN the number of False Negatives.

Before we start the testing, we examine the sensitivity of our approach to the training input by performing a ten-fold cross-validation on D_{train}. The assessment yields a combined Precision of 0.998 and Recall of 0.998 (one FN and one FP). We conclude that our approach is robust to the training data.

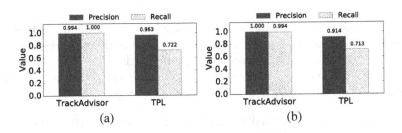

Fig. 2. Classification results for HTTP requests (a) and domains (b)

E. Evaluation of classification on D_{test}. First, we check the URLs of D_{test} against Tracking Protection Lists. As shown in Fig. 2(a), TPL achieves a Precision and Recall of 96.3 % and 72.2 % respectively (13 FPs and 134 FNs). In contrast, TrackAdvisor achieves perfect Recall and nearly perfect Precision (0 FPs and 2 FNs).

One possible reason why TPL has so many False Negatives could be that TPL is better tuned to recognize the trackers more relatively well-known to the community, as it relies significantly on user reports to populate the list.

F. Possible evasive tactics from third-party trackers: An inquisitive reader may ask why we simply did not use only ValueLength and Lifetime as features for the classifier even though as we have shown in Fig. 1 that the ValueLengths and Lifetimes of non-tracker cookies are different from those of tracker cookies. The reason is that a classifier built from only ValueLength and Lifetime is ineffective against two possible evasive tactics from third-party trackers:

T1. Cookie Chunking: Instead of using a single cookie that contains an identifier, third-party trackers can chop it into multiple cookies with different *names* that will be combined later when the HTTP requests are processed at the server. This way, they can reduce the lengths of the cookies and help them avoid detection.

T2. Lifetime Reduction: Instead of setting a large value for the expiration of the cookies, trackers can use smaller values depending on their own *popularity*. For example, a very popular website like Google can set their cookie lifetime to a month or even a week instead of a year because Google knows people visit the site frequently.

We have conducted extensive experiments on the robustness of TrackAdvisor against **T1** and **T2** where we (a) identify every tracker cookie in each HTTP request (in both D_{train} and D_{test}) that we manually label as going to third-party trackers, (b) either split them up according to **T1** or reduce their lifetimes according to **T2**, and (c) re-train our classifier on D_{train} and re-test on D_{test}. We cannot describe the experiments in details due to space limitation but we find that TrackAdvisor's performance is unchanged even when we execute **T1** and **T2**.

5   The Pervasiveness of Third-Party Trackers

In this section, we quantify the extent of third-party tracking by analyzing the Alexa Top 10 K websites. Overall, we find a significant presence of third-party tracking that would be disconcerting to privacy advocates.

(A) 46 % of the Alexa Top 10 K websites have at least one third-party tracker on them. By applying TrackAdvisor on our entire dataset, we found that 46 % of the Alexa Top 10 K websites had at least one third-party tracker on them. We use the term "target website" to refer to the Alexa website that was explicitly visited by the user in each request as we explained earlier. We plot the cumulative coverage in terms of unique target sites as a function of the number third-party trackers in the order of decreasing activity in Fig. 3(a). In more detail, for each third-party tracker t, let S_t be the set of websites in our dataset that are tracked by t. On the x-axis, we order the trackers in decreasing order in terms of the number of sites on which they appear: $|S_{t_i}|$. The y-axis is the cumulative coverage (C_{t_i}) of the first i trackers in that order. $C_{t_i} = | \cup_{k=1}^{i} S_{t_k}|/N$ where $N = 10,000$ is the total number of target websites.

We can see from Fig. 3(a) that:

- 46 % of the Alexa Top 10,000 websites have at least one tracker on them.
- The top 5 most common trackers cover 30 % of the top 10,000 sites.
- Google alone (doubleclick.com and google.com) covers 25 % of the sites. The doubleclick.com domain is responsible for advertisements and google.com is where other websites download widgets and libraries.

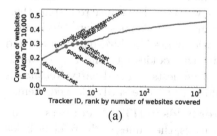
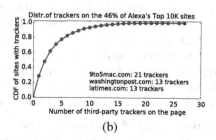

(a)   (b)

Fig. 3. (a) Cumulative coverage of top 10K Alexa sites as a function of third-party trackers in the order of decreasing tracking presence in our dataset. (b) The distribution of the number of trackers on the Alexa top 10 K sites.

B. The majority of tracked sites are tracked by more than one tracker.
Equally interesting is the fact that a website that has third-party tracking is
likely to contain multiple trackers. In Fig. 3(b), we plot the CDF of the distribution of third-party trackers on the Alexa websites that have at least one tracker.
For example, we see in the plot that 28 % of websites have one tracker, which
means that there are at least two trackers present on each of the remaining
websites (72 %).

We also find that 29 % of the websites that are tracked by at least five third-
party trackers. For a visitor that means that five different entities become aware
of her web-surfing preferences. It is equally worrisome to see that some popular
websites such as latimes.com and washing-tonpost.com have upwards of 10 third-
party trackers.

The well-known Google Analytics is not on the list in Fig. 3(b), because
by contract, Google Analytics provides statistics only to the first-party websites
and the cookies set by Google Analytics are always associated with the domains
of the first-party websites and therefore are not third-party cookies. Furthermore,
the same user who visits different websites monitored by Google Analytics will
likely receive different IDs, which makes tracking him or her non-trivial.

C. Third-party interactions: 37 % tracking versus 63 % benign. Recall
from Sect. 4 that our dataset contains a total of 202,556 third-party HTTP
requests, which includes both third-party tracking and benign third-party interactions. Using our approach, we identify 75,849 (37 %) of them as third-party
tracking interactions. This is of interest in considering counter-measures to third-
party tracking, since there is a large number of interactions with benign third-
party websites, as we discuss in the next section.

6   Possible Solutions Against Third-Party Trackers

Here, we discuss some potential solutions that can be implemented in a browser
fairly easily to block third-party trackers from collecting user information.

A. Blocking all third-party cookies. One can consider labeling as trackers
all third-party websites that exchange cookies with the user's computer. On the
one hand, this type would allow a user to block 100 % of the trackers with a
false positive rate of 12.6 %. On the other hand, that comes at the expense of
the degraded browsing experience. There are websites that refuse to display their
content unless the user's browser accepts third-party cookies. More specifically,
with third-party cookies disabled, iFrames, widely used in third-party games and
apps on social networks, cannot read their own cookies [10] and cannot work.
As we saw in Sect. 5, the majority (63 %) of requests to third-party websites is
benign. A complete blocking solution would have unnecessarily blocked them.

B. Removing/Anonymizing the referrer fields in HTTP requests. Apart
from the cookies that can uniquely identify users, the values of the referrer fields
of the HTTP requests are important to the third-party websites' ability to partially construct a user's browsing history. Therefore, using TrackAdvisor to identify HTTP requests carrying identifying information and then either removing

the referrer information or replacing it with bogus values is one way to protect the user's privacy. To the best of our knowledge, third-party websites have tried to withhold content from the users only in the case where the browsers would not accept the cookies and no efforts at all have been invested in validating the referrers as a condition to provide content.

Here we only provide suggestions for possible defense methods against third-party trackers. The full evaluation of the two methods is, however, beyond the scope of this paper and may be tackled in a future work.

7   Related Work

Although much attention has been devoted to studying the phenomenon of third-party trackers using cookies to track users [14,16,18], there exists no practical solution that leverages cookies as a means to detect third-party tracking. To the best of our knowledge, all existing practical solutions such as AdBlock Plus [1], Microsoft's Tracking Protection Lists [7], Collusion [3], and Ghostery [5] rely on corporate- and community-maintained black lists (sometimes called block lists) to block HTTP requests to well-known third-party trackers. AdBlock Plus is an improvement to the original AdBlock that also blocks third-party trackers in addition to advertisements. Ghostery and TPL focus on blocking trackers instead.

All other related work have been focused on uncovering other types of cookies (aside from the standard HTTP ones) that could be used to track users but did not propose countermeasures like we did. In [12,17], the authors documented the use of Flash cookies, which are Locally Shared Objects similar to cookies. Advertisers can create a pair of cookies, an HTTP one and a Flash one, with identical content, where the latter can "re-spawn" the former even after the former has been deleted. Fortunately, the practice of using Flash cookies have been on the decline because there have been lawsuits against the advertisers, who essentially re-spawned the HTTP cookies against the users' will.

There is a form of cookie-less tracking, which is cache-based and utilizes ETags [6,12]. An ETag, assigned by the website and unique for each user, is associated with an object on a web page (like an image) that can tell the server if the object in the browser cache is the same as the one on the server. An advertiser then can have exactly the same objects on many websites and track the users just like they would with cookies. This method is not popular, as users can just clear the browser caches frequently.

Most modern browsers offer a "Do Not Track" option which is nothing more than a request and the websites can ignore it if they choose to. The most recent high-profile website that decided to not honor "Do Not Track" is Yahoo [11]. The Electronic Frontier Foundation then responded by releasing Privacy Badger [8], a browser add-on that detects third-party trackers. It keeps tracks of all cookies as the user visits websites and blocks cookies that are *previously seen*. This is a promising development, but, given that this was released only in May 2014, there are no reports yet as to how well Privacy Badger works, if it degrades user experience, and how much overhead it may add in terms of memory due to the large number of cookies that need to be tracked.

Finally, there exists a form of tracking using the *fingerprint* [13] of the browsers. This form of tracking relies on the information that the browser sends to the remote website (such as IP address, User-Agent, System fonts, screen resolution etc.). The remote website then can use all of this information to uniquely identify the browser that the request comes from. However, because the overhead that incurs is very high for browser fingerprinting, we would make the argument that third-party trackers are unlikely to adopt it as a means to track the browsing behaviors of users.

8 Conclusion

We present TrackAdvisor, a Machine Learning-based method designed to detect third-party trackers and become the basis for protecting the users' privacy from third-party trackers. TrackAdvisor's novelty is its focus on the interactions between the browsers and the remote websites to detect when the user's browsing privacy is being leaked instead of relying on black lists. TrackAdvisor exhibits high Precision (99.4) and Recall (100 %) in contrast with a Recall of 72.2 % by Microsoft's Tracking Protection Lists, which is a black list-based component in the widely used Internet Explorer.

Towards protecting user privacy, we evaluate two potential countermeasures: (a) removing user identity in tracker cookies and (b) removing the referrer information from the HTTP requests sent to third-party trackers. We find that the second method achieves the goal of protecting user privacy while not "breaking" the functionalities of the web pages.

Finally, we present a study on the pervasiveness of third-party trackers. Our study shows that 46 % of the websites on Alexa's Global Top 10,000 list contain at least one tracker each and 25 % of the 10,000 are tracked by a single entity: Google, as its doubleclick ad service is very popular and many websites use the code libraries provided by Google itself to add functionalities.

References

1. AdBlock Plus. https://adblockplus.org
2. Alexa, the Web Information Company. http://www.alexa.com
3. Collusion, browser extension. https://chrome.google.com/webstore/detail/collusion-for-chrome/ganlifbpkcplnldliibcbegplfmcfigp
4. FourthParty Firefox Extension. http://fourthparty.info
5. Ghostery. https://www.ghostery.com/
6. HTTP ETags. http://en.wikipedia.org/wiki/HTTP_ETag
7. Microsoft's Tracking Protection Lists. http://ie.microsoft.com/testdrive/Browser/p3p/Default.html
8. Privacy Badger. http://www.theregister.co.uk/2014/05/02/eff_privacy_badger/
9. Selenium, Web Browser Automation. http://docs.seleniumhq.org/

10. Third-party iFrames can no longer read their own cookies when "Block third-party cookies and site data" is enabled. urlhttps://code.google.com/p/chromium/issues/detail?id=113401

11. Yahoo declines to honor "Do not track". http://yahoopolicy.tumblr.com/post/84363620568/yahoos-default-a-personalized-experience

12. Ayenson, M., Wambach, D., Soltani, A., Good, N., Hoofnagle, C.: Flash cookies and privacy II: now with HTML5 and etag respawning. Social Science Research Networks (2011)

13. Eckersley, P.: How unique is your web browser? In: Atallah, M.J., Hopper, N.J. (eds.) PETS 2010. LNCS, vol. 6205, pp. 1–18. Springer, Heidelberg (2010)

14. Leon, P., Ur, B., Shay, R., Wang, Y., Balebako, R., Cranor, L.: Why Johnny can't opt out: a usability evaluation of tools to limit online behavioral advertising. In: Proceedings of the SIGCHI Conference on Human Factors in Computing Systems, pp. 589–598. ACM (2012)

15. Mayer, J.: Tracking the Trackers: Self-help tools. http://cyberlaw.stanford.edu/node/6730

16. Mayer, J.R., Mitchell, J.C.: Third-party web tracking: policy and technology. In: 2012 IEEE Symposium on Security and Privacy (SP), pp. 413–427. IEEE (2012)

17. McDonald, A.M., Cranor, L.F.: A survey of the use of adobe flash local shared objects to respawn http cookies. J. Law Policy Inf. Soc. **7**, 639–721 (2012)

18. Weinberg, Z., Chen, E.Y., Jayaraman, P.R., Jackson, C.: I still know what you visited last summer: leaking browsing history via user interaction and side channel attacks. In: 2011 IEEE Symposium on Security and Privacy (SP), pp. 147–161. IEEE (2011)

19. Witten, I.H., Frank, E., Trigg, L.E., Hall, M.A., Holmes, G., Cunningham, S.J.: WEKA: practical machine learning tools and techniques with Java implementations

Exploring Miner Evolution in Bitcoin Network

Luqin Wang[1](✉) and Yong Liu[2]

[1] Department of Computer Science and Engineering,
NYU Polytechnic School of Engineering, New York, USA
`lukelwang@gmail.com`
[2] Department of Electrical and Computer Engineering,
NYU Polytechnic School of Engineering, New York, USA

Abstract. In recent years, Bitcoin, a peer-to-peer network based crypto digital currency, has attracted a lot of attentions from the media, the academia, and the general public. A user in Bitcoin network can create Bitcoins by packing and verifying new transactions in the network using their computation power. Driven by the price surge of Bitcoin, users are increasingly investing on expensive specialized hardware for Bitcoin mining. To obtain steady payouts, users also pool their computation resources to conduct pool mining. In this paper, we study the evolution of Bitcoin miners by analyzing the complete transaction blockchain. We characterize how the productivity, computation power and transaction activity of miners evolve over time. We also conduct an in-depth study on the largest mining pool F2Pool. We show how it grows over time and how computation power is distributed among its miners. Finally, we build a simple economic model to explain the evolution of Bitcoin miners.

Keywords: Bitcoin · Measurement · Network analysis

1 Introduction

Bitcoin [1] is known as *the first decentralized digital currency in the world* [2]. Unlike any traditional currency issued and regulated by a sovereign bank, Bitcoin is not controlled by any institution or country. It circulates globally without boundary and is free from financial regulation systems due to its decentralized P2P accounting and transaction design. Debuted in 2009 and after five years' development, Bitcoin exchange price has risen from nothing to over $100 per coin through mid 2013, surged to its peak at $1,242 on Nov. 29, and is wobbling between $350 and $600 in today's market. Till September 2014, the market capitalization of Bitcoin has increased to around 6 billion US dollars; and the Bitcoin network runs over 60,000 transactions daily. Along with Bitcoin network's capitalization and volume, a variety number of derivative services have been developed and legalized. Exchange markets, i.e., Coinbase [3] and Bitstamp [4], allow users to buy and sell Bitcoins using regular currencies globally. Online merchants, e.g., Dell and Overstock, are now accepting Bitcoin as a payment method. Governments of several countries, such as Canada and Thailand, have

© Springer International Publishing Switzerland 2015
J. Mirkovic and Y. Liu (Eds.): PAM 2015, LNCS 8995, pp. 290–302, 2015.
DOI: 10.1007/978-3-319-15509-8_22

approved fully-legal Bitcoin exchange and issued tax guidance on Bitcoin transactions. Different from a regular currency, there is no central bank or authority who decides how many Bitcoins to be issued and distributed. According to the Bitcoin protocol, there are only a finite amount of Bitcoins. In addition to buying Bitcoins from others, the only way for a user to acquire Bitcoins is to contribute her computation resources to pack and verify new transactions. We call this process *Bitcoin mining* and users who participate in mining as *Bitcoin miners*. The Bitcoin protocol is designed so that new Bitcoins are mined at a steady rate until all Bitcoins are mined. The surge of Bitcoin price motivates Bitcoin miners to invest on more and more powerful hardware for faster mining. Due to the dramatic growth in both the number of Bitcoin miners and the computation power of their hardware, it has become increasingly difficult to mine Bitcoins. For an individual miner, even with powerful hardware, it now takes a very long time for her to get Bitcoins if she does mining by herself, the so-called *solo mining*. Similar to pooling money to buy lottery, majority of the miners choose to pool their computation resources to mine Bitcoins together, the so-called *pool mining*. Pool mining gives individual miners steadier payouts than solo mining.

Bitcoin network is a P2P system that peers can obtain direct financial incentives by contributing their computation resources. While the Bitcoin price is constantly driven by various economic, politic and legal factors, we are interested in finding out how Bitcoin price evolution drives the miners' mining behaviors. Towards this goal, we conduct a measurement study on the evolution of Bitcoin miners by analyzing the complete transaction blockchain of the Bitcoin network from its very first transaction in 2009 to March 2014. We first characterize how the productivity, computation power and transaction activity of miners evolve over time. We then conduct an in-depth study on the largest mining pool F2Pool [5]. We characterize how it grows and how the computation power is distributed among its heterogeneous members. Finally, we build a simple economic model which explains the evolution of miners by considering the Bitcoin price and the computation race between miners.

The rest of the paper is organized as follows. We review the related work in Sect. 2. A short survey of Bitcoin network and the mining process is presented in Sect. 3. We present our methodology of analysis and the characterization results in Sects. 4 and 5, respectively. The paper is concluded in Sect. 6.

2   Related Work

Although Bitcoin network has a short history, as a P2P based digital currency system, it has drawn lots of attentions of researchers from different fields. Babaioff et al. [6] studies the incentive for Bitcoin users to disseminate transactions. Decker and Wattenhofer [7] measured and modeled how transactions are propagated in Bitcoin network. Ron and Shamir [8] examined the entire transaction graph of Bitcoin network to study its statistical properties. Meiklejohn et al. [9] measured and clustered Bitcoin accounts owned by the same user by grouping input addresses from the same transaction. Freid and Harrigan [10] explored the limits of user anonymity. Eyal and Sirer [11] and Kroll et al. [12] discussed the vulnerabilities of Bitcoin network on how powerful adversaries can potentially manipulate mining mechanism. Huang et al. [13] studied how malwares steal users' computation power to mine Bitcoin. Becker et al. [14] estimated the typical cost structures in Bitcoin network and discussed the general viability of proof-of-work approach.

3   Survey of Bitcoin Network

3.1   Account and Transaction

Bitcoin network is a peer-to-peer network without central authority. A Bitcoin account is simply a pair of public/private keys. An account ID is derived from its public key. The private key is used to generate digital signature for authentication. There is no cost to create a Bitcoin account. So each Bitcoin user can create as many accounts as she wishes. Transaction is the mechanism for users to transfer Bitcoins to each other. A transaction consists of a set of senders and a set of receivers (denoted by their account IDs), the amount from each sender, and the amount to each receiver. For example, if Alice wants to send 3 Bitcoins (BTCs) to Bob. She might send from two of her accounts: one account A_1 has 1 BTC and the other account A_2 has 2 BTCs. Suppose Bob has only one account B_1, thus this transaction is simply: 1 BTC from A_1, 2 BTCs from A_2, and 3 BTCs to B_1. Finally, all senders will sign the transaction with their private keys, and the signed transaction is broadcast to the entire Bitcoin network. Any user who receives this transaction will first verify whether the senders have the amount of BTCs indicated in the transaction. Different from the traditional banking systems, there is no central database to maintain the Bitcoin balance of each account. Instead, the whole Bitcoin network stores and verifies all the transactions using a shared blockchain. Any user can check the balance of any account by backtracking the blockchain to retrieve all transactions associated the account. Invalid transactions will be discarded, and valid ones will be stored in memory to be packed and appended to the blockchain.

3.2   Block and Blockchain

The blockchain is a public ledger shared in the whole Bitcoin network. As the name suggests, the blockchain contains a chain of chronologically ordered blocks, each of which contains transactions within a time window of ten minutes and a generation transaction indicating which account packed this block. Each user downloads and synchronizes a copy of the blockchain in her local machine to verify incoming transactions. All newly confirmed transactions are packed into a new block, which will be broadcast to the whole network. Whenever a user receives a block, she will validate all the transactions in this block using the current blockchain. If any transaction is invalid, she will discard the block. Otherwise, this block will be confirmed and appended to the current blockchain.

3.3 Bitcoin Mining

Bitcoin network depends on the computation resources on users to maintain the integrity of the blockchain. Each user can volunteer to verify and pack new transactions to blocks. While a lot of users are doing the verification and packing work simultaneously, only the newest valid block will be confirmed by all users and appended to the current blockchain. The user (miner) who created this block will get rewarded with some BTCs (the current reward is 25 BTCs/block). To achieve this, a proof-of-work mechanism is introduced. When packing new transactions to a block, a miner first generates a special transaction indicating that the network sends her the mining reward. Along with all other transactions, she repeatedly generates a random number nonce, put them together and runs a hash function. If the hash value is below a target value, the user claims she created the block and broadcasts the block and the nonce. Other users can easily perform the same hash function with the published nonce to verify the block.

According to Nakamoto's protocol [1], the total number of BTCs that can be mined is 21 million and the last BTC to be mined is in block #6, 929, 999 near year 2140. By default, a new block is created approximately every ten minutes, no matter how much aggregate computation power is in the network. To control the new block creation speed, a *difficulty value* is introduced. The target value for block hash calculation is inversely proportional to the difficulty value. As a result, the higher the difficulty value, the more hash calculations each miner has to conduct to find a hash value below the target. As detailed in [15], at a given difficulty value D, for a miner with computation power of H hashes per second, the expected time for the miner to generate a new valid block is:

$$E[T] = \frac{D \times 2^{32}}{H} \text{ s.} \tag{1}$$

The difficulty value is updated every 2, 016 blocks based on the speed at which the past 2, 016 blocks were generated. The difficulty value is stored in each block. Knowing how many BTCs are generated in the whole network in one day, given the difficulty value, we can also calculate the total hash rate of the system.

Solo and Pool Mining. In the early days of Bitcoin, miners mined blocks individually. We call this approach *solo mining*. The advantage of solo mining is whenever a block is created by the miner, she gets all the rewards. However, as more and more computation resources are injected to the Bitcoin network, the difficulty value has to be increased significantly to control the new block creation speed. Now it takes a powerful miner years to create a block. Pool mining is a way for miners to pool their resources together to obtain steady payouts. A pool assigns a lower difficulty value to each of its members. It becomes easier for each miner in the pool to solve the hash problem and prove their work. Each pool miner submits her own hash values under the pool target value (called shares) to the pool for verification. If a share is under the network target value, a block is claimed by the pool and pool operator will distribute the reward to every pool miners. The most popular payout approach for pool mining is pay-per-share, in which miners are rewarded proportionally to the number of shares they submitted to the pool. With pool mining, the expected payout for a minor is the same as solo mining, but the variance of payout is largely reduced.

4   Methodology

4.1   Data Collection

As described in Sect. 3, all transactions in Bitcoin network are stored in the blockchain. When a user wants to make a transfer, she must first connect to the Bitcoin network and synchronize with the current blockchain. We ran the Bitcoin client in our local machine to get the latest blockchain. After collecting the blockchain, we parsed it to blocks and transactions. Each block has its hash value, height (block ID), hash value of the previous block, generation time (in UTC timestamp), the amount of new BTCs created, target difficulty, nonce, and all transactions in the block. For each transaction, inputs include the previous transaction hashes of the senders and the associated signature scripts; outputs include the receiver account IDs and their corresponding amounts. We use the previous transaction hash to retrieve the transaction history and the balance of each sender by iteratively backtracking the blockchain. We synchronized the complete blockchain in March 2014 and parsed the data. The raw data includes all blocks and transactions from 2009/01/03 (the very first Bitcoin block created) to 2014/03/11. We retrieved 290,089 blocks and 34,646,076 transactions. We then parsed all blocks and transactions field-by-field and stored all the parsed information into a MYSQL database.

4.2   Solo Miner Analysis

Pool mining only started on 16th December 2010 [16]. All previous miners were solo miners. After the introduction of pool mining, each pool also uses one unique ID to mine Bitcoins. We first treat each unique Bitcoin ID who successfully created a block as a solo miner. As a result, we treat pools as solo miners for now. Using block timestamps, we count the number of BTCs mined by miners each month in the network. Also, using Bitcoin exchange market data [3] we calculate the monthly USD (we assume BTCs were exchanged to USD at market price immediately after they were mined) generated in the network. Moreover, we also obtain the distribution of how many BTCs each miner mined over time.

Besides the earnings, we can also estimate the aggregate computation power of all miners. With a given difficulty value of D, if N blocks were mined in a day, based on (1), the aggregate daily hash rate of the entire Bitcoin network can be estimated as:

$$H_{total} = \frac{N \times D \times 2^{32}}{86,400} \qquad (2)$$

Similarly, we can estimate a miner's daily hash rate by replacing N with the number of blocks the miner mined in a day.

We are also interested in whether the miners cashed out their mined BTCs after mining. However, it is hard to collect IDs of all Bitcoin exchange markets so as to track all transactions between the miners and the exchange markets. Instead, we track for each miner the interval between the time when she mined some new BTCs and the time when her next transaction was issued. This time interval serves as a lower bound for her cash out lag.

4.3   Pool Miner Analysis

To study how Bitcoin mining pool evolves, we collect pool data from our database. We choose miner IDs with top hash rates in the network and manually classify them. Most of these IDs belong to well-known mining pools according to Blockchain.info, an online Bitcoin statistics website. To analyze pool mining behaviors, we choose F2Pool, a China-based mining pool whose payout rule is clear and the payout transactions are easy to obtain. In our data up to March 2014, F2Pool ranked 7th in terms of the total computation power in the network. According to the newest statistics in [17], in September 2014, F2Pool grows to the largest mining pool, having over 25 % of the overall computation power.

We query transactions having F2Pool's account ID and classify them as input or output. For transactions having F2Pool ID as the only receiver, we identify whether they are block generation transactions. For a transaction having it as the only sender, we validate whether the transaction is used to distribute payouts to pool miners. Pools have different approaches to send payouts to pool miners. The simplest way is that the pool sends out payouts to all pool miners in one transaction immediately after each block is created. However, none of the ten pools we checked use this approach. Some pools use a binary tree like iterative payout approach which pays one pool miner and transfer the remaining balance to a new ID at each iteration. And some pools randomly choose a number of miners to pay in one transaction and transfer the remaining balance to a new ID, and then distribute the remaining balance in subsequent transactions. When F2Pool mines a block, it will send out the payouts in the next day. It used to send out payouts to all members using a single transaction, but changed to two transactions recently. Knowing the payout mechanism, we can calcualte how many BTCs each pool miner earns each day using pool payout transactions.

4.4   Simple Economic Model for Miners

To become a miner, a user first needs to invest on hardware, ranging from regular computers in early days, to graphics card, GPUs, and specially designed ASIC chips, and incur the *capital cost*. After she joins the network for mining, she needs to pay the bill for electricity, air conditioning, housing and maintenance etc., and incur the *operational cost*. Since miners are driven by profits derived from the mined Bitcoins, the economic question is *whether and how soon their revenues can cover their capital and operational costs?* We build a simple economic model. For a hardware with hash rate H, based on (1), assume the hardware works 24 h per day, the expected number of BTCs it can mine daily is:

$$N(t, H) = \frac{H \times 86,400}{D(t) \times 2^{32}} R, \tag{3}$$

where $D(t)$ is the difficulty value in day t, R is the number of BTCs rewarded for each block. If the hardware's power consumption is P kw, and the electricity price is $\eta(t)$ per kwh, the daily electricity bill is $24P\eta$. Given the Bitcoin exchange price of $\rho(t)$ in day t, if we only consider electricity operational cost, the daily profit rate $r(t)$ for the hardware with hash rate H and power consumption P is:

$$r(t, H, P) = N(t, H)\rho(t) - 24P\eta(t). \tag{4}$$

Obviously, a miner prefers places with low electricity price $\eta(t)$, and will shut down her hardware whenever the profit rate becomes negative. Based on (3) and (4), to maintain a positive profit rate, the hardware's computation-over-power efficiency should satisfy:

$$\frac{H}{P} > K\frac{\eta(t)D(t)}{R\rho(t)}, \tag{5}$$

where K is a constant. As $D(t)$ increases, hardware with low computation-over-power efficiency will be quickly kicked out of the mining game.

To obtain high profit rate, minors should go for specialized mining hardware with high computation-over-power efficiency. Those hardware come at high prices, though. If the miner purchased a piece of expensive hardware at day t_0 with price C, the time τ it takes her to recover the capital cost should satisfy:

$$\int_{t_0}^{t_0+\tau} r(t, H, P) \times I[r(t, H, P)]dt = C, \tag{6}$$

where $I[x]$ is the indicator function which equals to 1 if $x > 0$, and 0 otherwise.

4.5 Limit of Computation Race

According to (4), miners are highly incentivized to increase their computation power to obtain higher profit margin. The Bitcoin network has witnessed exponential computation power growth in the past few years. But at the same time, the number of Bitcoins that can be mined each day is deliberately set to a fix value. If the Bitcoin price is kept flat, the total mining profit that miners can obtain from the network is a constant. All miners are essentially playing a zero-sum computation race game: each miner increases her computation power, then the total computation power in the network increases; consequently the system increases the difficulty value $D(t)$ to maintain a steady Bitcoin creation speed, which in turn reduces the Bitcoin mining rate of individual miners, according to (3). This is a unfortunate and unavoidable *tragedy-of-common* phenomena that has been observed in the Bitcoin network. Such a race will automatically end when the profit margin hits zero. We can predict the equilibrium point by

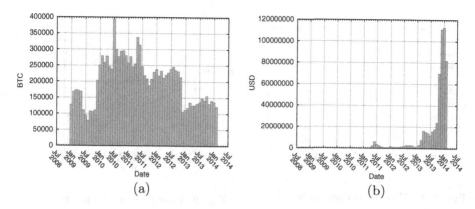

Fig. 1. (a) Monthly BTCs generated, (b) Monthly USD generated

extrapolating on our simple economic model in the previous section. Namely, let ξ_0 be the highest computation-over-power efficiency (in unit of hash-per-second/kilowatt) that the future computation technology can achieve, η_0 be the lowest electricity price in the world, and ρ_0 be the steady state exchange price of Bitcoin, then we can immediately calculate the maximum sustainable computation power $\mathcal{H}$ in the whole Bitcoin network as:

$$\frac{\mathcal{H}}{\xi_0}\eta_0 = 6R\rho_0, \quad \Rightarrow \quad \mathcal{H} = \frac{6R\xi_0\rho_0}{\eta_0}, \tag{7}$$

where the left-hand side of the first equation is the minimum electricity charge for one-hour mining with the most efficient mining hardware, and the right-hand side of the first equation is the expected hourly total payout in the whole network at the target mining rate of one block every ten minutes. If the total computation power goes above $\mathcal{H}$, the expected profit margins of all miners become negative, some of them will start to drop out the mining race, which in turn brings back the profit margin to positive. So far we ignored the capital cost and other operational costs. Therefore (7) gives us an upper bound on the maximum sustainable computation power at any fixed Bitcoin price ρ_0, given the highest feasible computation efficiency ξ_0 and the lowest electricity price η_0.

5   Characterization Results

Figure 1a plots the total Bitcoins generated each month. In 2009, the numbers are not stable because the Bitcoin client was newly released and the size of the network was relatively small. In December 2012, the reward R for each block was reduced from 50 BTCs to 25 BTCs, resulting in the number of BTCs was reduced by half in the latter months. Figure 1b shows how much USD are generated monthly according to the daily Bitcoin to USD exchange price.

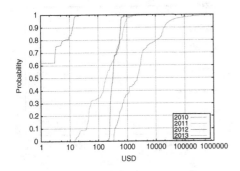

Fig. 2. CDF of miners' annually earning

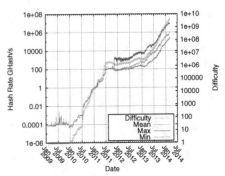

Fig. 3. Bitcoin network hash rate

Table 1. Fraction of frozen miners and average transfer lag of active miners

	Frozen miners	Active transfer lag
2009	66.36 %	138 Days
2010	20.13 %	102 Days
2011	1.89 %	19 Days
2012	0.49 %	7 Days
2013	0.96 %	1.5 Days

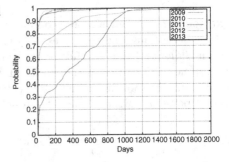

Fig. 4. Transfer lag distribution

5.1 Solo Miners

Figure 2 illustrates the distribution of solo miners' annually earnings. Before August 2010, there is no market data and the estimation of BTC value is $0. The earnings in latter years are tremendously greater than in the earlier years due to the exchange price went up rapidly. In addition, top miners became more and more powerful and were responsible for the most blocks created. Similar to (3), we estimate the hash rate of each solo miner based on the number of blocks she created. Figure 3 shows the minimum, maximum and mean hash rate of solo miners together with the system regulated difficulty value in logarithm scale. It shows that the computation power are evenly distributed among miners at the early stage, then become highly skewed with a small number of very powerful miners as the Bitcoin network evolves. As will be studied next, those top miners are indeed mining pools.

We now examine how fast miners transfer out mined Bitcoins. We measure the time lag between a miner claimed a block and her next transaction. If a miner has no subsequent transaction in our trace, we tag the minor as frozen. For active miners, we calculate the average and distribution of their transfer lags. As shown in Table 1, a large fraction of early miners were frozen and never

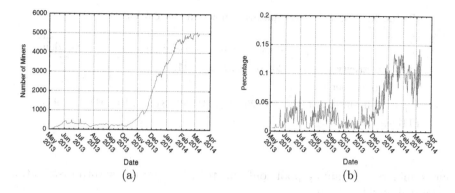

Fig. 5. (a) F2Pool miner growth, (b) F2Pool computation share

touched their mined Bitcoins, even after the Bitcoin price surge in 2013. Our conjecture is that those early miners were casual early adopters of Bitcoin as a fun technology, and they were not motivated by the potential financial value of Bitcoin. When Bitcoin became valuable, they might have, unfortunately, lost their account IDs, so that couldn't cash out. This suggests that lots of Bitcoins mined in the first two years might have been lost permanently! Things changed completely in 2011, not surprisingly, this is in sync with the value increase of Bitcoin. Not only almost all miners are active, the lag for transfer gets shorter and shorter. The slight increase in frozen ratio from 2012 to 2013 is due to the artifact that our trace ends in March 2014. Figure 4 further illustrates the decrease trend of transfer lags as time evolves. This suggests that later miners were explicitly driven by profits and diligently transferred out mined Bitcoins.

5.2   Pool Mining

Figure 5a shows the evolution of the number of miners in F2Pool. We can see that from May to October 2013, the number of pool miners is relatively stable. This is due to the stable Bitcoin price around $120 in that period. Figure 5b plots the ratio between F2Pool's computation power over that of the whole network. The ratio is also relatively stable from May to October 2013. Starting from November 2013, motivated by the price surge of Bitcoin, the number of miners increased more than ten times till March 2014. As illustrated in Fig. 5b, F2Pool's computation share also increases dramatically. This indicates that more miners chose to join pool mining in the face of increasingly tense competition between minors. In Fig. 6, we estimate the mean and median hash rate of F2Pool miners, and how much computation power is controlled by the top 10 % powerful pool miners. The mean is larger than the median and the top 10 % miners dominate the computation power of the pool. This is because the hash rates of the top pool miners are significantly larger than the low-end miners. Since the earning of a minor in a pool is proportional to her hash rate, the earning distribution

Table 2. Sustainable computation power under current Bitcoin price

Country	Italy	UK	Belgium	US	Sweden
Average electricity price in 2013 (cent per kwh)	20.56	13.61	11.77	9.33	8.25
Computation power bound (THash/s)	473,325	715,031	826,812	1,043,041	1,179,584

among miners in a mining pool conforms to the power law wealth distribution in the real world.

5.3   Economic Considerations

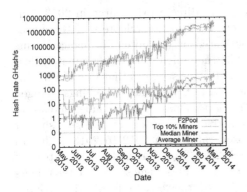

Curious in knowing whether miners can get their investment back, we choose two mining hardwares released in 2011 and 2013 respectively. The first one is MSI Radeon HD 6990 graphics card with 750 MHash/s and 410 W. The price for this card at release was $699. From 2010, mainstream miners started to use graphics cards to do mining instead of CPUs. We set a starting date on 07/01/2011. We cal-

Fig. 6. F2Pool miner hash rate vs. pool hash rate

culate the card's profit rate according to (4) using the real Bitcoin price and electricity prices in US and Italy respectively. As shown in Fig. 7a, this card generates positive profits in US, breaks even (earns $699 back) on 2013/04/30, and continues to make money till September 2013. Then the daily profit becomes negative even though the Bitcoin price kept increasing. This is because as more minors joined the system, the difficulty value increased at a faster pace than the Bitcoin price. According to (5), the card's computation-over-power efficiency can no longer sustain a positive profit rate. Meanwhile, due to higher electricity price (see Table 2), mining in Italy seldom gets positive profit. There is no way for the miner to recover her capital cost. In late 2012 and early 2013, powerful ASIC mining hardware started to occupy the mining market. We estimate BFL SC 5 G/s mining cube, a 5,000 MHash/s and 30 W advertised ASIC chip for just $274. We find that if it were purchased on 2013/07/01, no matter in US or Italy, it would have broken even with less than one month. The major reason is that the computation-over-power efficiency of this new card is about one hundred times higher than MSI Radeon HD 6990 graphics card.

Finally, we estimate the computation power upper bound of Bitcoin network according to (7). We use the current Bitcoin price and the average electricity

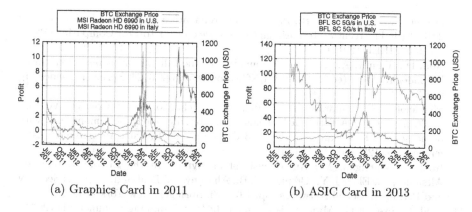

(a) Graphics Card in 2011   (b) ASIC Card in 2013

Fig. 7. Daily mining profit rate and break-even time.

prices in different countries [18] to estimate mining cost. We choose the current best hardware SP35 YUKON ASIC chip, which has 6 THash/s and 3,500 W. Table 2 shows as the electricity price varies, the network computation power upper bound can differ by a factor of 2.5. The current Bitcoin network has a computation power of 248,116 THash/s. There is still room for growth. Since in average the network computation power doubles every two months, our conjecture is that the network will saturate in about half year, given that the Bitcoin price and mining hardware efficiency stay still.

6   Conclusion

In this paper we characterized the evolution of Bitcoin miners' productivity, computation power and transaction activity by analyzing the full blockchain in Bitcoin network. We showed how the largest mining pool in Bitcoin grows over time and how computation power is distributed among its miners. We also built a simple economic model that explains the evolution of mining hardware and predicts the limit of the computation race game between miners.

References

1. Nakamoto, S.: Bitcoin: A peer-to-peer electronic cash system (2008). http://www.bitcoin.org/bitcoin.pdf
2. bitcoin.org: Frequently asked questions. https://bitcoin.org/en/faq. Accessed 10 September 2014
3. Coinbase.com. https://www.coinbase.com. Accessed 10 September 2014
4. Bitstamp.com. https://www.bitstamp.net. Accessed 10 September 2014
5. F2Pool.com. https://www.f2pool.com. Accessed 10 September 2014
6. Babaioff, M., Dobzinski, S., Oren, S., Zohar, A.: On Bitcoin and red balloons. In: Proceedings of the 13th ACM Conference on Electronic Commerce, pp. 56–73. ACM (2012)

7. Decker, C., Wattenhofer, R.: Information propagation in the Bitcoin network. In: 2013 IEEE Thirteenth International Conference on Peer-to-Peer Computing (P2P), pp. 1–10. IEEE (2013)

8. Ron, D., Shamir, A.: Quantitative analysis of the full Bitcoin transaction graph. In: Sadeghi, A.-R. (ed.) FC 2013. LNCS, vol. 7859, pp. 6–24. Springer, Heidelberg (2013)

9. Meiklejohn, S., Pomarole, M., Jordan, G., Levchenko, K., McCoy, D., Voelker, G.M., Savage, S.: A fistful of Bitcoins: characterizing payments among men with no names. In: Proceedings of the 2013 Conference on Internet Measurement Conference, pp. 127–140. ACM (2013)

10. Reid, F., Harrigan, M.: An analysis of anonymity in the Bitcoin system. In: Altshuler, Y., Elovici, Y., Cremers, A.B., Aharony, N., Pentland, A. (eds.) Security and Privacy in Social Networks, pp. 197–223. Springer, New York (2013)

11. Eyal, I., Sirer, E.G.: Majority is not enough: Bitcoin mining is vulnerable (2013). arXiv preprint arXiv:1311.0243.

12. Kroll, J.A., Davey, I.C., Felten, E.W.: The economics of Bitcoin mining, or Bitcoin in the presence of adversaries. In: Proceedings of WEIS, vol. 2013 (2013)

13. Huang, D.Y., Dharmdasani, H., Meiklejohn, S., Dave, V., Grier, C., McCoy, D., Savage, S., Weaver, N., Snoeren, A.C., Levchenko, K.: Botcoin: monetizing stolen cycles. In: Proceedings of the Network and Distributed System Security Symposium (NDSS) (2014)

14. Becker, J., Breuker, D., Heide, T., Holler, J., Rauer, H.P., Böhme, R.: Can we afford integrity by proof-of-work? Scenarios inspired by the Bitcoin currency. In: Böhme, R. (ed.) The Economics of Information Security and Privacy, pp. 135–156. Springer, Heidelberg (2013)

15. Bitcoinwiki: Bitcoin difficulty. https://en.bitcoin.it/wiki/Difficulty. Accessed 10 September 2014

16. bitcoin.cz: World's first mining pool celebrates 3rd year with 0% fee. https://mining.bitcoin.cz/news/2013-12-16-pool-celebrates-3rd-anniversary. Accessed 10 September 2014

17. blockchain.info: an estimation of hashrate distribution amongst the largest mining pools. https://blockchain.info/pools/. Accessed 10 September 2014

18. statista.com: Felectricity prices in selected countries in 2013 (in u.s. dollar cents per kilowatt hour). http://www.statista.com/statistics/263492/electricity-prices-in-selected-countries/. Accessed 10 September 2014

Wireless and Embedded

Measuring the Performance of User Traffic in Home Wireless Networks

Srikanth Sundaresan[1]($^{\boxtimes}$), Nick Feamster[2], and Renata Teixeira[3]

[1] ICSI, Berkeley, USA
srikanth@icsi.berkeley.edu
[2] Princeton University, Princeton, USA
feamster@cs.princeton.edu
[3] Inria, Paris, France
renata@inria.fr

Abstract. This paper studies how home wireless performance characteristics affect the performance of user traffic in real homes. Previous studies have focused either on wireless metrics exclusively, without connection to the performance of user traffic; or on the performance of the home network at higher layers. In contrast, we deploy a passive measurement tool on commodity access points to correlate wireless performance metrics with TCP performance of user traffic. We implement our measurement tool, deploy it on commodity routers in 66 homes for one month, and study the relationship between wireless metrics and TCP performance of user traffic. We find that, most of the time, TCP flows from devices in the home achieve only a small fraction of available access link throughput; as the throughput of user traffic approaches the access link throughput, the characteristics of the home wireless network more directly affect performance. We also find that the 5 GHz band offers users better performance better than the 2.4 GHz band, and although the performance of devices varies within the same home, many homes do not have multiple devices sending high traffic volumes, implying that certain types of wireless contention may be uncommon in practice.

1 Introduction

Many home networks use 802.11 wireless as a predominant mode of communication; in fact, many consumer devices in home networks connect exclusively over a wireless connection. Despite increasingly widespread deployment of home wireless networks, there is little information about their performance in real homes, particularly as it relates to that of real user traffic and end-to-end performance. Understanding how wireless performance affects end-to-end user performance will become increasingly important as the throughput of residential access links continues to increase and the home wireless network becomes more likely a bottleneck.

There is an extensive set of previous work studying wireless network performance in many settings, including conferences, enterprise networks, and even apartment complexes [1,3,6,9,10,12]. These studies have measured either layer-2

© Springer International Publishing Switzerland 2015
J. Mirkovic and Y. Liu (Eds.): PAM 2015, LNCS 8995, pp. 305–317, 2015.
DOI: 10.1007/978-3-319-15509-8_23

performance metrics (such as wireless bitrates and retransmissions) or layer-3 performance such as TCP throughput over the wireless link. Yet, wireless network performance is extremely variable, even on short timescales, and mapping layer-2 performance to higher-level performance metrics such as throughput or latency is challenging. Additionally, active measurements can only capture the wireless network performance at one point in time; these measurements may not correspond to the performance that users see in practice for their actual application traffic.

In this paper, we explore the relationship between wireless performance metrics and TCP performance of user traffic. To do so, we *passively* measure wireless performance metrics on user traffic as it passes through the home wireless access point and correlate these metrics with the TCP performance of user traffic. We implement a measurement tool that runs on a commodity home wireless access point, which permits a widespread deployment and the ability to differentiate wireless versus wide-area performance. The routers that we use for our study have both 2.4 and 5 GHz radios, which allows us to compare the performance of these two bands. The deployment on commodity hardware poses strict design constraints: (1) the devices are resource-constrained, which limits the amount of collection and processing we can do; (2) each home has only a single measurement vantage point; and (3) we aim to use unmodified drivers to avoid interfering with the very environment that we are trying to measure. We measured the performance of wireless networks in 66 home networks around the world; we passively measure user traffic to extract both the performance of active TCP connections and wireless statistics such as frame bitrate and retransmissions. Our study both confirms results from previous studies and reveals new phenomena. Specifically, we find:

- As access link capacity increases, wireless performance plays a greater role in the TCP throughput that users observe.
- Latency inside the home is a significant contributor to end-to-end latency.
- The 5 GHz channel performs better than the 2.4 GHz (in particular, latency over the wireless is larger for 2.4 GHz); we also find that bitrates are generally low and retransmission rates high on 2.4 GHz.
- Within the same home, different devices experience different wireless performance.
- It is rare for devices in a home to send significant traffic volumes simultaneously.

As content providers continue to place content closer to users and governments and companies continue to invest in increasing access link throughput, understanding how users' home wireless networks relate to the performance that their traffic experiences will become critical for improving user experience. Our findings are a first step towards understanding the relationship between wireless performance metrics and TCP performance of user traffic. The results from this paper may ultimately be useful for designing a system to detect and isolate performance problems in home wireless networks.

2   Method

We describe the passive measurement tool that we developed for home access points, and the TCP and wireless performance metrics we used.

2.1   Measurements

We perform passive measurements of user traffic from commodity home wireless access points and correlate those measurements with the wireless metrics for the corresponding traffic. In contrast to active measurements, passive measurements more accurately reflect the actual performance that users experience. Further, passive measurements do not introduce contention or other artifacts that could affect the conditions that we seek to characterize. A measurement tool that operates on commodity access points facilitates both a widespread deployment, which can take advantage of an installed base of access points, and the ability to differentiate wireless versus wide-area performance. Ultimately, such a tool could operate in practice for a large user population. On the other hand, both the resource limitations of commodity access points and the bandwidth constraints in real home networks introduce design constraints that preclude using existing network diagnostic tools.

We collect packet traces of connections from the WAN interface and both wireless interfaces on the access point using pcap. Packet traces from the WAN interface provide information about wide-area TCP connections and IP packets that traverse the access point. We configure the wireless interfaces in monitor mode to capture radiotap headers [11]. For each frame, the radiotap headers provide the source and destination MAC addresses, the received signal strength (RSSI), and the frame control bits (the bitrate used, and whether the frame was retransmitted).

Deployment: We deploy our measurements on BISmark [2,17], which uses Netgear's WNDR 3700/3800 access point. This device has an Atheros chipset with a 450 MHz processor, one 802.11gn radio and one 802.11an radio. The 3800 has 128 MB of RAM, and the 3700 has 64 MB of RAM. The devices run OpenWrt with the ath9k wireless driver that uses the Minstrel rate adaptation algorithm with the default setting to a maximum bitrate of 130 Mbps. To respect user privacy, we do not collect payloads, and we anonymize all IP addresses and MAC addresses using SHA-256 and a per-access point secret salt as the data is collected on the router. Figure 1 summarizes our IRB-approved deployment and the characteristics of the home networks in this deployment; we collected data from 66 homes in 15 countries for one month in 2013.

Limitations: Our collection methods limit the types of wireless performance problems that we can study. First, continuous data collection from multiple interfaces on a commodity access point imposes significant CPU and data requirements. Thus, the router collect data only every five minutes on average for 15 seconds per iteration. The router exports only flow summaries, to reduce upload bandwidth requirements. This level of sampling precludes analyzing fine-grained characteristics (*e.g.*, transient faults, other conditions that frequently vary) or characteristics that derive from complete TCP flows. Second, because we anonymize device MACs and IP addresses, finer-grained analysis of the impact of certain types of application flows on certain devices (video in mobile devices, for example) is not possible. It is also not possible to account for device-specific issues, such as buffering in mobile devices. Third, we only have a single vantage point from which to collect our measurements, because typically homes only have a single access point. In contrast, other studies collect and correlate data from multiple radios [10] or multiple vantage points [3,6,12]. Finally, due to a driver limitation in the deployed devices, we could not scan for nearby access points. Scanning caused persistent disconnections for a small number of users; since this had a direct impact on users (BISmark devices are intended to be used as the primary access point), we did not scan the medium.

2.2 Metrics

We use the passive traffic traces to extract both TCP-level performance metrics and wireless performance metrics.

TCP Performance Metrics. The access point runs `tcptrace`, which processes the pcap traces to provide TCP statistics. We study the *average download TCP throughput* achieved during the captured lifetime of the flow. We use this metric to compute the *aggregate throughput* at every one-second interval by summing the average throughput of all active flows downloading traffic through a given access point during that interval. For reference, we compare the aggregate throughput with the access link capacity, which we measure using BISmark's active measurements. BISmark performs a multi-threaded TCP throughput test approximately every two hours [16,17]. We define the *access link capacity* as the 95th percentile of the multi-threaded throughput test measurements. We also study the round-trip time (RTT) of TCP connections, which `tcptrace` computes as the difference between the time of the data and SYN packets and its corresponding acknowledgments (`tcptrace`'s analysis algorithm already handles many corner cases, such as delayed acknowledgments). Running `tcptrace` at the access point allows us to measure both the RTT between the access point and the home devices (the *LAN RTT*) and the RTT between the access point and destinations in the wide-area (the *WAN RTT*).

Wireless Performance Metrics. We use the bitrate, retransmission rate, and received signal strength indication (RSSI) as our indicators of wireless performance problems because we can obtain these metrics easily from packet headers. IEEE 802.11 bitrate adaptation techniques adjust the transmission bitrate as wireless channel conditions change. Although these techniques usually adapt rates even under benign conditions to determine the channel quality, rate adaptation is typically more frequent when the channel quality is poor, because wireless senders typically reduce the bitrate in response to bit errors [8]. Thus, we also use the *normalized bitrate*, which is the average wireless bitrate computed over one second intervals, normalized by the maximum bitrate supported by that channel, as an indicator of a poor wireless channel. Normalized bitrate tends to be low when the wireless channel quality is poor. When bitrate adaptation does not adjust the bitrate (*e.g.*, due to varying channel conditions or contention), the normalized bitrate might not indicate channel quality, but in these cases retransmission rates are still high. We also compute the *retransmission rate* as the fraction of frames with the retransmit bit set in any given one-second interval.

3 Results

We present the results from our measurement study. We first measure the throughput and RTTs of user traffic in home networks and how these performance metrics relate to wireless performance metrics. We then explore the wireless performance characteristics of user traffic in more detail.

Total # of homes	66
Total # of countries	15
2.4 GHz	
Active devices	192
Average devices per home	2.9
5 GHz	
Active devices	66
Average devices per home	1.0

Fig. 1. Data collected for this study.

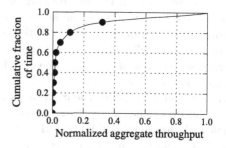

Fig. 2. The fraction of time that the collection of active flows receive a particular ratio of flow throughput to access link throughput.

3.1 Correlating TCP and Wireless Performance

We explore the achieved throughput of user traffic and the contributions of the home wireless network to this performance. Then, we study RTTs of user traffic and how the poor wireless network performance can result in higher LAN RTTs. This finding is relevant in light of the many recent efforts by service providers to reduce latency to end-to-end services with myriad optimizations and careful placement of content.

User Traffic Rarely Achieves the Full Access-Link Throughput. Figure 2 shows the fraction of time that the sum of TCP throughput for all flows in a home (the "aggregate throughput" as defined in Sect. 2.2) achieves a particular value relative to the access link throughput, as measured with BISmark's active throughput test (the *normalized aggregate throughput*). The results show that the user traffic rarely saturates the available access link throughput. Of course, the TCP traffic might not saturate the access link throughput for many reasons: for example, user traffic demand may be insufficient (in fact, previous studies have shown this phenomena is often the case [15]), or flows may be short enough that they fail to saturate the access link, which could happen if many short Web transfers are the dominant traffic type. Unfortunately, we have only the flow statistics exported by `tcptrace`, so we cannot run a tool like T-RAT [18] to identify with certainty when the application, as opposed to the network, was limiting TCP throughput. Nevertheless, it is remarkable that the access link is so underutilized so often. We suspect that one reason for lower utilization of the access link (when there is sufficient demand to saturate it) may be the presence of wireless bottlenecks in the home network. The rest of this section explores this possibility.

Achieved Throughput Often Correlates with Wireless Performance Metrics. To explore the relationship between the TCP throughput of user traffic in homes and access-link throughput, we measure how the aggregate throughput correlates with the bitrate and the retransmission rate. We normalize the aggregate throughput by the access link capacity (*normalized throughput*) and correlate this value with each of the wireless performance metrics. When we consider all traffic flows, TCP throughput does not correlate with any of the wireless performance metrics: the correlation coefficient between retransmission rate and normalized throughput is −0.01; for bitrate, the correlation coefficient is −0.02; and for RSSI, the correlation is 0.06.

However, when we explore the correlation for the subset of flows whose normalized throughput is greater than 0.1 (*i.e.*, for which we determine there is sufficient user demand), correlation between wireless metrics and access link throughput is stronger. This correlation increases with the access link throughput. In Fig. 3a we show how the correlation coefficient between aggregate throughput and retransmission rate varies as we only consider users with access link throughput above a certain value; we see as this value increases, the correlation becomes stronger. Figure 3b shows a similar trend when we correlate

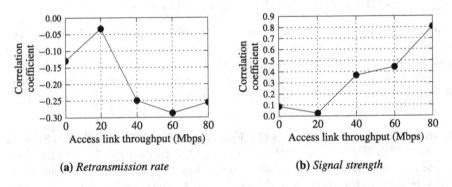

(a) *Retransmission rate*   (b) *Signal strength*

Fig. 3. Correlation of wireless metrics to normalized throughput at different access link throughput levels.

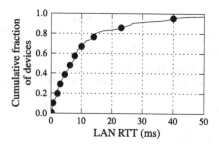 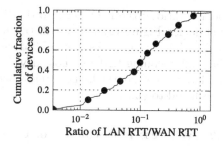

(a) *Distribution of TCP round-trip time between the access point and client across all devices in our study.*

(b) *The distribution of the median ratio of the LAN TCP round-trip time to the WAN TCP round-trip time across all flows for that device, across all devices.*

Fig. 4. Round-trip latency of flows.

RSSI with normalized throughput (though, obviously, the opposite trend holds; normalized throughput is positively correlated with RSSI). This result makes sense: wireless is more likely to introduce a bottleneck as access link throughput increases. The coefficient for bitrate follows a similar trend, but correlation is weaker for access links whose speeds exceed 60 Mbps, where the wireless network may be operating closer to its capacity. (The default setting of the access points supports a maximum bitrate of 130 Mbps, which translates to a TCP throughput of about 85 Mbps under excellent conditions; actual throughput will likely be less.) Patro *et al.* [10] also show in a more limited setting (dense deployments in two apartment complexes) that achieved throughput is highly correlated with the above wireless metrics.

The Latency Inside a Home Network is Often a Significant Contributor to Overall Round-Trip Time. The TCP round-trip time between the wireless access point and a wireless client should be on the order of one millisecond. As this RTT increases, it not only signifies that the wireless link is bottlenecked due to buffering or medium access delays, but it can have an adverse impact on performance, especially for applications that are latency sensitive. Figure 4a plots the distribution of the median LAN RTT (as defined in Sect. 2.2) across all devices in our study. The median device on the local wireless network sees a median wireless latency of about 8 ms, but nearly 30 % of the devices experience local TCP round-trip latencies greater than 15 ms. Buffering affects latency, particularly for mobile devices that sleep more frequently. While we cannot distinguish mobile devices in our dataset (because we anonymize MAC addresses and do not look into the payload), we try to minimize this issue by considering the mean of the RTTs, and only for flows with at least 25 packets in the downstream direction.

We also analyze the performance of the home network relative to the wide-area network performance; we compare the round-trip times between the devices and the access point to the round-trip times from the access point to the wide-area destination for each flow. We define the *median latency ratio* for a device as the median ratio of the LAN RTT to the WAN RTT (Sect. 2.2) across all flows for that device. Figure 4b shows the distribution of the median latency ratio across all devices. The result shows that 30 % of devices have a median latency ratio greater than 0.2, meaning that for those devices, at least half of the flows have end-to-end latencies where the home wireless network contributes more than 20 % of the overall end-to-end latency.

3.2   Wireless Performance of User Traffic

We now characterize wireless performance in our deployment. Our preliminary findings include: (1) the 5 GHz wireless band consistently achieves better performance than the 2.4 GHz band; (2) the performance of a home wireless network varies across individual wireless devices within the same home; and (3) multiple devices in the same home network rarely send high traffic volumes at the same time.

The 5 GHz Band Performs Better than the 2.4 GHz Band. We analyze the performance that devices in home wireless networks achieve and how performance varies depending on whether devices are on the 2.4 GHz band or the 5 GHz band. Our hypothesis was that devices on the 5 GHz band would perform better because there are generally fewer devices (and surrounding access points) in the 5 GHz band, and that the 5 GHz band also has less non-WiFi interference (*e.g.*, microwaves, baby monitors). As shown in previous studies, devices on 2.4 GHz experience both WiFi and non-WiFi interference [10].

Figure 5a shows the impact of spectrum on flow throughput for flows that have throughput greater than 1 Mbps. We present the normalized flow throughput to eliminate any bias related to the access link capacity. Flows to devices on the 5 GHz spectrum have higher normalized throughput than those on 2.4 GHz. Similarly, we see in Fig. 5b that the LAN RTT for flows in 2.4 GHz are much higher than for flows in 5 GHz. The distribution of normalized flow throughput in each spectrum is similar between the 2.4 GHz and 5 GHz when we consider

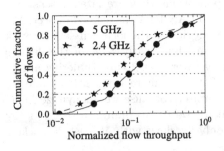

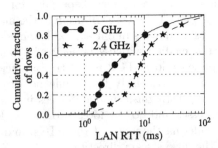

(a) *Flows in the 5 GHz band achieve higher throughput.*

(b) *Flows in the 2.4 GHz band experience higher LAN RTT.*

Fig. 5. Characteristics of flows in the 5 GHz vs. the 2.4 GHz spectrum.

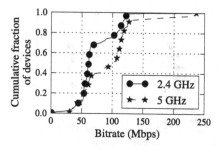

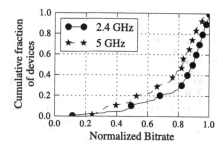

Fig. 6. Distribution of wireless bitrates for devices in both the 2.4 GHz and 5 GHz spectrums, for all devices in the deployment. Devices in the 2.4 GHz spectrum see lower bitrates.

Fig. 7. Distribution of median normalized bitrates, for devices in both the 2.4 GHz and 5 GHz spectrums. Devices do not achieve maximum bitrate, especially in the 2.4 GHz range.

flows whose normalized throughput is less than 0.1. We are investigating this phenomenon, but these could include cases where we suspect that there is not enough application demand. Even in those cases, however, the LAN RTTs are smaller for devices connected over 5 GHz.

Figure 6 plots the CDF of the median bitrate for all devices in all homes, for both the 2.4 GHz band and the 5 GHz bands. Only 30 % of 2.4 GHz devices see median bitrates above 65 Mbps; in contrast, more than 50 % of devices in the 5 GHz spectrum see bitrates greater than 100 Mbps. It is worth noting that the wireless bitrates do not correspond to the actual throughput. Even under perfect conditions, a wireless bitrate of 130 Mbps corresponds to an actual TCP throughput of about 80 Mbps. The bitrate values thus reflect a loose upper bound on the achievable end-to-end throughput.

Figure 7 shows the median bitrate per device for each home network, normalized by the maximum supported bitrate of the corresponding wireless protocol (between 65 Mbps and 300 Mbps for 802.11n, and 54 Mbps for 802.11a/g). Many devices, especially those in the 2.4 GHz range, often operate close to the maximum bitrate supported by the protocol, more so than 5 GHz devices. However we also see that the maximum bitrates of 5 GHz devices are higher. This discrepancy can be explained by the fact that many devices in the 2.4 GHz channel could be small mobile devices with single antennas that restrict their maximum bitrates to 65 Mbps. Also, attenuation is higher on 5 GHz, which could lead to more active bitrate adaptation.

Figure 8 shows the retransmission rates for all devices across all homes; the result shows similar trends with respect to the 2.4 GHz and 5 GHz ranges: retransmissions are more common in the 2.4 GHz band, with about 20 % of devices having retransmission rates above 10 %.

Within a Single Home Network, Individual Devices Can Experience Very Different Wireless Performance. We also studied the performance of individual devices in a home network and the extent to which wireless performance varies across devices in the same home network. We found many cases where the median wireless retransmission rates for a device was high. For the

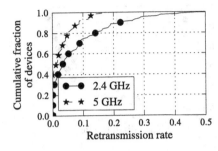
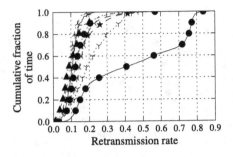

Fig. 8. Median retransmission rates, for devices in both the 2.4 GHz and 5 GHz spectrums. Retransmissions are higher in the 2.4 GHz spectrum, where nearly 30 % of devices see a median retransmission rate greater than 10 %.

Fig. 9. The retransmission rates between the access point and clients in a single home network. In this home retransmission rates are high. Interestingly, one device has a significantly higher retransmission rate.

devices in the home shown in Fig. 9, nearly all of the devices have median retransmission rates greater than 10 %. Interestingly, one device experiences a high retransmission rates nearly all of the time, suggesting a persistent problem that may result from device placement, interactions between the access point and that device's driver, or some other cause.

To study how wireless performance varies across devices in a single home, we measure the K-S distance of the distributions of raw wireless bitrates between each pair of devices in each home. Figure 10a plots the median and the maximum pairwise K-S distance in each home. We find that more than 80 % of homes have at least one pair of devices with a K-S distance of more than 0.6, indicating that most homes have at least one poorly performing device (due to either poor placement, poor hardware, or poor drivers). We investigate the variance of RSSI across different devices and we see similar differences (Fig. 10b). Future work could involve investigating the disparate performance across devices further and determining whether the variability in device performance is caused by any single factor.

Simultaneous Communication is Infrequent. Most of the homes in our deployment had more than one active device during our study. Interestingly, however, these devices often were not highly active at the same time. We measured one-second intervals and observed the number of times that multiple devices were sending at least 25 packets within the one-second interval. To our surprise, simultaneous communication was rare: for 85 % of the one-second intervals on the 2.4 GHz band and 93 % of the intervals on the 5 GHz band, we observed at most one device sending at least 25 packets in the interval. This observation relates to wireless contention and may imply that certain types of wireless contention are infrequent. This finding contrasts with previous work that shows that contention is a factor in wireless performance [10]. This discrepancy may result from differences in either deployment locations or in measurement method and warrants further exploration.

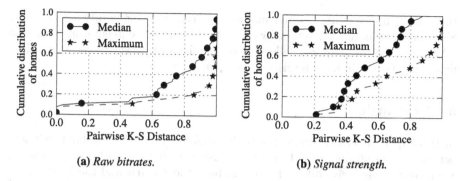

(a) *Raw bitrates.*   **(b)** *Signal strength.*

Fig. 10. The pairwise K-S distance between devices within a home network, across all homes.

4 Related Work

We focus our survey of related work on studies of wireless performance in real deployments and on attempts to detect and characterize common wireless performance problems.

The WiSe project is most similar to our efforts [10]; WiSe is a deployment of multiple wireless monitors in a diverse set of home environments that are configured with custom measurement and monitoring software. In this deployment, each access point is a custom OpenWrt-based embedded device with two network interface cards: one that forwards traffic and another that monitors the quality of the wireless channel. Because each WiSe access point has two interfaces, the deployment sees a much more complete picture of the wireless spectrum. The deployment is also concentrated in two dense residential complexes; our deployment is larger and more diverse, but it does not use custom hardware with multiple network interfaces, which limits our ability to collect certain types of measurements. The work also designs an estimator for TCP performance based on wireless performance metrics; validating this model in our own testbed is part of our ongoing work. Other efforts have deployed dense monitors to study wireless in conferences, and university buildings [3,5,6]; these studies explore similar characteristics but do not focus on home network settings, which are generally lightly managed (or unmanaged) and hence potentially more chaotic. Papagiannaki *et al.* [9] deploy and measure wireless performance characteristics in three homes.

Other work has characterized wireless performance problems using custom hardware or active measurements. Rayanchu *et al.* [13] detected non-wireless interference using custom hardware. Kanuparthy *et al.* [4] developed a tool to detect wireless performance problems (*e.g.*, low signal-to-noise ratio, congestion, hidden terminals) using both active probes and an additional passive monitor deployed within the network. Other techniques have also studied different types of wireless performance problems. Manweiler *et al.* build a tool to detect hidden interference in homes and adjust channel selection to minimize interference [7];

the tool requires a custom kernel and does not run on a commodity access point. Shrivastava *et al.* develop a tool for estimating interference in enterprise wireless LANs [14]; the tool requires collection and analysis of packet traces at multiple access points within an enterprise to perform diagnosis.

5 Conclusion

In this paper, we characterized the performance of user traffic in home wireless networks from 66 homes in 15 countries using passive network measurements. We analyzed passively collected traces in both the 2.4 GHz and the 5 GHz spectrum. One of the more significant challenges in executing this study involved designing a measurement tool that could operate within the tight constraints of a commodity home router and draw reasonable inferences from a single vantage point without a second monitor radio. Our study of this real user traffic in home networks revealed that most TCP flows in home networks achieve only a small fraction of the available access link throughput, that wireless characteristics have a greater effect on the performance of user traffic as access link throughput increases, that the 5 GHz channel exhibits better performance than the 2.4 GHz band, and that distinct devices within the same home can see very different wireless performance. We plan to build on these insights to create a diagnostic tool that can identify both the location of the network bottleneck link and the underlying causes of the bottleneck, should it lie in the wireless network. Finally, although wireless performance often suffers as a result of transient factors, such as microwaves, passing humans, or even minute changes in orientation of devices, many wireless performance problems are persistent. Our ability to monitor wireless performance over longer time periods in many homes may shed light on the persistent performance problems, which could offer a more holistic picture of wireless network performance problems.

References

1. Adya, A., Bahl, P., Chandra, R., Qiu, L.: Architecture and techniques for diagnosing faults in IEEE 802.11 infrastructure networks. In: MobiCom 2004, pp. 30–44. ACM, New York (2004). http://doi.acm.org/10.1145/1023720.1023724
2. BISMark: Broadband Internet Service Benchmark. http://projectbismark.net/
3. Cheng, Y.C., Afanasyev, M., Verkaik, P., Benkö, P., Chiang, J., Snoeren, A.C., Savage, S., Voelker, G.M.: Automating cross-layer diagnosis of enterprise wireless networks. SIGCOMM Comput. Commun. Rev. 37(4), 25–36 (2007)
4. Kanuparthy, P., Dovrolis, C., Papagiannaki, K., Seshan, S., Steenkiste, P.: Can user-level probing detect and diagnose common home-WLAN pathologies. SIGCOMM Comput. Commun. Rev. 42(1), 7–15 (2012)
5. Kotz, D., Essien, K.: Analysis of a campus-wide wireless network. Wirel. Netw. 11(1–2), 115–133 (2005)
6. Mahajan, R., Rodrig, M., Wetherall, D., Zahorjan, J.: Analyzing the MAC-level behavior of wireless networks in the wild. In: SIGCOMM 2006, pp. 75–86 (2006)

7. Manweiler, J., Franklin, P., Choudhury, R.: RxIP: monitoring the health of home wireless networks. In: INFOCOM, 2012 Proceedings IEEE, pp. 558–566, Mar 2012
8. Minstrel rate adaptation algorithm. http://goo.gl/5xPSC
9. Papagiannaki, K., Yarvis, M., Conner, W.S.: Experimental characterization of home wireless networks and design implications. In: Proceedings of the IEEE INFOCOM, Barcelona, Spain, Mar 2006
10. Patro, A., Govindan, S., Banerjee, S.: Observing home wireless experience through WiFi APS. In: MobiCom 2013, pp. 339–350. ACM, New York (2013)
11. Radiotap. http://radiotap.org
12. Rayanchu, S., Mishra, A., Agrawal, D., Saha, S., Banerjee, S.: Diagnosing wireless packet losses in 802.11: separating collision from weak signal. In: INFOCOM 2008, pp. 735–743, Apr 2008
13. Rayanchu, S., Patro, A., Banerjee, S.: Airshark: detecting non-WiFi RF devices using commodity WiFi hardware. In: IMC 2011, pp. 137–154. ACM, New York (2011)
14. Shrivastava, V., Rayanchu, S., Banerjee, S., Papagiannaki, K.: PIE in the sky: online passive interference estimation for enterprise WLANs. In: NSDI 2011, p. 25. USENIX Association, Berkeley (2011)
15. Siekkinen, M., Collange, D., Urvoy-Keller, G., Biersack, E.W.: Performance limitations of ADSL users: a case study. In: Uhlig, S., Papagiannaki, K., Bonaventure, O. (eds.) PAM 2007. LNCS, vol. 4427, pp. 145–154. Springer, Heidelberg (2007)
16. Sundaresan, S., de Donato, W., Feamster, N., Teixeira, R., Crawford, S., Pescapè, A.: Broadband internet performance: a view from the gateway. In: Proceedings of the ACM SIGCOMM, Toronto, ON, Canada, Aug 2011
17. Sundaresan, S., Burnett, S., de Donato, W., Feamster, N.: BISmark: a testbed for deploying measurements and applications in broadband access networks. In: Proceedings of the USENIX Annual Technical Conference, Philadelphia, CA, June 2014
18. Zhang, Y., Breslau, L., Paxson, V., Shenker, S.: On the characteristics and origins of internet flow rates. In: Proceedings of the ACM SIGCOMM, Pittsburgh, PA, Aug 2002

Enabling Wireless LAN Troubleshooting

Ilias Syrigos[1]([✉]), Stratos Keranidis[1], Thanasis Korakis[2],
and Constantine Dovrolis[3]

[1] University of Thessaly, Volos, Greece
{ilsirigo,efkerani}@uth.gr
[2] NYU Polytechnic School of Engineering, New York, USA
korakis@uth.gr
[3] Georgia Institute of Technology, Atlanta, USA
constantine@gatech.edu

Abstract. Particular WLAN pathologies experienced in realistic scenarios are hard to detect, due to the complex nature of the wireless medium. Prior work has employed sophisticated equipment, driver modifications, or even application-layer techniques, towards diagnosing such pathologies. The key novelty of our approach lies in the identification of metrics able to characterize the root causes of individual pathologies, while also being directly extractable from MAC-layer statistics available in today's wireless equipment. Through the development of the proposed framework as application-layer software on top of commercial hardware and its experimental evaluation, we validate the efficiency and applicability of our approach.

1 Introduction

With home WLANs becoming increasingly popular and the plethora of wireless devices operating in the limited unlicensed spectrum, the performance degradation experienced by end-users is almost inevitable. Common home WLAN pathologies are related with low-quality channel conditions. However, even high quality links may suffer from anomalies that are inherent to the operation of the 802.11 standard, such as contention for medium access. In addition, the well-known 802.11 impairments of *"Hidden-Terminal"* [1] and *"Capture-effect"* [2], which are identified in dense topologies, frequently appear in closely spaced WLAN environments.

As administrators/users of home WLANs are not aware of such pathologies, performance issues are usually interpreted incorrectly and the blame is attributed to ISPs. Troubleshooting WLAN performance is hard, due to the complex and dynamic nature of the wireless medium and requires collection of low-level information hardly interpreted even by experts.

Prior work in diagnosing wireless networks performance has considered a variety of approaches, ranging from in-depth studies [3–5] of specific pathologies through sophisticated equipment, to solutions [6] relying on vendor-specific drivers or modifications and application-layer frameworks [7] that are directly

© Springer International Publishing Switzerland 2015
J. Mirkovic and Y. Liu (Eds.): PAM 2015, LNCS 8995, pp. 318–331, 2015.
DOI: 10.1007/978-3-319-15509-8_24

applicable to commercial WLAN devices. Considering the different categories of approaches, a tradeoff exists between the achievable detection accuracy and the applicability in common home WLAN setups. Towards bridging this gap, novel frameworks need to be developed that combine the advantages of both worlds.

In this work, we develop user-level detection mechanisms, which exploit low-level information that can be revealed by commercial Access Point (AP) devices. MAC-layer statistics are collected and updated as part of the Physical layer (PHY) rate adaptation mechanism. These statistics include, but are not limited to, the number of transmission attempts as well as the number of which were successful. The key novelty of our approach lies in the identification of metrics based on the aforementioned statistics that are able to characterize the root causes of WLAN pathologies. Through extensive experimentation, we concluded in the identification of unique trends that performance experiences, in terms of the proposed metrics, when 802.11 links are affected by different WLAN pathologies. Our detailed findings have been incorporated in a combined detection methodology that has been implemented on commercial APs from different vendors. The main outcome of our research is an application-layer framework that is automatically activated upon the detection of degraded performance to accurately determine the underlying pathology and report it to the end user. Our work intends to highlight the importance of having MAC-layer statistics accessible from the application-layer through a standardized way and encourage all manufacturers of 802.11 equipment to adopt this approach.

2   Related Work

A great variety of research approaches has proposed mechanisms towards diagnosing common WLAN pathologies. Several works have focused on the detection of specific pathologies, such as distinguishing between frame losses resulting due to low signal or collisions in [3], or the identification of device types generating cross-technology interference in [4,5,8,9]. Another class of approaches [10,11] has proposed advanced anomaly detection frameworks that provide increased accuracy by combining measurements obtained from several nodes. In addition, [9,12,13] are based on the elaboration of multiple monitoring devices and require the application of synchronization protocols [9,13], hence rendering them applicable only to centrally managed WLAN deployments. On the other hand, [6,14] are based solely on observations derived from a single node, thus being applicable in independently owned home WLANs.

The various aforementioned approaches also differ on the specified implementation requirements. More specifically, in [4,5] the use of sophisticated equipment is necessitated, while the approaches presented in [3,6,12,14] require vendor-specific drivers or modifications. The main drawback of the aforementioned approaches is that they are not hardware agnostic. In [7], the first user-level approach able to infer the MAC-layer effects of common home WLAN anomalies is proposed. In our work, we take a step further by developing a systematic approach able to detect the root causes of an extended list of pathologies, by taking advantage of the detailed information offered by MAC layer statistics, while still being accessible by the application layer.

3   MAC-Layer Statistics

Commercial 802.11 devices that are developed by major vendors of wireless products, such as Atheros and Intel can be controlled through well-known Open-Source drivers (ath9k, iwlwifi, Mad-WiFi and ath10k [15]). Such drivers constantly collect detailed MAC-layer statistics that are updated as part of the PHY rate adaptation procedure, including among others, information related to the total number of attempted frame transmissions and retransmissions.

In this work, based on this information we define and utilize two metrics. Firstly, the *Normalized Channel Accesses* : $NCA = CA/MCA$ where CA and MCA denote the attempted Channel Accesses and Model-Based Channel Accesses per second respectively, for a specific PHY rate and a specific frame length. MCA is calculated according to the 802.11 a/g performance model presented in [16]. We validated these values with experiments on various types of wireless chipsets under idle channel conditions at the fixed frame length of 1500 bytes. The NCA metric characterizes the access (uninterrupted or not) to the wireless medium by a station willing to transmit data frames. Secondly, we define the *Frame Delivery Ratio* : $FDR = ST/CA$ where ST denotes the number of Successful Transmissions per second. The FDR metric is an indicator of the link quality which is responsible for the successful or not delivery of a frame.

In the following Sections, we present how these metrics can be exploited towards characterizing the impact of commonly identified pathologies on WLAN performance.

4   IEEE 802.11 Related Pathologies

Performance of 802.11 stations first depends on the availability of channel access opportunities and second on the efficiency of frame delivery, whenever medium access is granted. We build our pathology identification mechanism on top of this initial observation and categorize pathologies into two classes. The first one considers pathologies occurring in cases that the transmitter identifies the medium as busy and thus defers from transmitting (**Medium Contention**). In the second category, we group pathologies occurring in cases that the medium is detected as idle, thus enabling the transceiver to proceed with frame transmissions that fail to be delivered at the receiver (**Frame Loss**). We present the taxonomy of the considered pathologies in Fig. 1.

4.1   Medium Contention

Contention-based pathologies frequently occur in dense WLAN deployments, where multiple 802.11 devices concurrently attempt to access the medium. However, as the unlicensed spectrum is also exploited by other wireless protocols (e.g. Bluetooth, Zigbee) and a large range of RF devices (e.g. cordless phones, security cameras), the medium is further congested due to non-802.11 emissions.

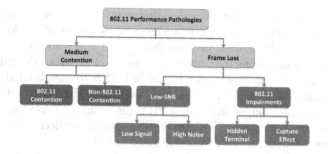

Fig. 1. Taxonomy of IEEE 802.11 pathologies

The resulting decrease in available channel access opportunities is directly dependent both on the channel airtime captured by 802.11 transmissions, as well as the transmission Duty Cycle (DC) of non-802.11 RF devices.

The crucial impact of medium contention is clearly highlighted in cases of contending stations that utilize diverse PHY rate configurations, which leads to performance anomaly [17]. The high bitrate stations observe a higher throughput degradation in comparison with the lower rate nodes. This degradation is a result of the low number of CA attempts due to the high channel airtime utilization by the low bitrate stations. Consequently, we expect the NCA metric to decrease across increasing PHY rate configurations of the concerned station. However, regarding the FDR metric, higher bitrates should result in higher number of collisions, due to simultaneously expiring back-off timers, and thus to a decrease in FDR, but not in that extent of considering it as a significant trend.

In case of non-802.11 contention, devices with fixed transmission DC, such as microwave ovens, can be interpreted as low bitrate stations which do not comply with the 802.11 standard and hence do not perform a *"Backoff"* procedure. As a result we expect a decrease in NCA metric across increasing PHY rates, as it happens in 802.11 contention. Another consequence of the absence of backoff mechanism in non-802.11 devices is that collisions can occur in the middle of a frame transmission and so higher PHY rates will result in lower probability of collisions. Taking that into consideration, we expect an increasing trend in the FDR metric.

4.2 Frame Loss

In this category, we group pathologies generated in scenarios that the 802.11 *"Channel Sensing"* mechanism constantly identifies the medium to be idle and grants uninterrupted medium access. However, conditions experienced at the receiver side may lead in reduced probability of successful Frame Delivery and subsequent doubling of the Contention Window (CW) parameter. As the reduced MAC-layer Frame Delivery Ratio (FDR) is the root cause of this phenomenon, we identify it as the key metric for characterizing the impact of Frame Loss related pathologies.

Fundamental causes of receiver side underperformance are usually related with the *low-SNR conditions* experienced as a consequence of the low Received Signal strength, resulting from channel fading and shadowing or due to high-Power non-802.11 emissions that result in Noise level increase. Considering that complex modulation schemes require higher link SNR to ensure reliable communication, in comparison with basic schemes, we expect the FDR performance to significantly decrease across increasing PHY rates, under low-SNR conditions. Furthermore, the decrease in FDR would also lead in an decrease in the NCA metric, as the doubling of the CW results in fewer CAs.

In addition, significant frame delivery inefficiencies may also be attributed to *802.11 impairments*, phenomena appearing in cases that concurrent channel access and subsequent frame collisions cannot be avoided through the 802.11 *Channel Sensing* mechanism. More specifically, the *"Hidden-Terminal"* anomaly occurs in cases that the receiver node lies within the transmission range of two active 802.11 nodes that are mutually hidden and cannot sense each other resulting in frame collisions. In cases that no remarkable difference is observed in the received signal strength of colliding frames at the intermediate node, the *"Hidden-Terminal"* phenomenon appears symmetrically for both flows. However, the most frequently observed case is the *"Capture-effect"* phenomenon, in which case a considerable difference in RSSI values is observed, resulting in a higher probability of successful decoding for the high-power frames. As a result, the link *"capturing"* the medium experiences lower collision probability accessing the medium more frequently and resulting in higher performance penalty for the affected links.

Longer duration transmissions experiencing higher probability of collision, so we expect to see an FDR increase across increasing PHY rate values of the affected link. However, hidden nodes suggest longer distances from the AP and consequently an underlying low-SNR pathology, so we also expect an FDR decrease in high PHY bitrates. In overall, we should identify a highly varying FDR metric across PHY rates and additionally more notable variations under *"Capture-effect"* scenarios where the impact is more severe. As regards the NCA metric, although the underlying low-SNR conditions should impose a decreasing trend, the impact of FDR variation, which as mentioned before is higher under *"Capture-effect"* scenarios, would enforce NCA to not display a clear trend.

5   Detection Methodology

Having defined the key metrics of NCA and FDR, we next focus on developing a detection methodology able to identify unique trends on the way each individual pathology affects performance of both metrics. Before that, we need to decide upon the existence or not of a pathology. This is accomplished by a simple throughput test of fixed length frames at the maximum PHY rate, the result of which is compared to the analytical value calculated by the aforementioned model in [16]. In case that achieved throughput is lower than the 80 % of the theoretical one, we initiate our proposed framework presented below. By taking advantage of the relation between the PHY rate of the affected link and the proposed metrics, we design an active probing mechanism that probes the WLAN channel with multiple packet trains, where each train consists of several packets that are transmitted at varying PHY rates. We call the proposed test as *Varying Bitrate Probing* and each train is transmitted in each one of the 802.11a/g compatible PHY rates, selected from the vector $R = (6, 9, 12, 18, 24, 36, 48, 54)$ Mbps. Each train provides a unique sample - we need multiple samples to make any statistical inference. In parallel with the probing procedure, the NCA and FDR metrics are calculated per each configured PHY rate.

Next, we apply the non-parametric *Theil-Sen Slope* estimator on the collected samples to identify trends in the relation between the two metrics and the PHY rate of the affected link. The output of the *Theil-Sen Slope* estimator consists of the slope estimation with 95 % confidence interval, plus the p-value, where both aid in determining the existence of a trend and its characterization as increasing or decreasing. P-values are interpreted as follows: $p < 0.01$ indicates very high significance and $p < 0.05$ is considered significant and the null hypothesis (of the slope being equal to zero) is rejected in both cases. P values greater than 0.05 indicate failure to reject the null hypothesis and thus no trend is detected.

In such occasions, we have to distinguish between two further cases, where in the first case, data points present highly varying values and partially present both significantly increasing and decreasing trends, while in the second the considered input data is roughly constant and result in approximately zero estimated slope. Although in the first case, no specific trend can be reliably detected, several scenarios might present high start-to-end variation, a trend that we also need to identify. To this aim, we enhance our test, by employing the *Pairwise Difference Test* metric $S_{PDT} = \frac{FDR^8 - FDR^1}{\sum_{k=2}^{8} |FDR^k - FDR^{k-1}|}$, where $k \in \{1, 2, ..., 8\}$ denotes the configured PHY rate. It is obvious that $-1 \leq S_{PDT} \leq 1$. If there is a strong trend, either increasing or decreasing, S_{PDT} approaches 1 or -1. Identification of the second case is based on the evaluation of statistical dispersion through the measure of standard deviation. We consider specific standard deviation thresholds, as derived from our experimentation and described in the following section.

6   Experimentation with Proposed Metrics

The experimental setup that is used as the basis of our experimentation consists of a single communicating pair of nodes that we refer to as System under Test (SUT). Both nodes feature the Intel 5300 chipset, implement the 802.11a/g protocol and operate in infrastructure mode, through the *iwlwifi* driver. In the following experiments, we reproduce each considered pathology and investigate how the performance of the SUT link is affected in terms of the NCA and FDR metrics, while it performs the *Varying Bitrate Probing* test. The devices participating in the following experiments are closely located within a double floor indoor office environment at the University of Thessaly premises, as depicted in Fig. 2. A representative subset of the various executed experiments that replicate each individual pathology is detailed in the following Sections.

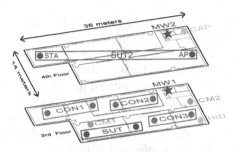

Fig. 2. Testbed topology

6.1   Contention with 802.11 Terminals

Through this first experiment, we aim at investigating the impact of medium contention with 802.11 compatible devices, and for this purpose we establish 3 contending links in close proximity and on the same channel with the SUT link. More specifically, we use Ch. 44 of the 5 GHz band that is totally free of transmissions in the testbed premises.

In the first 2 Scenarios, we activate only the CON1 link to transmit 5 Mbps of traffic load, at the PHY rates of 6 Mbps and 54 Mbps accordingly. Figure 3(a) depicts the NCA performance and shows a significant decreasing trend across increasing PHY rates in Sc.1. due to the *"802.11 performance anomaly"*, while in Sc. 2 only minimal variation is detected across increasing PHY rates, as a result of the high PHY rate. In Sc. 3, we still activate only the CON1 link to transmit at the PHY rate of 24 Mbps with 20 Mbps of traffic load. We observe that in Sc. 3, the NCA values per PHY rate have decreased in comparison with

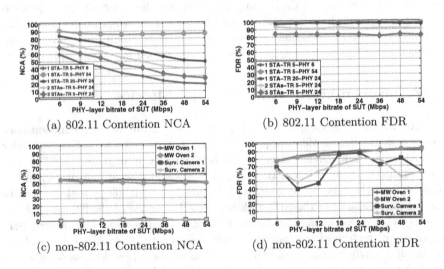

Fig. 3. NCA and FDR performance of medium contention related pathologies

Sc. 2, while a significant decreasing trend is clearly identified. Finally, in Sc. 4, we simultaneously activate links CON1 and CON2 to transmit 5 Mbps of traffic load, at the PHY rate of 24 Mbps, while in Sc. 5 we replicate the configurations of Sc. 4, but simultaneously activate the 3 links CON1, CON2 and CON3. In both cases, significant decreasing trends are identified by the Theil-Sen estimator. Summarizing the above scenarios, a significant decreasing trend is detected with a p-value of 0.01 except for the Sc. 2 where the p-value of 0.4 is derived and thus no trend is detected. Figure 3(b) plots the resulting FDR performance across all the considered Scenarios and presents only minimal variation across different PHY rates (standard deviation of 0.95). We notice that the increasing number of contending stations results in decreased FDR, as also observed in [18], a fact related with the increased probability of collisions when the back-off timers of multiple terminals simultaneously expire.

6.2   Contention with Non-802.11 Devices

In this second experiment, we aim at characterising the impact of different types of non-802.11 devices. More specifically, we consider a Microwave Oven (MW) that typically emits high RF energy in 2.44–2.47 GHz frequencies with DC of 0.5 and a Surveillance Camera that constantly (DC = 1) transmits with 10 dBm power, occupying 18 MHz of bandwidth on various frequencies of the 2.4 GHz band. The two devices are located at positions MW1 and CM1 of the 3rd floor accordingly. We set the SUT link to operate on the commonly configured Ch. 6 (2437 MHz) and the camera on 2432 MHz.

In Fig. 3(c), we clearly observe that the continuously emitting Surv. Camera results in NCA values that are close to zero across PHY rates, as the SUT link constantly detects the medium to be busy. On the other hand, the MW that is activated with the DC of 0.5, provides a fixed amount of time available for medium utilization per period. This phenomenon affects performance in terms of the NCA metric, in a way similar to the "802.11 performance anomaly", thus leading the NCA values to decrease across increasing PHY rates. The resulting FDR performance is depicted in Fig. 3(d), where in the case of the MW, an increasing trend is observed with the p-value of 0.01. Considering the FDR evaluation of the Surv. Camera, no specific trend is identified, as the FDR highly fluctuates due to the extremely low number of attempted transmissions.

6.3   Low SNR

In this experiment, we jointly investigate the impact of low-SNR conditions resulting either in *Low Signal* or *High Noise* scenarios. Considering the *Low Signal* case, we generate varying low-SNR topologies, by establishing a remote 802.11 link (SUT2) on the 4th floor and properly tuning the transmitter's Power, to result in links of 15 dB, 10 dB and 5 dB SNR. In Fig. 4(a) and (b), we observe that performance regarding NCA and FDR is unaffected as long as the SNR provides for robust communication at the given PHY rate. However, in cases when the SNR requirement of the configured bitrate exceeds the SUT's link

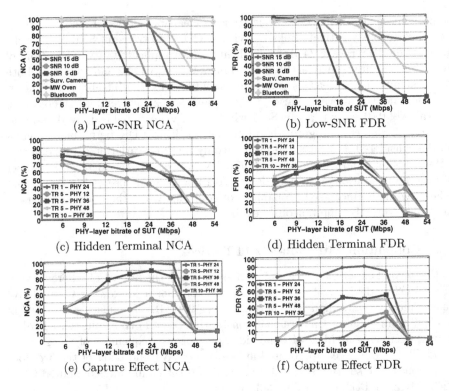

Fig. 4. NCA and FDR performance of frame loss related pathologies

SNR, a remarkable drop in NCA and FDR is noticed resulting in a decreasing trend (p-value 0.01) for both metrics. Towards experimenting under High Noise conditions, we use the SUT link of the 3rd floor and activate the MW at position MW2 of the 4th floor, along with the Surv. Camera at position CM2 of the 3rd floor. In both scenarios, the high power emissions of the remotely located interfering devices are not detected to exceed the high Energy Detection threshold at the location of the SUT link. However, due to their high DC, the *Noise level* is constantly increased, hence generating low-SNR conditions and approximating the performance obtained in *Low Signal* scenarios, in terms of both metrics.

6.4 Hidden Terminal

Towards experimenting with *"Hidden-Terminal"* scenarios, we establish a hidden to the SUT2 link, by activating the transmitter at position HID of the third floor and resulting in equally received signal strength at both link receivers. In the first scenario we measure the impact of 1 Mbps traffic load, transmitted at the PHY rate of 24 Mbps. As shown in Fig. 4(c), the NCA metric presents a decreasing trend, across increasing PHY rates, while no specific trend is identified for the FDR metric, as depicted in Fig. 4(d). More specifically, a small increase across the first PHY rates is followed by a sharp decrease due to the underlying low-SNR pathology. In the next three scenarios, we fix the traffic load at 5 Mbps and vary the PHY rate of the hidden link, between 12, 24 and 48 Mbps respectively. Across all the tested scenarios, identical trends as in Sc. 1 are detected. In Sc. 5, we fix the PHY rate of 36 Mbps and transmit at the traffic load of 10 Mbps, noticing similar performance as in previous scenarios. In all scenarios a decreasing trend is detected regarding the NCA metric with p-value of 0.01, while the null hypothesis regarding FDR is rejected (p-value > 0.05).

6.5   Capture Effect

In this last set of experiments, we examine the performance fluctuations under various scenarios experiencing the *"Capture-effect"* phenomenon. For this purpose, we use the node located at position CAP of the 4th floor, as the interferer of the SUT2 link. In Sc.1, we start by injecting the light traffic load of 1 Mbps in the wireless medium, while configuring the interfering link at the PHY rate of 24 Mbps. As presented in Fig. 4(e) and (f), similar trends are observed as in the considered *"Hidden-Terminal"* scenarios. In Scenarios 2, 3 and 4, we increase the traffic load of the interfering link to 5 Mbps and vary the PHY rate among 12 Mbps, 36 Mbps and 48 Mbps, while in Sc. 5 the traffic load is further increased to 10 Mbps and the PHY rate is fixed at 36 Mbps. Across all the considered scenarios, the NCA metric presents no significant trend, as the calculated p-values lie above 0.05. As regards to FDR, no trend is detected in all Scenarios (p-values above 0.23), although the high performance penalty in comparison to *"Hidden-Terminal"* is depicted with close to zero FDR values. Regarding the performance obtained in Sc. 1, we remark that as both 802.11 impairments pose similar impact on both metrics under low traffic load conditions, discrimination between the two phenomena will be challenging under such cases.

6.6   Framework Enhancement and Result Summary

In many cases of frame loss pathologies, Theil-Sen estimator falsely concludes that the existing pathology is the hidden terminal one. For that reason, the introduction of the aforementioned PDT metric enhances our test with further refinement of the identification of trends. More specifically, in cases where the Theil-Sen estimator detects decreasing trend in NCA attempts and no trend in FDR metric, we apply the PDT metric in FDR statistics. Through extensive experimentation, we concluded that $S_{PDT} < -0.8$ denotes low-SNR pathology, $-0.8 \leq S_{PDT} \leq -0.32$ denotes hidden terminal pathology and $S_{PDT} > -0.32$ denotes capture effect pathology. The outcome of our study is presented in Table 1, which lists the specific trends that can be detected through the proposed methodology. Not every combination of metrics' trends is mapped to a specific pathology and that cases may correspond to the existence of multiple simultaneous pathologies, which we do not consider in our current work. The derived findings have been incorporated in an application-layer framework

Table 1. Identified trends per considered pathology

		Frame Delivery Rate (FDR)			
		Constant	No Trend	Increasing	Decreasing
Normalized Channel Accesses (NCA)	Decreasing	802.11 Contention	Hidden Terminal	Non-802.11 Contention DC < 1	Low SNR
	No Trend		Capture Effect		
	Constant		Non-802.11 Contention DC = 1		

that is automatically activated upon the detection of degraded performance to uniquely determine the underlying pathology.

7   Framework Evaluation

In this section, we extensively evaluate the detection performance of the developed framework, under two specifically designed sets of experiments. In each set, we replicate a specific anomaly under various scenarios and by measuring the number of true positives we quantify the perceived detection accuracy. In the first set, we generate scenarios of contention with 802.11 devices, while in the second we experiment with low-SNR scenarios and 802.11 impairments. For the sake of completeness we also examine cases, where our throughput test does not consider as pathologies.

7.1   Contention with 802.11 Terminals

We start by configuring 3 different topologies, consisting of 1, 2 and 3 contending stations that coexist within the 3rd floor of the testbed. We replicate 36 different scenarios in each different topology (108 in total), by varying both the configured PHY rate and traffic load parameters to generate diverse medium utilization conditions. Through an extra wireless node, we monitor the percentage of Airtime that is captured by the contending links in each topology, towards highlighting the impact of Airtime Utilization on the resulting detection accuracy. In Fig. 5, we clearly observe that the detection performance improves across increasing medium utilization conditions as the impact of contention is becoming more evident. More specifically, as medium utilization increases above 25 % the mechanism successfully detects the 802.11 contention pathology, across all the corresponding scenarios in the 3 different topologies. Low medium utilization conditions (below 15 %), however, are always detected as no pathology by the initial throughput test and thus are not considered as detection failures.

7.2   Frame Loss

In this set of experiments we evaluate the detection performance under low-SNR scenarios, by placing the transmitter of the SUT link at the 3rd floor

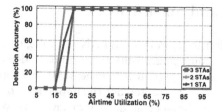

Fig. 5. Detection performance across different 802.11 contention scenarios.

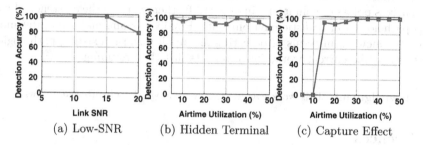

(a) Low-SNR   (b) Hidden Terminal   (c) Capture Effect

Fig. 6. Detection performance across frame loss related pathologies.

and the receiver across 20 different locations at the 4th floor. We also vary the transmission Power of the SUT transmitter to further vary the SNR levels in each link and result in 80 different topologies. For each different topology, the SUT link executes our detection mechanism, in order to investigate whether the low-SNR conditions are detected. The resulting scenarios are grouped in 5 different SNR classes. We observe in Fig. 6(a) that the detection accuracy is 100 % for all SNR classes, except for the 25 dB case, which poses no significant impact and is not detected as pathology from the initial throughput test.

Towards replicating the Hidden-Terminal and Capture Effect phenomena, we activate an interfering link at a fixed position in the 4th floor which is hidden to the transmitter of the SUT. By observing the RSSI values of the transmitted frames, we notice that 4 of the topologies lead to nearly equal (approximately 0–3 dB of difference) values between SUT's transmitter and interfering link's transmitter and consequently are vulnerable to the hidden terminal pathology. Furthermore, 9 links present a notable (>15 dB) difference in RSSI values and hence are vulnerable to the capture effect phenomenon. We evaluate our algorithm in the corresponding topologies that potentially suffer from 802.11 impairments, while inducing traffic of varying load and PHY bitrate at the interfering link and consider 36 different scenarios for each topology. In Fig. 6(b), we observe that the Hidden Terminal pathology is successfully detected across the various tested scenarios that are presented in order of airtime utilized by the Interfering link. In the case of the capture effect pathology, we notice in Fig. 6(c) that the obtained accuracy presents low performance for low airtime utilization, due to the pathology causing similar impact upon the suffering nodes as the *"Hidden-Terminal"* one does.

8   Conclusions and Future Work

The proposed detection framework of WLAN pathologies causing performance degradation showed encouraging results by accurately detecting all the considered pathologies. Our approach of utilizing the MAC-layer statistics offered from some wireless devices' vendors pointed out the importance of making these accessible, as they are already implemented, to user-level. As we demonstrated this will be of great advantage to WLANs administrators in their effort of troubleshooting low performance. As future work, we seek to integrate our framework with access points of volunteers, in order to further evaluate the existence of various pathologies in realistic environments. Finally, we aim at the improvement of our framework in terms of detecting all simultaneously existing pathologies, contrary to the current work, which reports just the prevailing one.

Acknowledgment. This work was funded by a Google Faculty Research Award.

References

1. Feilu, L., Jian, L., Zhifeng, T., Korakis, T., Erkip, E., Panwar, S.: The hidden cost of hidden terminals. In: Proceedings of ICC (2010)
2. Lee, J., Kim, W., Lee, S., Jo, D., Ryu, J., Kwon, T., Choi, Y.: An experimental study on the capture effect in 802.11a networks. In: Proceedings of WinTECH (2007)
3. Rayanchu, S., Mishra, A., Agrawal, D., Saha, S., Banerjee, S.: Diagnosing wireless packet losses in 802.11: separating collision from weak signal. In: Proceedings of INFOCOM (2008)
4. Gollakota, S., Adib, F., Katabi, D., Seshan, S.: Clearing the RF smog: making 802.11N robust to cross-technology interference. In: Proceedings of SIGCOMM (2011)
5. Lakshminarayanan, K., Sapra, S., Seshan, S., Steenkiste, P.: RFDump: an architecture for monitoring the wireless ether. In: Proceedings of CoNEXT (2009)
6. Lakshminarayanan, K., Seshan, S., Steenkiste, P.: Understanding 802.11 performance in heterogeneous environments. In: Proceedings of HomeNets (2011)
7. Kanuparthy, P., Dovrolis, C., Papagiannaki, K., Seshan, S., Steenkiste, P.: Can user-level probing detect and diagnose common home-WLAN pathologies. SIGCOMM CCR **42**(1), 7–15 (2012)
8. Rayanchu, S., Patro, A., Banerjee, S.: Airshark: detecting non-WiFi RF devices using commodity WiFi hardware. In: Proceedings of IMC (2011)
9. Rayanchu, S., Patro, A., Banerjee, S.: Catching whales and minnows using WiFiNet: deconstructing non-WiFi interference using WiFi hardware. In: Proceedings of NSDI (2012)
10. Cheng, Y., Bellardo, J., Benkö, P., Snoeren, A., Voelker, G., Savage, S.: Jigsaw: solving the puzzle of enterprise 802.11 analysis. In: Proceedings of SIGCOMM (2006)
11. Chandra, R., Padmanabhan, V., Zhang, M.: WiFiProfiler: cooperative diagnosis in wireless LANs. In: Proceedings of MobiSys (2006)

12. Sheth, A., Doerr, C., Grunwald, D., Han, R., Sicker, D.: MOJO: A distributed physical layer anomaly detection system for 802.11 WLANs. In: Proceedings of MobiSys (2006)
13. Shrivastava, V., Rayanchu, S., Banerjee, S., Papagiannaki, K.: PIE in the sky: online passive interference estimation for enterprise WLANs. In: Proceedings of NSDI (2011)
14. Giustiniano, D., Malone, D., Leith, D., Papagiannaki, K.: Measuring transmission opportunities in 802.11 links. IEEE/ACM Trans. Netw. **18**(5), 1516–1529 (2010)
15. Wireless Chipsets Drivers. http://wireless.kernel.org/en/users/Drivers
16. Jangeun, J., Peddabachagari, P., Sichitiu, M.: Theoretical maximum throughput of IEEE 802.11 and its applications. In: Proceedings of NCA (2003)
17. Heusse, M., Rousseau, F., Berger-Sabbatel, G., Duda, A.: Performance anomaly of 802.11b. In: Proceedings of INFOCOM (2003)
18. Bianchi, G.: Performance analysis of the IEEE 802.11 distributed coordination function. IEEE JSAC **18**(3), 535–547 (2000)

Improving the Packet Send-Time Accuracy in Embedded Devices

Ricky K.P. Mok$^{(\boxtimes)}$, Weichao Li, and Rocky K.C. Chang

Department of Computing, The Hong Kong Polytechnic University,
Hong Kong, China
{cskpmok,csweicli,csrchang}@comp.polyu.edu.hk

Abstract. A number of projects deploy Linux-based embedded systems to carry out large-scale active network measurement and network experiments. Due to resource constrains and the increase of network speed, obtaining sound measurement results from these low-end devices is very challenging. In this paper, we present a novel network primitive, OMware, to improve the packet send-time accuracy by enabling the measurement application to pre-dispatch the packet content and its schedule into the kernel. By this pre-dispatch approach, OMware can also reduce the overheads in timestamp retrievals and sleeping, and the interference from other application processes.

Our evaluation shows that OMware can achieve a microsecond-level accuracy (rather than millisecond-level in a user-space tool) in the inter-departure time of packet trains, even under heavy cross traffic. OMware also offers optimized call for sending back-to-back packet pairs, which can reduce the minimum inter-packet gap by 2 to 10 times. Furthermore, OMware can help reduce the error of replaying archived traffic from 40 % to at almost 19 %.

1 Introduction

Linux-based embedded devices are ubiquitous. For example, many homes use home routers or WiFi APs for sharing the residential broadband access. Some of them run OpenWrt [27], a popular Linux distribution for networked embedded devices, which allows developers to re-use the software tools implemented for the PCs via cross compilation. Due to their low cost, several projects, such as BISMark [1], SamKnows [8], and RIPE Atlas [6], employ them as vantage points to measure the Internet performance or gauge the network service quality of residential broadband. ARM-based single-board computers, such as Raspberry Pi [5], are also used in sensor network and embedded cloud research.

Obtaining sound measurement results from these resource-constrained devices is however very challenging. A fundamental requirement is to send out (probe or archived) packets onto the wire according to their pre-determined schedules. Inaccurate packet send times will distort the scheduled probe patterns (e.g., Poisson, periodic, and Gamma renewal) in active measurement which may result in non-optimal probing [9]. Inaccurate packet send times can also directly affect the

© Springer International Publishing Switzerland 2015
J. Mirkovic and Y. Liu (Eds.): PAM 2015, LNCS 8995, pp. 332–344, 2015.
DOI: 10.1007/978-3-319-15509-8_25

measurement results for timing-sensitive measurement, notably packet-pair capacity [12,20] and available bandwidth [19].

A major source of send-time inaccuracy is the high overhead for these devices to move packets between user and kernel space and in executing the sleep and timestamping function calls. These overheads will widen the gap between the scheduled send time and the actual time of delivering the packet to the wire. Another problem is to contend resources with other running processes (E.g., firewall, NAT, and DNS request forwarding in a residential broadband router). Due to the CPU context switching, the measurement tool will experience highly fluctuated overheads which cannot be calibrated easily. A traffic generator may even fail to send the expected pattern when the CPU consumption is high [10].

In this paper, we propose OMware, a new network primitive to improve the send-time accuracy. Its main novelty is on utilizing the sleep period typically required for a packet sending process to copy packets from user space to kernel and construct the sk_buff structure [24] for the network card driver. As a result, the first pre-dispatching phase "absorbs" these operations' overheads. In addition, OMware offers optimized function calls for sending back-to-back packet pairs, which can improve the accuracy of capacity and available bandwidth measurement [11,12,20,21].

We evaluate OMware with two OpenWrt routers (NETGEAR WNDR 3800 and TP-LINK WR1043ND) and perform a set of experiments under different levels of cross traffic to investigate the improvement in network measurement. The results show that OMware can achieve a microsecond-level accuracy (rather than millisecond-level in a user-space tool) in the inter-departure time (IDT) of packet trains even under heavy cross traffic. Besides, the packet sending delay can be significantly reduced by 0.2 ms. Furthermore, OMware can reduce the IDT in a back-to-back packet pair by 2 to 10 times, therefore enabling the embedded device to measure a much higher capacity.

2 Related Works

There are generally two approaches to increase the packet I/O performance—hardware and kernel. The hardware approach adopted by SoNIC [23], NetFPGA [4], and [14] uses programmable network interface cards to improve the precision of packet sending time and receiving timestamp. However, these cards are usually expensive, thus prohibiting them from being used in embedded devices, such as residential broadband routers. Intel recently proposes the DPDK library [18] to boost packet processing performance. However, this library is only supported by their Xeon series CPU which is not available in many embedded systems.

The kernel approach runs on commercial PCs and optimizes the operating system's kernel to increase the performance. Examples include PF_RING [15] for improving packet capturing performance, and nCap [16], netmap [29], and kTRxer [30] for improving both sending and receiving speed. Epoll in Linux and kqueue in FreeBSD are mainly for improving the event notification mechanism, which can enhance the performance of packets reception. On the other hand, pktgen [26] aims at a high-speed packet sending. However, they do not consider the accuracy of packet send time. Using real-time Linux (RTLinux [7]) is a possible solution to increase the packet send-time accuracy. For example, Kiszka et al. propose RTnet [22] for hard real-time networking. However, running RTLinux on residential broadband router may significantly affect the performance of running other network services.

In wireless sensor network community, Österlind and Dunkels [28] proposed to pre-copy packet to improve the packet forwarding throughput in 802.15.4 networks, but the application cannot send packets at any dedicated time.

3   Background

Linux-based embedded devices, such as home routers and private NASes (Network Access Storage), can be found in many homes today and of low cost. Some of them support OpenWrt, which is one of the popular and active Linux distributions specifically for embedded devices. Furthermore, the packages of several network measurement tools, including D-ITG, `httping`, and `hping`, are readily available on public repositories. Developers can also run their own tools via cross compilation. However, the computational power of these devices are far lower than commodity PCs. Table 1 shows the detailed configurations of three testing devices, including NETGEAR WNDR 3800, which has the same configurations as a BISMark-enabled router, and a reference PC.

Table 1. The configurations of the testing devices.

Device Model	CPU/Chipset (Clock Freq.)	RAM
Raspberry Pi	BCM2835 (700 MHz)	512 MB
TP-LINK WR1043ND	AR9132 (400 MHz)	32 MB
NETGEAR WNDR3800	AR7161 (680 MHz)	128 MB
Reference PC	Intel Core2Duo (1.86 GHz)	2 GB

Note: All embedded devices are running OpenWrt 12.09.1.
All devices expect Raspberry Pi support 1 Gbps Ethernet.

Due to resource limitations, the performance and accuracy of these devices are not satisfactory, especially in today's high speed network. We have identified three basic operations—timestamp retrieval, sleep, and packet transmission—could cause performance degradation. These operations are commonly used in network tools. In the following, due to page limitation, we can only show the performance issues in packet transmission, which cause the most significant impact.

3.1   Packet Sending Performance

We define the packet sending performance by the time period between the calling of `sendto()` and the packet is put on wire, because some tools may regard the

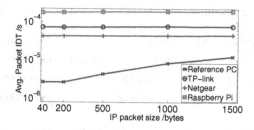

Fig. 1. The average packet IDT against packet size on all devices.

calling of `sendto()` as the packet sending time. Previously, Rizzo showed that the time period 950 ns in his high-end FreeBSD host (Intel i7-870 with 10 Gbit NIC) [29]. However, we found that tens of microseconds are required in the embedded devices.

Instead of forcing the functions to return early [29], our benchmark program repeatedly flushes out 100,000 identical TCP packets using the raw socket (i.e., `sendto()`). Besides, the packet's TCP/IP header and checksums are pre-computed to mitigate any overhead from these operations. We repeat the experiment with five packet sizes, which are {40, 200, 500, 1000, and 1500} bytes. All the packets are captured by an endace DAG card directly connected to the device. We then analyze the IDTs between packets to estimate the overall sending performance.

Figure 1 shows the average packet IDTs against the packet sizes. We can see that the performance of the three embedded devices is about one order of magnitude slower than a commodity PC. For example, the average packet IDT for 40-byte packets is 2.64 μs, while the NETGEAR router is 41.7 μs. The Raspberry Pi performs the worst among the embedded device, because the Raspberry Pi's ethernet interface connects to CPU via the USB interface and results in poor performance. Unlike the reference PC, the performance is fairly stable across the packet sizes in all three embedded devices. The average packet IDTs for TP-LINK and NETGEAR only respectively increase by 5 % and 8 % as the packet size increases from 40 bytes to 1500 bytes.

4   Pre-dispatch Programming Model

We survey several network tools listed in Table 2. We find that these tools are often implemented with similar kind of function calls in packet I/O, sleep and timestamp retrieval. We further investigate their source code and programming flows. These tools often adopt a *sequential* programming model to schedule the sending of packets. Figure 2(a) and (b) illustrate a timeline comparison between the sequential model and our proposed pre-dispatch model, respectively. The application in the figures refers to a network tool running on the user space. For both model, at time t_0, we assume the application has prepared the packet content to be sent at a future time, t_s. The packet appears on the wire at

Table 2. Examples of function calls used in network tools.

Tools	Packet I/O	Sleep	Timestamp Retrieval
D-ITG [13]	POSIX Socket	select() and polling	gettimeofday()
httping [2]	POSIX Socket	usleep()	gettimeofday()
Iperf [3]	POSIX Socket	nanosleep()	gettimeofday()

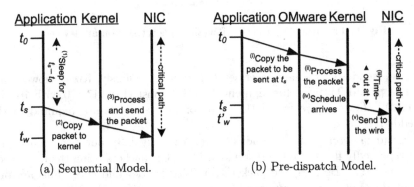

(a) Sequential Model.   (b) Pre-dispatch Model.

Fig. 2. Timeline comparison between the sequential and pre-dispatch approaches.

$\{t_w, t'_w\}$ in {sequential, pre-dispatch} model. Therefore, the sending time errors are $(t_s - t_0)$ or $(t'_s - t_0)$ for sequential or pre-dispatch model, respectively.

We first consider the sequential model in Fig. 2(a). The applications using this model are usually implemented using POSIX socket for packet I/O and a family of sleep() functions for spacing out packets. We summarize this model into three major steps.

(1) The application prepares the packet content, computes the sleep period (i.e., $t_s - t_0$, for $t_s > t_0$) and goes into sleep mode.
(2) After the sleep period is over, the packet content is copied to the kernel using socket.
(3) The packet headers are filled by the TCP/IP stack and finally sent to the network card.

On the other hand, our pre-dispatch model, as shown in Fig. 2(b), divides the packet sending process into two major phases. The tool first prepares and copies the packet to the OMware before the scheduled sending time, t_s. Then, the OMware sends the packet when t_s arrives. We can describe the details with five steps:

(i) Once the packet is ready and the sending time is determined, the application can immediately invoke the packet sending call in the OMware API, which takes the pointer of packet and the sending time as the input.
(ii) The OMware processes the packet, which includes adding ethernet header and constructing sk_buff structure.

(iii) If the packet sending time does not arrive (i.e., current time $< t_s$), OMware will add the packet sending operation as a kernel task triggered by a high resolution timer. Otherwise, the packet should be sent immediately.
(iv) When the scheduled send time t_s arrives, an interrupt will be generated to trigger the callback routine of sending the processed packet.
 (v) As the packet has been processed, it can be put onto the wire quickly. The OMware API then acknowledges the application on whether the process is successful.

The major difference between the two models is when the program starts to wait (i.e., (1) and (iii)) for the scheduled time. The pre-dispatch model utilizes part of the sleep time to handle time consuming operations, such as (i) and (ii). Therefore, the system can take a shorter critical path in sending packets and improve the throughput.

5   Evaluation

In this section we evaluate the packet send-time accuracy, pre-dispatching period, packet-pair accuracy, and packet send timestamp accuracy on a testbed. To support the pre-dispatch model, we have implemented OMware, which is a loadable kernel module for Linux. OMware provides a set of APIs for network tools. We cross-compile OMware, so that our experiments can run on two home routers, NETGEAR WND3800 and TP-LINK WR1043ND, both of which are installed with OpenWrt 12.09.1.

5.1   Testbed and Test Suite

We setup a testbed, as shown in Fig. 3, to emulates a network environment with cross traffic. The WAN port of the OpenWrt router, $D0$, is directly connected to an endace DAG Card 4.5G2 [17] with 1 Gbps Ethernet for capturing the traffic sending from $D0$. The server installed with the DAG card, $S0$, runs the dagfwddemo program, so it can forward the traffic from $D0$ to a Linux host, $S1$, and the cross traffic. $X0$ and $X1$ are two Linux hosts for generating cross traffic using D-ITG, where $X0$ is behind the NAT provided by $D0$. The cross traffic is unidirectional UDP flows generated by D-ITG [13]. Each flow is configured with Pareto distributed packet inter-arrival times and uniform distribution of packet

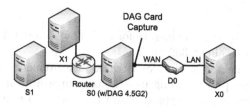

Fig. 3. Testbed for the performance tests.

Table 3. The test suite for evaluating OMware.

Methods	Packet pattern	Library	Model	Description
OIR	Packet train	OMware	OMware (initial pre-dispatching)	The tool prepares all the probe packets and their sending timestamps in advance and sends them to OMware for pre-dispatching the sending of the packets
OFR	Packet train	OMware	OMware (on-the-fly pre-dispatching)	The tool uses clock_nanosleep() with absolute timestamp to sleep until ϕ μs before the scheduled send time. Then, it prepares the probe packets and sends them to OMware for pre-dispatching the sending of the packets
OSM	Packet train	OMware	Sequential	This method is a special case of *OFR* method where ϕ is zero
RSM	Packet train	POSIX	Sequential	This method uses raw socket for sending packets. Similar to *OSM*, clock_nanosleep() with absolute timestamp is used for spacing the probe packets
TOM	Packet pairs	OMware	OMware	This method employs the packet pair sending function in OMware to send a sequence of packet pairs with initial pre-dispatching
TRW	Packet pairs	POSIX	Sequential	This method uses raw socket to send a sequence of packet pairs

size over $\{40, 1500\}$ bytes. The bitrate for each flow is about 2200 kbps, and the packet sending rate is about 352 packets/s.

We have implemented a simple network measurement tool running with OMware and different programming models for comparing the performance and timing accuracy between our approach and raw socket. Table 3 lists the details of a test suite. The packet train tests send a train of evenly spaced TCP data packets to the WAN port. According to their memory capacities, the train has 100 packets for the NETGEAR router and 50 packets for the TP-LINK router. The packet pair tests send 50 and 25 pairs of back-to-back packets to the WAN port. Both tests use different packet sizes, inter-departure times between packets or packet pairs, and degree/ direction of cross traffic. The parameters used are listed in Table 4. The packet send time is recorded by both the measurement tool using OMware and the DAG card.

Table 4. The parameters used in evaluating packet sending performance.

Parameters	Values
No. of cross traffic flows, ρ	0, 1, 5, 10, 20, 30
Direction of cross traffic, ρ	WAN→LAN, WAN←LAN
IP packet size, λ (bytes)	40, 200, 500, 1000, 1500
Expected inter-departure time, α (μs)	0, 10, 100, 1000, 10000, 100000
Pre-dispatching period for the OFR method, ϕ (μs)	0, 100, 500, 1000

5.2 Packet Send-Time Accuracy

We use the timestamps from the packet capture to compute the actual packet IDT sent from the router by $IDT = ts_{n+1} - ts_n$, where ts_n represents the timestamp of the nth packet in the packet train. Figure 4 shows a log-log plot of average packet IDT against the expected IDT, α, in the idle NETGEAR router. The error bars plot the 95 % confidence interval of data. We can see that the OIR method outperforms the other three, especially in very small packet IDT (10 and 100 μs). But the variation for 10 μs case is quite large, as this IDT is close to the limit of the system. The OFR method becomes more accurate when the expected IDT increases to 100 μs as the pre-dispatching can take place after sending the first fesw packets. The OSM and RSM methods improve their accuracy when the IDT is larger than 1 ms.

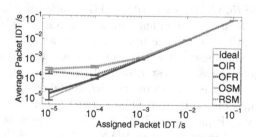

Fig. 4. The log-log plot of measured average packet IDT against assigned one for OIR, OFR ($\phi = 1000$ μs), OSM, and RSM ($\rho = 0$, $\lambda = 40$ bytes, $\alpha \geq 10$ μs, NETGEAR).

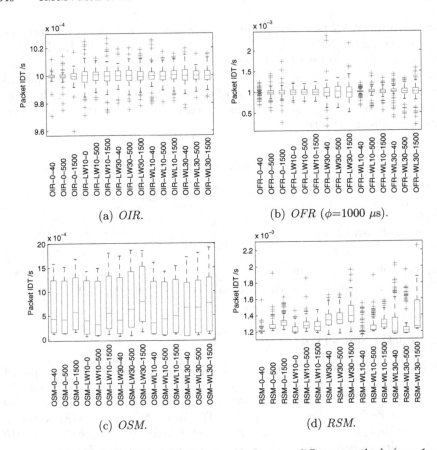

Fig. 5. The box-and-whisker plots of packet IDTs using different methods ($\alpha = 1$ ms, NETGEAR router).

Figures 5(a) to (d) are four box-and-whisker plots respectively showing the summary of data of the *OIR*, *OFR*, *OSM*, and *RSM* methods where the expected packet IDT is set to 1 ms. In each box-and-whisker plot, the top/bottom of the box are given by the 75th/25th percentile, and the mark inside is the median. The upper/lower whiskers are the maximum/minimum, respectively, after excluding the outliers. The outliers above the upper whiskers are those exceeding 1.5 of the upper quartile, and those below the minimum are less than 1.5 of the lower quartile. Each figure shows 15 test cases with different degrees/directions of cross traffic and packet sizes. For example, *OIR-0-500* on the x-axis in Fig. 5(a) represents the results obtained from *OIR* method under '0' cross traffic (idle) and sending 500-byte IP packets; WL*XX* or LW*XX* represents the experiment runs with *XX* flows of cross traffic in WAN→LAN or WAN←LAN direction, respectively.

We can see that the *OIR* method is the most stable against the cross-traffic. Most of the IDTs fall within ±20 μs of the true value. The *OFR* method also shows an accurate median value. But the cross traffic slightly affects this method's accuracy. The inter-quartile range increases with the number of cross traffic flows. Without adopting the pre-dispatching technique, the *OSM* method shows even larger inter-quartile range (about 1 ms) for all cases, which is caused by the inaccuracy of sleep function. Finally, the *RSM* method shows the worst result. All the IDTs suffer from at least 0.2 ms inflation. Besides, this method is also susceptible to cross traffic interference. When the WAN←LAN cross traffic is heavy (e.g., LW30), the inter-quartile range shows a six-fold increase. To summarize, traditional method (*RSM*) experiences larger delay and variance in sending packets than OMware-based methods.

5.3 Pre-dispatching Period

Another important issue is the length of pre-dispatching period in the *OFR* method. Some stateful measurement tools, such as OneProbe [25], requires the information from the previous probe packets to generate a new one. Preparing all probes packets at the beginning of the measurement becomes infeasible. As shown in the previous section, OMware cannot pre-dispatch probes if the packet send time is too close to the current time. Therefore, we test four different pre-dispatching periods and examine their effects on the packet send-time accuracy.

Figures 6(a) and (b) show the CDFs of the packet IDTs with different pre-dispatching periods using an expected packet IDT of 10 μs and 1000 μs, respectively. When the expected packet IDT is very small (e.g., $\alpha = 10$ μs), the pre-dispatching period cannot improve the accuracy. It is because the requested IDT is insufficient for OMware to finish the pre-dispatching phase before the scheduled send time. However, when the expected packet IDT increases to 1 ms, the fluctuation of the packet IDTs can be significantly decreased when the pre-dispatching period increases to 500 μs (as shown in Fig. 6(b)). We also found similar pattern in other cases. Therefore, we conclude that the pre-dispatching period of 500 μs is sufficient for completing the first part of packet dispatchment in this router.

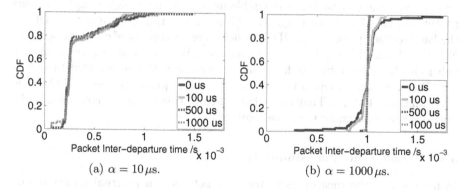

(a) $\alpha = 10\,\mu s$.   (b) $\alpha = 1000\,\mu s$.

Fig. 6. The CDFs of packet inter-departure time of the OFR method with different pre-dispatching period ($\rho = 0$, $\lambda = 1500$ bytes, NETGEAR router).

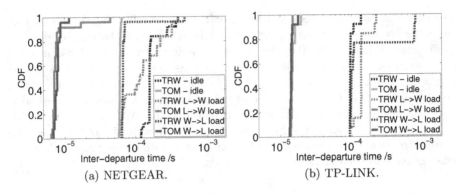

(a) NETGEAR.   (b) TP-LINK.

Fig. 7. The CDFs of back-to-back packet pairs' inter-departure time. ($\alpha = 1\,\text{ms}$ and $\lambda = 40\,\text{bytes}$).

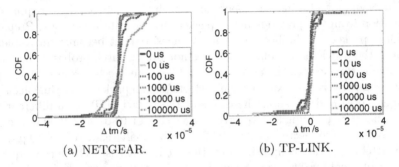

(a) NETGEAR.   (b) TP-LINK.

Fig. 8. The CDF of the difference between packet IDTs computed by the DAG card capture and send timestamps reported by OMware ($\rho = 0$ and $\lambda = 40\,\text{bytes}$).

5.4   Packet-Pair Accuracy

OMware provides a dedicated API for sending back-to-back packet pairs. A smaller gap between the two packets can enable us to measure a higher capacity using packet pair based methods (e.g., [11,20]). Figures 7(a) and (b) plot the CDFs of the back-to-back packet pairs' IDTs under different degrees of cross traffic in the NETGEAR and TP-LINK router, respectively. We set a 1 ms gap between each pair to mitigate the influence from the previous pair. We can see that the NET-GEAR router can achieve a minimum IDT of 6.44 μs, while the TP-LINK one only can reach 13.6 μs. They can achieve 2 to 10 times improvement against the raw socket version under the same condition.

5.5   Packet Send Timestamp Accuracy

In most cases, the measurement tools cannot rely on external timestamping device, such as DAG card, to provide precise packet send timestamp. The tools have to rely on the send timestamp reported by OMware. To appraise the accuracy of the timestamps, we subtract the packet IDTs computed by two time sources, $\Delta tm = IDT_{OMware} - IDT_{DAG}$, where IDT_{OMware} and IDT_{DAG} are the packet IDTs of the same pair of packets, but computed using the timestamps reported by the OMware and those captured by the DAG card, respectively. Figures 8(a) and (b) show the CDFs of Δtm for the NETGEAR and TP-LINK routers. We can see that the packet IDT difference computed by the two time sources are very close. OMware's timestamp accuracy can generally reach micro-second level. Therefore, the measurement tools can use OMware's timestamp to compute accurate results.

6 Conclusions

This paper proposed a novel network primitive to improve the packet send-time accuracy. The model employs a two-phase approach to allow pre-dispatch of packets to reduce the impact from the low packet sending performance. Our implementation, OMware, allows the tools to buffer probe packets and their send times in the kernel before their actual send time. Hence, the packet send-time accuracy and sending rate can be significantly improved.

Our testbed evaluation results showed that using OMware to pre-dispatch packets can provide accurate packet send times. Comparing to raw socket, OMware can reduce the minimum packet inter-departure time by ten times and reduce the variation by 6 times under heavy load cross traffic. In the future, we will compare the performance of OMware in more embedded devices and investigate the performance impact to other applications.

Acknowledgements. We thank three anonymous reviewers for their valuable comments. We also thank Lei Xue, McKeith Kwok, and Jack Chan for their help in programming the prototype of OMware and carrying out experiments. This work is partially supported by an ITSP Tier-2 project grant (ref. no. GHP/027/11) from the Innovation Technology Fund in Hong Kong.

References

1. Bismark. http://www.projectbismark.net
2. httping. http://www.vanheusden.com/httping/
3. Iperf - The TCP/UDP Bandwidth Measurement Tool. http://iperf.fr/
4. NetFPGA. http://netfpga.org/
5. Raspberry Pi. http://www.raspberrypi.org/
6. RIPE Atlas. https://atlas.ripe.net/
7. RTLinux. https://rt.wiki.kernel.org/
8. Samknows. http://www.samknows.com
9. Baccelli, F., Machiraju, S., Veitch, D., Bolot, J.C.: On optimal probing for delay and loss measurement. In: Proceedings of ACM IMC (2007)
10. Botta, A., Dainotti, A., Pescapé, A.: Do you trust your software-based traffic generator? IEEE Commun. Mag. **48**(9), 158–165 (2010)

11. Chan, E., Chen, A., Luo, X., Mok, R., Li, W., Chang, R.: TRIO: measuring asymmetric capacity with three minimum round-trip times. In: Proceedings of ACM CoNEXT (2011)
12. Chan, E., Luo, X., Chang, R.: A minimum-delay-difference method for mitigating cross-traffic impact on capacity measurement. In: Proceedings of ACM CoNEXT (2009)
13. Dainotti, A., Botta, A., Pescapè, A.: A tool for the generation of realistic network workload for emerging networking scenarios. Comput. Netw. **56**(15), 3531–3547 (2012)
14. Degioanni, L., Varenni, G.: Introducing scalability in network measurement: toward 10 Gbps with commodity hardware. In: Proceedings of ACM IMC (2004)
15. Deri, L.: Improving passive packet capture: beyond device polling. In: Proceedings of SANE (2004)
16. Deri, L.: nCap: wire-speed packet capture and transmission. In: Proceedings of IEEE E2EMON (2005)
17. Endace. DAG packet capture cards. http://www.endace.com
18. Intel. Packet processing on intel architecture. http://www.intel.com/content/www/us/en/intelligent-systems/intel-technology/packet-processing-is-enhanced-with-software-from-intel-dpdk.html
19. Jain, M., Dovrolis, C.: End-to-end available bandwidth: measurement methodology, dynamics, and relation with TCP throughput. IEEE/ACM Trans. Netw. **11**, 537–549 (2003)
20. Kapoor, R., Chen, L.-J., Lao, L., Gerla, M., Sanadidi, M.Y.: CapProbe: a simple and accurate capacity estimation technique. In: Proceedings of ACM SIGCOMM (2004)
21. Kim, J.C., Lee, Y.: An end-to-end measurement and monitoring technique for the bottleneck link capacity and its available bandwidth. Comput. Netw. **58**, 158–179 (2014)
22. Kiszka, J., Wagner, B., Zhang, Y., Broenink, J.: RTnet - A flexible hard real-time networking framework. In: Proceedings of IEEE ETFA (2005)
23. Lee, K.S., Wang, H., Weatherspoon, H.: SoNIC: precise realtime software access and control of wired networks. In: Proceedings of USENIX NSDI (2013)
24. Linux Foundation. sk_buff. http://www.linuxfoundation.org/collaborate/work-groups/networking/skbuff
25. Luo, X., Chan, E., Chang, R.: Design and implementation of TCP data probes for reliable and metric-rich network path monitoring. In: Proceedings of USENIX ATC (2009)
26. Olsson, R.: pktgen the Linux packet generator. In: Proceedings of Linux Symposium (2005)
27. OpenWrt. https://openwrt.org/
28. Österlind, F., Dunkels, A.: Approaching the maximum 802.15.4 multi-hop throughput. In: Proceedings ACM HotEmNets (2008)
29. Rizzo, L.: Netmap: a novel framework for fast packet I/O. In: Proceedings of USENIX ATC (2012)
30. Xue, L., Luo, X., Shao, Y.: kTRxer: A portable toolkit for reliable internet probing. In: Proceedings of IEEE IWQoS (2014)

Software Defined Networking

What You Need to Know About SDN Flow Tables

Maciej Kuźniar[1]([✉]), Peter Perešíni[1], and Dejan Kostić[2]

[1] EPFL, Lausanne, Switzerland
maciej.kuzniar@epfl.ch
[2] KTH Royal Institute of Technology, Stockholm, Sweden

Abstract. SDN deployments rely on switches that come from various vendors and differ in terms of performance and available features. Understanding these differences and performance characteristics is essential for ensuring successful deployments. In this paper we measure, report, and explain the performance characteristics of flow table updates in three hardware OpenFlow switches. Our results can help controller developers to make their programs efficient. Further, we also highlight differences between the OpenFlow specification and its implementations, that if ignored, pose a serious threat to network security and correctness.

1 Introduction

Background. In OpenFlow-based Software Defined Networking (SDN) deployments [2,5], SDN developers and network administrators (developers for short) write network programs at a logically centralized controller to control the network. The control plane involves the controller communicating with the switches' OpenFlow agents to instruct them how to configure the data plane by sending flow modification commands that place rules in the forwarding tables. OpenFlow's transition from research to production means that the new frameworks are taking reliability and performance [6,12–15] to new levels that are necessary in the production environment. All of these assume quick rule installation latency, and rely on the switches to confirm successful rule installations.

Measuring switch performance is a challenging task. The biggest issue is that each switch under test has many "quirks" which result in unexplained performance changes. Therefore, the thorough evaluation and explanation of these phenomena takes a substantial effort and cannot be easily automated. For example, a switch may have vastly different performance characteristics for similar experiment setups and finding the responsible parameter and its value requires many tests. Same applies to trying out combinations of rule modifications.

Our goal. In this paper, we set out to advance the general understanding of OpenFlow switch performance. Specifically, our focus is on analyzing control plane processing times and flow table update rate in hardware OpenFlow switches that support version 1.0 of this protocol. This paper is *not* about data

© Springer International Publishing Switzerland 2015
J. Mirkovic and Y. Liu (Eds.): PAM 2015, LNCS 8995, pp. 347–359, 2015.
DOI: 10.1007/978-3-319-15509-8_26

plane forwarding performance. Our contributions are as follows: (*i*) we go a step further in measuring OpenFlow switch control plane performance and its interaction with the data plane (for example, we dissect rule installation latency in a number of scenarios that bring the switch to the limit), (*ii*) we devise a more systematic way of switch testing, *i.e.*, along many different dimensions, than the existing work, and (*iii*) we believe we are the first ones to report several new types of anomalous behavior in OpenFlow switches.

Related work. Curtis *et al.* [3] identify and explain the reasons for relatively slow rule installation rate on an HP switch. OFLOPS [16] observed that some OpenFlow agents did not support the barrier command. OFLOPS also reported some delay between the control plane's rule installation and the data plane's ability to forward packets according to the new rule. Huang *et al.* [4] perform switch measurements while trying to build High-Fidelity Switch models, and report slow flow setup rates. Relative to these works, we dissect switch performance at a finer grain, over a longer period of time, and more systematically in terms of rule combinations, initial parameters, etc. In addition, we identify the thresholds that reveal previously unreported anomalous behavior. Jive [11] proposes to build a proactive OpenFlow switch probing engine, and store switch behavior in a database. We show that the switch performance depends on so many factors that such a database would be difficult to create. NOSIX [17] optimizes commands for a particular switch based on its capabilities and performance. However, the authors do not analyze dynamic switch properties as we do; our work would be useful in improving the NOSIX optimization process.

Key findings and impact. Our key findings are as follows: (*i*) control plane performance is widely variable, and it depends on flow table size, priorities, batching of commands and even rule update patterns; (*ii*) switches might periodically or randomly stop processing control plane commands for up to 400 ms; (*iii*) data plane state might not reflect control plane—it might fall behind by up to 400 ms and it might also manifest rule installations in a different order; (*iv*) seemingly atomic data plane updates might not be atomic at all.

The impact of our findings is multifold and profound. The non-atomicity of seemingly atomic data plane updates means that *there are periods when the network configuration is incorrect despite looking correct from the control plane perspective.* The existing tools that check the control plane configuration [7–9] are unable to detect these problems. Moreover, the data plane can fall behind and unfortunately *barriers cannot be trusted.* Thus, the approaches for performing consistent updates need to devise a different way of defining when a rule is installed; otherwise they are not providing any firm guarantees. Our results show that interoperability between switches and controllers cannot be taken for granted. We hope that SDN controller and framework developers will find our findings useful in trying to ensure consistent performance and reliability from the variety of switches they may encounter. Also, efforts that are modeling switch behavior [4] should consult our study.

2   Measurement Methodology

Tools and experimental setup. The main requirements for our tool are (*i*) portability, (*ii*) flexibility, and (*iii*) sufficient precision. First, since the switches we test are often in locations with limited physical access, the measuring tool cannot use customized hardware (*e.g.*, FPGAs). Our previous experience suggests that switches behave unexpectedly, and thus we need to tailor the experiments to locate and dissect problems. Finally, as the tested switches can modify at most a couple thousands of rules per second, we assume that a millisecond measurement precision is sufficient. To achieve the aforementioned goals we built a tool that consists of three major components that correspond to the three benchmarking phases: input generation, measurement and data analysis (Fig. 1).

First, an input generator creates control plane rule modification lists as well as data plane packet traces and saves them to text and pcap files. Unless otherwise specified, the rules match packets based on IP src/dst and forward to a single port. Because we noticed that some switches optimize updates for the same rule, we use consecutive IPs for matches (to make sure we modify different rules), but we also cross-check our results using random matches and update patterns.

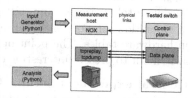

Fig. 1. Overview of our measurement tools and testbed setup.

We refer to the control plane measurement engine as the controller as it emulates the behavior of an OpenFlow controller. We implement it as a module in the NOX controller platform that can issue rule updates at a much higher rate than what the hardware switches can handle.[1] The engine records time of interactions with the switch (*e.g.*, flow modification sent, barrier reply received).

Our experiments require injecting and recording data plane packets to precisely measure when the flow table is updated. We rely on tcpreplay and tcpdump tools to send packets based on a pcap file and record them. To avoid time synchronization issues, the switch is connected to a single host. The host handles the control plane and generates and receives data plane traffic.[2] Network RTT between the host and the switches is between 0.1 and 0.5ms. Finally, an analysis tool reads the outputs and computes the metrics of interest. Modularity lets us easily analyze different aspects of the captured data.

Switches under test. We benchmark three switches with OpenFlow 1.0 support: HP ProCurve 5406zl with K.15.10.0009 firmware, Pica8 P-3290 with PicOS 2.0.4, and Dell PowerConnect 8132 F with beta[3] OpenFlow support (both P-3290 and 8132F belong to the newest generation of OpenFlow switches). They use ProVision, Broadcom Firebolt and Broadcom Trident+ ASICs respectively.

---

[1] Our benchmark with software OpenVSwitch handles ~42000 rule updates/s.

[2] Note that we do not need to fully saturate the switch data plane, and thus a conventional host is capable of handling all of these tasks at the same time.

[3] The software is going to be optimized and productized in a near future.

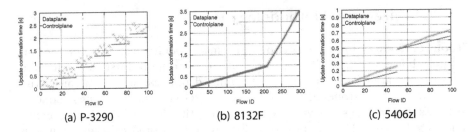

Fig. 2. Control plane confirmations and data plane probes. Data plane updates may fall behind the control plane acknowledgments and may be even reordered.

Such switches have two types of forwarding tables: software and hardware. While hardware table sizes (about 1500, 2000, and 750 rules, respectively) and levels of OpenFlow support vary, we make sure that all test rules ultimately end up in hardware tables. The point of this study is not to advertise or discredit any switch but to present interesting characteristics and to highlight potential issues.

General experiment setup. In most experiments in this paper we use the following generic setup and modify only particular parameters. At the beginning of each experiment we prepopulate the switch flow table with R default priority, non overlapping rules forwarding packets matching flows number $1 - R$ to 0 to port A. After the switch applies this update in the hardware flow table, the measured run starts. We send B batches of rule updates, each batch consisting of: B_D rule deletions, B_M rule modifications and B_A rule insertions followed by a barrier request. In the default setup $B_D = B_A = 1$ and $B_M = 0$. Batch i deletes the rule matching flow number $i - R$ and installs a rule that matches flow i and forwards packets to port A. Note that the total number of rules in the table is stable during the experiment (in contrast to previous work that measures only the time needed to fill an empty table). If the experiment requires injecting and capturing data plane traffic, we send packets that belong to flows F_{start} to F_{end} at a rate of about 1000 packets/s. For clarity, when describing an experiment we change only one parameter. In reality we vary different parameters as well to confirm the observations. Finally, unless an experiment shows variance greater than 5 % across runs, we repeat it three times and report the average.

3   Data Plane

While the only view the controller has of the switch is through the control plane, the traffic forwarding happens in the data plane. In this section we present experiments where we monitor rule updates in the control plane and at the same time send traffic to exercise the updated rules.[4]

---

[4] While experimenting and digging deep to understand the root causes of various behaviors we made other, less critical observations described in a tech report [10].

3.1 Synchronicity of Control and Data Planes

Many solutions essential for correct and reliable OpenFlow deployments (*e.g.*, [12,15]) rely on knowing when the switch applied a given command *in the data plane*, and they resort to using the barrier message for the task.[5] However, as authors of [16] already hinted, the state of the data plane may be different than the one advertised by the control plane. Thus we set out to measure how do these two views correspond to each other at a fine granularity.

We use the default setup extended with one match-all low priority rule that drops all packets[6] and we inject data plane flows number F_{start} to F_{end}. For each update batch i we measure the time when the controller receives a barrier reply for this batch and when the first packet of flow i reaches the destination. To work around the limited rate at which the testing machine can send and capture packets (100000 packets/s), we send traffic in 100-flow parts. Since the results for 5406zl and P-3290 are similar for each part we show plots for only one range. For 8132F we merge the results for three ranges to show the change in behavior.

Results for $R = 300$, $B = 500$, $F_{start} = 1$ with $F_{end} = 100$ (5406zl and P-3290) and $F_{end} = 300$ (8132F) are in Fig. 2. Each switch behaves differently.

5406zl: The data plane configuration of *5406zl is slowly falling behind* the control plane acknowledgments – packets start reaching the destination long after the switch confirms the rule installation with a barrier reply. After about 100 rule updates (we observed that adding or deleting a rule counts as one update, and modifying an existing rule as two), the *switch stops responding with barrier replies for 300 ms*, which allows the flow tables to catch up. After this time the process of diverging starts again. The divergence increases linearly and, in this experiment, reaches up to 82 ms, but *can be as high as 250 ms* depending on the number of rules in the flow table. The 300 ms inactivity time is constant across all experiments we run, but happens three times more often (every 33 updates) if there are over 760 rules in the flow table. Moreover, the frequency and the duration of this period do not depend on the rate at which the controller sends updates, as long as there is at least one update every 300 ms. The final observation is that *5406zl installs rules in the order of their control plane arrival.*

P-3290: Similarly to 5406zl, P-3290 stops responding to barriers in regular intervals. However, unlike 5406zl, it is either processing control plane (handling update commands, responding to barriers), or installing rules in TCAM and never does both at the same time. Moreover, *despite the barriers, the rules are not installed in hardware in the order of arrival.* The delay between data and control plane reaches *up to 400 ms* in this experiment. When all remaining rules get pushed into hardware, the switch starts accepting control plane commands again. We confirmed with a vendor that because the synchronization between

---

[5] As specified, after receiving a barrier request, the switch has to finish processing all previously-received messages before executing any messages after the barrier request. When the processing is complete, the switch must send a barrier reply message [1].

[6] We need to use such a rule to prevent flooding the control channel with the PacketIn messages caused by data plane probes or flooding the probes to all ports.

the software and hardware table is expensive, it is performed in batches and the order of updates in a batch is not guaranteed. When the switch pushes updates to hardware, its CPU is busy and it stops dealing with the control plane.[7]

8132F: Finally, *8132F makes sure that no control plane confirmation is issued before a rule becomes active* in hardware. There are also no periods of idleness as the switch pushes rules to hardware all the time and waits for completion if necessary.[8] Interestingly, the switch starts updating rules quickly, but suddenly slows down after 210 new rules installed and maintains this slower speed (verified up to 2000 batches). However, even after the slowdown, the control plane reliably reflects the state of the data plane configuration.

Summary: To reduce the cost of placing rules in a hardware flow table, vendors allow for different types (e.g., falling behind or reordering) and amounts (e.g., up to 400 ms) of temporary divergence between the hardware and software flow tables. Therefore, the barrier command does not guarantee flow installation. **Ignoring this problem leads to an incorrect network state that may drop packets, or even worse, send them to an undesired destination!**

3.2 Rule Modifications Are not Atomic

Previously, we observed unexpected delays for rule insertions and deletions. A natural next step is to see if modifying existing rules exhibits a similar behavior.

A gap during a FlowMod: As before, we prepopulate the flow table with one low priority match-all rule dropping all packets and $R = 300$ flow specific rules forwarding to port A. Then, we modify these 300 rules to forward to port B. At the same time, we send data plane packets matching rules 101–200 at a rate of 1000 packets/s per flow. For each flow, we record a gap between when the last packet arrives at the interface connected to port A and when the first packet reaches an interface connected to B. Expected time difference is 1ms because of our measurement precision, however, we observe gaps lasting up to 7.7, 12.4 and 190ms on P-3290, 8132F and 5406zl respectively. At 5406zl the longest gaps correspond to the switch inactivity times described earlier (flow 150, 200).

Drops and unexpected actions: To investigate the forwarding gap issue further we add a unique identifier to each packet to detect if they are being lost or reordered. Moreover, to get higher precision, we probe only a single rule (number 151 – a rule with an average gap, and number 150 – a rule with a long gap on 5406zl) and increase our probing rate to 5000 packets/s.

We observe that P-3290 does not drop any packets. A continuous range of packets arrive at port A and the remaining packets at B. On the other hand, both

---

[7] The vendor claims that this limitation occurs only in firmware prior to PicOS 2.2.

[8] We observe periods when the switch does not install rules or respond to the controller, but these periods are rare, non reproducible and seem unrelated to the experiments. We think they are caused by periodic background processing at the switch.

Table 1. Priority handling of overlapping rules. Only 8132F behaves as defined in the OpenFlow specification.

Switch	Observed/inferred behavior
P-3290	May temporarily reorder for overlapping matches (depending on wildcards). OK for the same match.
8132F	OK (Note: May temporarily reorder if not separated by a barrier)
5406zl	Ignores priority, last updated rule permanently wins

8132F and 5406zl drop packets at the transition period for rule 151 (3 and 17 packets respectively). For rule number 150, 5406zl drops an unacceptable number of 782 packets. When we replace the drop-all rule with a rule that forwards all traffic to port C, identifiers of packets captured on port C for both 5406zl and 8132F fit exactly between the series at ports A and B. This suggests that the *update is not atomic*—a rule modification deactivates the old version and inserts the new one, with none of them forwarding packets during the transition.

To further investigate this behavior, we repeat the experiment with no low priority rule at all. Both switches flood packets to all ports during the transition. While it follows the no match behavior of 8132F, it is surprising for 5406zl, since by default non-matching packets cause PacketIn messages. The only imperfection of P-3290 is that if the output port of the same rule gets updated between ports A and B frequently, some packets arrive at the destination out of order.

*Summary: Two out of three tested switches have a transition period during a rule modification when the network configuration is neither in the initial nor the final state. **The observed action of forwarding packets to undesired ports is a security concern.** Non-atomic flow modification contradicts the assumption usually made by controller developers and network update solutions. Our results suggest that either switches should be redesigned or the assumptions made by the controllers have to be revisited to guarantee network correctness.*

3.3 Priorities and Overlapping Rules

The OpenFlow specification clarifies that, if rules overlap (*i.e.*, two rules match the same packet), packets should always be processed only by the highest priority matching rule. Since our default setup with IP src/dst matches prevents rule overlapping, we run an additional experiment to verify the behavior of switches when rules overlap. We install rules that can match the same packet: R_{hi} that has a higher priority and forwards to port A, and R_{lo} that forwards to B. R_{hi} is always installed before and removed after R_{lo} to prevent packets from matching R_{lo}. Initially, there is one low priority drop-all rule and 150 pairs of R_{hi} and R_{lo}. Then we send 500 update batches, each removing and adding one rule: $(-R_{lo,1}, +R_{hi,151}), (-R_{hi,1}, +R_{lo,151}), (-R_{lo,2}, +R_{hi,152}), \ldots$ We send data plane traffic for 100 flows. If a switch works correctly, no packets should reach port B.

Table 2. Dimensions of experimental parameters we report in this section. Note that we also run experiments for other combinations to verify the conclusions.

Experiment	In-flight batches	Batch size (del+add)	Initial rules R
In-flight batches	1–20	1+1	300
Flow table size	2	1+1	50 to max for switch
Priorities	as in Flow table size + a single low priority rule in the flow table		
Access patterns	2	1+1	50 to max for switch + priorities
Working set	as in Flow table size, vary # of rules that are not updated during the experiment		
Batch size	2	1+1 to 20+20	300

Table 1 summarizes the results. First, as we already noted, 8132F does not reorder updates between batches and therefore, there are no packets captured at port B. The only way to allow some packets on port B is to increase the batch size – the switch freely reorders updates inside a batch (which is allowed by the specification) and seems to push them to hardware in order of priorities. On the other hand, P-3290 applies updates in the correct order only if the high priority rule has the IP source specified. Otherwise, for a short period of time—210 ms on average, 410 ms maximum in the described experiment—packets follow the low priority rule. Our hypothesis is that the software flow table data structure sorts the rules such that when they are moved to hardware the ones with IP source specified are pushed first. Finally, in 5406zl, only the first few packets of each flow (for 80 ms on average, 103 ms max in this experiment) are forwarded to A and all the rest to B. We conclude that the switch ignores priorities in hardware (as documented for the older firmware version) and treats rules installed later as more important. We confirm this hypothesis with additional experiments not reported here. Further, because the priorities are trimmed in hardware, installing rules with the same match but different priorities and actions causes an error.

Summary: *Results (Table 1) suggest that switches may permanently or temporarily forward according to incorrect, low priority rules.*

4   Flow Table Update Speed

The goal of the next set of experiments is to pinpoint the most important aspects that affect rule update speed. From the previous section we know that although the control plane information is imprecise, in a long run the error becomes negligible (all switches synchronize the data and control plane views regularly). We first identify various performance-related parameters: the number of in-flight commands, current flow table size, size of request batches, used priorities, rule access patterns. Then we sample the whole space of these parameters and try to identify the ones that cause some variation. Based on the results, we select a few experimental configurations which highlight most of our findings in Table 2.

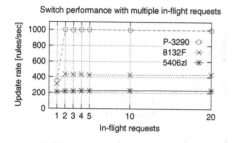

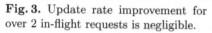

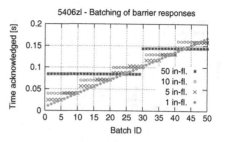

Fig. 3. Update rate improvement for over 2 in-flight requests is negligible.

Fig. 4. 5406zl barrier reply arrivals. It holds replies for up to 29 requests.

4.1 Two In-Flight Batches Keep the Switch Busy

The number of commands a controller should send to the switch before receiving any acknowledgments is an important design decision [14]. Underutilizing or overloading the switch with commands is undesired. Here, we quantify the tradeoff between rule update rate and the servicing delay (time between sending a command and the switch applying it) to find a performance sweet spot.

We use the default setup with $R = 300$ and $B = 2000$ batches of rule updates. The controller sends batch $i + k$ only when it receives a barrier reply for batch number i. We vary k and report the average update rate, which we compute as $(1 + 1) * B$ (because each batch contains one add and one delete) divided by the time between sending the first batch and receiving a barrier reply for the last.

Figure 3 shows the average rate across eight runs. The rule update rate with one outstanding batch is low as the switch is idle for at least a network RTT. However, even two in-flight batches are sufficient to saturate all tested switches given our network latencies. Thus, we use 2 in-flight batches in all experiments.

Looking deeper into the results, we notice that with a changing number of in-flight batches 5406zl responds in an unexpected way. In Fig. 4 we plot the barrier reply arrival times normalized to the time when the first batch was sent for $R = 300$, $B = 50$ and a number of in-flight batches varying between 1 and 50. We show the results for only 4 values to improve readability. If there are requests in the queue, the switch batches the responses and sends them together in bigger groups. If a continuous stream of requests is shorter than 30, the switch waits to process all, otherwise, the first response comes after 29 requests.

Summary: We demonstrated that with LAN latencies two in-flight batches suffice to achieve full switch performance. Since, many in-flight requests increase the service time, controllers should send only a handful of requests at a time.

4.2 Current Flow Table Size Matters

The number of rules stored in a flow table is a very important parameter of a switch. Bigger tables allow for a fine grained traffic control. However, there is a

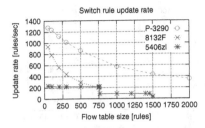

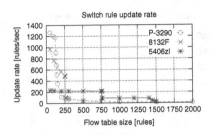

Fig. 5. Update rate decreases when the number of rules in the flow table grows.

Fig. 6. Priorities cripple performance. One low-priority rule significantly decreases update rate.

well known tradeoff—TCAM space is expensive, so tables that allow for complex matches usually have limited size. We discover another, hidden cost of full flow tables. We use the default setup fixing $B = 2000$ and changing the value of R.

In Fig. 5 we report the average rule update rate. There are two distinct patterns. Both P-3290 and 8132F express similar behavior—the rule update rate is high with a small number of entries in the flow table but quickly deteriorates as this number increases. As we confirmed with one of the vendors and deduced based on statistics of the other switch, there are two reasons why the performance drops. First, even if a switch installs rules in hardware, it keeps a software flow table copy as well. The flows are first updated in the software data structure which takes more time when the structure is bigger. Second, the rules need to be pushed into hardware (the switch ASIC), which may require rearranging the existing entries. On the other hand, 5406zl maintains a lower, but stable rate following a step function with a breaking point around 760 rules in the flow table. This stability is caused by periods of inactivity explained in Sect. 3.

Summary: The performance of all tested switches drops with a number of installed rules, but the absolute values and the slope of this drop vary. Therefore, controller developers should not only take into account the total flow table size, but also what is the performance cost of filling the table with additional rules.

4.3 Priorities Decrease the Update Rate

Next, we conduct an experiment that mimics a situation where a lowest priority all-matching rule drops all packets that do not match any other rule. The experiment setup is exactly the same as the one described in Sect. 4.2 with one additional lowest priority drop-all rule installed before all flow-specific rules.

Figure 6 shows that for a low flow table occupancy, all switches perform comparably as without the low priority rule. However, P-3290 and 8132F suffer from a significant drop in performance at about 130 and 255 installed rules respectively. After this massive drop, the rate gradually decreases until it reaches 12 updates/s for 2000 rules in the flow table for P-3290 and 30 updates/s for 750 rules in the flow table for 8132F where both switches have their tables almost full.

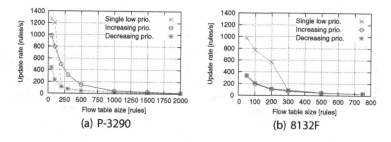

Fig. 7. Switch rule update performance for different rule access patterns.

Interestingly, 5406zl's update rate does not decrease so much, possibly because it ignores the priorities. We confirm that the results are not affected by the fully wildcarded match or the drop action in the low priority rule by replacing it with a specific IP src/dst match and a forwarding action.

Finally, we rerun the experiments from Sect. 4.1 with a low priority rule. The absolute rates are lower, but the characteristics and the conclusions hold.

More priorities: Now, we check what is the effect of using different priorities for each rule. We modify the default set-up such that each rule has a different priority assigned and install them in an increasing or decreasing order.

Switches react differently: P-3290's and 8132F's performance follows a similar curve as in the previous experiment, but there is no breaking point (Fig. 7). In both cases the rate is higher with one different priority rule until the breaking point, after which they equalize. Moreover, P-3290 updates rules quicker in the increasing priority order (consistent with [11], but the difference is smaller as for each addition we also delete a rule). 5406zl is unaffected by the priorities, but our data plane study shows a serious divergence between the control plane reports and the reality for this switch in this experiment (see Trivia in [10]).

Working set size: Finally, we check what happens if only a small subset of rules in the table (later referred as "working set") is frequently updated. We modify the default setup such that batch i deletes the rule matching flow $i - W$ and installs a rule matching flow i. We vary the value of W. In other words, the first $R - W$ rules never change and we update only the last W rules.

The results show that 5406zl's performance remains the same as presented in Figs. 5 and 6. Further, for both P-3290 and 8132F a small update working set makes no difference if there is no low priority rule. For a given R (1000 for P-3290 and 500 for 8132F in Fig. 8), the performance is constant regardless of W. However, with the low priority rule installed, the update rate characteristic changes (Fig. 8). For both switches, as long as the update working set is smaller than their breaking point revealed in Sect. 4.2, the performance stays as if there was no drop rule. After the breaking point, it degrades and is marginally worse compared to the results in Sect. 4.2 for table size W.

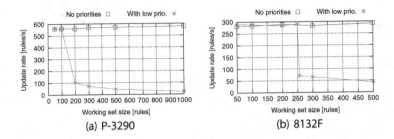

Fig. 8. Size of the rule working set affects the performance. For both P-3290 and 8132F with low priority rule, the performance depends mostly on the number of rules constantly updated and not on the total number of installed rules.

Summary: The switch performance is difficult to predict—a single rule can degrade the update rate of a switch by an order of magnitude. Controller developers should be aware of such behavior and avoid potential sources of inefficiencies.

4.4   Rule Modifications Are Slower than Additions and Deletions

We run the same experiments as described in previous subsections, but modifying existing rules instead. Because the results are very similar, we do not report them here in detail. All plots follow the same curves, but in general the update rate is between 0.5x and 0.75x of the rate for additions and deletions for P-3290 and 8132F. For 5406zl the difference is much smaller and stays within 12 %.

5   Conclusions and Future Work

In this paper we try to shed light on the state of OpenFlow switches – an essential component of relatively new, but quickly developing Software Defined Networks. The main takeaway is that despite a common interface, the switches are more diverse than one would expect, and this diversity has to be taken into account when building controllers. Because of the limited resources, we obtained sufficiently long access only to three switches. In the future, we plan to keep extending this study with additional devices to obtain the full picture.

Acknowledgments. We thank Marco Canini, Dan Levin and Miguel Peón for helping us get access to the tested switches. We also thank Pica8 and Dell representatives for quick responses and explanations. We thank the reviewers, who provided excellent feedback. The research leading to these results has received funding from the European Research Council under the European Union's Seventh Framework Programme (FP7/2007–2013) / ERC grant agreement 259110.

References

1. OpenFlow Switch Specification. http://www.openflow.org/documents/openflow-spec-v1.0.0.pdf
2. Ethernet Switch Market: Who's Winning? (2014). http://www.networkcomputing.com/networking/d/d-id/1234913
3. Curtis, A., Mogul, J., Tourrilhes, J., Yalagandula, P.: DevoFlow: scaling flow management for high-performance networks. In: SIGCOMM (2011)
4. Huang, D.Y., Yocum, K., Snoeren, A.C.: High-fidelity switch models for software-defined network emulation. In: HotSDN (2013)
5. Jain, S., Kumar, A., Mandal, S., Ong, J., Poutievski, I., Singh, A., Venkata, S., Wanderer, J., Zhou, J., Zhu, M., Zolla, J., Hölzle, U., Stuart, S., Vahdat, A.: B4: Experience with a globally-deployed software defined WAN. In: SIGCOMM (2013)
6. Katta, N.P., Rexford, J., Walker, D.: Incremental consistent updates. In: HotSDN (2013)
7. Kazemian, P., Chang, M., Zeng, H., Varghese, G., McKeown, N., Whyte, S.: Real time network policy checking using header space analysis. In: NSDI (2013)
8. Kazemian, P., Varghese, G., McKeown, N.: Header space analysis: static checking for networks. In: NSDI (2012)
9. Khurshid, A., Zou, X., Zhou, W., Caesar, M., Godfrey, P.B.: VeriFlow: verifying network-wide invariants in real time. In: NSDI (2013)
10. Kuźniar, M., Perešíni, P., Kostić, D.: What you need to know about SDN control and data planes. Technical report EPFL-REPORT-199497, EPFL (2014)
11. Lazaris, A., Tahara, D., Huang, X., Li, L.E., Voellmy, A., Yang, Y.R., Yu, M.: Jive: performance driven abstraction and optimization for SDN. In: ONS (2014)
12. Liu, H.H., Wu, X., Zhang, M., Yuan, L., Wattenhofer, R., Maltz, D.A.: zUpdate: updating data center networks with zero loss. In: SIGCOMM (2013)
13. Mahajan, R., Wattenhofer, R.: On consistent updates in software defined networks. In: HotNets (2013)
14. Perešíni, P., Kuźniar, M., Canini, M., Kostić, D.: ESPRES: transparent SDN update scheduling. In: HotSDN (2014)
15. Reitblatt, M., Foster, N., Rexford, J., Schlesinger, C., Walker, D.: Abstractions for network update. In: SIGCOMM (2012)
16. Rotsos, C., Sarrar, N., Uhlig, S., Sherwood, R., Moore, A.W.: OFLOPS: an open framework for openflow switch evaluation. In: Taft, N., Ricciato, F. (eds.) PAM 2012. LNCS, vol. 7192, pp. 85–95. Springer, Heidelberg (2012)
17. Yu, M., Wundsam, A., Raju, M.: NOSIX: a lightweight portability layer for the SDN OS. ACM SIGCOMM Comput. Commun. Rev. 44(2), 28–35 (2014)

Software-Defined Latency Monitoring in Data Center Networks

Curtis Yu[1]([⊠]), Cristian Lumezanu[2], Abhishek Sharma[2],
Qiang Xu[2], Guofei Jiang[2], and Harsha V. Madhyastha[3]

[1] University of California, Riverside, USA
cyu@cs.ucr.edu
[2] NEC Labs America, Princeton, NJ, USA
[3] University of Michigan, Ann Arbor, USA

Abstract. Data center network operators have to continually monitor
path latency to quickly detect and re-route traffic away from high-delay
path segments. Existing latency monitoring techniques in data centers
rely on either (1) actively sending probes from end-hosts, which is
restricted in some cases and can only measure end-to-end latencies, or
(2) passively capturing and aggregating traffic on network devices, which
requires hardware modifications.

In this work, we explore another opportunity for network path latency
monitoring, enabled by software-defined networking. We propose SLAM,
a latency monitoring framework that dynamically sends specific probe
packets to trigger control messages from the first and last switches of a
path to a centralized controller. SLAM then estimates the latency distribution along a path based on the arrival timestamps of the control
messages at the controller. Our experiments show that the latency distributions estimated by SLAM are sufficiently accurate to enable the
detection of latency spikes and the selection of low-latency paths in a
data center.

1 Introduction

Many data center applications such as search, e-commerce, and banking are
latency-sensitive [3,7]. These applications often have several distributed components (*e.g.*, front-end, application server, storage) that need to communicate
across low-latency network paths to reduce application response times. To effectively manage data center networks and provide fast paths, operators must continually monitor the latency on all paths that the traffic of an application could
traverse and quickly route packets away from high-delay segments [1,5].

Operators can monitor path latency *from the edge* by sending probes (*e.g.*,
ICMP requests) between servers and measuring response times. However, three
factors complicate this approach. First, some data centers (e.g., collocation centers [14]) restrict access to customer servers. Second, end-to-end probes cannot
monitor the latency on path segments between arbitrary network devices, which
is helpful in identifying sources of high delay. Finally, operators are reluctant

© Springer International Publishing Switzerland 2015
J. Mirkovic and Y. Liu (Eds.): PAM 2015, LNCS 8995, pp. 360–372, 2015.
DOI: 10.1007/978-3-319-15509-8_27

to repeatedly run expensive measurements from the edge and prefer to allocate server resources to customer VMs [12].

The alternative is to monitor latencies *from inside the network* by capturing information about paths directly from network devices. Trajectory sampling [6] and *l2ping* are examples of this approach. Such solutions incur the overhead of performing real-time local coordination and aggregating measurements captured at many devices. Recent work proposes to instrument switches with a hash-based primitive that records packet timestamps and measures network latency with microsecond-level accuracy [10, 11]. However, these methods need hardware modifications that may not be available in regular switches anytime soon.

In this paper, we explore another opportunity to monitor path latency in data center networks, enabled by software-defined networks (SDNs). We develop SLAM, a framework for **S**oftware-defined **LA**tency **M**onitoring between any two network switches, that does not require specialized hardware or access to end-hosts. SLAM uses the SDN control plane to manage and customize probe packets and trigger notifications upon their arrival at switches. It measures latency based on the notifications' arrival times at the control plane.

SLAM is deployed on the network controller and computes latency estimates on a path in three steps. *(setup)* It installs specific monitoring rules on all switches on the path; these rules instruct every switch to forward the matched packets to the next switch on the path; the first and last switches also generate notifications (*e.g.*, PacketIn) to the controller. *(probe)* SLAM sends probes that are constructed to match only the monitoring rules and that traverse only the monitored path. *(estimate)* It estimates the path's latency based on the times at which the notification messages (triggered by the same probe) from the first and last switches of the path are received at the controller.

SLAM offers several advantages over existing latency monitoring techniques. First, by exploiting control packets inherent to SDN, SLAM requires neither switch hardware modifications nor access to endhosts. Second, SLAM enables the measurement of latency between arbitrary OpenFlow-enabled switches. Finally, by computing latency estimates at the controller, SLAM leverages the visibility offered by SDNs without needing complex scheduling of measurements on switches or end-hosts. Moreover, SLAM's concentration of monitoring logic at the controller is well-suited to the centralized computation of low latency routes that is typical to SDNs. Compared to OpenNetMon [15], a similar approach, SLAM detects and adjusts for real-world deployment issues.

We address three key issues in our design of SLAM. First, latencies on data center network paths are small—on the order of milli- or even micro-seconds—and vary continually, due predominantly to changing queue sizes. As a result, any single latency estimate may become invalid between when it is measured by SLAM and when it is used to make rerouting decisions. Therefore, instead of a single latency estimate for a path, we design SLAM to infer the latency distribution over an interval. A latency distribution that shows high latencies for a sustained period of time can be more instrumental in inferring high-delay segments in the network.

Second, since SLAM's latency estimation is based on the timings of PacketIn's received at the controller, the accuracy of latency estimates depends on both end switches on the path taking the same amount of time to process notification messages and send them to the controller. However, in reality, the delay incurred in a switch's processing of the action field of a matched rule and its subsequent generation of a notification (*i.e.*, PacketIn) depends on the utilization of the switch CPU, which varies continually. Moreover, switches are generally not equidistant from the controller. To account for these factors, for every switch, SLAM continually monitors the switch's internal control path latency and its latency to the controller (via EchoRequest messages) and adjusts its estimation of the latency distribution.

Lastly, despite SLAM's benefits, its probing overhead is the same as that associated with probes issued from end-hosts. To alleviate this cost, we also explore the feasibility of SLAM in a reactive OpenFlow deployment, where new flows always trigger PacketIn messages from every switch. The key idea is for SLAM to use the existing OpenFlow control traffic without requiring monitoring probes to trigger additional PacketIn messages. We use a real enterprise network trace to show that SLAM would be able to capture latency samples from most switch-to-switch links every two seconds by relying solely on PacketIn's triggered by normal data traffic.

We deploy and evaluate a preliminary version of SLAM on an OpenFlow-based SDN testbed and find that it can accurately detect latency inflations of tens of milliseconds. SLAM works even in the presence of increase control traffic, showing a median latency variation of a few milliseconds when the switch has to process up to 150 control messages per second. Although not suitable to detect very fine variations in latency, SLAM is quick and accurate in identifying high-delay paths from a centralized location and with little overhead.

2   Background

We first describe the operation of a typical OpenFlow network and discuss the factors that contribute to the latency experienced by a packet that traverses it.

2.1   OpenFlow

We consider a network of OpenFlow-enabled switches, connected with a logically centralized controller using a secure, lossless TCP connection. The controller enforces network policies by translating them into low-level configurations and inserting them into the switch flow tables using the OpenFlow protocol.

The network configuration consists of the forwarding rules installed on switches. Every rule consists of a bit string (with 0, 1, and * as characters) that specifies which packets match the rule, one or more actions to be performed by the switch on matched packets, and a set of counters which collect statistics about matched traffic. Possible actions include "forward to physical port", "forward to controller", "drop", etc.

The controller installs rules either proactively, *i.e.*, at the request of the application or the operator, or reactively, *i.e.*, triggered by a PacketIn message from a switch as follows. When the first packet of a new flow arrives, the switch looks for a matching rule in the flow table and performs the associated action. If there is no matching entry, the switch buffers the packet and notifies the controller by sending a PacketIn control message containing the packet header. The controller responds with a FlowMod message that installs a new rule matching the flow into the switch's flow table. The controller may also forward the packet without installing a rule using a PacketOut message.

2.2 Data Center Path Latency

A packet traversing a network path experiences *propagation delay* and *switching delay*. Propagation delay is the time the packet spends on the medium between switches and depends on the physical properties of the medium. The propagation speed is considered to be about two thirds of the speed of light in vacuum [16]. The switching delay is the time the packet spends within a switch and depends on the various functions applied to the packet. In general, the switching delay in an OpenFlow switch has three components: lookup, forwarding, and control. We describe them below and use Fig. 1 to illustrate.

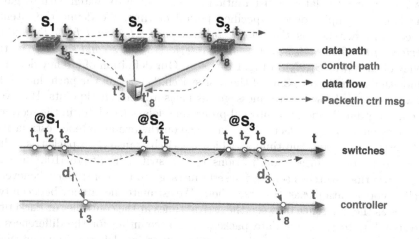

Fig. 1. Latency computation using control message timestamps. Consider a packet traversing a path comprising switches S_1, S_2, and S_3. The packet arrives at these switches at t_1, t_4, and t_6 and leaves at t_2, t_5, and t_7. The true latency between S_1 and S_3 is $t_7 - t_2$. The matching rule at switches S_1 and S_3 has the additional action "send to controller" to generate PacketIn's (the red dotted lines). t_3 and t_8 are the times when the PacketIn's leave S_1 and S_3, and they arrive at the controller at t'_3 and t'_8. d_1 and d_3 are the propagation delays from switches S_1 and S_3 to the controller. We use $(t'_8 - d_3) - (t'_3 - d_1)$ to estimate the latency between S_1 and S_3, after accounting for the processing times in each switch (see Sect. 3) (Color figure online).

Lookup. When a switch receives a packet on one of its input ports, the switch looks for a match in its forwarding table to determine where to forward the packet. This function is usually performed by a dedicated ASIC on parts of the packet header.

Forwarding. A matched packet is transferred through the internal switching system from the input port to an output port. If the output link is transmitting another packet, the new packet is placed in the output queue. The time a packet spends in the queue depends on what other traffic traverses the same output port and the priority of that traffic. In general, forwarding delays dominate lookup delays [16]. The intervals $[t_1, t_2]$, $[t_4, t_5]$, and $[t_6, t_7]$ represent the combined lookup and forwarding delays at switches S_1, S_2, and S_3 in Fig. 1.

Control. If there is no match for the packet in the flow table or if the match action is *"send to controller"*, the switch CPU encapsulates part or all of the packet in a PacketIn control message and sends it to the controller. The control delay is the time it takes the PacketIn to reach the controller ($[t_2, t_3']$ and $[t_7, t_8']$ in Fig. 1).

3   Latency Monitoring with SLAM

SLAM computes the latency distribution for any switch-to-switch path by gathering latency samples over a specified period of time. We define the latency between two switches as *the time it takes a packet to travel from the output interface of the first switch to the output interface of the second switch*, e.g., the latency of the path (S_1, S_3) in Fig. 1 is $t_7 - t_2$. Our definition of latency does not include the internal processing of the first switch, $t_2 - t_1$, on the path due to the way we use OpenFlow control messages as measurement checkpoints. However, since we continually monitor internal processing delays (see later in the section), we can account for any effects they may have on the overall latency estimation.

Directly measuring the time at which a switch transmits a packet is either expensive [6] or requires modifications to the switch hardware [10]. Instead, we propose that switches send a PacketIn message to the controller whenever a specific type of data packet traverses them. We estimate the latency between two switches as the difference between the arrival times at the controller of PacketIn's corresponding to the same data packet, after accounting for the differences in internal processing of the two switches and propagation delays to the controller. In Fig. 1, the estimated latency is $(t_8' - d_3) - (t_3' - d_1)$.

We incorporate these ideas into the design of SLAM, an OpenFlow controller module that estimates the latency distribution between any two OpenFlow switches in a network. Next, we discuss how to generate and send probes that trigger PacketIn messages and how to calibrate our latency distribution to the differences in control processing latency between switches. We then describe the design of SLAM.

3.1   Latency Monitoring

To estimate latency on a path, SLAM generates probe packets that traverse the path and trigger PacketIn messages at the first and last switches on the path. To guide a probe along an arbitrary path, we pre-install forwarding rules at switches along the path, whose action field instructs the switch to send matched packets to the next-hop switch. In addition, to generate PacketIn's, the rules at the first and last switch on the path contain "send to controller" as part of their action set. SLAM sends monitoring probes using PacketOut messages to the first switch on the path. Our method is similar to the one proposed by OpenNetMon [15], but we explore the implications of using such a system, including its issues, and quantify this effect on the final result.

An important requirement is that the monitoring rules we install to guide the probes do not interfere with normal traffic, *i.e.*, only our probes match against them. For this, we make the rules very specific by not using wildcards and specifying exact values for as many match fields as possible (*e.g.*, VLAN tag, TCP or UDP port numbers, etc.). To save space on switches, we also set the rules to expire once the monitoring is finished by setting their hard timeout.

3.2   Control Processing

We define the *control processing time* of a switch as the time it takes a switch to process the action included in the rule that matches a packet, generate a PacketIn, and send it to the controller. In Fig. 1, $t'_3 - t_2$ and $t'_8 - t_7$ are the control processing times for S_1 and S_3. Control processing times determine when PacketIn messages arrive at the controller. If processing times vary across the first and last switch, the latency estimation on the path is skewed.

Control processing consists of slow path delay and control channel delay. The slow path delay is the time it takes the switch to transfer the packet along its internal circuits from the ASIC where the match is performed to the switch CPU that generates the PacketIn. As shown in prior work [4], the slow path delay depends on what other operations (*e.g.*, flow installations, stat queries) are performed simultaneously on the switch. The control channel delay is the propagation delay from the switch to the controller.

We adapt to the variations in control processing across switches by constantly monitoring both the slow path and control channel delays. To monitor the slow path delay of a switch, we send packet probes to the switch using PacketOut, use a carefully placed rule to trigger a PacketIn, and then drop the probe without forwarding it to other switches. This resembles our path latency estimation method described above, with the modification that the path to be monitored consists of one switch. We discard latency samples obtained during periods when the slow path delays of the first and last switches on a path vary. Predicting how each variation affects our latency estimate is subject of future work.

To monitor the control channel delay on a switch, we send EchoRequest Open-Flow control messages to the switch and measure the delay in its replies. We find that the control channel delay from the controller to switch is more predictable.

Thus, if we discover that switches are not equidistant to the controller, we simply adjust the estimated latency by the difference in their control channel delays, as hinted earlier in the section.

3.3   Monitoring Design

We have developed SLAM, a framework for latency monitoring in SDNs, based on the methods enumerated above. SLAM combines four components—rule generator, traffic generator, traffic listener, and latency estimator—that run on the network controller (Fig. 2).

Given a path to monitor, SLAM identifies the first and last switches on the path. It then installs a specific rule on each switch on the path to guide measurement probes, as explained above. The traffic generator then sends a stream of packet probes along the monitored path using OpenFlow PacketOut messages. These packets match the specific rules installed in the previous step. Normal traffic is processed by the original rules on the switches and is not affected by our monitoring rules. In addition, the measurement module generates probes to monitor the slow path and control channel delays of the first and last switches on a monitored path.

The traffic listener captures control packets received from switches and records their arrival timestamps. To obtain a latency sample, it then correlates PacketIn messages associated with the same probe packet and triggered by different switches. By aggregating the latency samples obtained from multiple probes sent on a path, SLAM computes a latency distribution for the path.

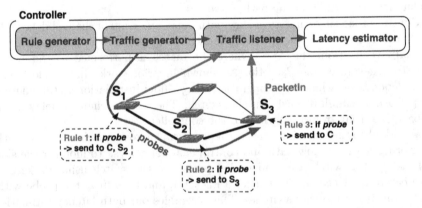

Fig. 2. SLAM design. SLAM generates probe packets along the path to be monitored. The probes are guided by carefully specified rules and trigger PacketIn messages at the first and last switches on the path. SLAM analyzes PacketIn arrival times and estimates path latency.

4   Evaluation

We implemented SLAM as a module for the POX OpenFlow controller and deployed it on our 12-switch network testbed. We evaluate SLAM from three aspects: (1) the accuracy of its latency estimates, (2) its utility in selecting paths based on latency, and (3) its adaptiveness to network conditions.

Ground truth estimation. To evaluate the quality of SLAM's path latency estimates, we must first measure the real path latency (*i.e.*, the ground truth). As we cannot directly time packet arrival and departure on switches, we use the following setup to measure ground truth, similar to that used for OpenFlow testing by Rotsos *et al.* [13] and by Huang *et al.* [8]. We create another physical connection between the first and last switches on a path and the controller in addition to the already existing control channel and put the controller on the data plane.

We use the controller to send probe packets along the path to be monitored. When a probe arrives at the first switch, the action of the matching rule sends the packet both to the next switch on the path and to the controller on the data plane. Similarly, at the last switch, the matching rule sends probe packets back to the controller. We obtain the ground truth latency by subtracting the two arrival times of the same probe at the controller. This method is similar to that used by SLAM, with the difference that no packet ever crosses into the control plane. Although the computed latency may not perfectly reflect the ground truth, it does not contain the effects of control processing, and hence, can be used as a reasonable estimate to compare against SLAM's estimated latency distribution.

Experiments. To evaluate SLAM's performance under different network conditions, we perform three sets of experiments: low latency (*Exp L*), medium latency (*Exp M*), and high latency (*Exp H*). We estimate latency between the same pair of switches in our testbed, but each of the three experiments takes place on a different path between the switches. There is no background traffic for the low latency experiment. For medium and high latency experiments, we introduce additional traffic using *iperf* and simulate congestion by shaping traffic at an intermediate switch on the path. We use 200 Mbps *iperf* traffic with 100 Mbps traffic shaping in *Exp M*, and 20 Mbps *iperf* traffic with 10 Mbps traffic shaping in *Exp H*. In each experiment, we run both SLAM and the ground truth estimator concurrently for 10 min with a rate of one probe per second.

4.1   Accuracy

First, we seek to understand how similar to ground truth is the latency distribution computed by SLAM. To compare two latency distributions (of different paths or of the same path under different conditions), we use the Kolmogorov-Smirnov (KS) test [9]. The KS test computes a statistic that captures the distance between the empirical cumulative distribution functions (CDFs) of the two sets of latencies. The null hypothesis is that the two sets of latencies are drawn from the same distribution. If we can reject the null hypothesis based on the test

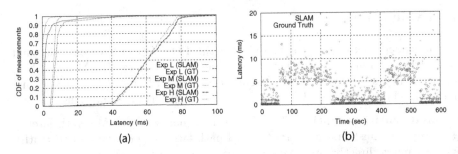

Fig. 3. (a) SLAM vs. Ground truth latency empirical CDFs. (b) SLAM with bursty traffic. As path latency increases, SLAM is able to correctly detect the increase.

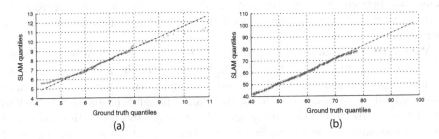

Fig. 4. Quantile-Quantile plots for SLAM vs. ground truth in (b) *Exp M*, and (c) *Exp H*. The quantiles for SLAM's estimates are close to the quantiles for ground truth estimates, indicating that SLAM is able to detect millisecond-level path latency variations.

statistic, then this implies that the two distributions are not equal. Further, we can compare the quantiles of the two distributions (*e.g.*, median) to determine if one path has lower latencies than the other. Figure 3(a) shows that, although SLAM overestimates the ground truth for under-millisecond latencies, it is able to match the ground truth latency distribution as the path latency increases. Indeed, the KS test does not reject the null hypothesis for *Exp M* and *Exp H*.

Figures 4(a) and (b) show the Quantile-Quantile (Q-Q) plots for *Exp M* and *Exp H*, respectively. We remove outliers by discarding the bottom and top 10 % (5 %) of SLAM's latency estimates for *Exp M* (*Exp H*). Except for a small number of very low and high quantiles, the quantiles for SLAM's estimates are equal or close to the quantiles for ground truth estimates; most of the points in the Q-Q plot lie on the $y = x$ line.

4.2 Filtering Out High Latency Paths

SLAM can help network operators identify low-latency paths. For a collection of paths, we can use the pairwise KS test to first select a subset of paths whose distribution are different from each other, and then filter out paths with high latency quantiles. Similarly, when monitoring a path, an operator can first use the KS test to determine if its latency distribution has changed (*e.g.*, due to

Table 1. Comparison of the 50th, 75th, 90th, and 95th percentile values for *Exp M* and *Exp H*.

Exp #	50th %tile	75th %tile	90th %tile	95th %tile
Exp M	7.47 ms	8.66 ms	11.6 ms	19.2 ms
Exp H	60.0 ms	71.9 ms	76.8 ms	78.0 ms

change in traffic) and then use the latency quantile values to decide whether to continue using it or switch to a different path. For instance, in our experiments, when we compare samples from *Exp M* and *Exp H*, the KS test rejects the null hypothesis, *i.e.*, the latency distribution on the monitored path has changed due to change in traffic. Table 1 shows that four quantiles for the two samples differ significantly. This is confirmed by Fig. 3(a), where empirical CDFs of the measurements collected by SLAM for *Exp M* and *Exp H* are clearly different. SLAM's use of KS test, in combination with latency quantiles, is more robust because an operator can be confident that the difference in latency quantiles across paths or on the same path over time is statistically significant.

4.3 Sensitivity to Network Conditions

Next, we study SLAM's accuracy in the presence of bursty data traffic and increased control channel traffic.

Data traffic. To see if variable traffic affects SLAM's latency estimates, we repeat *Exp H*, but instead of running *iperf* continuously, we run it in bursts of variable size. Figure 3(b) shows how latency varies over time as we introduce and remove traffic from the network. SLAM's estimates adapt well to changes in the ground truth latency triggered by introducing congestion in the network. Like the results shown in Fig. 3(a), SLAM over-estimates latency when path latency is low but accurately captures latency spikes. These results further confirm SLAM's effectiveness in enabling data center networks to route traffic away from segments on which latency increases by tens of milliseconds.

Control traffic. We monitor the slow path delay of switches in our network while we introduce two types of control traffic: FlowMod, by repeatedly inserting forwarding rules, and PacketIn, by increasing the number of probes that match a rule whose action is "send to controller". We varied the control packet rate from 1 to 20 per second and observed a median increase of 1.28 ms. Varying the amount of concurrent rule installations from 0 to 150 rules per second resulted in a median increase of 2.13 ms. Thus, the amount of unrelated control traffic in the network does not influence SLAM's effectiveness in detecting high-delay paths.

5   Reactive OpenFlow Deployments

So far, we considered a proactive OpenFlow deployment for SLAM, where normal data packets always have a matching rule and do not trigger PacketIn messages. Another option is to use a reactive deployment, in which switches notify the controller of incoming packets without a matching rule by sending a PacketIn control message. Because too many such control messages could overload the controller and make the network unusable [2], reactive deployments are limited to smaller enterprises and data centers with tens of switches or when the network must react to traffic changes automatically.

Reactive networks provide a significant advantage for SLAM: it can use existing PacketIn messages to compute path latency distributions. This eliminates the need to insert expensive probes to trigger PacketIn's and reduces the cost of monitoring by using already existing control traffic [17]. However, there are two disadvantages, which we discuss at large next.

5.1   Variations in Control Processing

Using reactive PacketIn's at both ends of a path to capture its latency means that normal data packets are delayed at the first switch until the controller tells the switch what to do with them. This introduces an additional delay in the path of a packet described in Fig. 1: the time it takes the controller to process the packet and reply to the switch (either with FlowMod or PacketOut) and the time it takes the switch to forward the packet to the out port once it learns what to do with it. SLAM can estimate the controller processing time and the controller-to-switch delay as described in Sect. 3.2. However, the switch forwarding time depends on the load on the switch CPU and what other traffic is traversing the switch; this is more difficult to estimate accurately. In practice, SLAM can use the approach in Sect. 3.2 to infer variations in switch processing and discard measurements performed during times when variations are high.

5.2   Frequency of Control Traffic

The accuracy of SLAM's estimated latency distribution depends on the frequency of PacketIn's from switches at both ends of the measured path. This is affected by the overall distribution of traffic in the network and by the structure of rules used to guide the traffic. For example, because switches on a backup link see little data traffic, they trigger little control traffic for SLAM to use. Similarly, forwarding rules with long timeouts or with wildcards limit the number of PacketIn messages.

To evaluate the frequency of PacketIn measurements, we simulate SLAM on a real-world enterprise trace. We use the *EDU1* trace collected by Benson *et al.* [2], capturing all traffic traversing a switch in a campus network for a period of three hours. We identify all network flows in the trace, along with their start time. The collectors of the trace report that the flow arrival rate at the switch is on the order of a few milliseconds [2].

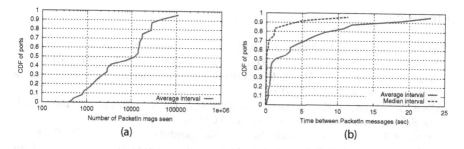

Fig. 5. (a) No. of PacketIn's each link in a 24 port switch sees in three hours. (b) Average and median time between PacketIn's per link on a 24 port switch.

Since only PacketIn's associated with traffic that traverses the same path are useful, we need to evaluate the flow arrival rate for each input port of the switch. Our traffic trace does not contain input port information, therefore we simulate a 24-port switch using the following heuristic. We first associate every distinct /p prefix (where p is, in turn, 32, 30, 28, 20, or 24) of source IP addresses in the trace with a port and then assign each individual flow to the link (or input port) associated with its source IP /p prefix. We group flows by prefix because routing in the Internet is typically prefix-based. Below, we present results for p = 28; results for other prefix lengths are qualitatively similar.

We compute both the number and the frequency of PacketIn messages that each link receives during the measurement period. Figure 5(a) shows that most links see more than 10,000 PacketIn's during the three hour span, which is equivalent to a rate of around one PacketIn per second. Figure 5(b) presents the average and median time between consecutive PacketIn's for each link of the switch. SLAM would capture samples from most links every two seconds and 80 % of all links would be measured less than every 10 seconds.

To summarize, our analysis on a real-world enterprise trace shows that, in a reactive SDN deployment, SLAM would be able to capture latency measurements once every two seconds on average without requiring any additional generation of probes. We are currently investigating the design of an adaptable SLAM that would rely on existing PacketIn's when control traffic volume is high and generate probes that trigger artificial PacketIn's when control traffic is scarce.

6   Conclusion

We presented SLAM, a path latency monitoring framework for software-defined data centers. SLAM uses timestamps of carefully triggered control messages to monitor network latency between any two arbitrary switches and identify high-delay paths. SLAM's measurements are accurate enough to detect latency inflations of tens of milliseconds and enable applications to route traffic away from high-delay path segments.

References

1. Al-Fares, M., Radhakrishnan, S., Raghavan, B., Huang, N., Vahdat, A.: Hedera: dynamic flow scheduling for data center networks. In: USENIX NSDI (2010)
2. Benson, T., Akella, A., Maltz, D.: Network traffic characteristics of data centers in the wild. In: ACM IMC (2010)
3. Chen, Y., Mahajan, R., Sridharan, B., Zhang, Z.-L.: A provider-side view of web search response time. In: Proceedings of ACM SIGCOMM (2013)
4. Curtis, A.R., Mogul, J.C., Tourrilhes, J., Yalagandula, P., Sharma, P., Banerjee, S.: DevoFlow: scaling flow management for high-performance networks. In: Proceedings of ACM SIGCOMM (2011)
5. Das, A., Lumezanu, C., Zhang, Y., Singh, V., Jiang, G., Yu, C.: Transparent and efficient network management for big data processing in the cloud. In: HotCloud (2013)
6. Duffield, N., Grossglauser, M.: Trajectory sampling for direct traffic observation. In: Proceedings of ACM SIGCOMM (2000)
7. Flach, T., Dukkipati, N., Terzis, A., Raghavan, B., Cardwell, N., Cheong, Y., Jain, A., Hao, S., Katz-Bassett, E., Govindan, R.: Reducing web latency: the virtue of gentle aggression. In: Proceedings of ACM SIGCOMM (2013)
8. Huang, D.Y., Yocum, K., Snoeren, A.C.: High-fidelity switch models for software-defined network emulation. In: Proceedings of HotSDN (2013)
9. Kolmogorov, A.N.: Sulla determinazione empirica di una legge di distribuzione. Giornale dellIstituto Italiano degli Attuari 4(1), 83–91 (1933)
10. Kompella, R.R., Levchenko, K., Snoeren, A.C., Varghese, G.: Every microsecond counts: tracking fine-grain latencies with a lossy difference aggregator. In: Proceedings of ACM SIGCOMM (2009)
11. Lee, M., Duffield, N., Kompella, R.R.: Not all microseconds are equal: fine-grained per-flow measurements with reference latency interpolation. In: Proceedings of ACM SIGCOMM (2010)
12. Moshref, M., Yu, M., Sharma, A., Govindan, R.: Scalable rule management for data centers. In: Proceedings of USENIX NSDI (2013)
13. Rotsos, C., Sarrar, N., Uhlig, S., Sherwood, R., Moore, A.W.: OFLOPS: an open framework for OpenFlow switch evaluation. In: Taft, N., Ricciato, F. (eds.) PAM 2012. LNCS, vol. 7192, pp. 85–95. Springer, Heidelberg (2012)
14. RagingWire. http://www.ragingwire.com
15. van Adrichem, N.L.M., Doerr, C., Kuipers, F.A.: OpenNetMon: network monitoring in OpenFlow software-defined networks. In: IEEE NOMS (2014)
16. Varghese, G.: Network Algorithmics. Elsevier/Morgan Kaufmann, Amsterdam (2005)
17. Yu, C., Lumezanu, C., Zhang, Y., Singh, V., Jiang, G., Madhyastha, H.V.: FlowSense: monitoring network utilization with zero measurement cost. In: Roughan, M., Chang, R. (eds.) PAM 2013. LNCS, vol. 7799, pp. 31–41. Springer, Heidelberg (2013)

Author Index

Printed in the United States
By Bookmasters